INDUSTRIAL ECONOMICS

INDUSTRIAL ECONOMICS

A.K. Sharma

ANMOL PUBLICATIONS PVT. LTD.
NEW DELHI - 110 002 (INDIA)

ANMOL PUBLICATIONS PVT. LTD.
H.O.: 4374/4B, Ansari Road, Darya Ganj,
New Delhi-110 002 (India)
Ph.: 23278000, 23261597
B.O.: No. 1015, Ist Main Road, BSK IIIrd Stage
IIIrd Phase, IIIrd Block,
Bangalore - 560 085 (India)
Visit us at: www.anmolpublications.com

Industrial Economics

First Published, 2006

PRINTED IN INDIA

Printed at Mehra Offset Press, Delhi.

Contents

Preface

"Industrial Economics" as a paper is being taught at M.A.Eco., M.B.A. and other Management Courses at various universities and institutions. This book is designed as an introductory text to the above paper, encompassing vital information on all pertinent aspects. Thus the material presented here would be of interest as well as of great use to the students, teachers and professionals of Management Courses. This book will provide complete knowledge of the nature and characteristics of industrialisation, industrial location, market structure and its performance, price determination under different conditions, small and cottage industries, foreign capital and industrial finance, public sector and policies, role of MNCs, economic policies etc. to the students.

The major topics dealt in this book are—Introduction to Industrialisation; Industrial Location; Market Structure and Performance; Price Determination and Policies; Small Scale and Cottage Industries; Industrial Finance and Foreign Capital; Public Sector and Policies; Role of Multinational Corporations; New Economic Policy etc.

It is hoped that all those will benefit from the contents of this book for whom it is meant. The author will feel amply rewarded, if motive is achieved.

Editor

1

Introduction to Industrialisation

Industrialisation is inevitable in a developing economy. But what is industrialisation. Pei Kang-Chang has said that, "industrialisation in a way is a process of developing as well as widening of capital." Eugene Staley has linked industrialisation with high productivity and has said that "High productivity produces industrialisation and that industrialisation produces high productivity." Prof. S.C. Kuchhal has said that, "industrialisation is also treated as a process in which the economic gains of industrial progress, mainly in the nature of increasing returns are continuously created and wholly or partially realised." In UNESCO "industrialisation means an absolute and relative growth in the importance of factories, mills, mines, power plants, railways and so on of manufacturing and closely related activities, especially activities involved in the building and operation of a modern economic infrastructure." Industrialisation has also been defined as use of more capital per unit of output.

Industrialisation and Per Capita Income

Living standard of a people is adjudged by the per capita income of the people. Needless to say that this income is directly linked with the industrialisation. It is industry which provides employment to the skilled, semi-skilled and un-skilled labourers. No one can deny that vast difference between low per capita income of undeveloped and developing countries on the one hand and high rate of consumption and per capita income of developing countries is primarily due to industrialisation.

Industrialisation and Economic Development

Industrialisation and economic development always go hand in hand. In the words of Myrdal, "In advanced countries the development of manufacturing industry has been concomitant with these countries' spectacular economic progress and rise in the levels of living: many of its products are indeed almost symbolic of a high living standard." Industrialisation helps providing employment, raising paying capacity of the masses, national productivity and income. It also provides a viable solution to the ever-increasing economic problems of the countries faced with population explosion. It is industrialisation alone which can help in proper exploitation of natural resources of a country to the best advantage of the natives themselves.

Patterns of Industrialisation

Patterns of industrialisation vary from one country to the other. In England, France and the USA by and large industry is in private sector whereas in China and USSR it is in public sector. In India we have mixed economy, where both public and private sectors are free participants in industrialisation. Another pattern of classification can be whether process of industrialisation is evolutionary or revolutionary though it is in fact very difficult to clearly democrate between the two. It is commonly believed that the pattern of industrialisation in USSR was revolutionary whereas the one in the USA evolutionary. In an evolutionary pattern and process enterprising spirit, personal freedom and technology are main generating forces.

Processes of Industrialisation

Each society had to pass through different stages before it became industrially progressive and advanced. Industrialisation process is linked with social system on the one hand and rate of economic development and growth on the other. Whole process also proceeds from simple to the complex and that too passes through different stages, though the time taken may not be the same at every stage. The time would always depend on available resources, availability of manpower, attitude of the government and its policies and programmes and also social system favouring or disfavouring industrialisation. Industrialisation process and policy cannot however be framed in isolation.

Industrialisation is a continuous process and usually passes through three stages. In the first stage secondary industry concerns itself with the processing of primary products *e.g.* milling grains and tanning leather etc. In the second stage secondary industry begins to transfer material to somewhat finished goods *e.g.*, preparation of bread and confectionery etc. In the third stage machine and equipment is used not for direct satisfaction of any want but for facilitating future process of production. Where there is first stage of industrialisation, the country will be exporting bulk of its output whereas at the second stage the industry will be capable enough to serve its local needs. Most of the developing countries have only reached second stage of industrialisation. Third stage of industrialisation indicates industrial maturity of the nation. At this stage the nation is in a position to not only satisfactorily meet its own needs and necessities but to export goods to other countries to meet their requirements as well.

Industrialisation has become today motto and watch word of every developing nation. Those nations which have recently won freedom are making every effort to industrialise themselves. Of course the task is not easy, because the process of industrialisation needs vast men and material resources and needs of the society are many which need immediate tackling.

EVOLUTION OF INDIAN INDUSTRIES

In 1919 first world war came to an end and with that economic depression started, which continued all over the world upto 1933. But inspite of this in the country, there was progress on the industrial front. Production of Steel ingot rose from 1.3 lakhs in 1922 to 10.42 lakhs in 1935, which was a rise of about 800%. Similarly production of Cotton goods increased from 1714 million yards, which was about 250%; output of Match industry went up by 38%, that of Paper by 180% and that of Cane Sugar by about 400%. There was considerable increase in production of Engineering goods and those of the electrical goods also started.

Second World War and Indian Industry

Inspite of economic depression, industries in India made some progress, though as compared with the consumption, population and area, the output on the industrial field was negligible. It was at this difficult time that second world war broke out. Indian industries now received bulk orders for the supply of the goods to meet day to day demands of the armies, which included not only British soldiers, but soldiers all over the world. In fact, India became one of the important centres of supplies of war material. Production of goods increased but only in limited sphere. In order to meet needs, particularly war needs, new industrial enterprises were started. Extra plants were set up. In order to increase production, factories were made to work in two shifts. Similarly organisational and technical improvements were made to get better production. Every machine was made to work to its fullest capacity. Where necessary, new plants were added to the existing ones. Industrial production on the whole increased from 104% in 1938 to 100% in 1945; base year 1937 being equal to 100. Some of new industries which were started during World War II included Ferro Silicon, ferro manganese, copper, copper sheets, wires, cables, diesel engines, pumps, bicycles, machine tools, cutting tools, textile, tea, caustic soda and chlorine etc. On the whole number of companies in 1945 went upto 14,859 from 11,114 in 1939. Similarly, capital investment in the industries also increased from Rs. 290 crores in 1939 to Rs. 389 crores in 1945. During this period new industries were also started. But if this progress is viewed impartially, it will be observed that it was very slow and attention was paid and development was made only in respect of industries which were useful for the production of raw material. No attempt was made to produce material, which was of either day to day use or with which common man was concerned. Thus the needs of common man were completely ignored and Industrial growth had nothing to do with the millions spread all over the country. Moreover there were certain adverse effects on the industrial economy, due to certain forces, which were very active during war period and very adversely influenced industrial growth. Some of the important factors were:

1. Heavy Strains on the Industry. During war period industry was put under heavy strains. The machines were put to work from morning till night. Every plant machinery deteriorated and there was heavy wear and tear of machines.

2. Ignoring of Consumption Goods. During war days every effort was made to produce only such goods which were useful for meeting war needs. The result was that production of consumption goods was completely ignored. There was inflation in the market and purchasing capacity of the people considerably went down. Thus whatsoever was available, that also could not be purchased by the poor and weaker sections of the society. There were also controls and corruption in society.

3. Exploitation of Workers. During this period every labourer and worker was required to produce more and more, because there was heavy demand for the goods. But they were not paid their due share in the profits. Their wages too kept very low. The result was that they were exploited and the owners got profit out of their miserable conditions.

4. Ignoring Long Term Factors. While setting up new industries during war period no long term factors which were taken into consideration. The only factors which were taken into consideration included scarcity of resources and the problems created by raw material. This proved very harmful for the industries in the long run.

5. Large Scale Inter-locking of Funds. During the war days many industrial units gained heavy profits. The result of this was that the money got blocked up in the hands of few industrialists. The concentration of wealth in few hands resulted in many social evils and malpractices. The few powerful people who thus emerged began to control whole industrial system of the country. They formed groups and joint stock companies. Similarly they cared more for their own interests rather than the interests of the shareholders and the workers.

6. No Balanced Growth. No care was taken about ensuring that the growth was balanced and quite well planned. On the other hand an attempt was made to set up industries as quickly as possible, so that war efforts were not slackened. Though immediate needs were met, yet the society had to pay for this ill planning during the year which followed after war period.

Forms of Organising Industry

There are mainly four forms of business organisation which are as under:

1. Sole tradership
2. Partnership
3. Joint Stock company
4. Co-operative organisation

While starting a business one has to choose one out of these different forms. However, the following factors will be taken into account while selecting a suitable form of business organisation:

1. Type and Nature of Business Activity *i.e.*, trading or manufacturing. Trading business generally requires small capital and managerial ability and can be easily managed by a sole trader while manufacturing should be better organised on partnership or joint stock company basis.

2. Volume of Business. Large volume of business needs large finance and can be managed by companies or partnerships. Small volume of business suits sole proprietary business.

3. Financial Requirements. Business requiring large amount of finance are undertaken by joint stock companies.

4. Government Control. If a person wants to avoid government interference and control he should adopt sole tradership or partnership. In companies there is too much government regulation.

5. Area of Operation. If business is widely scattered, it is difficult for a sole trader or partnership to manage it. Companies with large network are better equipped to manage such a business.

6. Limitation of Liability. On account of unlimited liability in sole traderships and partnerships it is very difficult to undertake very risky businesses. Company form suits better for risky adventures because of limited liability of its members.

7. Tax Considerations. On account of doubt taxation in companies, it is not preferred. First of all company has to pay income tax on its profit and then shareholders have to pay income tax on their dividend incomes.

Sole Proprietorship

One man business or sole proprietorship is the oldest form of business organisation from ownership point of view. In this type of business an individual introduces his own capital, uses his own skill and efficiency; solely manages the affairs of the business and is himself responsible for the results of its operations. In simple words, this type of business is completely owned and controlled by one person. Though it is the oldest form, still it is the most common form of business organisation even today. All that a person has to do is to decide the type of business one wants to do and arrange for the necessary amount of capital.

This type of business has no separate legal entity and the total reward and risk is to be fully assumed by the owner himself. His liability is also unlimited.

Thus the following features of a sole proprietorship emerge from the above discussion:

(i) It is owned by one individual.

(ii) It is managed and controlled by one person.

(iii) The liability of owner is unlimited.

(iv) The owner has to fully bear the risk.

(v) There is not much government regulation to interfere.

Advantages

One man business is considered to be the best because of the following advantages:

1. Easy Formation. There are no legal formalities to be performed for the formation of this type of business. Any person can decide to form one man business and start without the interference of anybody else. Thus, it is the easiest of all types of ownership form of organisations.

2. Full Control. The proprietor has the exclusive right of managing and controlling the affairs of the business. There is no problem of consulting any partner or anybody else. His decisions regarding his business are final. He can avail of any opportunities and meet crisis as he deems fit.

3. Personal Relation with Customers and Employees. As a sole trader business is generally small in size, the owner is in a position to be in close touch with his customers and his employees and cater to their needs and tasks. Individual attention to customers results in their increased satisfaction and thus results in increased sales and more profits.

4. Motivation. The main objects of business is to earn maximum profits. In proprietary business there is a direct relationship between effort and reward. This serves as a powerful incentive because the proprietor knows that the entire reward of his efforts will go to him. He therefore works harder to earn extra profits.

5. Personal Goodwill. A sole proprietor can build a grand goodwill on the basis of his personal resources.

6. Quick Decisions. For efficient operation of a business sometimes situations arise whereby a businessman has to take prompt decisions to take advantage of certain opportunities. This is an added advantage of one man business where there cannot be delay in taking decision for want of consulting anybody else.

7. Secrecy. As secrecy is very important for the success of a business, the sole proprietor is in a special position to take full advantage of being a single person to maintain his business secrets.

8. No Government Regulation. Unlike companies, there is no interference and regulation of the government regarding sole tradership. Of course, he has to comply with tax laws, labour laws etc. but there is no special Act dealing with sole tradership.

Disadvantages

Of course the advantages explain as to why one man business is the best in the world, but no man is big enough to control everything. However, it has the following disadvantages:

1. Limited Financial Resources. Being an individual, his financial resources are limited to meet the needs of the growing business. As he can depend only on his savings the size of the business remains small and it takes quite long for him to expand the size of the business.

2. Limited Managerial Ability. The managerial skill of the single owner is also limited as there is no one who can sincerely advise him on his business problems. Today business is full of complications and one man finds it quite difficult to meet the problems because of the limited managerial skill of an individual.

3. Unlimited Liability. The sole proprietor has to bear the entire financial burden and risk of the business. As his liability is unlimited not only the assets of business, but also his private property and estate can be used for discharging the liabilities of business. This also works as a disincentive to expand his business.

4. Uncertainty of Duration. The sole tradership form of business comes to an end with the death or insolvency of the owner. Thus, this type of business can abruptly come to an end.

From the above we can conclude that one man business suits in the following types of businesses:

(i) Where limited amount of capital is needed.

(ii) Where risk is not heavy.

(iii) Where business is not complicated so that one person can conveniently manage.

(iv) Where personal attention should be given to customers.

5. Partnership. The partnership business is very often an outgrowth of sole tradership concerns. In the same way, private limited companies are generally formed out of partnership concerns. A partnership is the relation between persons who have agreed to share the profits of a business, carried on by all or any of them acting for all." Some of the basic features of partnership are as follows:

1. In order to form a business firm, there must be at least two persons, but not more than 20.

2. Partnership is the result of a contract between the partners.

3. Profits or losses in a partnership are to be shared equally by all the partners unless stated otherwise.

4. Each partner can participate in the management of the business except sleeping partners.

Advantages of Partnership in Comparison to Sole Proprietorship

However, partnership enjoys the following advantages as compared to sole tradership.

1. Larger Financial Resources. The combined resources or savings of many individuals would be certainly larger than the limited capital of the sole proprietor.

2. In case of death of a sole trader, his business comes to an end. But in the case of partnership, the death, insolvency or accident of any one of the partners, the business continues.

3. Being a small business, a sole trader is quite ineffective in exerting nay controlling influence both as a buyer and as a seller.

4. Division of Labour. Benefits of specialisation may be derived by a partnership firm by distributing work among the partners in such a way that each of the partner may specialise in one of the functions like production, purchasing, marketing, finance etc. But this is not possible in sole tradership.

5. Better Managerial Ability. Partnership gets the benefit of combined managerial ability of a number of partners. Such managerial ability is quite limited in sole proprietorship business.

Thus it will be seen that most of the advantages and limitations of sole tradership are overcome by a partnership firm.

Joint Stock Company

Joint stock company form of business organisation is the most popular form of which has helped modern industries by providing enormous capital to the industry. The fundamental principle of a joint stock organisation is that the capital is contributed by a large number of people, known as shareholders who have very restricted powers and have hardly any say in the managerial affairs of the business. A company has been defined by C.J. Marshall as "A corporation is an artificial being, invisible and existing only in contemplation of law. Being a mere creation of law it possesses only the properties which the charter of its creation confers upon it either expressly or as incidental to its very existence." The above definition makes it clear that the individuality of the company is different from its constituents and the company exists in the eyes of law as a separate entity.

However, the following are the distinctive characteristics of a joint stock company.

1. Distinct Entity. A company is not a natural person. It is an artificial person which exists only in the eyes of law. Being a creation of law, it has a distinct legal entity. Its entity is different from the persons who are its members. A company is created with a purpose of enabling a group of persons to conduct some activity in some more convenient way than would have been possible by retaining their identity as individuals. A shareholder who is its partner, being a distinct person can sue a company and be sued by the company.

2. Limited Liability. The liability of the members of a joint stock company is limited to the nominal value of their shareholdings. In other words, unlike partnership and sole-tradership, the private estates of the shareholders are not liable towards the debts of the Company. Therefore, whereas a shareholder stands to lose the amount invested in the shares of a company, he cannot be called upon to pay any thing from his private property in order to help the company in its financial crisis.

3. Perpetual Succession. The existence of the company is not affected by death of any or all of its members. Members may transfer their shares but the company continues in the same name. It is well said that members may come and members may go, but the company goes for ever. As the company is brought into existence by law, it is law alone that will bring the life of the company into an end.

4. Command Seal. As a company is an artificial person, it cannot sign on any documents. Common seal with the name of the company engraved on it is used as a substitute for its signatures. The law requires every company to have a seal of its own. The fact that the seal of the company should not be misused by anyone, the directors who work as agents of the company are required to sign alongwith the seal of the company.

5. Transfer of Shares. The shares which are the constituents of the share capital of the company are freely transferable. A shareholder can anytime sell his shares in the open market without the consent of anyone.

6. Divorce between Ownership and Management. As a company is a distinct legal entity from that of shareholders, the shareholders cannot bind the company by their acts. The management of the company is entrusted to an elective body known as Board of Directors.

Advantages

The main advantages of the company form of organisation are clear from the above discussion of the characteristics. However, a list of advantages is given below:

1. Large Financial Resources. A company can have unlimited number of shareholders. These shareholders contribute huge amount of funds towards the capital of the company. This is an outstanding advantage of the company that it allows the vast amount of capital flown into it that would have otherwise little chance of being used. As shares of the company are of small value, a person with small resources can become a member of a company by purchasing only as many shares as capacity permits.

2. Transfer of Shares. Shares in a company are conveniently transferable without having to obtain anybody's consent. The shares of the companies are dealt with at stock exchanges and immediate buyers and shares of all shares easily available here. Thus stock exchanges provide an added attraction to invest in shares.

3. Diffused Risk. The risk of loss in a company is spread over a large number of investors each of whom will share only a small portion of the loss if any. This advantage is from the point of view of the individual shareholder.

4. Democratic Management. The Board of Directors is an elective body to which the management of the company is entrusted. The law provides for democratic norms for the election of the directors and the functioning of the company.

5. Limited Liability. This is an added advantage to the shareholders. As already stated above the liability of the shareholders is limited, a person who buys shares in a company cannot be called upon to pay more than the nominal value of shares. This puts a limit to the risk that the members of the company are subjected to.

6. Greater Efficiency. As professional managers can be employed by companies, greater efficiency of management is possible.

7. Stale Existence. The company enjoys a perpetual existence and it is not affected by the death, retirement or insolvency of any or all the members of the company.

8. Aid in National Development. The company form of organisation assists in the development and progress of industries of the nation by stimulating enterprise making available large capital for industries.

9. Tax Benefit. The Income Tax also provides for many tax benefits to joint stock company. This chief advantage is that the rate of income tax is on a flat rate and not on a slab system.

TYPES OF INDUSTRIES

In every country, industries are given encouragement so that these flourish and national needs and necessities are met from within the country. But industries are of different types and kinds which may briefly be discussed as under:

(1) Cottage Industries. These are the industries in which not much capital or space is required. Usually a craftman or few of them combine together work at their residence or with small accommodation which they manage to get on rent or have their own. The members of the family assist the craftman in his work. Once the goods have been produced, the craftman himself manages to sell them to his self-created customers. In some advanced countries of the world, like Japan and Switzerland, cottage industries play a very important role in national economy. The greatest advantage of cottage industries is that manpower is not wasted and the people engage themselves in these industries usually in their spare time.

(2) Small Scale Industries. 'Small' scale industry is a comparative and relative term. But usually such an industry is an individual's adventure. A person with some capital starts the industry and employes people to work under him. In small scale industries it is not the craftsmanship or the manual power which counts, but it is machine and technical knowhow which gets preference.

(3) Private Sector Industry. Then comes private sector industry. It is a kind of industry which is set up by few individuals with their own capital. They manufacture such commodities, which according to them, will be readily accepted by the society and through which they will get maximum profit. In such an industry profit or loss is that of the individual or individuals who have set up the industry. Such an industry has considerable freedom in the personnel policy.

(4) Large Scale Industries. Large scale industries are the nerve centre of a nation. These industries need large capital, machine and space. In it there is great respect for technical experts. There is clear division of labour and each one is required to confine oneself to a particular job allotted to him. Similarly whole industry works under a well organised system. The contacts between the management and the employees are impersonal rather than personal. Large scale industries are usually faced with problems of employer-employee relations.

(5) Public Sector Industry. But today many states feel that private sector industries do not take social needs into consideration. It is also felt that these industries exploit their employees to the maximum. Accordingly in very many states of the world the states themselves have set up important industries. The money needed in setting up such industries is spent by the state. The profit or loss in running such industries is borne by the society as a whole.

(6) Joint Sector Industry. It is a type of industry in which capital and control is neither exclusively in the hands of the state nor that of the private individuals, but in it both the state and the private individuals combine together. In such an industry usually the share capital and investment of state is more than that of the private individuals thereby giving the former a weightage or an upper hand over the later.

These are some of the important types of industries in every society. But the greatest need for every new industry is that it should be given sufficient protection so that it is in a position to face competition from the outside world. In case no protection is given, the result will be that it will not survive competition from more developed countries and be killed in its infancy.

CHARACTERISTICS OF MODERN INDUSTRY

Modern industrial organisation is quite different from the past. In the past, there was direct, close and personal relationship between the employers and the employees. In many cases crafts men used to work at their residences engaging all the members in the work, in one way or the other. They also used to take pride in the nature of their work. There was no division of labour and also no problem of distribution or consumption. The producer himself was the distributor. Where an employer engaged others to do work for him, iron law of wages was applied. The employee was paid so little that it was not only difficult but rather impossible for him to make his both ends meet. He was not allowed to raise his voice and there was no job security and his job was always threatened and ever in risk.

But in so far as modern industry is concerned conditions are quite different. Modern industry has its own characteristics which may briefly be discussed as under:

1. Big Industries. Our modern industries are usually quite big in which a large number of people are employed all belonging to different caders holding high and low positions, skilled, semi-skilled and un-skilled.

2. Trade Unionism. Those who work in an industry usually organise themselves into trade union. These organised people then try to bargain with the management for better working conditions, better emoluments and for getting other facilities.

3. Impersonal Character. In modern industry worker has no close affiliation or association with the goods which he is producing. It is primarily because one who starts the work does not finish it. It is to pass through various stages before it completely becomes a finished products. The top bosses meet together and have personal contacts only and do not know much about workers.

4. Amenities. In every industry employer is supposed to provide amenities to the employees. He is to see that the employees have all such amenities which are conducive for efficient working. Similarly he is also to see that safety has been provided to them, if they are working on dangerous machines.

5. Headache of Management. When interests of the workers themselves clash it becomes the headache of management to settle them. Not only this, but the management is required to create capital, to make arrangements for the continued supply of raw material and sale of the finished products.

6. Need for Money. A good modern industry cannot run without finances. In the past a craftman could mange with little money, but today heavy finances and amounts are needed to keep the industry running.

7. Stress on Organisation. In industry today, the employer lays more stress on organisation rather than the employee. He will try to popular his brand rather than the craftsman. What he believes is that once his organisation is sound and his brand has become popular, the things will go smooth, whether there is one craftman or the other working on that.

8. Division of Labour. In the past there used to be no division of labour in the industry. But today there is clear division of labour. Each person is required to do only a particular type of job, leaving the rest to the care of the others. One does not know through how many stages raw material will pass before taking the shape of finished product.

9. Problem of Sale. In the past craftmen used to produce very limited number of goods, which he could very easily sell in the market. But today articles are purchased in bulk. Bulk production has created problem of sale in the market. Little slowness in sale will mean hoarding of stocks, which will in turn create problem of raising additional capitals, for keeping the factory moving.

10. Need for Specialisation. Each industry tries to have specialisation in one field or the other. It is with this end in view that need and necessity of specialists in each industry is increasing and they are commanding more and more respect.

11. Desire for Monopoly. Still another feature is that every industry wants to have less competition and more monopoly conditions. It wants to avoid wastage of money and human resources in competition. But inspite of this desire, almost every industry is faced with competitions from other industries.

12. Adequate Wages. In our industry of today iron law of wages cannot apply. Today it is believed that an employee, must get adequate wages, so that he can pull on reasonably well, along with his family. The industry should pay him enough so that he can maintain his social status.

13. Stress on Profit. An industrialist of today cares more for his product than for any thing else. He wants to be sure that minimum is spent and maximum is saved so that his margin of profit increases. More an industrialist saves, happier he feels.

14. Less Manual Labour. In an advanced and developed industry there will be less manual labour. It is because today it is believed that machine can work with more accuracy, uniformally and quickly as compared with the manual labour.

15. Stress on Human Relations. Then in our industry of today much stress is laid on establishing and having happy and healthy human relations. The employer will try to approach every problem on human grounds, if really today he wants to progress and prosper.

16. Rise of Industrialists. Today, needs and necessities of the society have become very complex and complicated. In order to meet these needs, a class of industrialists, who have sufficient wealth, has come into existence. These people invest and try to add to their wealth by earning. These people are socially respected and enjoy great social status.

INDUSTRIALISATION IN INDIA

India for long has remained and continues to be predominantly an agricultural country, nearly 70 per cent of the country's population derives their livelihood from agriculture.

In the case of agriculture, the operation of the law of diminishing returns starts operating at a relatively early stage compared with industries. In the case of India, nearly 70 per cent of the country's labour force is engaged in the Agricultural Sector. Agricultural land in India just cannot absorb such vast number of workers in a productive and profitable way even with the present traditional techniques of production, not to speak of mechanised form of agriculture which in the United States employ just around 4 per cent of the labour force in the country. It is said that the marginal productivity of labour in agriculture in India is zero, which means that there is much disguised unemployment in Indian agriculture. The workers outwardly appear to be employed, but in fact they add nothing to agricultural production; and even if a substantial amount of labour force is withdrawn from the agricultural sector, production of agricultural commodities will not decline.

Absorption of Displaced Workers

Only the industrial sector can absorb workers displaced from agriculture; without large, medium, and small-scale modern industries, India will not be in a position to solve her problem of mass unemployment and mass poverty.

Even if agriculture is modernised and made more progressive, it must be realised that it would mean more displacement of labour by machines, and demand for agricultural commodities and especially for foodgrains is fairly inelastic. India cannot export increasing quantities of foodgrains and other agricultural commodities like tea, coffee, etc. to Western developed countries because of the low income elasticity of demand for agricultural commodities, especially foodgrains.

Indian Agriculture

It must be realised that developed countries have not only modern industries, but they have also developed agriculture which is another reason why, if India remains a purely agricultural country and modernises her agriculture, she will not be in a position to sell her agricultural commodities in increasing quantities in the markets of developed and industrialised countries.

The demand for Indian agricultural commodities is declining in some cases, because developed industrial countries are going in for synthetic substances like man-made fibres for cotton yarn, synthetic rubber for natural rubber, plastic wrappings for jute bags and so on.

There is another reason why demand for Indian agricultural produce and other natural raw materials for developed countries will decline. Natural materials like iron ore and other metals are playing a decreasing role in finished industrial goods. Thus, instead of iron and steel, many motor and machine parts are at present being made of plastic and instead of natural metals various artificial substances are being increasingly used as substitutes.

Mass Unemployment

Industrialisation is the only answer to India's mass unemployment and poverty. In industries, the law of increasing returns operates over a longer range than in the agricultural sector. This means that industries have a very large potentiality to provide productive employment opportunities to Indian people who today for want of any employment opportunities are thrown back on agriculture where their marginal productivity is zero. Thus, industries will provide employment to vast masses of people and provide income and help alleviate mass poverty and ensure a vast number of people rising standard of living.

Increases in Demand

Rapid industrialisation of India would mean increasing demand for foodgrains and other industrial raw materials produced by the agricultural sector (such as cotton, jute, tea, coffee, rubber, fruits, etc.) Thus, with industrialisation of the country, demand for agricultural commodities will rise ensuring higher prices and thus ensuring more income to people engaged in the agricultural sector.

Abundance of Raw Material

Another reason why there should be industrialisation in India is that India has vast industrial raw materials like cotton, jute, oilseeds, leather, tea, coffee, fruits, fish and so on. Instead of sending industrial raw materials abroad and importing finished goods from them paying substantial price for them, India herself can build a vast network of various industries for which abundant raw materials are available in the country.

Wrong Impression

Very often when the terms agriculture and industry are mentioned, there is the impression that the two sectors are somehow opposed to each other and that one sector can prosper only at the cost of the other sector. Nothing can be farther from the truth.

Increase in Supply

Increase in the supply of industrial goods like tractors, electrical and diesel engines and pumpsets and other agricultural implements and chemical fertilisers will help modernise agriculture and increase per acre and per capita production in the agricultural sector.

People displaced from the agricultural sector, because of modernisation of Indian agriculture, can be provided employment opportunities in the industrial sector. That is how displaced persons from the agricultural sector were absorbed by the industrial sector in presently developed countries.

Defence System

Industrialisation is also extremely desirable for another important reason. The entire modern defence system is based on the foundation of modern industries—automatic guns and rifles, canons, warships, bombers, missiles and various other defence equipments which can be produced in the country only if the country has a vast network of modern industries. Thus, defence and protection of the country from foreign aggression require that India possesses a strong industrial base which alone can supply thousands of defence items.

Modernised Agriculture

With developed and modernised agriculture and a vast network of large, medium and small scale modern industries, India will be less dependent on foreign countries for her vital needs. Dependence on foreign countries for an essential article like foodgrains or industrial commodity like crude oil or for defence equipment can produce disastrous political consequences for India, resulting in the loss of her independence. For example, when food was being imported from the united States under P.L. 480 during the 1950s and 1960s, as otherwise there would have been a mass disaster, the United States tried to bring political pressure on India to make it yield to Pakistan on the Kashmir issue. Modernisation of agriculture and industrialisation will mean more self-reliance which is welcome both from economic and political points of view.

Change in Value-System

Industrialisation also means a change in the value-system. Industrialisation will introduce new industrial culture—discipline, hard work, competitiveness, team work, self-reliance, adaptability, inventiveness and organisational ability.

It will be observed that India's agricultural population is characterised by idleness, superstitituousness, extreme dependence on natural forces, fatalism, etc. These qualities will hardly make a country prosperous in modern times. Industrialisation is wanted in India because many features of industrial culture which will accompany the country's industrialisation are essential elements, if India is to live successfully in modern times and in a highly competitive world.

FACTORS HAMPERING RAPID INDUSTRIAL DEVELOPMENT

For rapid economic development and modernisation of Indian society, for providing increasing opportunities of employment, for making maximum use of indigenous resources, for raising the income of the people and their standard of living and thus solving the problem of mass unemployment and mass poverty prevalent in developing countries like India, rapid industrialisation is necessary, not only from the economic point of view but even from socio-political point of view.

While the objective of rapid industrialisation is extremely desirable in developing countries like India, there have been operating in these countries a number of factors that hamper the process of rapid industrialisation.

Classification of Factors

These factors may be classified into four categories:

1. Economic Factors. Rapid development of modern industries in a developing country like India badly needs development and provision of certain infrustructural facilities which may be absent or inadequate for quite some time, thus creating severe bottlenecks in the way of rapid industrialisation.

A basic necessity for rapid industrialisation is an efficient network of transport and communications system. The transport system brings raw materials from various centres to factories and carry produced goods to different markets in a short time. This makes large-scale production of goods and services possible. It follows that absence of an adequate and efficient transport and communications system would put hurdles in the way of movement of raw materials and finished goods making large-scale production difficult as the produced goods cannot be quickly and efficiently moved to different markets in the country. Developing countries including India suffer from inadequacy of transport and communications facilities (made up of roads and motor transport, railways, airways, inland and oceanic shipping, telephone and telegraph, and so on) hampering rapid industrial development. Transport has proved a bottleneck in the process of industrial development of the country.

Hurdle of Power

Another hurdle is power or energy (as, for example, supplied by coal, hydro and thermal and nuclear electricity, petroleum and so on). Without energy or power, the wheels of industry will not move. Most developing countries including India have been suffering from shortage of energy which is hampering their rapid industrial development. For example, in India while the supply of electricity has been increasing fairly rapidly since independence, demand for it far exceeds the supply.

Trouble with Transport

The trouble with transport and electricity sectors is that vast investments are necessary for their development and governments in developing countries having limited financial resources are not in a position to invest substantial amounts in power generation. Secondly, the projects of transport and electricity sectors require long gestation period. Another difficulty is that transport facilities and electricity generation cannot be increased when demand for it goes up. There is a minimum scale which must be adopted in both these sectors, whether there is or is not adequate demand for full capacity production in those sectors.

Infrustructural Facilities

Then there are other infrustructural facilities like training institutions to prepare hundred types of skill needed for modern industries. Their absence or inadequacy poses a serious handicap. India for long had to employ foreign technicians who had to be paid high salaries (part in foreign currencies) and who may not be found suitable for work in a totally different socio-cultural background.

Another infrustructural facility is the network of financial and banking institutions and stock exchanges with enough financial resources to meet the investment needs of various industries that are to be set up.

Thus, transport, power, skills of various types, educational, financial, banking and professional institutions, which constitute or make for necessary industrial environment may be absent or may not have been adequately developed in countries wanting to rapidly industrialise and that might hamper rapid industrial development.

Network

Fortunately, India has developed since independence in 1947 a broad network of all these institutions that are helping industrial growth and development. But there is a feeling that except in metropolitan areas and big towns, in district and taluka places and in rural areas of the country, these institutions are not developed to the extent necessary, hampering rapid industrial development of the country.

2. Socio-Demographic Factors. Rapid growth of population in a developing country may effectively hinder rapid industrialisation of the country. Rapid growth of population would mean that additional production of wealth would be used mainly for consumption by the additional number of people, thus adversely affecting the rate of saving and investment which are crucial to industrial and economic growth. Additional population in a developing country would mean low per capita income, low rate of saving and therefore, low rate of investment and again as a consequence, low per capita income, and thus the vicious circle of poverty would continue with continually adverse effect on the rate of saving and investment which are two critical elements of industrial growth.

Division of Society

For example, in the case of India, her society is characterised by caste, class, religion, etc. which have divided the community into water-tight compartments. Each caste has several sub-castes and each such caste and sub-castes have their own mode of eating, clothing, living and pattern of life. This results in hampering mass production of goods for wide markets, because markets in India are fragmented on the basis of religion, caste and sub-caste. Also, caste and religions rivalries have divided Indian community into factions which find it difficult to unite for a common cause such as rapid industrial development. This division, for example, would make trade unions weak with little bargaining power as these labour unions will come to be based on castes and religions. The same would be true in other professions and trades. This stratification of society, by making inter-caste and inter-religious communication difficult, makes implementation of any common programme of rapid industrialisation difficult. For long, only certain castes and communities were associated with industry and commerce.

Cultural Values

Much more damaging to rapid industrialisation is the long-prevailing cultural values in India. Due to long foreign rule over the country, precarious monsoon and prevailing poverty which Indians have experienced for centuries, Indian mentality or outlook on life is generally characterised by fatalism, otherworldliness, attitude of resignation to one's fate or destiny (due to the acceptance of the Theory of Karma) which holds the view that your life in the present world is determined by your sins or meritorious deeds in the past lives and no amount of efforts would change what you are fated to become during your present life-time. And, therefore, Indian culture has for long come to be characterised by absence of a strong desire to improve one's material conditions of life, considering material wealth as something sinful, and a simple life with only a few essential wants meritorious and worth emulation. With this sort of value-system which shuns material prosperity, rapid industrialisation would be practically impossible. And, therefore, rapid industrialisation of India would require radical changes in the attitude of the people and their value system with emphasis on material prosperity, personal profit motive, inventiveness, strong faith in modern sciences and technology, on cooperative efforts, hand work and discipline in individual and social life, and ability to take risks by experimenting with new products and processes all of which go to make what may be called modern industrial culture. Industrialisation does not mean just establishing a few industrial establishments here and there; it means building up an extensive industrial structure based or sound foundations of industrial culture.

3. Public Administrative Machinery. Developing countries like India suffer from scarcity of various resources, especially human resources necessary for bringing about rapid industrialisation and economic development. With a view to make the best use of available resources, these countries have rightly adopted economic planning as an instrument of rapid economic development, with emphasis on rapid industrialisation. But economic planning and its effective implementation require a vast network of skilled and administrative personnel. But it so happens that an underdeveloped country like India also has an underdeveloped administrative structure.

Administrative Structure

Thus, India has erected an enormously big administrative structure and has entrusted the administrative personnel with the gigantic task of administering hundreds of controls and issuing of licences, handling of vast funds and public enterprises. Lacking developmental culture, the administration has failed in properly implementing various schemes which together constitute Five Year Plans of India. The administration in India is characterised by lack of development culture, lack of decision making ability and by bureaucratic delays, corruption, waste of various types of resources and inefficient implementation of developmental schemes. Thus, India has an expanding public sector, there being in 1991, 246 Central Government Public Sector Undertakings with a total investment of Rs. 1,13,234 crores, apart from State-level public sector enterprises like the State Transport Corporations and State Electricity Boards.

Failure of Public Sector

Thus, underdeveloped public administration has been hampering rapid industrialisation of the country. The public sector which has command over basic and vital infrastructural facilities has failed to keep up its pace of development with adverse effects on the development of industries, both in the public and private sectors.

4. International Environment. Absence of favourble international environment would impede rapid industrial development in developing countries like India and it so happens that these forces are outside the control of most of the developing countries, including India.

Developed countries may put restrictions on exports of capital goods and equipment needed for rapid industrial development of developing countries like India, or raise their prices or they may prohibit export of latest technology or send inappropriate technology or impose hard conditions for selling patent rights or may send experts of inferior quality and who cannot give their best in totally different socio-cultural environment. Developed countries may restrict flow of financial capital into developing countries, thereby creating foreign exchange problems for countries like India; or they may charge prohibitive rates of interest or put other harsh conditions hampering industrial and therefore, economic development of countries like India. Also, developed countries may follow policies, fiscal and trade, that hamper exports from developing countries or making the terms of trade adverse against them.

SOCIAL PROBLEMS AND CONSEQUENCES

Industrialisation very deeply effects social patterns and processes. It changes our social outlook and approach to social problems. It influences family, religion and whole of our urban and rural pattern and set up. Some of the important social effects may be discussed as under:

1. **Social Adjustment.** Industrialisation creates great problem of social adjustment. In a rural economy usually there is village solidarity and spirit of collectiveness. There is less of competition and more of co-operation. But with industrialisation spirit of collectivism is replaced by individualism. Not only this, but village loses its family character.
2. **Setback to Customs and Traditions.** The villages all over the world have their own customs and traditions. These develop after long years of labour. Industrialisation changes whole outlook of the people towards these customs and traditions to the disadvantage of the society.
3. **Effect on Family System.** Agricultural pattern favours joint family system, whereas industrialisation not only discourages the system but makes that impossible because every village boy who manages to get a job in the industry cannot take his whole family with him.
4. **Problem of Moral Standards.** Usually the old and young in a family live in a hut built by the workers around the factory. This creates moral problems for the grown up children both boys and girls.

5. **Problem of Taxation Structure.** Pattern of taxation in agricultural economy is definitely different than the one which can be in industrialised society..Agriculture cannot be taxed to the extent to which industry can be taxed. Similarly agriculture can afford to have more direct taxation than the industry.

6. **Health Problems.** Industrialisation creates as well as solves many health problems. It can produce goods, which help in maintaining cleanliness etc. But usually it creates health problems. Industries fail to provide good accommodation to their low paid employees, who are forced to live in huts and shanties without proper drainage and water facilities. The smoke of the health is in itself a disease trap. Even there is problem of inhaling and exhaling. Thus industry creates its own health problems as well.

7. **Setback to Handicrafts.** Handicarafts receive serious setback. Industry can produce goods quickly, in a better manner and with less cost. The goods produced by machine are better to look at. The people thus prefer to purchase machine made goods rather than handicrafts resulting in loss of income to the villagers and also lowering their living standard, making their lives economically miserable.

8. **Deterioration in Urban Environment.** While discussing social effects of industrialisation, Prof. Kuchhal has said "During a period of rapid industrialisation there may be time lag between establishment of factories in the urban areas and making associated investments in public utilities, road and means of transport, housing, sanitation schools, hospitals and recreation facilities. It may lead to a deterioration in urban environment, creation of slum conditions, overtaking of facilities and consequent reduction in the standard of living."

9. **Dis-proportionate Urban-Rural Development.** When there is Industrialisation naturally more stress is laid on the

development of urban areas where the industries are located rather than the rural areas where there are no industries. The problem of urban-rural development is created. Urban areas develop only at the cost of rural areas, which in turn creates its own problems.

It will thus be observed that industrialisation results in the creation of many social problems. It influences our family and religion. In fact there is no aspect of life which is not influenced by industrialisation either in one way or the other.

INDUSTRIALISATION INFLUENCE

Influence of Industrialisation on Internal Trade

In an agricultural economy pace of trade inside the country is very slow. Whatsoever is produced is locally consumed but, if there is at all any surplus production that is consumed in the nearby areas and localities without much bargaining. In an agricultural economy except agricultural goods there is no commodity in excess supply.

Bulk Production becomes Possible. But industrialisation gives a new fillip to trade. With the establishment of new industries more and more goods are produced. It becomes then possible to produce goods in bulk so that demands of the consumers are met. An industrialist will then try to monopolise and ensure, that his brand reaches every nook and corner of the country. The result of all this is that trade becomes brisk and more the industries are set more brisk the trade becomes. The whole nation then gets activitised with business activities and nation becomes a centre of trade.

Trade Pattern Changes. In an agriculture economy, whatsoever is surplus is sent out as raw material, because the chances of internal consumption do not exist. But when country is industrialised, whole trade pattern changes. Raw material is consumed by the industry itself. Then there is no need to trade with outside market. The trade in these goods in the country becomes brisk.

Effects on Foreign Trade Restrictions on Import of Goods. But effects of industrialisation are more on foreign rather than on internal trade. One of the important effects is that with the production of indigenous goods, and because of emergence of industrial area, import quota is considerably reduced. Thus every effort is made to put every restriction on the import of goods which are being manufactured in the country. This is done with two main objects in view. The first object is that the newly set up industry is protected from competition of already established industries in the market. If newly set up industries are required to face world competition, these are bound to be ruined. Then another objective is that foreign exchange is saved. Since each nation is always short of foreign exchange, therefore by putting ban on import of these goods, foreign exchange is saved. But one adverse effect of this policy is that extent of foreign trade comes down.

Diversification in Trade. As long as the country is not industrialised, it is to depend on foreign market, for the purchase of only those commodities which are most essentially needed by the society. Thus trade is confined to few commodities only and that too, to a limited extent because limited foreign exchange availability does not permit to increase its scope. But when country becomes industrialised it becomes self-sufficient in some respects and is in a position to save some foreign exchange. Money thus saved can be used for the purchase of other goods and commodities.

Both way Trade. Still another effect is that the trade becomes both ways traffic. Before industrialisation, a nation is to depend on other countries. It is only to take and not to give. The exporting country is always in a better bargaining position and quotes terms to suit its convenience. On the other hand importing country has nothing to export or bargain. But with industrialisation the situation changes.

Dependence on Capital Goods. Dependence for spare parts and capital equipments increases, in so far as countries going to be industrialised are concerned. For the establishment of industry machines and spare parts are needed. These are not manufactured in the country and ought to be imported from the countries which can provide them. In this way industrialisation brings dependence on capital goods in foreign trade.

Industrialisation in fact, influences balance of international trade. There are many instances to quote that those countries which were having adverse balance of trade before industrialisation had a favourable trade balance after industrialisation. Not only this, but after industrialisation many nations emerged as exporters instead of remaining as importers only.

APPROPRIATE INDUSTRIAL TECHNOLOGY

1. Technology Factors. There is no doubt that technological factors contribute very substantially to the raising of industrial productivity. In fact, it is the single most powerful factor with the greatest impact on industrial productivity. Just compare production of cloth by a worker with the aid of a handloom, a powerloom and automatic loom and one can notice what difference technological factors have made to productivity. Thus, "The application of motive power and mechanical improvement to the processes of production have accelerated the pace of industrialisation to an unprecedented degree, and have given us the vision of the past and unexplored frontiers that still lie ahead of us in the realm of science and technology." Mechanical power, highly complicated and sophisticated machines, efficient integration of various processes of production, specialisation of work have all tremendously increased industrial productivity. If Ford could produce just about six cars per month when the factory was established in the beginning of the present century, the same factory can now turn out, a car per minute, thanks to the unprecedented advances in sciences and technology and assembly line production system.

Increase in Productivity. But it is very difficult to measure exactly how much increase there has taken place in industrial productivity due to technological progress and advances, though its tremendously favourable impact on industrial productivity is undoubted.

If, in developing countries like India, industrial productivity is relatively low compared to that in the developed countries, one very important reason is obsolete machinery, lack of spare parts, absence of or inadequate skills for handling machines, inadequate power supply and comparative neglect of Research and Development which are the very foundation and basis of technological progress and continual advances.

Technological Aspect of Production. So far as technological aspect of rationalisation is concerned, it involved standardisation of product, simplification of process of production wherever possible, mechanisation of process of production, intensification of efforts by labour, and specialisation of work.

Standardisation. Standardisation implies a judicious process of selection of materials and products. It means fixing of certain standards, eliminating unsuitable sizes (for example, two or three standard sizes of toilet soaps rather than having hundreds of sizes of different shapes and forms). Elimination of undesirable sizes would increase productivity of existing industrial units and of capital equipment.

Simplification. Simplification implies rendering complex industrial productive processes simple. On the basis of experience and experimentation complex technical process can be reduced to simple processes. With the simplification of technical operations, workers would find it easy to acquire the skills and, thus, become more efficient and productive.

Standardisation of a product would be beneficial from the point of view of retailers who will have to keep a smaller stock and also beneficial from the point of view of consumers as they will have to choose from among a fewer but better varieties of a product.

Mechanisation. Mechanisation implies mechanical operations in place of manual handling of production process. Mechanisation ensures uniformity, accuracy and regularity of supply. Mechanisation helps to bring about standardisation of products and thus helps to reap all the advantages of standardisation.

Intensification. Intensification implies increasingly rapid speed of execution. The main objective of 'intensification' is increasing the rapidity of productive processes by removing inefficiency and slackness.

Mechanisation also results in specialisation or helps to bring about specialisation with increasing efficiency of labour and productivity and lower costs of production and prices of goods.

Thus, it would be observed that standardisation, simplification, mechanisation with increasing efficiency of labour and productivity and lower costs of production and prices of goods.

2. Organisational Aspect. On the organisational front, rationalisation implies some sort of agreement and coordinated action by all the producers in an industry with a view to coordinate total supply with total.

Labour Intensive Technology. Under-developed and undeveloped countries are always faced with many serious problems in so far as industry and economy are concerned.

Labour Intensive Techniques: Those who favour labour intensive techniques argue as under:

(a) ***Providing of Employment.*** One of the most serious problems of poor countries is that of providing employment to millions of its people. In case labour intensive production techniques are adopted, main stress shall be on the labour and thus many people will get employment. This will increase employment opportunities and the nation will be in a position to solve this problem at least to some extent.

(b) ***Helps in the Proper use of Raw Material.*** Each nation has some raw material locally available to it. If labour intensive techniques are adopted then the very raw material is very usefully utilised *e.g.*, cotton can be used for manufactured of cloth at village level with labour intensive techniques.

(c) ***Necessity of Capital is Reduced.*** Poor countries are always short of capital due to various reasons. The people have low per capita income and as such their saving capacity is very low. The rate of capital formation is equally slow. The result is that these countries are forced to borrow from foreign countries. The nation is required to pay heavy interests. At the time of repayment, the nation is heavily strained and forced to have further borrowing.

(d) ***Encouragement to Cottage Industries.*** Cottage and small scale industries are complementary ot large scale industries. These also pay a very significant role in the economic life of a nation. In countries like Japan and Switzerland cottage industries play a more important role than large scale industries. If labour intensive techniques are adopted, then cottage and small scale industries will receive encouragement for the betterment of the nation as a whole.

(e) ***Helps in Raising Standard of the Family.*** When labour intensive techniques are adopted with that cottage and small scale industries are run with the help of locally available raw material. In these industries then the women and children all get an opportunity to participate and join. Thus all the members of family become earning hands.

(f) ***Urbanisation is Checked.*** In case labour intensive techniques are adopted, then jobs will be locally available, because raw material is locally available. When the workers can get the job at their own place of living, they will never think of migration to cities. In this way urbanisation is checked, which is of course a major problem of our modern society.

(g) ***Much of National Income is Saved.*** Usually when the people migrate to cities, because of capital oriented techniques of production, a huge amount is spent by the state on providing amenities, security and facilities to them. If they remain in the villages then no such expenditure is incurred and it becomes available to the society for investment in the industry and for additional production. But when there is labour oriented technique of production, the people are not required to leave their villages.

(h) ***Quick Results Available.*** Usually when capital intensive techniques of production are adopted, there is gap between production and investment. The people are till then supposed to wait. on the other hand in labour intensive techniques there is no gap between investment and production. The labour begins to work with the available skill and the society gets the product.

(i) ***Inflation is Checked.*** Capital intensive techniques mean spending more and more capital in the industry. When more money is available in the market and gets circulated, then evil effect is that the economy cannot bear it. There then starts inflation. But on the other hand when there is labour intensive technique of production then no capital comes in the market and the nation is not faced with the problem of inflation.

(j) ***Monopolies Checked.*** Capital intensive techniques of production ultimately result in the creation of monopolies. Every effort will be made to create a situation, when distribution, sale and production of a commodity is controlled by only one person or a group of persons. But if labour intensive techniques of production are adopted then there is no question of creation of monopoly situation and the society will be saved from the evils of monopoly situation.

(k) ***No Concentration of Power.*** When there is labour intensive technique of production, the changes of concentration of economic power in the hands of few persons are reduced to the minimum. The workers and labourers work on small scale and cottage industries and whatsoever they produce they keep the reward with themselves. On the other hand when there is capital oriented or capital intensive industry, capital gets concentrated in few hands and those who manage to get power begin to control social, economic and political life of the country and thus create problems for the whole nation.

(l) ***Discouragement to Capitalism.*** Capital intensive techniques of production encourage capitalism, because those who have wealth will only be in a position to produce. We however, know that capitalism is now an outdated concept. But in labour intensive techniques of production, there is no danger of capitalism raising its ugly head.

(m) ***Advantages of Decentralisation.*** Usually in capital intensive techniques of production, the industries get concentrated in few areas to get the advantage of external economies. In these days when wars and internal disturbances can break out at any time, if one area in which industries have concentrated, becomes a trouble spot, whole nation gets dislocated. There is always a desire that there should be decentralisation of industries. This helps in maintaining supplies partially, even in difficult times.

(n) ***Upliftment of the Poor.*** In labour intensive techniques the poor workers are the real beneficiary. Firstly because they get employment, secondly they are not forced to migrate to cities where they would have been forced to pay heavily on rent and for maintaining themselves and lastly by not paying to the middle man, may that be even an industrialist or a capitalist. When they keep their earnings, with themselves obviously, their living standard rises and the poor get a chance to rise in life.

(o) ***Consumption of Goods Increases.*** In capital intensive techniques of production, purchasing capacity of only few persons increases. In this way even if the industry is in a position to produce, it cannot have consumer market and thus producing capacity of the industry remains idle to a great extent. But when the poor have purchasing capacity due to labour intensive techniques of production, then consumer market gets widened and the industry gets encouragement more and more goods are produced to the advantage of the nation.

Economists like Dobb, are of the opinion that capital intensive technique of production has its own advantages. Some such advantages which have been mentioned in this regard are follows:

1. Quicker Rate of Growth. When capital is available, new machinery can be set up. The nation proceeds on the path of industrialisation. The rate of growth is both faster as well as quicker. The result of all this is that nation is in a position to become self-sufficient very quickly and in many ways.

2. Bulk Production Possible. In labour intensive techniques it is not possible to produce the goods in bulk. The labourers have their own limited capacity to produce. It is only bulk production which can meet the needs of the society. But in capital intensive production it becomes possible to produce goods in bulk, with which both national as well as international needs can be met.

3. Possible to Produce Goods at Cheap Rates. One of the advantages of bulk production is that the goods are produced at cheap rates. In the case of labour intensive technique of production goods are bound to be costly and if the consumer is to purchase costly goods, then in the long run he is the sufferer.

4. More Amount Available for Re-investment. When there is labour intensive technique of production, very little amount is saved for re-investment in the industry. We know that unless money for reinvestment from internal resources is available, no nation can progress. But the nation is not faced with this type of problem when capital intensive technique of production is adopted.

5. No indifference to Technological Inventions. If labour intensive techniques of production are adopted then the nation will have to go on using old obsolete methods of production. We know that those nations which do not take advantage of latest techniques of production made available to the society by scientific and technological inventions, will in the long run be the sufferer and continue to remain backward.

6. Quality Goods become Available. In so far as quality is concerned goods produced manually cannot be of same high quality, as the goods which are produced with the help of machines to which capital intensive technique of production gives birth. Thus the society gets better quality goods with the help of capital intensive techniques of production.

7. No Stagnation in Economy. Once the nation remains scientifically and technologically backward, then whole economy will become stagnant. A stagnant economy would obviously mean poor living standard of the people, less chances of employment, less respect in the international field and so on. From our actual practice we find that every nation is always keen to break the economic backwardness created by stagnant economy.

8. No Surplus Labour. Though in the beginning it may appear that in labour intensive technique more workers are getting employment but in the long run one will find that if the life of the plant is taken as a span, then more people will be absorbed under capital oriented than labour oriented technique.

9. Possible to Cope with the Increasing Population. In poor countries population is very rapidly increasing. For this increasing population, output per head must be raised. If labour intensive techniques are adopted chances of output coping with increased population are very low.

Both labour intensive and capital intensive techniques have their own advantages as well as disadvantages. A poor country cannot decide which of the two is better. Therefore, the nation cannot think in terms of 'either' or 'or' but must combine both the systems together, in such a way that the benefits of both are available to the society.

FACTORS TO PROMOTE INDUSTRIALISATION

Process of industrialisation is not very easy. The difficulties are of course great, but it is wrong to think that these are insurmountable. Though it may take time but gradually a determined nation will be in a position to industrialise itself. Some of the factors which promote industrialisation may briefly be discussed as under:

1. Availability of Natural Resources. A country which wishes to industrialise itself will be in a position to do so soon in case natural resources are available in the country and the nation is not to depend on other nations for making these available. Natural resources provide basic raw material needed for the promotion of industry. It is then left to the Government to arrange and to see that these resources are properly exploited and made available to the industry as such low rates that it can afford to produce goods at cheap rates for the nation as whole.

2. Entrepreneurial Ability. A country having able entrepreneurs will always go faster on the path of industrialisation, as compared with a country, which has no able managers. It is the responsibility of the country to produce able managers. The nation should also see that those who are trained in industrially advanced countries do not become a class among themselves, but provide sufficient training to others in the country so that stream of trained people flows in the country itself.

3. Facilities to Labourers and Workers. Industrialisation becomes easy where facilities to labourers and workers are available in the industries and they feel attracted and tempted to join these. These facilities should be so alluring and attractive.

4. Setting up of Corporations. One method which can promote industrialisation is that Industrial Development Corporations should be set up, which should be exclusively responsible for the development of different sectors in the industry and should ensure that problems which come on the path of industrialisation are immediately removed so that whole process becomes smooth.

5. Availability of Labour. In the countries where manpower both skilled and unskilled is available, path of industrialisation will be easy, as compared with the industries, where it is not available.

6. Availability of Capital. In underdeveloped and undeveloped countries the capital for setting up new industries is usually very short and shy. It is preferred to be spent on purchase of agricultural land, because more prestige is attached to that. Moreover whereas returns from agricultural lands are sure, these are speculative in the case of industrial investments. The government can promote industrialisation by providing incentives to the shy capital by way of guaranteeing return of capital used in setting up industries or by giving some minimum profit on the investments made so that the problem of risk in investments is solved.

7. Role of International Organisations. In the process of industrialisation international bodies play a vital role. It is with the help of these bodies that the exchange of expertise, technical knowhow and difficulties of foreign exchange are considerably solved. Who does not know that such international bodies as World Bank; International Finance Corporation; International Development Association; International Monetary Fund and International Fund for Economic Development have played a vital role in the industrialisation of non-industrialised countries.

8. Role of Industrially Advanced Countries. Industrially advanced countries can play a big role in the complex and difficult task of industrialisation. This they can do by:

(a) technical personnel to train the untrained people of less advanced countries;

(b) by providing training facilities to the students of developing countries in their own country;

(c) by providing them machinery and where necessary funds as well;

(d) by assuring non-industrialised nations that supply of spare parts of the machinery being supplied to them will be continued;

(e) by way of long term loans, thereby not taxing their limited resources;

(f) by assuring countries that situation will not be allowed to develop in which good produced will not be consumed.

9. Easy Availability of Foreign Capital. In case foreign capital is easily available, then industrialisation becomes easy. It helps in two ways; firstly foreign exchange becomes easily available and secondly it becomes possible to fully utilise internal available resources for industrialisation. In many cases though the nation may spare finances from internal resources, yet their utilisation might not become possible because necessary foreign capital for setting up industry is not available.

10. Arrangements for Providing Protection. It is essential that newly set up industries should be given protection, from foreign manufactured cheap but good goods till these come of age and are in a position to complete with advanced countries of the world.

11. Checking of Inflation. Industrialisation needs heavy investments, for which money can raised both by internal resources and with the help of foreign nations. Usually less advanced countries of the world are not in a position to bear the burden of this extra investment resulting in inflation. This makes masses vehemently oppose industrialisation. It is therefore, essential that investment in industrialisation should be made only to the extent to which economy can bear that and inflationary tendencies are effectively checked.

12. International Trade. Each nation today has international trade both for development and survival. It is with its help that foreign exchange becomes easily available, and nation can procure machinery and spare parts. Consumption of goods produced is facilitated.

13. Industrial Planning. Industrialisation of non-industrialised nations needs proper planning. Industrial planning must clearly specify the extent to which the nation is prepared to industrialise, itself and also the ways and means of industrialisation. It should decide priority areas of industrialisation. But greatest care to be taken is that different sectors of industrial economy do not clash with each other and are harmoniously allowed to grow.

14. Government's Fiscal Policies. If a nation wants to go industrially fast, it enjoins upon the Government of that nation to follow a fiscal policy which is sound and conductive for industry. The policy should discourage speculative investment, bring about an increased investment; increase in number of subsidiary industries and provide for tax concessions in re-investment.

These are some of the steps which promote industrialisation, but all these cannot be taken all at once. It takes a very long time to formulate industrial policy and still more to implement that, because no industrially backward nation can successfully launch programme of industrialisation without active co-operation of international organisations on the one hand and industrially advanced countries on the other. In the wake of industrialisation, cottage industries receive a setback and importance of agriculture is reduced to a considerable extent.

EFFECTS OF PARTITION OF INDIAN ECONOMY

1. Change in Location Factors. Before partition of the country there were certain locations which were considered very useful and advantageous for location of industries. Some of these areas and it was considered unsafe to locate industries in those areas. In this way the country lost the advantages of the locations of these areas for industrial purposes.

2. Dislocation of Transport Facilities. Immediately after the partition of the country there was complete dislocation in transport facilities. The whole system was put under heavy strains due to migration of the people from one part of the country to the other. Similarly people employed in running transport system migrated to Pakistan from India and vice versa thereby creating gaps at all levels, both technical and non-technical.

3. Loss of Many Industries. Partition of the country resulted in the loss of many industries to India, which were very vital for development. Indian industries of jute and cotton received a serious set back, whereas before partition, the country enjoyed monopoly in these industries. From a supplier nation, India now became a dependent nation for raw jute and raw as well as medium staple cotton.

4. Attitude of Pakistan. Unfortunately after the partition of the country, attitude of Pakistan was not very favourable towards India. It always remained hostile. Thus the nation had to spend a lot of money on the defence of the country, which otherwise would have been made available for industrial development of the nation.

5. Short Supply of Foreign Capital. After the partition of the country, there was political instability in the country. The result was that there was no foreign capitalist, who was prepared to invest in Indian industries. Growth of industries also suffered for want of foreign capital.

6. Import of Food Grains. With the partition of the country food producing areas went to Pakistan. Though undivided India was deficit in food, yet this dependency considerably increased. The result was that the nation had to spare her limited foreign exchange for the import of food, instead of importing machinery for industrial growth and development.

7. Shortage of Raw Material. Immediately after the partition of the country raw material became in short supply. Without raw material no industry can run. In this way shortage of raw material adversely effected growth of industries in India.

8. Loss of Market. After the partition of the country, India lost a very good market for her industrial goods. India lost her market for cotton, textile, glass, rubber and vegetable oil goods. In addition to this, India also lost her market in rubber goods, brass, copper and foot wear. Loss of market for these goods, very adversely effected the growth of these industries.

9. Loss of Skilled Labour. The Muslim labourers had an expertise in certain types of industries *e.g.* hosiery goods, woollen goods, metal works etc. With the partition of the country, most of the skilled workers in these industries decided to migrate to Pakistan, creating a big gap. In order to even maintain these industries, trained persons were needed. Need of these persons went still high when the problem of development of these industries came to the front.

10. Unfavourable Balance of Trade. Before the partition of the country, India had favourable balance of trade. It is estimated that at the time of partition, India had accumulated sterling balance to the extent of 17330 million and repatriation of pre-war sterling debt of Rs. 4200 millions. With this foreign exchange available to the nation, she could import any machinery, which could help in the growth of Indian industries. But soon after the partition, India had to import raw jute and food grains, which put heavy strains on the economic resources of the country.

11. Problem of Settlement of Refugees. Unfortunately with the partition of the country there started influx of refugees. The number of persons who migrated to India and thus needed immediate settlement ran into millions. They were to be provided jobs and settlements. Attention and resources of the nation were diverted to their settlement, with the result that for long time to come the nation could not spare time and resources for the growth and development of industries.

These were some of the adverse effects of partition on the industrial development and growth of the country. There were however, certain favourable effects as well, which may briefly be discussed as under:

(a) ***Advantages of Industrial Establishments.*** At the time of partition India got 91% of the total industrial establishments, whereas only 9% went to Pakistan. Similarly 93% of the total industrial workers employed in these industries remained with India and only 7% decided to migrate to Pakistan. It will be appreciated, that it was no less an advantage for India at that critical time. At the time of partition, there was not a single industry in Pakistan, whereas the number of such industries in India which employed one lakh or more persons was six.

(b) ***Advantages of Mineral Resources.*** After partition, India was put in advantageous position in mineral resources. India got major resources in coal, mica, maganese, iron are

and other minerals. India got 97% of the mineral resources of undivided India, whereas Pakistan got only 3% of these resources. India was thus in an advantageous position in this regard as well.

(c) ***Advantage of Entrepreneurial Skills.*** As compared with Pakistan, India had many diversified industries which attracted even Muslims entrepreneurs as well as managerial persons. These people either did not migrate from India or soon after migration again came back to India. In this way India was placed in an advantageous position. No one can deny that big entrepreneur and qualified and competent managerial personnel contribute a lot in the growth and development of Indian industries.

GUIDING PRINCIPLES OF INDUSTRIALISATION

When India won freedom, its industrial scenario was indeed grim. Of course, there were a few consumer goods industries and one or two steel mills, basic industries were largely neglected and capital goods production was insignificant. Further, most of the industries were largely concentrated in a few regions while most parts of the country were without any industry worth the name. Plans for industrialisation had therefore to rectify these imbalances by bringing about integrated and balanced development of industries in various regions of the country. The guiding principles or main objectives of the programmes of industrial development had therefore been:

(a) To bring about a faster pace of industrialisation for achieving a rapid growth of the economy.

(b) To develop basic, heavy and capital goods industries to fill the gaps in our industrial structure.

(c) To provide basic infrastructure for rapid growth of industry.

(d) To create employment opportunities.

(e) To promote balanced regional development.

(f) To help in promoting import substitution with a view to limiting imports and saving foreign exchange.

Having set the above guiding principles, the Government of India took upon itself the task of providing basic infrastructure for rapid industrial development. Rail transport, electricity, heavy electricals, chemicals, machine tools, iron and steel, etc. were sought to be directly developed by the state under the Public Sector. Private sector was provided necessary incentives and concessions in the government's policy and given financial accommodation by the public financial institutions. In brief, there was an all around effort, both public and private, to put India on the industrial map of the world.

The industrial progress that the country has made over the past four decades is commendable. India is now counted among the top ten industrial nations of the world. Contribution of manufacturing sector to the GDP has gone up from a bare ten per cent in 1950-51 to nearly twenty per cent now. The industrial sector as a whole (comprising manufacturing, electricity, gas and water supply and mining and quarrying) accounts for nearly 27 per cent of GDP as against barely 15 per cent in 1950-51.

Shortcomings of Industrial Development

However, it must be accepted that industrial development in India has not been strictly in accordance with the guiding principles and it has failed to achieve some of the cherished objectives.

An important shortcoming of industrial growth has been its unequal distribution between various regions. The areas which already had important industries have provided nucleus for further concentration of industry. Not only traditional industrial cities have become overcrowded causing environmental degradation, but also traditional industrial states have attracted more industries thereby causing regional imbalances. For example, nine States viz., Andhra Pradesh, Bihar, Gujarat, Karnataka, Madhya Pradesh, Maharashtra, Tamil Nadu, Uttar Pradesh and West Bengal, account for about 80 per cent of industrial activity in India. Industries contribute about three-fourths of value added and eighty per cent of employment in these States. All other States outside this group of nine have thus very little industrial output and employment. This shows that the objective of regional balanced growth through industrialisation has remained unfulfilled and that industrial development of the past four decades has further accentuated regional imbalances.

Another weakness of industrial development in India has been in the field of employment generation. Industrial expansion was sought to be the means of eradicating unemployment. However, the manufacturing sector or the large industries have failed to generate employment significant enough o make any dent into the unemployment problem. In India, labour force has been growing at a rate of about 2.5 per cent per annum but industrial employment growth rate has been only around 1 per cent thus causing pressure on non-industrial activities such as agriculture, trade and service sectors.

An important consequence of industrial development in India has been the rapid growth in industries producing consumer durables. The growth rate of industries producing such goods a consumer electronics has been faster than those producing goods for mass consumption. This shows that industry is catering more and more to the requirements of the rich rather than those who really need to benefit from industrial growth.

Yet another snag with industrial development of India has been the unwieldy and inefficient growth of the public sector. Though initially conceived as the vehicle of industrial growth and an instrument to prevent concentration of economic power in the private hands, the gigantic growth of the public sector and its inefficient functioning has been a drain on Indian economy. These enterprises have not much to show by way of efficient performance; a large majority of them have been making perpetual losses thus causing a continued drain on tax-payers' money. Reforms are now under way to improve functioning of public enterprises by incorporating some element of privatisation through public sector disinvestment in their equity that is being offered to the private sector.

The overall picture of India's industrial development is thus a mixed one. Over the years industry has grown at a reasonably high rate but there have been wide variations in annual growth rates from one decade to another. There has been expansion of the basic industries and the capital goods sector, but also the production of consumer durables has been faster than the goods of mass consumption. The industrial expansion has also failed to eradicate unemployment or mitigate regional inequalities.

INDUSTRIAL PRODUCTIVITY

Factors Causing Low Productivity. One of the factors making for low productivity is constraints on production. It is useful here to note the trends in capacity utilisation in the industrial sector. Surprisingly, in spite of the importance of the subject, very few systematic studies exist, especially at the aggregate level. Given this position, the results put out by the Centre for monitoring the Indian economy on capacity utilisation in manufacturing industries come too handy. According to these results, in 1980 capacity utilisation in manufacturing industries was 74.4 per cent, suggesting that capacity is underutilised to the extent of a maximum of 25 per cent.

Falling Capital Utilisation. Another disturbing Act is that capacity utilisation is exhibiting a falling trend. During the decade of the seventies capacity utilisation has fallen from 85.2 per cent in 1970 to 74.4 per cent in 1980. Butt the data also threw up some beautiful signs since the trend can be broken up into two distinct phases, the first one from 1970 to 1974 exhibiting a market fall in capacity utilisation.

At this stage, it would be instructive to note the rationale for fall in capacity utilisation. The overall growth in capacity during the period has been around 88 per cent as compared to a growth of 64 per cent in production. Capacity growth of the order of 6.5 per cent per annum could not by any reasonable criteria be considered excessive.

Capacity Utilisation. Information of capacity utilisation presented in ICICI's financial performance of companies for 1979-

80, is also interesting. According to data presented in the study, the median value of capacity utilisation for a sample of 238 public limited companies was 67 per cent in 1979-80, showing a marginal decline from the previous year. The utilisation was specially low in companies in the machinery manufacture industries.

Factors Causing Low Utilisation of Capacity This lower utilisation of capacity not only in industry but also in agriculture could be traced to many factors. In some sectors, inadequate demand, as currently in textiles, could be the constraint. But it is now widely recognised that quite some part of under-utilisation of cap[acity could be accounted for by deficiencies in the basic infrastructure of power, coal and transport. Many of these are being attended to and many of the lagging sectors have shown improved performance lately.

Stagnation in Productivity. Stagnation in productivity can also be overcome by improving the incentives to work and lessening industrial disputes. However, one of the unfortunate elements in a situation where productivity is to be stepped up is the loss in mandays due to unhealthy industrial relations. Since 1951 there has been an increasing number of loss of mandays. This is an area where action could bring quick results by way of increased-production to boost productivity. Recent measures to limit strikes should be considered as only the first step to provide the breathing time necessary to create an atmosphere where the basic causes leading to the need for strikes are less end as it is difficult to completely eliminate them.

INDUSTRIAL SICKNESS

Industrial sickness refers to that state of industry when industrial units continue to accumulate perpetual losses and thus become economically unviable propositions. The symptoms of industrial sickness include failure to pay statutory liabilities like the Provident Fund, ESI contribution and failure to pay timely instalments of principal and interest on loans taken from financial institutions and through public deposits. Increase in inventories with a large number of slow moving items, high rate of rejections of goods manufactured, low capacity utilisation and frequent industrial disputes are among the causes of industrial sickness.

Incidence of Sickness in Indian Industries. The problem of industrial sickness has assumed quite serious dimensions over the past years. Some of our traditional industries like cotton textiles, jute and sugar have a large number of sick units. Even some units in the non-traditional industries like engineering and chemicals have also fallen prey to this disease. Cement and rubber industries too suffer from industrial sickness. Apart from the large and medium sized industrial units, many of small scale enterprises suffer from industrial sickness. Regionwise, Maharashtra and West Bengal show the highest incidence of industrial sickness.

The number of sick and weak industrial units (both the large, medium and small scale industrial units), which was 24,530 in 1980 with an outstanding bank credit of Rs. 1808 crores, went up to 2.23 lakh in 1991 and the outstanding bank credit locked up in them was high of Rs. 10768 crores. The position further worsened and at the end of March, 1998, the number of sick industrial units stood at 2.37 lakh and the outstanding bank credit against them increased to Rs. 13787 crores.

Besides locking up of funds, which could be otherwise fruitfully utilised, the phenomenon of industrial sickness tends to aggravate the problem of unemployment and also creates adverse climate for further industrial growth. In order to provide a focal point to handle the task of rehabilitation of such units, the Industrial Reconstruction Corporation of India has been reconstituted as the Industrial Reconstruction Bank of India (IRBI). The IRBI is now the principal agency for the reconstruction and rehabilitation of sick industrial units. The approach towards rehabilistion is very selective and only potentially viable units are taken up for rehabilitation.

Under the Sick Industrial Companies (Special Provision) Act, 1985 (SICA), the Government of India has set up a Board for Industrial and Financial Reconstruction (BIFR) in January 1987 that became operational on May 15, 1987. The BIFR determines the preventive, ameliorative, remedial and other measures which are required to be taken in respect of sick industrial companies and takes steps to assure expeditious enforcement of these measures.

Causes of Industrial Sickness

Industrial sickness is not something that suddenly befalls an industrial unit; it is a gradual crippling of an enterprise that manifests in the form of slow down of sales, reduced production, erosion in capital base, difficulties in honouring loans and bills and interest payable, piling up of excessive inventories and even difficulties in meeting wage bill and salary expenses. All such features of sickness set on the enterprise slowly over time and finally culminate in industrial sickness. The factors that bring about such problems of sickness may be external and beyond control of the enterprise or internal to it, or a combination of both. Some such factors are:

(A) External Factors

(i) Decline in market demand for the goods produced by the industrial unit due to a shift in taste and preference of the consumers or due to their reduced purchasing power consequent to the crippling effect of inflation, unemployment or market recession. Or shift in demand to substitute products.

(ii) Decline in market share due to entry of new firms, increased competition and emergence of excess capacity in the industry as a whole and its individual production units.

(iii) Excessive government control, regulation and restrictions on product mix, industrial location, price controls, minimum wage laws and inability to retrench excessive workers have all contributed to high cost of production and the consequent losses due to inability to sell at market prices.

(iv) Increased costs of production due to such bottlenecks as inadequate power supply, non-availability of raw materials at reasonable prices, costly finance etc. The producers fail to sell their high cost products at the prevailing market prices and hence incur continuous losses.

(v) Government levies such as high excise duties, higher other taxes and charges by the government have also added to the cost of production. Such taxes and levies could not be recovered from the market by raising product prices as upward revision of per unit prices has, in most cases, led to fall in demand, lower sales revenue and the consequent losses.

(B) Among the internal factors contributing to industrial sickness are:

(i) Poor maintenance of plant and machinery, lack of technological upgradation and modernisation, non-replacement of worn-out machines on time.

(ii) Lack of managerial and financial expertise, unjustified and excessive expenditure on overheads, improper use of materials and manpower, incompetent financial planning, absence of quality control and improper coordination of various production and distribution processes have all led to high cost production.

(iii) Wrong choice of location, technology or product coupled with frequent labour disputes, strikes, lockouts and non-cooperative attitude of trade unions lead to lower production and higher per unit cost and thus reduce economic viability of the industrial unit.

These are the more general causes of industrial sickness; they all contribute to the malady though the intensify and combination of these factors may differ from one enterprise to another. In many cases it could be the demand shrinkage while in others it is primarily labour unrest. It could be a combination of both. In some cases natural disasters like fire, accident, etc. could be the cause while others may get sick due to inadequacy of funds or unwillingness of management, modernise industrial units. Irresponsible management, wilful manipulation of funds, policy of declaring excessive dividends without retaining adequate reserves, lack of sensitivity and alertness on the part of management to heed to repeated signals about ill health of the industry and thus not taking any timely and strong remedial measures, all contribute to industrial sickness. Irresponsible or unscrupulous managements may borrow excessive funds at uneconomic interest rates without regard to their ability to make payment of interest or repayment of loans on time have landed many enterprises into the lap of sickness.

Consequences of Industrial Sickness

It is obvious that sick industrial unit, unless they are revived and restored to health by sound financial measures and managerial rejuvenation, are likely to close down sooner or later. In the case of closure of such units, whose number may continue to swell year after year, the worst affected sections are the working classes, *i.e.* the labourers working in these industries who face unemployment and the loss of means of living. Industrial sickness also represents the work of capital resources locked in them, which by no means is desirable in a capital poor country. Industrial sickness also spreads from one industry to another through input-output relationship and thus threatens to engulf many industries. It generally creates on adverse investment climate for the domestic as well as the foreign investors. The government certainly cannot ignore the adverse consequence of industrial sickness on the economy and thus adopts many preventive as well as rehabilitative measures to put these industries back on the rails.

PROBLEMS OF UNDERDEVELOPED COUNTRY

Industrialisation creates its own problems and that perhaps is the reason that in many countries it is opposed. There are many causes responsible for that which might briefly be discussed as under:

(1) Lack of Transport Facilities. In non-industrial countries, which wish to industrialise themselves, transport facilities are badly needed. Lack of these facilities hinders the whole process. It is because even the choice of location of an industry becomes very difficult. Not only this but consumption of goods produced, as well as cost of production are dependent on location and in the initial stages of industrialisation, both these factors very much count in the spread or slowing down of whole process.

(2) Non Availability of Power. One of the major reasons why non-industrialised and underdeveloped countries take a long time for industrialisation is that they lack availability of power. This holds growth and expansion of large scale industries and also expansion of domestic industries as well.

(3) Size Local Market. If the local market for the consumption of goods produced by the industry is quite sufficient then the industry is encouraged and the process of industrialisation becomes both easy as well as quick. But when there is no or small local market, industrialists are discouraged, because they feel that they will have to face international market for consumption of goods. The investment then is slow and with that the whole process becomes slow.

(4) Lack of Trained Persons. Most of the advanced countries are usually not prepared to train people of unindustrialised countries. They are not willing to part with their technical knowhow because that decreases their importance.

(5) Absence of Facilities to the Workers. One of the problem of industrialisation is that the workers must be kept satisfied and happy so that they can produce more. To begin with each industry finds it difficult to provide many facilities to the workers with the result that good workers do not feel attracted towards industry. Thus lack of facilities discourages the workers and slows down the process of industrialisation.

(6) Lack of Repair Facilities. To begin with in every country machines will be imported from industrially advanced countries. The plants once imported need both repairs and spare parts. For this they are to depend on the exporting nation. Many a times due to one reason or the other repair facilities are either delayed and not made available, with the result that the machines slow down and the whole process of industrialisation is also slowed.

(7) Lack of Subsidiary Industries. When large-scale industries are set up these can successfully function only when there are also subsidiary industries which provide raw material and also use the waste sent out by these industries. In their absence cost of production goes very high and in many cases it becomes prohibitive.

(8) Rapid Population Growth. In case population growth is not checked, industrialisation will seriously suffer. Each nation has limited resources and in case these are constantly employed for meeting the need of ever-increasing population, the result will be that no money will be available for setting up new industries and the pace of industrialisation will become very slow.

(9) Low Per Capita Income. When the people have very low per capita income Industrialisation suffers. The people then have no capacity to set industries. Even if they manage to set up industries, they will have no purchasing power.

(10) Problem of Capital. One more serious problem regarding Industrialisation is lack of capital. Without huge capital no new industry can be set up. In the public sector the state can set up industries only by saving money from some other item of expenditure and how far this can be done and capital raised is a very serious problem. Similarly private sector will not spend capital on industry unless it is sure that it will have its returns. As we know that capital is very shy for coming out in the market.

(11) Lack of Banking and Credit Facilities. Industry needs heavy finances. Though the industrialists try to manage from their economic resources, yet times frequently come in the life of an industry when it is to depend on credit facilities. If these are available the problem does not arise, but if these facilities are not available, industry seriously suffers and industrialists get discouraged.

(12) Social Resistance. In some societies industrialisation is not a welcome. The society opposes industrialisation due to one reason or the other, with the result that industrialisation in such societies becomes problematic and does not proceed smoothly.

(13) Problem of Literacy. In most of the cases in under-developed countries the people are illiterate. They therefore, find it difficult to adjust themselves in the urban environments when they find job in the industry. Illiterate workers also take comparatively long time to pick up work in the factories.

(14) Social Restraints. In some societies occupational mobility has social restraints. These restraints result in slow labour turnover and flow of workers to the industry so as to avoid the displeasure of the society. In such societies rate of absenteeism is also very high. This also creates problem of industrial labour instability.

(15) Lack of Industrial Leadership. In societies where there is opposition to industrialisation, there is always lack of industrial leadership with the result that in case such nations decide to industrialise themselves, these feel considerably handicapped for want of proper leadership in the industry. Lack of proper industrial leadership also stands on the path of industrialisation.

(16) Strains on Public Administration. In many countries public administration is usually under heavy strains. The number of competent officials available for handling the jobs are usually few, as compared with the volume of work. By over-loading there can be no efficiency and because of concentration of power in few hands, chances of corruption increase many fold. In this way industry is either neglected or becomes victim of centralisation and in both the cases industrialisation suffers.

(17) Strict Licensing System. In many countries of the world resources are limited and it is essential that these should be judiciously used. These should be allotted in such a way that priority needs are met first of all. This is done by introducing licensing systems. When this system is applied very strictly and that too by corrupt officials, then supply becomes difficult for the industry, which finds it difficult to keep the machines running.

(18) Social Customs. In underdeveloped and undeveloped societies, social customs also stand on the way of industrialisation. Firstly in such societies saving is wasted on performance of social customs like marriage, birth and death ceremonies and thus very little surplus money is available. Then social prestige in societies is attached to owning land and residential accommodation and in many cases to ornaments as well than sparing money for industry thereby slowing down industrialisation in the country.

(19) Unforeseen Calamities. Then come some unforeseen and un-expected man made and natural calamities. These create devastation, destruction and divert all national energies to avoiding these rather than setting up new industries. Such calamities when frequent give a serious setback to the programme of industrialisation.

(20) Unfavourable International Conditions. On the attitude of developed countries very much depends growth of industrialisation in many undeveloped countries. They may not be very favourably inclined to spare machinery for installation; they may create artificial scarcity of spare parts; may put heavy restrictions on the export of machines and also may quote such high prices which the poor developing countries may not be in a position to afford.

(21) Inefficient Public Administration. Usually in under-developed countries public administration system is inefficient and corrupt with the result that industrial laws are not made on time and to meet the needs of the people. If enacted these are not properly enforced by corrupt officers on duty.

(22) Defective Tax Structure. When public administration goes in the hands of inefficient officers, then the whole tax structure becomes undependable. Such a structure might not suit the needs of industry and the industrialist might not feel tempted to set up new industries.

(23) Lack of Natural Resources. If the nation has no natural resources and still wants to industrialise itself, its dependence for raw material on imports increases which cannot be depended. When the supply of raw material is erratic, industry cannot progress or prosper and industrialisation becomes very difficult.

(24) Political Instability. Each one will like to set up an industry when one is sure about the attitude of production party in power and its approach to industrialisation. Political instability makes investment of capital very shy and as such industrialisation is very much discouraged.

CHARACTERISTICS OF AN UNDERDEVELOPED ECONOMY

An underdeveloped economy is defined by different economists from different viewpoints. There is no any common definition available. We give below some important definitions with their analysis:

The group of specialists appointed by the UNO, has defined an underdeveloped economy on the basis of 'Per Capita Real Income' considered as to be its standard measure. They say, "We use the term underdeveloped country to mean countries in which per capita real income is low when compared with the per capita real incomes of the United States, Canada, Australia and West Europe."

This cannot be regarded as the exact definition of an underdeveloped economy as it considers the per capita income of some countries as the standard, which is an indefinite base. On the basis of this definition, even it is possible that if some developed nation has a lesser per capita income than that of these given countries, it may be also called as an underdeveloped country, which is not right from any viewpoint.

Prof. Nurkse defines an underdeveloped economy as the following, "The so called underdeveloped areas as compared with the advanced ones are unequipped with capital in relation to their population and industrial resources." In this definition Nurkse has considered the deficiency of capital as the only reason and measure of underdevelopment. Shortage of capital is only one cause among the many causes and not the only cause of underdevelopment.

One other definition is given by Prof. Jacob Viner, who considered future potentials of development of a country as the standard. According to him, "If a country which has good potential prospects for using more capital or more labour or more available natural resources or all these to support the present population on a higher level of living or of its per capita income level is already fairly high to support large population, it can be termed as underdeveloped."

On the basis of all these definitions, we may define the underdeveloped economy as the following: "It is such an economy where the rate of capital formation is low. Peoples' standard of living is also low. Besides this there are unused human resources and unexploited natural resources. A constant attempt is being made to use them fully and skilfully."

Different featurse are seen in different underdeveloped economies, but some are common to all of them. These are as follows:

1. Low Per Capita Income. The per capita real income in these economies is very low when compared with the income levels of the advanced countries. It is difficult to mention the level which distinguishes between the underdeveloped and developed countries, however it can be said that in underdeveloped countries Per Capita Income is so low that most of the population live below the normal standard of living. According to the World Development Report 1991 of the World bank, all the world economies can be divided into three categories. *(i)* Low income economy, *(ii)* Middle income economy, and *(iii)* High income economy.

According to the Report the Per Capita Income in the low income economy is around 320 dollars, in the middle income economy it is 1930 dollars and in the high income economy it is around 17080 dollars. Hence, there is a very big gap between an underdeveloped country and a developed country in regard to their per capita real income. A low income economy has a per capita income which is only two percent of the per capita income of the developed economy. In the underdeveloped countries themselves there are severe disparities, because the potential prospects of different countries also differ. The main reasons of low per capita income in these countries are: *(i)* Bigger quantity of population, or *(ii)* Low level of National Income, or *(iii)* Both, Low National income is caused by low productivity, low savings and investment, backward techniques, underdeveloped resources etc.

2. Dominance of Agriculture. In an underdeveloped economy a large part of the population depends upon agriculture for living. Industries and Service Sectors provide livelihood only to a small portion of the population. This is the reason that industry and service sectors remain undeveloped. In the developed countries only 2% to 7% part of population depend upon agriculture whereas in an underdeveloped economy this percentage is around 72. Similarly in the developed countries total National Income received only 3% contribution from the agricultural sector while in the underdeveloped countries contribution from this sector is around 35%. In the exports of an undeveloped country also there is dominance of agriculture products and agro-based raw materials. Thus the economic growth of these countries, to a great extent, depends upon agriculture.

3. Population. In the underdeveloped countries, total quantity of the population as well as the growth rate of population are high. There are some countries where growth rate of population is low but quantity of population is much more. The main reason of over-population is that these countries adopt modern methods of sanitation and health-care, when they come in contact with the developed nations. Consequently the death-rate in these countries has declined. But these countries hesitate to adopt family planning measures because of poverty, ignorance and religious dogma. This results in the rapid growth of population. Most of the underdeveloped countries are passing through a stage called "Population Explosion". Overpopulation affects in many ways, such as *(i)* A constant growth of unemployment in the country, *(ii)* Peoples' standard of living remains below the poverty line.

4. Widespread Unemployment, Underemployment and Disguised Unemployment. There is a widespread unemployment in these countries because of overpopulation, low industrial development and lack of capital formation. There is a shortage of job opportunities caused by low industrial growth. Besides this there is a state of underemployment also in an underdeveloped economy because of the lack of job opportunities. In other words people do not get suitable jobs, they deserve or they do not get full-time jobs. In some sectors there is disguised unemployment, which means in these sectors (especially in Agriculture) the marginal productivity of the labourer is zero. Even if some labourers are removed from these sectors, the production will remain unaffected. This situation is found only in absence of the job opportunities.

5. Lack of Capital Formation. There is lack of capital formation in the underdeveloped countries. The main reason for this is the low per head income and dominance of consumption, resulting in a very low quantity of savings. Even those people who save, cannot use their savings in the proper manner, as there are no banks, insurance companies and other financial institutions through which they may invest. Besides this the economic and social structure is so backward that the markets are limited and lack efficient entrepreneurs, producers and traders. This causes low demand level of the capital. The Growth rate of capital stock is also low, in other words the rate of capital form is very low.

6. Distribution of Income. In the underdeveloped countries there is widespread disparity in the distribution of income. Though disparity in distribution of income is also found in the developed countries but it is very low. In underdeveloped countries, a large part of Total National Income is concentrated in the hands of a few people, while the larger parts of the population have to be content with a very meagre income. For example 20% population of India enjoys 50% of the Total National Income, whereas 40% people having low income receive only 16% of it. Different studies show that more the country is developed, lesser the disparity of income is there.

7. Low Labour Productivity. In underdeveloped countries, Labour Productivity is very Low. This is both, the cause and the effect, of low Standard of Living. Low productivity results in less national income. Income level of the population is also low, and a large part of the population lives in severe poverty. Low productivity of labour is caused by many factors (which are usually present in the underdeveloped countries) such as lack of availability of inputs other than labour, which are used by labour in the process of production, low standard of health, absence of work incentive and lack of institutional infrastructure.

8. Poverty. It has become obvious after the study of the poverty level in underdeveloped countries that in these countries, about 35% of population has only between 50 to 75 dollars per capita annual income. This can be called the minimum standard of living. In India 37% population is below such poverty line. The worse part of the situation is that in the recent years, in spite of increase in the income of these underdeveloped countries, the volume of poverty has also been increased.

9. Foreign Trade. In the underdeveloped countries contribution of foreign trade is meagre in the national income. The main reason is that these countries have been in the foreign rule for a long period. Consequently their foreign trade is formulated according to the wishes of their past masters. Their export trade is limited to some traditional goods, in which the agricultural products and raw materials have a major part. Their imports are dominated by manufactured goods. These countries have foreign trade mostly with a few chosen countries or regions. Because of the greater volume manufactured goods, the level of industrialisation in these countries is low. The other reason for their backwardness in foreign trade is the absence of sufficient technical development required for industrial production. Hence these economies are usually very much dependent on imports. Value of import is usually more than the value of exports, and these countries are usually in the crisis of foreign exchange and adverse balance of payments. In these countries government gives stress on export goods, rather than commodities for internal consumption.

10. Social and Economic Institutions. In underdeveloped countries, there are no sufficient financial and other institutions, such as banks, insurance, and other trade and finance agencies. Money market and capital market are usually undeveloped and unorganised. One part of the economy is well developed while the others are undeveloped. Various monetary and financial policies of the government have no effect on the undeveloped sector, which hinders the economic development. Similarly, in these economies, some social institutions like caste system, joint family system, illiteracy and superstition are present which stagnate the economic development.

11. Dual Economy. In the underdeveloped countries dual economy is found. In the dual economy two different types of economies exist side by side. One sector of the economy is fully organised and developed, while the other is unorganised and undeveloped. The organised sector is perfectly developed, using ultramodern techniques through foreign exchange. On the contrary the unorganised sector is undeveloped, using old outdated techniques and making exchange by barter. Unorganised sectors also hinder the development of the organised sector. This dual economy is obvious, both in the rural and urban sectors. In the urban areas there are small and labour intensive, family industries on the one hand, and modern industries with the most advanced techniques on the other.

12. Market. In the underdeveloped countries, Markets are imperfect and undeveloped. They are very small in size. Due to low production, the per head income in these countries is less. Consequently the level of collective demand is also low. Immobility of the resources and ignorance of the people give birth to the imperfect, ill-organised markets.

13. Weak Administrative Structure. The administration of underdeveloped countries is generally not only weak and inefficient, but also corrupt. The main reasons for this are the lack of managerial efficiency and organisational facilities and the condition of polity prevailing. Due to ignorance of people bureaucrats can successfully misuse their authority and powers.

14. Lack of Technological Knowhow. In the underdeveloped countries, even general education is not available in sufficient quantity. Technical education is almost absent. Due to poverty not much money is spent on research and invention. Even if some new technique is developed, it cannot be properly utilised due to the lack of capital resources and services of skilled personnel. In these countries generally technology is imported from the foreign countries, as well as the skilled personnel also. As the modern techniques are absent, production is made by old redundant techniques, which causes higher production cost. Besides this there is lack of interest about using new techniques, in these countries. Due to surplus labour force, labour also opposes the use of new techniques.

15. Non-utilization or Underutilization of Productive Resources. In the underdeveloped economy the productive resources are either unutilised or underutilised. In spite of abundance of natural resources, these are not properly exploited. There are many reasons for this, such as lack of capital, absence of technical know-how, illiteracy and ignorance, use of age-old techniques etc. In India inspite of abundant natural resources, their proper exploitation has not been taken place.

Causes of Rapid Growth

A rapid increase in population during the post-Independence period accounted for by the higher growth rates of population. Factors affecting the growth rates of population can be classified into two groups: *(1)* those responsible for high birth rate, and *(2)* those responsible for falling death rate.

1. High Birth Rate. In India, the birth rate has remained persistently high. In India, climatic, economic, social and religious factors combine together to keep the birth rate very high. We shall discuss these factors in the succeeding section.

(i) **Climatic Factors.** India has a hot climate. Girls get matured at an early age in such a climate. Their reproductivity period starts normally from 14 years, resulting in a larger reproductivity span.

(ii) **Economic Factors.** The incidence of pregnancy and the number of children born in a poor household is generally larger for the following reasons:

(a) Every addition to the family in a poor household is treated as an asset. Children at a very young age start helping their parents to raise the family income.

(b) Because of deficient diet, lack of medical facilities, unhygienic living conditions, etc., the infant mortality rate among the poor people is generally high. In order to ensure that some children do survive, poor people tend to have large number of children.

(c) Children also act like insurance for their parents. These children, when grow up, provide security to their parents in old age.

(d) Poor people are generally illiterate. They do not understand the real implications of a large family, and therefore, resist the acceptance of family planning.

(e) Poor people cannot afford the costly contraceptives and oral medicines for controlling the size of their families.

(iii) Social Factors. Social factors also influence the size of a family. Among the various social factors affecting the growth of population the more important are as follows:

(a) Marriage is a universal phenomenon in India.

(b) Child marriage in rural India is a rule rather than an exception. Marriage at an early age lengthens the reproductive age of women.

(c) The number of women in the reproductive age is very large.

(d) The number of children born per couple tends to increase when the couple is desirous of male progeny which is considered a must according to customs.

(e) The joint family system also provides a spurt to population growth. In such a system, children are not the responsibility of the couple alone but of the whole family.

(iv) Religious Factors. India is a country of many faiths and cultures. Some religions do not prefer and preach family planning. For example, according to Christianity, termination of pregnancy is a sin. Even Mahatma Gandhi, who influenced the political scene of India for about four decades, did not agree to the idea of family planning. He considered it as an immoral act.

2. Falling Death Rate. In India, the death rate has declined considerably during the last five decades or so. The major factors responsible for the declining death rate are as follows:

(i) Control over many dreadful and chronic diseases such as plague, cholera, small-pox, etc. These diseases used to take a heavy toll of human life.

(ii) Invention of antibiotics and other life-saving drugs.

(iii) There are no deaths on account of good shortages and famines.

(iv) Improvement in diet and standard of living has increased life span of the people.

(v) Improvement in sanitation and cleanliness.

(vi) The provision of better maternity and post-natal care has helped to bring down the infant mortality rate.

Population Control. Growing population will create problems not only for the individual households but for the whole country. If population is allowed to grow at its present rate, it will retard economic development of our country. It is, therefore, essential to check the growth of population. The following measures can be adopted for population control:

(i) Industrial and Agricultural Development. Some thinkers believe that 'development is the best contraceptive'. By raising industrial and agricultural productivity higher incomes can be ensured for the labour class. It is through this increase in income that the poor families will almost certainly experience a beneficial decline in their traditionally high fertility.

(ii) Urbanisation. Urbanisation is usually associated with low fertility. Urbanisation changes the value of life and the outlook of the people. People living in crowded towns can easily realise the norms and necessity of a small size family.

(iii) **Enhancing the Status of Women in the Society.** Malnourished mothers give birth to weak and unhealthy infants. Such infants often die. This leads to frequent pregnancies. Women hardly have any say in determining the size of families. Women are generally dependent on men and it is the will of the man that ultimately prevails. High status of women in the society will create a sense of confidence and security in them which will have a desired effect on the fertility rate.

(iv) **Expanding Basic Education.** Enlightenment of women is essential to lower the fertility rate. Basic education makes possible for both men and women and acquisition of information of family planning. It increases their exposure to mass media and printed material, and enables them to learn about modern contraceptives and their use.

(v) **Reducing Infant Mortality.** By improving the nutritional content of diet, hygienic conditions and health services, the rate of infant mortality could be reduced considerably.

(vi) **Propagation.** Through mass media, the people can be informed, educated and persuaded to accept family planning which would ultimately reduce the birth rate.

(vii) **Provision of Family Aids.** The government should provide simple, non-injurious and effective contraceptives at cheaper rates. It should set up family welfare centres for the needy couples. Research facilities relating to the discovery of new and effective contraceptives must be expanded.

(viii) **Incentives and Disincenties.** Incentives in the form of cash payments, promotions, housing and other facilities could be offered to the acceptors of family planning programmes, similarly, penalties can be imposed on the parents having many children.

To sum up, population control is essential for accelerating the pace of economic development. The Western thinking that 'development is the best contraceptive' is irrelevant in Indian conditions. It is only through propagation, adoption and persuasion that we can check the growth of India's population.

POPULATION PROBLEM IN INDIA

India is the second largest populated country in the world with the total population estimated at present at more than 94.5 crores. Whereas China with about 20 per cent of the world's population has about 7 per cent of the land areas, India has got only 2.4 per cent of the total land areas to feed about 16 per cent of the total population of the world.

Nature of Population Problem. Some of salient features of India's population problem can be summarised as follows:

(i) India has a large population base. The density of population is very high and the population is projected to increase further in future.

(ii) Increase the growth rate of population has been caused by the persistence of high fertility and declining mortality.

(iii) As a result of the persistence of high birth rate nd low death rate the dependency ratio in the economy has been very high.

(iv) In spite of the growing industrialisation of the economy, about 74.3 per cent population still lives in villages. It is indicative of the overall low productivity.

(v) The proportion of women in the total population has been gradually falling.

(vi) The quality of human capital in the country is very poor. About two-thirds of the total population is illiterate and the productivity of the Indian labour is very low as compared with productivity of the labour in the developed countries.

Population and Economic Development. Economists, demographers and scientists hold different viewpoints as regards the relationship between population and economic growth. While some of the thinkers hold the view that population is an engine of economic development and it promotes economic development, others opine that population retards it.

The protagonists of the growth economics believe that population is an important determinant of economic growth. They treat population as 'human capital' which helps in the proper exploitation of natural resources, and thus raises the production potential of a country. Large population, if gets suitable job opportunities, can raise the level of domestic output. Population also create demand for goods and services, which in turn determines the size of market level of investment, output and employment. Prof. Nurkse is of the opinion that even if with country suffers from the problem of disguised unemployment, it should not be a cause of anxiety because the disguised labour force has concealed saving potential. By shifting the disguised labour force to some construction activity, the concealed potential saving could be converted into real saving. Thus, population stimulates the level of capital formation which is a pre-condition to economic growth.

However, in case of India, the situation is quite different. Instead of promoting economic development, population has retarded it as would be clear from the following discussion:

(1) Rising population has largely offset increase in production both of agricultural and industrial goods; as a result, the per capita income is rising at slow pace. While the national income during the last 45 years has increased at an average annual rate of 4.2 per cent, the per capita income has risen at the rate of 2.0 per cent per annum.

(2) Rising population leads to an increase in consumption expenditure. A large part of the public expenditure has to be allocated for providing basic amenities of life and, therefore, very limited resources remain available for development projects.

(3) As a consequence of growing population, the pressure of population on land in increasing. There has been a sharp decline in the land man ratio. The per capital availability of the cultivable land which was 0.89 hectare in 1950 has come down to 0.34 hectare in 1994-95. The size of agricultural holdings has also decreased and it has adversely affected the farm productivity.

(4) With increase in population the per capita availability of food also declines. As against the minimum intake of foodgrains of 850-900 grams per individual per day, the availability of per capita foodgrains in India in 1997 was about 495 grams per day. In India, about 1 million children fall victim of malnutrition.

(5) Rising population leads to overcrowding, growth of slums, frequent traffic jams and sanitary problems. High rate of population growth disturbs the ecological balance, and thus adversely affects environment. According to an estimate, by the end of this century the country will need about 400 lakh new houses and repairs to about 190 lakh houses. The density of population is expected to rise from 274 per sq km in 1991 to 418 per sq km by 2,000 A.D.

(6) Rising population worsens the unemployment problem. The aggregate labour force in India is expected to rise from 213 million in 1921 to 1,000 million in 2000 AD. It would be very difficult for the country to create employment opportunities for such a large force. The number of unemployed persons has gone up from 40 lakhs in 1951 to about 198 lakhs in January, 1997.

(7) Population growth, through increased consumption of energy resources, aggravates the energy crisis. If each family has to use 40 watt electric bulbs, we shall have to put up new 259 MW power stations every three months.

(8) As a consequence of growing population, public services relating to health, education, transport, etc., are constantly

under pressure; imbalanced distribution of population often causes political and social conflicts apart from riots.

Economic Development and Population Control

Demographers of the world have suggested different measures to arrest the growth of population. Among these measures, economic development is regarded as an effective method of population control. "Development is the best contraceptive" was the slogan raised by the World Population Conference held in 1974 in Bucharest. Many European countries have contained the growth of their population through economic development. In India, however, things are different. European model of economic development to control population cannot be employed in India. It cannot be an effective and practicable method of population control.

While in the western countries the population increased at a slow pace without disturbing the equilibrium between the natural resources and population; in India, it has registered a high rate of growth and, thus, retarded the process of economic growth. Similarly, the western countries took undue long time to bring the death rate to a low level; in India, there has been sharp decline in the death rate. High birth rate and rapid fall in the death rate has led to sudden population explosion and, thus retarded economic development. According to a World Bank Study, "Developing countries are like long distance runners. In their race against time to eliminate poverty, rapid population growth is an additional burden, which regardless of their inherent strengths, slows them down." In India, the first and foremost problem is how to achieve economic development before formulating a strategy for population control.

POPULATION & ECONOMIC DEVELOPMENT

According to Richard T. Gill, "Economic development is not a mechanical process. It is a human enterprise and like all human enterprises, its outcome will depend finally on the skill, quality and attitude of the man who undertakes it." The above statement is absolutely correct in the context of the Indian economy. Had the number of people in the country been the sole determinant of economic development, perhaps China would have been the most developed country of the world followed by India. But, it is not only the size of population but also its composition and quality which actually promotes economic development.

Composition of population refers to the distribution of population according to different age-groups. Broadly speaking, the population in India is divided in three groups, viz., 0-14 years, 15-59 years, and 60 years and above. The working population of the country or the supply of labour force comes from the age group 15-59 years. Larger the number of people in the age group 15-59 years, more will be the possibility of labour force contributing to economic development.

Table 1: Age Composition of Indian Population

(Percentage to the total)

Age Group	1971	1981	1992	2000
0-14	42	39.72	35.66	32.72
15-59	52	54.07	57.60	59.70
60 and above	6	6.21	665	7.58

Table 1. shows that the percentage of population in the age group of 15-59 in 1971 was only 52. And in this age group also, all persons do not work. There may be school/college-going children, housewives, disabled and unemployed persons. The dependency ratio of the population works out to about 50 per cent. A high dependency ratio acts as a serious drag on production and improvement of living standards. Data for the year 2000 shows that the percentage of population in the age group 15-59 years is likely to increase and, therefore, we can expect higher level of productivity and development.

It is not only the percentage of population in the age group 15-59 years that determines the work participation rate, but it also depends upon the employment opportunities. According to the census 1991, the work participation rate in India in 1991 was 37.46 per cent.

Quality of Population also determines the level of economic development. The real wealth of a country does not lie in its lands, waters, minerals, forests, etc., but in healthy and efficient men, women and children. The quality of population is to be seen in terms of education, training, skill, efficiency, industriousness of the people.

According to the World Bank, "Developing countries with higher literacy rates have tended to grow faster, even after allowances are made for differences in incomes and physical investments, and they have had higher physical investment rates."

In India, the rate of literacy was only 16.7 per cent in 1951 which had gone up to 52.21 per cent in 1991. This clearly shows that with the increase in the literacy rate the Indian economy has advanced over the last three decades of planned economic development.

Life Expectancy is another factor reflecting upon the quality of population. The number of years for which people of a country expected to live at the time of birth is known as the average life expectancy of that country. Life expectancy in India was only 20.2 years in decade 1911-20. It went up to 32.1 years in 1951 and further to 59.0 years in 1991-92. Increase in the life expectancy increases the span of working period of the population and thus helps in generating larger income in the economy.

Economists use the Physical Quality of Life Index (PQLI) as an important and reliable measure of economic development. PQLI includes life expectancy, infant mortality and literacy. Whereas the PQLI in India in 1996 was 50, it was 99 in Sweden and 97 in the U.S.A. the corresponding per capita incomes of three countries amounted to $ 320, $23, 750 and $ 26,980 respectively.

In brief, age composition and quality of population have a great bearing on economic development.

THEORY OF DEMOGRAPHIC TRANSITION

Growth economists consider human resources as an important determinant of economic development. The Theory of Demographic

Transition explains the growth of population through three different stages of economic development.

Stages of Demographic Transition. There are three stages of demographic transition: The first stage relates to the most backward stage of a country in which both birth rate and death rate are high. High birth and death rates keep the growth of population either stagnant or very slow.

The second stage of demographic transition relates to a developing economy. At this stage birth rate continues to be high, whereas the death rate falls considerably. Birth rate is high because of social customs which do not change overnight, there is mass illiteracy and the people are not rich enough to practise family planning measures. Death rate, on the other hand, falls on account of improved medical and health facilities, fall in infant mortality rate, assured food supply, a better standard of living, and so on. A high birth rate matched with a sharp decline in the death rate causes a rapid increase in population.

The third stage of demographic transition relates to the developed countries where population is either stagnant or it increases at a low rate on account of low birth and death rates.

Indian Experience. India is currently passing through second stage of demographic transition. According to the 1991 Census, the birth rate has been estimated at 28.9 per thousand and death rate at 10.0 per thousand. The average annual growth rate of population works out to be 1.89 per cent. By all standards over 1.5 per cent growth rate of population is indicative of underdevelopment. If population grows at such a high rate it will have deterrent effects on economic development. Not only the per capita income will increase slowly, but the people in general will have to be contended with a low standard of living.

The theory of demographic transition (TDP) is being defied in most of the developing economies. According to this theory, 'economic growth is the best contraceptive'. It may be true in case of the developed economies of today during the early phase of their economic development. These countries had the opportunities to exploit their own resources and also the external resources. In case of developing countries like India the pressure of rising population is impeding economic growth. Population cannot be controlled by achieving high rate of economic growth. During 45 years of planned development, in spite of satisfactory rate of economic growth there has not been exprceptible rise in the standard of living of the poor people.

The true solution to the population problem in a developing economy could be found by formulating a realistic and rational population policy which emphasises the need of containing population through better education, improving the status of women, employment generation and larger participation of the masses in the population control programmes.

Population Policy. In order to solve the menacing problem of population it is essential to formulate a rational population policy which my contain the growing population. The Government did not come forward with a national population policy until the mid-seventies.

The present population policy aims at reducing the birth rate by adopting various measures such as:

(i) Raising the age of marriage to 18 years for girls and 21 years for boys.

(ii) Raising the level of female education.

(iii) Providing monetary incentives for the couples accepting family planning.

(iv) Providing suitable group incentive to medical profession, zila parishads, panchayat samitis, teachers, trade unions, etc.

(v) Providing facilities for primary health centres, sterilisations, distribution of local contraceptives and oral pills, etc.

The experience of the last few years shows that the voluntary controls have proved to be ineffective control of the population. On the one hand, the Government should educate people about the norms of small family and provide necessary facilities to practise family planning; on the other hand, it should discourage large families by adopting various administrative, monetary and fiscal measures.

CONTRIBUTION OF INDUSTRIALISATION

Industrialisation has come to be regarded as synonymous with economic development. Fast economic development everywhere has been possible essentially due to rapid industrialisation. The following is the contribution of industrialisation to the Indian economy:

(i) **Share in National Income.** The share of the secondary sector is the net domestic product of India, which was as low as 16.7 per cent in 1950-51, has now risen to 29.25 per cent. This is in spite of the fact that a large portion of the industrial capacity remains unutilised for various reasons.

(ii) **Contribution to Employment.** Industries offer large employment opportunities to the people. Employment in industrial sector grew very moderately by 1.55 lakhs during the First Plan period. In March, 1995, however, the number of workers employed in the industrial sector went up to 80.6 lakhs in the private sector and 194.66 lakhs in the public sector.

(iii) **Growth of Industrial Output.** Industrialisation has helped the country in producing not only the essential consumer goods but also the capital goods. A wide variety of goods are produced in India making the country least dependent upon the industrialised nations. The growth rate of industrial output which was only 5.7 per cent during the First Plan period has gone up to 8.7 per cent in 1981-82. The growth rate declined to 3.9 per cent in 1982-83 but reached 8.2 per cent in 1983-84. The growth rate of industrial production, however, declined in 1984-85 to 6.68 per cent, and further to 6.4 per cent in 1985-86. Lower growth rate of infrastructural industries, viz., electricity, coal, crude petroleum, saleable steel, etc. was responsible for this setback. However, during the past four years the rate of industrial growth has again picked up. In 1985-86, the rate of industrial growth was 8.7 per cent and in 1986-87, it went up to 9.1 per cent. In 1987-88 the rate of overall industrial growth was 7.3 per cent and estimated at 8.7 per cent in 1988-89. In 1989-90, it came down to 8.6 per cent and further declined to 8.3 per cent in 1990-91. General Index of Industrial Production showed a decline of 0.6 per cent in 1991-92. In 1992-93 also the industrial sector was slow to recover at 2.3 per cent. But, thereafter, the performance of the industrial sector has been very impressive. In 1993-94, the growth rate of industrial output was 6.0 per cent. It went up to 9.4 per cent in 1994-95, 11.6% in 1995-96 but expected to fall at 6.7 per cent in 1996-97.

Causes of Slow Growth of Industries

The data pertaining to the rate of industrial growth indicates that industrial growth was rapid during the first two decades, especially during the Second and Third Plans. Industrial growth, however, slowed down after the Third Plan. The scenario of consistent structural deterioration since the mid-sixties was primarily the result of policy actions and inactions including the downgrading of production process. The following factors account for the slow growth of industries since mid-sixties:

(i) **Fall in Savings and Capital Formation.** Both net domestic saving and net domestic capital formation steadily rose over the first three Plans period. Thereafter, the absolute level of net investment in real terms fell even below the First Plan level. For the ten years period from *i.e.* 1966-67 to 1976-77, the average growth rate in real investment worked out to 3.1 per cent per annum as against 12.6 per cent per annum during the preceding decade. In 1985-86, the growth rate of gross domestic capital formation rose to 24.6 per cent but it came down to 23.4 per cent in 1986-

87, and further to 22.1 in 1987-88. In 1989-90, 1990-91, 1991-92, 1992-93, 1993-94 and 1994-95 the growth rate of gross domestic capital formation rose but due to the stringent monetary and fiscal policies of the government the industrial growth rate decelerated.

(ii) **Slowing Down of Public Sector Investment.** The public sector is a major source of resource mobilisation in India. Investment in the public sector had slowed down after the Third Plan. Whereas the share of public sector in net domestic product steadily increased, the percentage of public sector saving to the sector's share in net domestic product declined considerably. The savings of the public sector have declined continuously from 3.2 per cent of gross domestic product in 1985-86 to 1.7 per cent in 1994-95. The declining trend of saving and capital formation in the public sector adversely affected the industrial growth.

(iii) **Relaxation of Industrial Controls.** It was a common feeling that the public sector is encroaching too much in the spare of industrial activities and the private sector is subjected to some unnecessary controls abolition of industrial licensing (except in case of 6 industries), automatic expansion of plant capacities, import relaxation, abolition of asset limit on MRTP companies etc., led to many distortions, and economic difficulties.

(iv) **Fall in Development Expenditure.** Development expenditure of the Central Government had formed about 60 per cent of the total expenditure in 1964-65; thereafter, it declined to such a low proportion as 45.2 per cent in 1973-74, but rose to 45.6 per cent in the Budget 1996-97. The disproportionate growth of non-development expenditure has been responsible for erosion in the development effort.

(v) **Shift in Terms of Trade.** Since mid-sixties a shift in terms of trade in favour of the agricultural sector has taken place.

Industrial stagnation has followed from the relatively more successful assertion of the bargaining strength of industrialist class by landlords and the rural rich in recent years.

(vi) **Centralisation of Capital.** Centralisation of capital takes place when large business houses take control of smaller companies by devices like intercorporate investment.

(vii) **Speculative Dealings.** Economic surplus concentrated in the hands of rich farmers and large industries has been used to a greater extent for speculative purposes. This has led to fall in resources for development.

(ix) **Political Instability.** After 1989 there has been a climate of political instability which has adversely affected both the domestic conditions following the unfortunate Ayodhya incidents have also affected industrial activities.

In brief, the Indian economy is suffering from the problem of structural retrogression which has slowed the pace of industrialisation. If the trend is to be reversed, what is imperative is that the rate of investment in the economy should be stepped up considerably.

CAUSES OF UNDERUTILISATION

Full utilisation of capacity is necessary to achieve higher rate of growth of output, employment, income, investment and to make the best possible use of the scarce capital resources.

Existence of underutilised capacity not only disturbs the input-output ratio but it also adversely affects the supply of goods.

Magnitude of the Problem

The problem of underutilised capacity has two aspects:

(i) The level of utilisation of capacity in the industrial sector is very low; and

(ii) The level of capacity utilisation in capital utilisation in capital goods industries over the years has fallen, whereas in consumer goods industries, it has increased.

In 1995-96, the capacity utilisation in manufacturing industries was 75.0 per cent suggesting that capacity is underutilised to the extent of minimum 25.0 per cent.

Causes of Underutilisation of Capacity

Several factors are responsible for the underutilisation of capacity, the more important among these are as follows:

(i) **Planned Excess Capacity.** While making investment decisions the entrepreneurs take into account not only the existing demand for goods but also the level of demand likely to emerge in the foreseeable future. As a result of planned excess capacity, there is some degree of underutilisation of capacity.

(ii) **Technological Indivisibilities.** There are some plants and equipment which can function at a given capacity. In case the plant is used to produce smaller output, some capacity would remain underutilised.

(iii) **Shortage of Inputs.** A shortage of inputs like raw materials, power, transport facilities, labour, etc., may cause underutilisation of capacity.

(iv) **Shortage of Foreign Exchange.** The shortage of foreign exchange for the import companies, raw materials and spare parts is undoubtedly the most important single factor limiting output in industries.

(v) **Breakdowns.** A plant needs periodical repairs and check-ups. Sometimes it may have to be closed down on account of failure and other unforeseen breakdowns.

(vi) **Deficiency in Demand.** Demand for industrial goods depends on the purchasing power of community. In India, the rate of growth of income has been very slow due to both lack of adequate expansion on non-agricultural employment as well as poor agricultural performance. The country has not been able to create sufficient demand for domestic products in the foreign markets.

(vii) **Government Policy.** Policy changes by the government in respect of industrial licensing, expansion of capacity, imports, project aid, foreign exchange, protection, etc., also leave industrial capacity underutilised.

(viii) **Labour Unrest.** Underutilisation of industrial capacity can also be attributed to labour troubles leading to work stoppages. Prolonged strikes and lockouts keep the industries closed for a considerable long period of time, and as a result, some of the industrial capacity remains underutilised.

Remedies for Improving Capacity Utilization

Underutilisation of capacity results from a number of causes; therefore, a number of measures can be adopted to improve the capacity utilisation. Some of these measures are discussed below:

(i) Financial resources should be made available to an industry taking into consideration its capacity.

(ii) There should be adequate supply of raw materials, power, labour and other inputs to the industries.

(iii) Infrastructural facilities should be provided to avoid bottlenecks in the production process.

(iv) The Government should devise a system of incentives so as to desist the management from keeping idle capacities.

(v) The Government should also penalise companies which make excessive profit by deliberately underutilising their capacities.

(vi) Automatic re-endorsement of licensed capacity at the minimum production achieved by an industrial unit during a particular period of time.

(vii) Broad-banding facility to exporting manufacturing enterprises to adjust their product mix in line with changing market conditions.

(viii) The import policy should be liberalised to enable domestic industry to procure essential raw materials and capital goods.

(ix) Fiscal concessions in the form of higher tax rebate and allowances should be made.

(x) Introduction of minimum economic capacities for a selected group of industries.

INDUSTRIAL DEVELOPMENT SINCE INDEPENDENCE

Industrialisation has an important role to play in the economic development of the underdeveloped economies. The tremendous gap in the per capita incomes of the developed and the underdeveloped countries is largely a reflection of the disparity in the structure of those economics. The former are largely industrial economies while the latter are predominantly dependent upon agriculture. That a bold programme of industrialisation was the crying need of our economy, was realised by the government while chalking out the programme of economic development. The process of industrialisation in the country started with the Second Five Year Plan in 1956. And within a period of four and a half decades growth and diversification of industries in India has been indeed remarkable. India may be said to have initiated the process of industrial revolution, which is bound to transform the Indian economy into a prosperous industrialised country in the coming years.

It would be no exaggeration to say that country has achieved in a short span of less than fifty years, such a rapid progress in industrialisation and diversification of industrial structure which is truly revolutionary when compared to the preceding century of slow, uneven and haphazard growth.

Table 1 shows the production levels attained in some selected industries over the period of development during last four decades. The production figures given in the table show a manifold increase in production in basic and key industries. More significant is the progress made in the field of steel, aluminium, chemicals and chemical fertilisers, petroleum products, engineering goods industries. There has, however, been successively reduced levels of production of the mill made cotton textiles. But expansion in production of cloth in the decentralised sector has largely compensated for the shortfalls in the mill sector production. The country is now, more or less, self-sufficient in the production of consumer goods and some basic items like iron and steel.

PHASES OF INDUSTRIAL GROWTH

Industrial development in India picked up its momentum with the onset of the Five Year Plans in 1951. The overall annual growth rate of industrial production, since then (also called the trend rate of growth) has been around 6 per cent. However, the actual year to year growth rate has shown wide fluctuations around this trend rate. There have been years of high growth and then years of retardation and thus we find different trend rates of growth in various sub-periods between 1950-51 and 1994-95.

Period of High Growth Rate: 1950-51 to 1965-66

During the period of fifteen years between 1950-51 and 1965-66, industry recorded successively higher growth rates. The industrial growth rates increased from around 5.5 per cent in 1951-52 to 7.2 per cent during the Second Plan (1956-61) and about 9.0 per cent over the Third Plan (1961-66). The trend growth rate over this fifteen-year period was about 8 per cent per annum. This growth rate was very satisfactory for a nation which had just embarked on the path of industrialisation.

Among the many factors that contributed to attainment of this high growth rate, the economic role of the government has been

Table 1: Production Trends in Some Major Industries

		1950-51	1960-61	1970-71	1980-81	1990-91	1995-96	1996-97	1997-98
Finished steel	(m.tons)	1.04	2.39	4.64	6.82	13.53	21.7	22.7	23.4
Hot metal	(m. tons)	1.69	4.31	6.99	9.55	12.15	17.8	18.8	19.2
Steel ingots	(m. tons)	1.47	3.48	6.14	10.33	N.A.	22.4	23.6	24.8
Iron ore	(m. tons)	3.0	10.9	32.5	42.2	53.7	65.9	66.1	71.5
Machine tools	(value in crores of Rs.)	0.30	0.80	43.0	169.2	773.1	11021	15687	18702
Coal and lignite	(m. tons)	32.3	55.2	76.3	119.0	225.5	292.3	308.2	319.0
Cement	(m. tons)	2.7	8.0	14.3	18.6	48.8	67.7	73.5	82.9
Nitrogenous fertilisers	('000 tons)	9	99	830	2164	6993	9228	8764	10538
Petroleum products	(m. tons)	0.2	5.7	17.1	24.1	48.0	54.6	58.4	60.7
Sugar	('000 tons)	1134	3029	3740	5158	12047	14781	15303	13160
Cotton Textiles	(m. metres)	4215	6738	7602	8368	15431	18900	19841	19992
Mill sector	(m. metres)	3401	4649	4055	3434	1889	2019	1957	1948
Decentralised sector	(m. metres)	814	2089	3547	4934	13572	16881	17884	18044

perhaps the most significant, Public Sector investment in the industry was stepped up. Many new industries were set up by the government. The government also made investments in infrastrucutre that provided inducements to the expansion of industry in the private sector as well. The government also set up financial institution to provide long term funds to private sector for industrial expansion. Scientific and industrial research facilities were also provided by the government.

PERIOD OF DECLARATION 1965-66 TO 1979-80

However after this, for the next fifteen years viz., 1965-66 to 1979-80, the industrial growth rate declined significantly. The annual average growth rate of industry during this period was around 4 per cent. This is therefore called a period of deceleration of industrial growth. Along with the slowing down of the growth of industrial output, the period also witnessed the growth in industrial goods used mainly by the richer classes such as consumer durables, synthetic fabrics, luxury goods, etc. relative to the goods consumed by poor masses. Therefore, this is also called a period of industrial retrogression.

Among the major causes of industrial deceleration were:

(i) unsatisfactory performance of agriculture coupled with occasional droughts that caused sharp fall in agricultural incomes and the consequent fall in demand for industrial goods;

(ii) slackening of real investment, particularly in public sector in the sense that while nominal investment was kept up but due to escalation in price of capital goods due to inflation, the real investment did not increase much causing a slow down in industrial production;

(iii) the state control over industry was tightened through licensing, MRTP Act, exchange controls, taxation, price controls and other regulatory devices which hampered industrial growth;

(iv) in the earlier period much of the industrial development had come in the wake of vigorous import substitution *i.e.*

emphasis in domestic production of goods that were hitherto imported. Over the period, however, the policy of import substitution was gradually slowed down that caused a slow down in the industry as well.

Period of Recovery and High Growth since 1980-81

During the next ten years viz., 1980-81 to 1990-91, the industrial activity again picked up. The average growth rate of industrial production was around 8 per cent during this period. The following table (Table 2) shows the annual growth rates of major sectors of industry since 1990-91:

Table 2: Annual Growth Rates

(Period	Mining	Manufacturing	Electricity	Industry as a whole)
1990-91	4.5	9.0	7.8	8.2
1991-92	0.6	-0.8	8.5	0.6
1992-93	0.5	2.2	5.0	2.3
1993-94	3.5	6.1	7.4	6.0
1994-95	7.6	8.5	8.5	8.4
1995-96	9.6	13.8	8.1	12.8
1996-97	-2.0	6.7	4.0	5.6
1997-98	5.9	6.6	6.6	6.6

Onset of liberalisation measures under the stewardship of the Late Prime Minister, Shri Rajiv Gandhi, deregulation of some industrial sectors, by taking them out of the purview of industrial licensing, inputs of capital goods for industrial expansion, improvements in technology through their imports and better utilisation of capacity were some of the factors that contributed to industrial recovery. But again in 1991-92, industrial growth rate tumbled down to 0.6 per cent; it recovered slightly to 2.3 per cent in 1992-93 and then improved to 6.0 per cent in 1993-94. There was a further jump in the growth rate to 8.4 per cent in 1994-95 and the growth rate reached its peak of 12.8 per cent in 1995-96. However, it came down to 5.6 per cent in 1996-97 and 6.6 per cent in 1997-98. The new economic policy with its liberalisation measures has now started making its positive impact on industrial growth rate which has gone much above the long term trend growth rate. Industrial growth during the plans is thus not a story of smooth success, it has been marked by a long period of deceleration, occasional slow downs and patches of stagnation.

PATTERN OF INDUSTRIALISATION: STRUCTURAL CHANGES IN INDUSTRY

One of the major shortcomings of industrial structure at the time of independence was that whereas India did possess some of the reasonably well developed consumer goods industries like cotton textiles, sugar, etc., capital goods industries like steel, heavy electricals, heavy engineering goods and machine making industries were practically absent. Thus, under the Plans special efforts were made to rectify this imbalance. Several steel plants, heavy electricals, machine tools and many other basic and key industries were set up. The gaps in industrial structure were, thus, sought to be filled up through massive expansion in capital goods industries.

Indian industry has undergone some significant structural changes since the era of modern industrialisation was ushered in during the Second Five Year Plan (1956-61). Some of these structural changes are discussed below:

Rapid Growth of Basic and Capital Goods Industries

One of the major handicaps of the Indian economy during the pre-independence days was the virtual lack of basic industries (steel, cement, etc.) and capital goods industries (industries producing machinery, equipment, etc.) Basic industries lay down the foundations on which the industrial superstructure stands while capital goods industries enlarge capacity for future production. The planning strategy incorporated in the Mahalanobis model of development which we adopted in the early years of planning and are still continuing with that in some modified form, lays all out emphasis on the capital goods sector and basic and heavy industries. Industrial and economic development based largely on this model has thus led to rapid growth of basic and capital goods industries. Though there have been fluctuations in the growth rate of these industries from one year to another, the trend rate of growth of the capital goods industries has been much higher than the average growth rate of the industrial section as a whole. This has immensely contributed to the expansion in our industrial capacity and laid down firm foundation of industrial development in the country.

Slow Growth of Consumer Goods Industries

A major weakness of the pattern of industrial development has, however, been a relatively slow growth of goods of mass consumption such as cotton textiles, sugar, vegetable oils, etc. An important factor responsible for this is that most of these consumer non-durable goods are agro-based products and consequently sluggish growth in agricultural output of cotton, sugarcane oilseeds, etc. is largely responsible for slow growth of these industries. Lower production and inadequate availability of these goods of mass consumption has led to rise in their prices and contributed to inflation in the country.

Table 3: Index Number of Industrial Production

(Base 1993-94 = 100)

	1994-95	1995-96	1996-97	1997-98
General Index	108.4	122.3	129.1	137.6
Basic goods industries	108.9	120.6	124.3	132.4
Capital goods industries	105.7	110.0	120.2	126.4
Intermediate goods industries	105.3	125.4	135.5	146.5
Consumer goods industries	111.8	125.6	132.1	139.6
Consumer durables	116.2	146.2	153.6	164.9
Consumer non-durables	110.8	121.1	127.5	134.1

Increased Production of Consumer Durables

An important outcome of the process of industrial development in India has been the rapid increase in the production of consumer durable goods such as automobiles, refrigerators, televisions, electrical and electronic goods. The production of such goods has recorded a four-fold increase between 1980-81 and 1994-95. There was further increases of around 65 per cent between 1994-95 and 1997-98. During the same period, there has been a very slow growth of non-durable goods, such as cloth and other items of daily use. This shows that resources are being rapidly diverted from the production of items of mass consumption (those used by common people) to the goods preferred by the rich and the upper middle class people.

The socio-economic consequences of this pattern of production are the economy is gradually becoming pro-rich *i.e.*, catering to the needs of the affluent persons and neglecting the basic requirements of the poor. Thus, while there may be a whole range of luxury goods available in the market, the poor persons still remain unclad and under-nourished. This is surely not a desirable pattern of production for a country like India where even now over a third of the people live below the poverty line. Such production pattern is only indicative of the further growth of inequalities which the Plans sought to reduce. Unless this pattern of production is modified in favour of the poor and lower middle class persons, social tensions and political instability are bound to grow further, thereby threatening the very fabric of our socio-economic structure.

Increasing Role of the Public Sector

One of the important developments in the field of industry during the Five Year Plans has been the rapid expansion of Public Sector in Indian Industries. While at the beginning of the Planning era in 1950-51 there were only 5 public sector undertakings under the Central Government with an investment of about Rs. 29 crores, by the end of March 1994 their number increased to 236 and their investment stood at Rs.2,02,000 crores. The public sector industries now occupy a very important place in the industrial economy of

India. Their production and sales turnover has multiplied manifold during the Plans.

Expansion in Infrastructure

Under the Plans, infrastructural facilities like power, transport, communications, etc. have shown a remarkable expansion and modernisation. There has been an all around increase in the production of energy; production of coal and lignite has increased over ten folds between 1950-51 and 1997-98. Installed capacity in power section has gone up about fifty times, power generation has increased about seventy five times and production of petroleum refinery products increased around 260 times over the period 1950-51 to 1997-98.

Growth of Small Scale Industries

A significant feature of industrial development during the Five Year Plans has been the special emphasis on small industrial sector. Consequently, the small industries have now come to occupy a pride of place in India's industrial structure. The number of small scale industrial units has increased from around 16 thousand in 1950-51 to 30.14 lakh in 1997-98. These industries now account for 40 per cent of the value added by the entire manufacturing sector, about 7 per cent of GDP and around 35 per cent of country's exports and employ a major part of working force in industrial sector.

To conclude, Indian industries have made a tremendous progress during the Five Year Plans. There has been a rapid expansion in industrial output, a substantial development in the basic and key industries and an impressive growth of mineral and energy resources. It is in view of the rapid developments in industry that India has now come to occupy a place among the major industrial economies of the world.

Overall assessment of industrial development shows that over the years Indian industry has been considerably modernised. Most of our products which suffered in the world market because of their high cost and low quality, are now developing a competitive edge and would soon be able to withstand foreign competition offered by these products from advanced industrial nations. We have also acquired a certain degree of self-reliance in the case of many industrial goods such as iron and steel, machinery, fertilizers, etc. Our industrial base has become quite sound. Investment climate has tremendously improved as both domestic as well as foreign investment is continuously increasing in various industrial sectors. However, out industry has failed to generate substantial employment and even today employs a very small fraction of our total labour face. High cost and inefficiency still pervade many industries and the incidence of industrial sickens is very high. To attain and maintain high industrial growth rates we have not only to improve our efficiency and competitive edge, but also develop new products, explore new markets and continue modernisation programmes with the choice of appropriate technology that does not sacrifice employment at the altar of rapid output growth.

NEW INDUSTRIAL POLICY

The government announced on July 24, 1991 a New Industrial Policy as part of a wider package of economic reforms and liberalisation programme. The New Industrial Policy of July 1991 seeks to drastically liberalise the economy and the industry by doing away with industrial licensing except for a few specialised cases, increasing the limit of foreign equity participation in industries and redefining the role of the public sector. The underlying objective behind all these changes is to 'unshackle the Indian industrial economy from the cobwebs of unnecessary bureaucratic controls'.

Broadly stated, the objectives of New Industrial Policy are:

(i) Removing regulatory system and other weaknesses.

(ii) Increasing the competitiveness of industries for the benefit of the common man.

(iii) Incentives for industrialisation of backward areas.

(iv) Enhanced support to small-scale sector.

(v) Ensure running of Public Sector Undertakings (PSUs) on business lines and cut their losses.

(vi) To link Indian economy to the global market so that we acquire the ability to pay for imports, and to make us less dependent on aid.

The New Industrial Policy deals with four main areas viz., Industrial Licensing, Public Sector, Foreign Investment and the MRTP Act.

Abolition of Industrial Licensing. The practice of licensing industries under Industries (Development and Regulation) Act, 1951] has been abolished for all industries except for a short list of 18 industries related to defence needs, social reasons (posing health or environmental hazards like cigarette, asbestos) and manufacture of luxury items.

The number of items in respect to which industrial licensing remains has now been reduced. At present, only five items of health, strategic and security considerations remain under the purview of industrial licensing. Thus, industry has been made free of the licensing requirements thereby removing the entry barriers and the ills associated with it.

Limiting the Role of Public Sector. De-reservation of Industries: Based on the Industrial Policy of 1956, the public sector in India expanded considerably to diverse fields of industrial and commercial activity. However, in the recent past, a number of problems surfaced in the working of many of the public sector enterprises. The most serious problem noticed was that many of them were regularly incurring losses which was being made good by the Government from revenues earned as a result of taxation or through borrowings. Not only this has drained the Government resources but it has also weakened the public sector as it has not been able to invest money for expansion, technological upgradation and in other development initiatives.

Under the New Industrial Policy only 8 items have been reserved for production by the public sector units as against 29 items reserved for this sector in the Industrial Policy of 1956. The number of industries reserved for the public sector has been further reduced to

4 *viz.*, defence products, atomic energy, railway transport and minerals used in generation of atomic energy. More and more private initiative is to be encouraged in the development of infrastructure like power, telecommunications, roadways, shipping, ports and civil aviation.

Enhanced Support to Small-Scale Sector. Government will provide enhanced support to the small-scale sector so that it flourishes in an environment of economic efficiency and continuous technological upgradation. A package of measures announced in this context provides for setting up of an agency to ensure that the credit demands of the small scale sector are fully met, allowing equity participation by other industries in small-scale sector not exceeding 24 per cent of the total shareholding. The tiny sector is to be provided priority in the government purchase programme. The government would also encourage the production of parts and components required by the public sector industries in the small scale ancillary industries.

Liberalised Policy Towards Foreign Investment. So far foreign investment had played only a minor role as a source of finance. Several developing and less advanced countries, with far less advanced economies of lesser size have received foreign capital several times more than India. This was mainly because they simplified their investment procedures. To attract foreign investment, the new policy provides for automatic approval in the high priority industries for direct foreign investment in Companies upto 51 per cent of share capital. In a major drive to simplify foreign direct investment procedures, Indian companies have been permitted to accept foreign investment under automatic approval route without obtaining prior permission from R~I. Foreign equity upto 100 per cent has been permitted in electricity generation and transmission, in construction of roads, ports and harbours.

Removal of Investment Control on large Business Houses: Change in MRTP Act. Hitherto, companies with certain assets limits (Rs. 100 crores since 1985) were required to get clearance under the Monopolies & Restrictive Trade Practices Act before starting new industries, or expanding existing units, appointment of directors, mergers or take-overs. Now, no such prior approval from Government is required.

Assessment of the New Industrial Policy

The New Industrial Policy of July 1991 makes a sharp departure from the Industrial Policy of 1956 that has governed the industrial development of India since mid-fifties. While the 1956 policy had presented a wider role for the state and closely controlled industries through strict industrial licensing system, the New Policy limits the role of state only to a few industrial sectors and frees the industry from licences and controls.

The major policy changes initiated in the industrial sector since July 1991 include removal of entry barriers, reduction of areas reserved exclusively for public sector, rationalisation of approach towards monopolistic and restrictive practices, liberalisation of foreign investment and encouraging the growth of employment in small scale and tiny industries.

According to the new policy, the role of the government should change from that of only exercising control over the entrepreneurs to providing help by making procedures transparent and by eliminating delays. The government has also withdrawn the mandatory clause converting loans to equity with regard to long-term loans from public financial institutions.

With regard to the public sector, the policy promises to strengthen its role in areas essential for the economy, but warns of a review in industries in areas which are unproductive and inefficient. The policy says, in 50's and 60's the public sector undertakings were used to control the commanding heights of the economy; now fiscal and monetary instruments will be used. Even in areas still reserved for the public sector, the private sector may also be invited. The areas retained for the public sector include arms and ammunition, atomic energy, rail transport and mining. Significant deletions from the earlier reserved list are steel, aircraft, telecommunications, power transmission & distribution and ship-building.

The Industrial Policy of July 1991 has opened a new chapter in India's economic history. Earlier reforms tinkered with licence-permit raj, but left it intact in all its essential aspects. The new policy finally and explicitly admits that the licence-permit raj has hampered instead of helping over development and, therefore, needs to be scrapped. The new policy, though it still retains some licensing, regulations and controls to serve the social ends, does away with much of the licence-permit raj and seeks to be more 'market friendly', which aims at making the government and the business as partners and not adversaries in the great national enterprise.

Criticism of New Industrial Policy

The critics of the New Industrial Policy have some apprehensions. They believe that so much of deregulation and liberalisation may lead to uncoordinated investments causing excess capacities in certain industrial sectors thus leading to waste of scarce capital resources. Again, they find no merit in allowing the big industrial houses to open up new industries or expand the existing ones with no need for any prior approval. This, they feel, would lead to further dominance of big industrial houses and cause undue concentration of economic power.

In spite of these reservations, the New Industrial Policy is expected to contribute substantially to a much faster growth of industrial sector. The past regime of regulations and controls through licensing had its adverse impact on investment and industrial expansion. Unnecessary and cumbersome procedures laid down for grant of licences discouraged many local and foreign investors from opening up new industries. Cornering of industrial licences by a few big industrial houses had created an oligopolistic market in the country. These oligopolists or semi-monopolistic enterprises dominating the market never felt any need to upgrade technology and improve efficiency because they knew that whatever be the cost or quality of their product, it is bound to be sold in the market that has been protected from competition from within (through licences) as well as outside through high tariff walls.

Expectations from New Policy

The New Industrial Policy by abolishing licensing has ushered in an era of competition. It is expected to release growth promoting forces of investment and enterprise by getting rid of unnecessary controls, and costly regulations. Competition among the domestic producers is bound to improve industrial efficiency and quality of production. And dismantling the tariff walls would open up the economy thereby exposing the domestic producers to foreign competition. This is again bound to improve efficiency. India with its abundant skilled cheap labour can capture world markets in many products and thus gain from globalisation only if our industry is willing to improve its efficiency to international standards. Being remained confined to protective tariff walls has rendered our industry inefficient. The new policy seeks to remove this obstacle to attain the competitive efficiency in the world market.

Opening up the economy for greater foreign investment under the New Industrial Policy by allowing greater equity participation to foreign investors would surely help industrial development by providing additional supplies of capital resources and advantages of modern world technology. Though there are some genuine fears that the entry of foreign multinational corporations would subject our domestic market to the control of these international oligopolies, by stifling growth of domestic industries, yet such fears seem to be unfounded in view of the fact that our industry has now acquired strength, maturity and sophistication so as to face competition from these foreign investors comfortably and confidently. However, it is necessary that the domestic industries are provided some additional benefits—tax concessions, investment rebates, etc. to reduce their costs so that they can face foreign competition with added vigour.

The industrial and other economic reforms pursued since middle of 1991 have brought out the competitive strength and resilience of the industrial sector. After a brief spell of restructuring and consequent lower growth rate, the industrial sector has emerged stronger rendering impressive growth with lot of strength to withstand the competition from other countries.

Agricultural Development Since Independence

The principal programmes of agricultural development taken up during the Plans related the increase in agricultural production by bringing about land reforms thereby changing the social and economic structure of the rural society. Education was imparted to the rural folk in the new methods and techniques of better farming, horticulture, etc. through a comprehensive programme of community development and national extension. Basic facilities like irrigation, transport and electricity were extended to the remotest parts of the countryside. Facilities for credit and marketing provision of price incentives and spread of literacy through adult education programmes were taken up to bring about a substantial rise in agricultural productivity.

The outcome of these programmes for agricultural development during the Five Year Plans are given in Table:

Table: Production of some Selection Agricultural Commidities

(In million tones)

Crops	1950-51	1960-61	1970-71	1980-81	1990-91	1996-97	1997-98
Rice	34.6	42.2	53.6	74:3	73.7	81.7	82.3
Wheat	6.4	11.0	23.8	36.3	54.1	69.4	65.9
Pulses	8.4	12.7	11.8	10.6	14.3	14.2	13.1
Total Food grains	50.8	82.0	108.4	129.6	176.4	199.4	192.4
Oilseeds	5.2	7.0	9.6	9.4	18.6	24.4	22.2
Sugarcane	57.1	110.0	126.4	154.2	241.0	277.6	276.3
Cotton	3.0	5.6	4.8	7.0	9.8	14.2	11.1
Jute and Mesta	3.3	5.3	6.2	8.2	9.2	11.2	11.1

In million bales of 170 kg each.

In million bales of 180 kg each.

Consequent to the heavy investment in the development of agriculture during the plans, output of both food and non-food crops has considerably increased, through much of the gain has accrued in the case of foodgrains production. From an extremely low output level of 51 million tones, foodgrains production increased to about 200 million tones in 1996-97. There was almost a ten-fold increase in wheat output and over two and a half times increase in rice production. The productivity of food crops, particularly wheat, increased substantially after 1967-68 with the onset of Green Revolution. Coarse grains too showed some good trends, but growth-in output of pulses has been extremely tardy, increasing from around 8 million tonnes in 1950-51 to 14 million tonnes in 1997-98. Among the non-food crops, sugarcane output increased sharply from 57 million tonnes in 1950-51 to around 280 million tonnes in 1997-98. Cotton and jute production showed a four-fold and three-fold increase respectively. Oilseeds too recorded a four-fold increase in output. Thus, there has been a significant progress in agriculture, though the growth rate has not been very promising. A better idea of growth in agriculture can be made from the index number of agricultural production given in Table.

Table : Index Number of Agricultrual production

(Base: Triennium ending 1981-82 = 100)

	1970-71	1980-81	1990-91	199-97	1997-98
Food grains	87.9	104.9	143.7	160.9	155.7
Rice	84.4	107.6	149.4	164.4	165.3
Wheat	67.7	103.2	156.6	197.0	187.2
Coarse Cereals,	105.4	99.8	113.1	118.2	107.5
Pulses	113.6	104.1	140.5	140.1	127.9
Non-Food grains	82.6	97.4	156.3	200.2	182.5
Oilseeds	97.1	95.1	179.5	229.6	203.1

Cotton	63.4	93.2	130.9	189.2	148.1
Jute	76.5	100.8	122.6	154.2	155.0
Sugarcane	81.2	98.8	154.3	177.4	166.5
All Commodities	85.9	102.1	143.0	175.4	164.9

Between 1950-51 and 1963-64, the agricultural production increased substantially. However, in 1964-65 and 1965-66, because of a severe crop failure the agricultural production substantially declined. But, since then, there has been a marked increase the agricultural production. The index of agricultural production for all commodities with triennium ending 1981-82 = 100), which stood at 85.9 in 1970-71 went up to 102.1 in 1980-81 and to .143.0 in 1990-91 indicating rapid growth of agriculture in this decade. In 1996-97, the index number of agricultural production stood at 175.4 before it came down to 164.9 in 1997-98.

The major outcome of agricultural development during the Five-Year Plans has been that India, which frequntly had to resort to heavy imports of food-grains, has now become self-sufficient in this field. However, this self-sufficiency is at rather a low level of per capita consumption. The per capita availability of food-grains has increased from about 395 grams per day in 1951 to only 484 grams per day in 1998. Within food grains. The per capita availability of pulses has declined from 61 grams per day in 1951 to about 33.2 grams in 1998.

Much of the agricultural development has however been concentrated in only some regions like Punjab, Haryana, Western Uttar Pradesh, parts of Rajasthan and Tamil Nadu. The crops that have gained most from the planned development process is largely the foodgrain crops, mainly wheat and rice and sugarcane among the cash crops. In the process the regional imbalance in agriculture growth rates has further widened and also the rich farmers in the well-to-do agricultural regions have cornored most of the gains of development. The rainfed (non irrigated) areas have not shown very satisfactory progress duirng the Plans as is clear from the fact that pulses, which are essentially grown in rainfed areas, are shown an extremely low rate of growth. It seems that most of the development efforts during the Plans have been concentrated on expansion of foodgrains so as to achieve self-sufficiency in food or to build up food security with much less concern for other crops.

Cause of Slow Growth in Agriculture. It may, however be pointed out that in spite of such a heavy investment in agriculture during our Five-Year Plans, the results in terms of output have not been highly satisfactory. There is scarcity of raw materials originating from agriculture. We are still dependent upon rainfall for irrigation of almost 70 per cent of our land. In brief we have not made much of progress in the field of agriculture although we have put in so much of money in this sector. The reasons for this failure on the agricultrual from may be easily found out in our faulty planning of agriculture. The rate of growth in our agriculture has been very slow because of the following factors :

1. Less Emphasis on Quick Yielding Projects. Unfortunately, in our planning much emphasis was placed upon those projects in agriculture which have a long gestation period. Quick yeilding projects were not given their due importance. for example, much ottention was paid to major irrigation projects while minor irrigation schemes were not given the place they deserved. Further, much attention was given to the increase in irrigation potential rather than looking after and maintaining the existing works. This has resulted in much loss of irrigation potential.

2. Inadequate Provision for Agricultural Inputs. While the need to have good and sufficient inputs in agriculture is fully felt, there is still on inadequate supply of the same. Irrigation facilities, though expanding, are still not enough and vast tracts are still dependent upon rains. We are still victims of floods and droughts, pests and plant diseases. Obvisously, not only should we arrange for much larger timely and sufficient supplies of the traditional inputs, but also develop locally available inputs.

3. Inadequate Credit facilities. The inadequacy of credit facilities has long been felt and regarded as one of the major drawbacks of our agriculture. For centuries, our farmers have been dependent upon non-institutional credit facilities with all the attendant limitations of the same. The development credit, till recently, has been rather slow while the need of credit has been mounting realising that the programme of development of agriculture cannot be carried out successfully unless there is a provision for credit facilities, the authorities are now trying their best to promote credit facilities. Co-operative credit is being boosted up; the Reserve Bank of India takes a special interest in development of co-operative credit, major commercial banks have been nationalised and are expanding their credit facilities to the rural areas. Regional Rural Banks have also been established and NABARD has been set up as an apex institution in the field of rural credit.

TECHNOLOGICAL CHANGE IN AGRICULTURE

Indian agriculture, which remained stagnant during the pre-independence years and was further incapacitated by the partition of the country in 1947, made some reasonably good progress during the past four decades, especially since the onset of the Green Revolution in the late sixties. The increase in production and productivity of major agricultural crops has indeed been commendable. Food grains production has expanded nearly four-fold since independence, wheat crop has witnessed revolutionary change in its production. General index of agricultural production has gone up from about 86 in 1970-71 (with the triennium ending (1981-82 = 100) to 175 in 1996-97 while that of wheat has gone up from 68 to 197 and that of rice from 84 to 165 over the same period. Non-food crops too recorded an over two-fold increase in production, The country has thus achieved a fair measure of self-sufficiency in food grains and in quite a few other agricultural products. The policy measures and programmes that have contributed to development of Indian agriculture can be categorised into two sets *viz.*, *(i)* technological changes and *(ii)* institutional and organisational changes. Both of them have played a significant role in putting Indian agriculture on a sound footing.

Technological Changes

Measures such as development and application of high-yielding varieties of seeds (HYV seeds), introduction of multiple cropping through sowing of short maturity crops, use of fertilisers (NPK) on an extended scale, expansion in the area under irrigation, application of pesticides and insecticides, use of machinery and other modern agricultural practices in various operations, continued research and development leading to better varieties of seeds useful for dry land farming and rainfed areas, etc. are among the major technological changes that have been made in agriculture. Such changes have no doubt made tremendous contribution to rapid agricultural growth in India. In fact, it is universally accepted, that India would not have witnessed this tremendous upsurge in agricultural output, particularly in the output of foodgrains if these technological changes had not taken place.

Institutional and Organisational Changes

The institutional changes mainly comprise changes in land tenure system viz., abolition of intermediaries, conferment of ownership on the tenants, security of tenure, land redistribution through ceiling on land holdings and consolidation of small scattered pieces of land into larger farming fields. Through such institutional changes the whole organisational structure of Indian agriculture has undergone a change. There are also changes in the spheres of agricultural credit where many institutional sources of finance such as cooperative societies and regional rural banks have expanded their network and financial activities to meet credit requirements of the farmers on easy and soft conditions thereby releasing him from the clutches of the greedy and exploitative moneylenders. Setting of regulated markets and promotion of cooperative marketing societies are also a part of organisational changes.

The institutional and organizational changes have also played their part in agricultural development. The abolition of zamindari system and the conferment of ownership rights on the tenants brought in the necessary incentives and will to do hard work on the farms which now belonged to the cultivators and not the ruthless zamindars. This directly contributed to growth of agricultural production. Land ceilings and land redistribution in the favour of landless also contributed similarly to agricultural growth. Prevention of exploitation of tenants through excessive rents charged by the landowners, giving them security of tenure by preventing their ejectment at will did create the necessary climate for hard work and farm improvements by the tenant cultivators. Consolidation of land holdings allowed for better land management and use of improved techniques.

But it is believed that the role of institutional and organisational changes in agriculture played only a limited role in its growth. This is because, firstly, these institutional reforms, particularly the land reforms, have not been implemented fully in letter and spirit; they largely remain on paper. Their tardy implementation due to opposition of powerful political pressure groups and vested interests did not release much growth generating forces. Secondiy, in the absence of technological breakthrough in agricultural operations, the institutional reforms could not contribute much to the growth of agriculture. Thus, whereas there was a high growth in agriculture during the first Plan, it tapered off during the Second Plan. The Third Plan saw the worst agricultural crisis in the country; the actual output of many agricultural goods such as food grains, oil seeds and raw cotton at the end of the Third plan was even lower than the output level at the end of the Second Plan.

Meanwhile, efforts were made to bring about a technological breakthrough in agriculture. New high-yielding varieties of seeds were discovered and used with substantial doses of fertilizers in irrigated areas. Mechanisation was also introduced and use of tractors, harvestors and other mechanised farm equipment was encouraged. The results were really revolutionary. There was manifold rise in agricultural productivity and output of food grains expanded sharply. Ever since the new technology was introduced in the late 1960's, there has been no looking back. Over the past years the country witnessed some periods of worst droughts, yet our agriculture has come out unscathed. fluctuations in yearly production have been minimised and beneath these fluctuations one could see the underlying increasing trend rate of production.

Technological changes have thus been largely responsible for our tremendous agricultural progress and upsurge in food production. Till the new technology was introduced, agricultural progress was extremely slow and uneven in spite of the major Institutional and organisational changes in this field.

But could technological changes alone bring about such revolutionary changes in agricultural scenario. The answer is no. How could the new technology be applied to small scattered and fragmented tiny pieces of land holdings. In what way could irrigation be developed on pieces of land that did not form a single farm. Thus, consolidation of landholdings, an important organistional change, helped application of new technology. Again in the absence of tenurial reformsabolition of zamindari and conferment of land ownership to the tenants, there were not many possibilities of adopting new technology. This is because the zamindars or the absentee landlords living in the luxury of city life could not have any inclination to spend on new production methods whereas the poor tenant cultivators had neither the means nor the incentive to buy modern technology. Again in the absence of organisational reforms in the field of agricultural finance, the poor formers could not get access to credit that has enabled him to go in for modern production methods. Thus, whereas technological change has made available modern production methods, institutional and organisational changes have provided an appropriate climate for their adoption and application. Without technological change, surely there could not be much development in agriculture; and hence it is a necessary condition of agricultural growth. But this technology may have remained largely unused if the necessary incentives and facilities for its use had not been provided by institutional changes. Thus, both the technological as well as the institutional reforms have played their role in agricultural development of India. But whereas the role of institutional changes has been a little bit controversial that of technology has been universally accepted. But no one can deny the role of institutional reforms in facilitating the adoption and application of modern agricultural technology; it would have remained largely ineffective or extremely limited without organisational and institutional changes.

MEASURES TO RAISE PRODUCTIVITY

Agrarian reforms are often considered equivalent to land reforms. Basically this is not so, unless land reforms are considered to include everything that should be done to improve agriculture in every sense. Basically, agrarian reforms would include the reforms connected with the land tenure system; and also include all other steps designed to improve agricultural productivity.

Intensive Cultivation of Land. Agriculture forms the backbone of our economy and a major portion of our working population is engaged in agriculture. Also another sizeable portion of population is dependent upon agriculture for its living in an indirect way. These factors are leading to a high degree of pressure upon land, a pressure which should be reduced if possible. Land is a factor which cannot be increased substantially. ..Therefore, the only long-term solution regarding the augmenting of land supply is to increase the intensification of its cultivation and increase in productivity. Each piece of land must be made to yield more than one crop and each crop yield must be more per hectare, so that in effect the supply of land is more even with the same geographical area.

Reducing Population Pressure. Reducing the pressure on land is connected with its productivity also. As it is, there is a large-scale disguised unemployment of labour in land. With an easing of pressure of population on land this disguise unemployment can also be reduced. As we know, disguised unemployment implies that the labour employed at the margin has a zero or negative marginal productivity so that a withdrawal of labour would lead to either an increase or no change in total output.

Consolidation of Land Holdings and Implementation of Land Ceilings. Productivity is very closely linked with size of the operational holdings. As it is, our agriculture is riddled with two extreme types of holdings. Some of them are very large and some of them are too small and fragmented. It is necessary that the operational holdings should more or less be such as would yield maximum yield per hectare. Currently, our agricultural productivity is very low. Very large farms are inefficient, partly due to the fact that there is a good deal of wastage in them. Similarly, very small farms are also inefficient because the small farmer cannot afford to use the necessary inputs. Accordingly, agricultural policy has to include a firm approach leading to the development of economic holdings which should be operationally most efficient. To this end, it has been thought fit to make sure that there are no holdings of too big areas; and that at the same time, very small holdings are consolidated. Hence, land ceiling laws have been passed and are being pursued vigorously. Similarly, the policy of consolidation of holdings is being implemented more effectively. The surplus land released through the implementation of ceiling laws is being distributed amongst landless labourers. But though this step will bring a sense of satisfaction to the poor agricultural labourers, it can retard agricultural productivity since these new owners will have very small holdings which may not be operationally very efficient.

Another aspect of improving land productivity concerns the provision of requisite inputs. Agricultural productivity is a matter of poper inputs and their use. In India, the supply of a number of important inputs is in short supply. We have still large areas which are dependent upon rain. It is desirable to have, instead, assured irrigation either through canal water, tank water, tube-wells or some other source. Currently, we are using only a small portion of our available water resources for irrigation purposes. More land should be brought under HYV seeds. Use of chemical fertilizers and pesticides must be further encouraged. Also, a proper agricultural policy has to make sure that the farmers' problems of credit and marketing are solved to their satisfaction so that they are assured of reaping the fruits of their efforts.

Reforms in System of Land Tenure. Another very important aspect of agricultural productivity which has received attention of the government right from the beginning, is the land tenure system. It is believed that ownership and the assurance that the fruits of one's labour would be available to oneself, go a long way in ensuring hard work and productivity. It is this and also the sense of social and economic justice that prompted the authorities to take steps to abolish zamindari system in the country. With the existence of zamindari, the tenants were subject tc all kinds of exploitation by the landlords and could be evicted from their lands at the will of the landlord. This created a great sense of insecurity in the tenants and they never felt interested in improving the productivity of land through investment, nor they were in a position to raise funds for such investment. The landlords, on their part, were basically interested in getting as much as possible out of the land and so they also never thought of investing in land. Thus, land reforms or reforms in the land tenure system were implemented. Landlordism was abolished and the tenants could purchase land from the government which took the possession of land on payment of compensation to the landlords. The implementation of these reforms had, however, been faulty.

Other Measures. The last plank of reforms to increase agricultural productivity would be concerned with social and economic justice. There is no reason why the fruits of agricultural workers and farmers should not be available to them. To this end, therefore absentee landlordism and intermediaries must be rooted out from wherever they still exist in Indian agriculture. Also the farmers must be freed from the clutches of money-lenders who exploit them in more than one ways. The custom of bonded labour has been abolished. The farmers should be assured of sufficient, timely and cheap credit for their farming activities. Various steps have been taken to this effect and it is hoped that very soon the rural scene would be transformed beyond recognition. In, the same way, implementing the provision regarding minimum wages to the agricultural workers, increasing the employment opportunities and reforming the agricultural marketing would go a long way in providing social and economic justice to the farmers and agricultural workers. If along with these reforms, subsidiary occupations like bee-keeping, dairy farming, poultry-farming and the like are developed, it would improve the economic conditions of the rural masses enable them to spare resources for investment, ease the pressure on land and act as a great deterrent against any kind of exploitation and thus keep in tremendously improving productivity in agriculture.

❑

2

Industrial Location

Though location of industrialisation has been a serious problem for our economists since times past, yet strange enough classical economists have not contributed much on the subject. Carl Joachim Friednich is of the view that, "from Adm Smith to Pigou, no adequate deductive treatment of the causes determining the economic location has been attempted, in spite of the fact that such an analysis may be capable of aiding in further refining the theories of monopolies, transportation rates and international trade." In fact these thinkers always felt that it was a problem not serious enough to call for any serious explanation. Location of industries means the methods and desirability of concentrating industries in different areas or localities. It is with the help of proper location that industrial efficiency becomes possible. Location of industry is a problem which is not only confined to new industries being set up, but is also concerned with the industries which are already in existence. It is, therefore, the responsibility of management of each industrial house to find out from time to time wheather favourable conditions still continue for the location of an industry or that these have in any way changed to a great extent.

Location and Localisation. Each industrialist will try to locate his industry at a place where he finds that the cost of production is lowest. It is called location of industries. On the other hand when the industries are concentrated in a particular area that is called localisation of industries, which can be due to many reasons including physical location, availability of raw material etc.

Location and Planned Location. The term planned location was first used by Lord Beveridge. According to him planned location meant giving each industrial area a variety of industries. It also meant that no large industry should be localised but dispersed. In the words of Sivayya and Dass, "Planned location of industries precedes as a first step to develop the country on regional considerations in order to check expansion of industrial cities and areas only in certain regions."

These days problem of industrial location is assuming great significance. It is primarily because every State wants that there should be no regional imbalances. Not only this but every industrial management wants to ensure that industries are located at a place, where the cost of production is the lowest and men, money and material are available without much difficulty.

INFLUENTIAL FACTORS OF LOCATION

Proper location of an industry is assuming great importance and significance these days. It is primarily because concentration of industry creates regional imbalances, whereas un-economic locational factor can discourage setting up of new industries. We have already seen that neither Weber's nor Florence's theory has come upto the mark and that both the theories suffer from some serious defects. Today it is believed that there are many factors which influence the location resources, availability of raw material psychology of the people etc. All these count a lot. The factors which influence location of an industry, may be discussed as under:

1. Historical Factors. A Beachman in 'Economics of Industrial Organisation' has perhaps rightly said that "When an industry is known to have concentrated in a particular area it is always easy to discover natural advantages attaching to the site" In many cases industries get located in an area because similar types of industries are already located there. Why these industries got located there, perhaps no reasonable explanation can be given for that and that it was either as a matter of chance, or due to certain peculiar circumstances, which existed at that time.

2. Assess to Markets. This factor is always taken into consideration by the entrepreneurs. This becomes essential when the industry is producing perishable goods, which cannot wait till long distances are covered. Similarly the industry will be discouraged, if sending of finished goods to the markets is a very costly affair. Proximity to markets helps in lowering down the sales price because over head charges are considerably reduced.

3. Availability of Raw Material. Concentration of industries near the centre of raw material is quite common. Cotton industry in India e.g. is located in Bombay and Ahmedabad simply because of easy availability of raw material. Jute and iron industries in India are also concentrated in the areas where necessary raw material is available. In the words of Saviyya and Dass, "in other words most of the agro-based and forest based industries are to be located in the vicinity of the sources of raw material supply.

4. Availability of Labour. For smooth running of industry it is essential that supply of labour must be adequately available and if possible it should be cheap as well. An industry can tap other regional resources for labour supply, but these are sure to be both costly and undependable. But Prof. Kuchhal is of the view that, "The importance of labour supply in influencing the location of industry is difficult to assess since non-availability of local labour is not likely to prevent a site which has great natural advantages for an industry." Since each industry is required to give minimum wages to the workers, therefore, the industry does not much worry whether the labour is locally available or has come from a distance.

5. Transport Facilities. Usually there are three modes of transport facilities namely road, water and rail. Each industry will try to locate itself where one of the modes of transportation is available. One finds that technical point of a mode of transport is usually centre of great activity. In the words of Edgar. M. Hoorer, "For each combination of material sources and market there must be a point or points at which the total transportation costs involved in assembling materials and delivering the products to the markets are less than they would be anywhereelse. In the absence of production cost differentials, the best location for the production process is at the point of minimum transport costs." In the past means of transportation were not very efficient as there are today with the result that choice in matters of location was very limited. Efficient means of transportation have however, made the choice very wide.

6. Power Resources. Power is essentially needed for running an industry. This has become still more essential because transport cost of coal is very heavy. Obviously the industry will have tendency to locaise itself at a place where power resources are easily available. Development of hydro-electricity has in our own times considerably changed locational distribution of industries. These days supply of power and electricity is considerably influencing dispersal and concentration of industries.

7. Cheapness of Site and Services. Quite a heavy sum of money is invested on the purchase of land for the construction of factory and providing other facilities needed for running the industry. Each entrepreneur will like to be tempted to set up a new industry at a place where site and services are very cheap. In fact he will like to be tempted to a place where services already exist so that his contribution is very low. Not only this, but one finds that when industries are concentrated at one place providing such services as setting up of joint research laboratories, providing educational and training facilities and providing other services becomes economical and easy.

8. Availability of Financial Facilities. No industry can run without availability of finances both for its existence and expansion. Finance is the only mobile factor of production. If a financier is not willing to invest in an industry unless that is located at a particular place, the industry may get discouraged or not even come up at all. For an industry capital can be raised both at national as well as international level.

9. Natural and Climatic Consideration. No industrialist will ever like to set up an industry at a place where there are unhygienic conditions or where natural environments are unfavovurable. An industrialist while setting up an industry will always take into consideration topography of a region, level of ground, drainage facilities available in the area, and facilities available for the disposal of waste products. If an industry wants steady supply of water in manufacturing process, obviously it will need a location where nature has provided enough water. Topography always is taken into consideration, because it helps in lowering down the cost of transportation, which ultimately helps in bringing down the cost of production.

10. Strategical Considerations. These days the targets of air attack e.g., are industries which are producing defence material. Obviously strategically these will have to be located at a place, where the changes of air attack are very remote. Moreover, strategically it is becoming important that industries of a type should not be concentrated at a particular place or in a particular area because at a difficult time when the nation is at war and if an area goes under the control of enemy other industries or nation as a whole may not suffer.

11. External Economies. These include growth of subsidiary activities when a particular industry is localised at a particular centre, which might have transport or shipping facilities. If large numbers of industrial units are localised at a place, that may be an additional inducement for setting up such industries in that particular area.

12. Personal Factor. An industrialist may have personal preferences and prejudices for a particular place. Such a consideration can be love for a home town or desire to develop a particular area and so on. Sometimes personal factors so much dominate that veen many economic considerations are ignored all together.

Locational Factors in Actual Working

In actual practice industries have been influenced either in one way or the other factors about its location. In so far as historical factor is concerned Barlow Commission in U.K. was of the view that cotton industry in U.K. grew and was located Lancashire simply because it was a historical incident that woollen industry was already located there. Similarly in India sugar and cotton industries are located in Bombay and Ahmedabad simply because raw material in huge quantity is available in these areas. As regards labour, Sivayya and Dass are of the view that, "For instance, watch making and provision instrument manufacturing industries are concentrated prominently in Switzerland because of their traditional skills. Similarly location of iron and steel industry in Jamshedpur was primarily because of easy availability of labour in that area. Paper mills are concentrated in Calcutta and Raniganj simply because of their proximity to the markets. Similarly many Calcutta factories manufacture stationary simply because ready market is available. Availability of transport facilities played a considerable role in deciding Visakhapatnam as location for the proposed Visakhapatnam steel plant." In fact there are many instances which can be quoted to prove that one factor or the other and in many cases more than one factor has played an important role in the location of an industry. Pilani in India would not have been so important a centre of development had not Birlas personal liking of the area. Similarly copper complex at Khetri would not have developed, held copper as raw material not been available in that area and so on.

Dynamics of Industrial Location

There are various factors which influence location of an industry, but none of these factors can continue to have its effectiveness for all times to come. A factor which might be very important today, might become less tomorrow or might even lose its usefulness altogether. We find that till yesterday economic considerations very much influenced location of an industry, but today these are being subordinated to strategic conditions. Similarly a site which might be ideally suited for the setting up of an industry today, might not be so tomorrow. Such a situation can arise because of technological changes and also changes in the means of production or changes in transportation facilities. Thus changes in different locational factors can bring a shift in the location of an industrial activity.

Though every state wants to have locational equiliblum in industrial development, yet usually that is not possible. Many a time locational changes do occur. E.M. Hoover has classified basic causes of locational changes as follows:

Seasonal Changes. Sometimes producers shift their location so as to meet changing seasonal needs and requirements. But the producer knows that in a particular season he will have to shift and as such he is quite prepared for that and can change location without much dislocation. Thus he is not taken unaware.

Secular Changes. A secular change is one which is not sudden but which involves a gradual alteration. Such a change continues for quite some time. It has also no tendency to reverse or repeat itself as it found in the case of seasonal or cyclical changes. A good example of this can be growth in population, which goes on bringing changes but gradually and slowly.

Structural Changes. Changes are also brought about because of development of new resources and techniques. Every major technological improvement is likely to bring about locational change. In the words of Prof. Kuchhal, "Modern technological innovations have made labour requirements less specialised and exacting. They also have involved decentralisation to new centres of production. Further, the vastly increased use of non human industry in production has been off set by improved techniques that make energy cheaper and more transmissible and tend to equalise the advantages of various location in respect of energy cost."

THEORY OF LOCATION

Alfered Weber a German economist was the first economist who gave scientific exposition to the theory of location and thus filled a theoretical gap created by classical economists. He gave his ideas in his Theory of Location of Industries' which was first published in German language in 1909 and translated into English in 1929. His theory, which is also known as 'Pure Theory' has analytical approach to the problem. The basis of his theory is the study of general factors which pull an industry towards different geographical regions. It is thus deductive in approach. In his theory he has taken into consideration factors that decide the actual setting up of an industry in a particular area.

Weber's Problems. Weber was faced with many serious problems. He wanted to find out why did industry move from one place to another and what factors determine the movement. After considerable thinking he came to the conclusion that causes be responsible for this migration could be Regional Factors Primary Causes) and Agglomerative and deglomerative factors (Secondary Factors). In so far as regional factors were concerned these, among other things, included cost of the ground, buildings, machines, material, power, fuel, labour, transportation charges and amount of interest that the capital would have earned.

Regional Factors (Primary Causes). According to Weber transportation costs play a vital role in the location of an industry. Each industry will try to find location at a place where transportation charges are the bearest minimum, both in terms of availability of resources and place of consumption. According to him transportation costs are determined by the weight to be transported on the one hand and distance to be covered on the other. Then the cost will also depend on the type of transportation system available and the extent to which it is in use, the nature of the region i.e. whether rocky, plain, connected or unconnected with roads etc. the kinds of the roads in the area where the goods are to be transported; nature of facilities required i.e. whether the goods are to be taken with great care, less care or even without any special care.

Locational Figure. While discussing regional factors. Weber has discussed the idea of locational figure. According to him every industry will try to see that it is located at a place where raw material is available nearest to the place of consumption on the one hand and most advantageously located material deposits on the other. According to Weber, "Thus locational figures are created. These locational figures, therefore, represent the first and most important basis for formulating the theory."

Classification of Material. Weber, before proceeding further, has classified raw material into different categories e.g.:

(a) Ubiquities material; which is suitable every where e.g. bricks, clay etc., and

(b) Localised material *e.g.*, iron ore, mineral etc. which is available in certain regions and not every where. Obviously the later play a bigger and important role than the former. He has also categoriesed raw material as 'Pure' and 'Weight Losing' raw material is one which impart its whole weight to the products e.g. cotton, wool etc. and weight losing materials are those in which only a part of the material enters into the weight.

Laws of Transportation

Weber, while discussing the theory of location, has also discussed laws of transportation. According to him material index measures the total weight to be moved. From material index he understood the portion of the weight of localised material to the weight of the product. According to him, "All industries whose material index is not greater than one and whose locational weight therefore, is not greater than two lie at the place of consumption."

Causes of Deviation of Location

Weber was faced with a serious problem namely why do the industries deviate from the centre of least transport costs. One such reasons could be differencs in the labour costs. This labour cost can be cheap either because of differing levels of efficiency and of wages of labour or because of differing levels of efficiency in the organisation and the technical equipment which the labour is required to use. Labour cost can go up and come down due to distribution of population as well. But whatsoever might be the reason for the low labour cost, According to Prof Kuchhal, deviation "will be possible only when the additional cost of transportation at the new centre is more than compensated by a saving in labour costs... When the labour costs are raried, an industry deviates from its transport locations in proportion to the size of its labour co-efficient". Weber himself has said that. With a high index of labour costs, a large quantity of labour costs will be available for comparison with correspondingly high critical isodapanes, and therefore we shall find a high potential attracting powers of the labour locations and vice versa". According to Weber's theory if the behaviour of each industry in respect of labour cost is to be measured than it is necessary to calculate the proportion of labour costs per ton of weight to be moved.

Agglomerative and Deglomerative Factory (Secondary Causes)

We have so far been discussing primary causes of industrial location. Weber has also discussed secondary causes responsible for industrial location. He has taken into account agglomerative and deglomerative factors. An agglomerative factor, according to him is a factor which provides an advantage in production or marketing a commodity simply because industry is located at one place. On the other hand deglomerative factor is one which gives such advantage because of decentralisation of production.

Agglomerative factors include gas, water etc. and are condusive for concentration of industry and deglomerative factors include land values and taxes and lead to decentralisation. Pulls of agglomerative factors are index of manufacture and locational weight. According to Weber ratio of manufacturing cost of locational weight is co-efficient of manufacture. According to Weber Agglomeration is encouraged with high co-efficient and deglomeration with low. According to him, "We shall do well to bear in mind that labour orientation is one form of deviation from the minimum point; agglomeration to another. When agglomerative forces appear in an industry oriented towards labour, there takes place a competition between the agglomerative deviation and the labour deviation, a struggle to create, locations for agglomeration, as compared with labour locations, both bearing upon the foundations of the transportational ground work.

Split in Location

Weber has considered the possibility of location of an industry at more than open one, particularly when production in an industry can be carried independently at more than one place. According to him in fact single location is an exception and split a rule. It is essential, according to him that all productive processes must go on at one and the same place and it is better that these be carried out at different stages and at number of places. Split is to occur in two stages. In the first stage it is elimination of waste and in the second working up of pure material.

Locational Coupling

Weber along with split in location has also given the idea of locational coupling, meaning thereby that different types of industries can be coupled in one and the same locality. According to him it is just possible to combine production of different articles in one plant because of the availability of several raw materials from the same source. This coupling can be possible either due to economic or technical reasons. It is also possible due to connection through material e.g., if the by product of one industry happens to be raw material for another then the two industries may select a single place of location. Locational coupling can also be due to market connection between two industries. In such a case product of one industry may enter into another industry without being used as material or half finished product.

Criticism of Weber's Theory

Weber's Theory of Industrial location has been put to several criticisms. Some such points of criticism are:

1. Unrealistic Assumptions. According to critics of this theory, Weber has unrealistically over-simplified the theory of industrial location. Many assumptions in the theory are unrealistic. According to them Weber has taken only two elements for determining the cost of transportation namely weight and distance. He has not given due to place to the type of transport, quality of goods to be transported, topography, character of region etc.

2. Labour Centres Notion Defective. Weber's ideas about labour centres have also not been accepted. He has started with the presumption that there are fixed labour centres with unlimited supplies of labour in each of them. Obviously both these assumptions are not correct. There cannot be fixed labour centres, because each industry creates new labour centres. Similarly there can never be unlimited supplies of labour in any centre.

3. Ideas About Fixed Points of Consumption. It is argued that Weber's this idea does not work well with the market conditions in a competitive structure. Consumers are always scattered all over the country and thus consumer centres always shift with a shift in industrial population. There can therefore be no fixed point of consumption.

4. Vague Generalisations. Weber, while expounding his theory of industrial location, has introduced, it is believed, certain vague generalisations. He has given no due place to non-economic factors of industrial location, which play a big role in this regard. Who can deny that there are certain historical and social forces which go a long way while deciding industrial location of an industry, but he has completely ignored them, which has made his theory very unrealistic.

5. Not a Deductive Theory. Andreas Predohl is of the view that Weber's Theory is only selective and not deductive. According to him he has made an artificial distinction between general and special factors which influence location of an industry. Such a distinction, in fact, has no logical significance. According to Weber transport costs and labour costs are only general costs. He has failed to explain why capital costs and management costs cannot be included or covered under it.

6. Defective Method of Analysis. Weber has tried to classify material into abiquities and fixed material. Again the division is arbitrary. According to Robinson who does not know that in actual practice materials are drawn from a large number of alternative fixed points.

7. Overburdened with Technical Considerations. Dennison is of the view that Weber's theory is heavily over burdened with technical considerations. It has not laid due stress on costs and prices and has over stressed technical co-efficients. According to him, 'The most important criticism about Weber's analysis is that it is lamentaly removed from all considerations of costs and prices and it is formulated mainly in terms of technical co-efficients."

Utility of the Theory

No doubt theory suffers from some serious defects, yet it cannot be denied that it has its own value, importance and significance. It is primarily because, the alternatives given are neither comprehensive nor complete. So far it is the only theory which is capable of universal application. Andreas Predohl has also given his ideas about industrial location and has come to the conclusion that every change of industrial location involves a change in the combination of means of production. But this theory, obviously does not provide any guidelines for locating new industries.

SARGANT FLORENCE THEORY

After Weber's Theory during recent years, Sargant Florence has given his theory about industrial location, which has become popular. He started with the idea that some of Weber's assumptions are not realistic. According to him geographical location of an industry is not as important, as the distribution of occupied population. His main consideration is that occupational distribution of population should be the main and primary factor for taking into consideration the location of an industry. His theory is mainly based on inductive analysis and while explaining location factor of an industry he has taken into consideration location factor and co-efficient of localisation. Now a question arises as to what is location factor. According to him, it is an index of the degree of concentration of an industry in a particular region. Now this raises another problem namely how to arrive at the index, to which Sargant has made a reference. According to Saviyya and Dass, 'This index is calculated by taking into consideration two ratios, namely, the percentage of workers of the industry in question found in the region under consideration and the percentage of all industrial workers in the country. In calculating index to find out the location factor the first one is divided by the second and if the quotient is one, the location factor is said to unity and it can be said that the industry is evently tributed over the whole country. If quotient is above unity, then the conclusion can be that the region under reference has higher share of industry.

Co-efficient of Localisation. By this he meant prosperity of an industry for concentration. It indicates an industry's tendency for localisation anywhere in the country. It is primarily concerned with a particular industry and not a particular region. It will thus be a single figure for the industry and also for the country as a whole. Coefficient of localisation can be found with the help of following formula.

(a) % age of all workers found in each region;

(b) % age of the workers of industry in question in each region;

(c) Positive deviations of (b) from (a) are to be added;

(d) Sum thus derived is to be divided by 100.

On the basis of coefficients it becomes possible to divide the industries into three categories namely high, medium and low. Thus coefficient helps in classifying industries according to their dispersion or concentration. While discussing the advantages of method Prof. Kuchhal says, "Thus the location significance of industries is shown and the problem of investigation becomes easier. Industries with low coefficient of localisation can thrive in different regions and are thus dispersed. Industries which show a high coefficient of localisation.... are centralised in particular regions."

Critical Assessment of the Theory

1. The theory is not in a position to explain the causes responsible for the choice of location of an industry. It can only help in finding out the existing state of industrial distribution in a country. It is said that the theory is only the investigation of status quo and nothing beyond that.

2. While finding out coefficient of localisation, the unit is political region, which it is said cannot be much justified in discussing an economic theory. Therefore, the unit should be economic region.

3. According to this theory number of workers is the only one factor as the indicator of concentration of an industry, but there is no logic in choosing this one factor alone for finding out concentration of an industry.

4. According to Florescence co-efficient of location for all the countries is the same. But it cannot be the same because distribution of workers in each country varies according to local conditions.

5. While formulating his theory, he has not given due place and consideration to various forces of concentration which have direct bearing on the location of industrial units namely the role of external economies or tax incentives etc.

Value of the Theory. Like Weber's theory, this theory also suffers from some defects, about which a mention has already been made. But the theory has its advantages too. The theory is of considerable use for studying location dynamics in any country. These indices help in guiding the trends of industrial development in a country.

Then another advantage is that coefficient of localisation helps in deciding the types of industries that may be dispersed under a scheme of regionalism. It then becomes possible to diversify industries with a medium coefficient of localisation over a wide area, according to factor equipment in each area.

Combination of the two Theories. Weber has given a pure theory about location of an industry, whereas Florence's theory is based on indices. Both the theories have their own values and advantages. At the same time both have their drawbacks as well. It is therefore, essential to have some balanced approach. Such an approach can help in finding out proper system and basis for location of an industry. This has become more essential because these days more and more attention is being paid to the problem of location of an industry. These days industrial location is not taken in a limited economic sense but in a wider perspective taking into consideration social and strategical aspects. In industrial location today maximum care is taken to see that location can secure maximum efficiency of production and distribution. In the past while locating an industry was considered that what was in the best interest of the industrialist, was also the best interest of the community. Obviously this attitude has now altogether changed. Now there is always a need for some kind of regional planning of industry. Such a planning should combine maximum efficiency with optimum distribution of industrial activity, based on broader economic, social and strategical considerations. The best objectives can be achieved by combining the theories. Weber's theory can be employed for the investigation of practical problems whereas Florence's theory can help for analysis of an existing state of location.

❐

3

Market Structure and Performance

The term market structure refers to the type constituents and nature of an industry. It includes the relative and absolute size of firms, active in industry, easiness in the entry into business, the demand curve of the firm products etc. There are two extremities of the market structure on this basis, on one end there is a market of perfect competition and on the other perfect monopoly market. In between these two extremities there are monopolistic competition, oligopoly, duopoly etc.

Elements of Market Conduct

(a) Seller and Buyer Concentration. Here seller concentration means in certain industry the number of active firms is very limited and these few firms produce a large part of the total supply. In other words, there firms possess the market power in a sense that any one of these firms can affect the market price by making change in the quantity of its product. In full competition, each firm produces a very small part of the total production. Hence, it cannot affect the market price. In this type of market, the seller concentration is zero. So, as we move from the perfect competitive market towards pure monopolist market, the quantity of seller concentration increase.

(b) Market Power. Every competitive firm attempts to get market power by making difference in the product. From economic point of view difference in the product or product heterogeneousness affects the market, structure significantly. In the position of homogeneous product when a seller makes even a slight change in the price of product the consumers begin to purchase the product sold by other producers. In other words the firm producing homogeneous product has to face the perfectly elastic demand curve. On the contrary in the position of heterogeneous products any single firm can increase some price without being affected due to the preferences of the consumer.

(c) Product Differentiation. In the perfect competition market all firms sell the same or homogeneous product. But in the market, in reality a single product is sold by the different producers, claiming that all products (such as toothpaste) are not same. The producers bring variety by means of brand name, packaging, size, colour, taste, weight etc. In spite of no locational differences, variety is seen by means of retailer service, home delivery, credit facility etc.

(d) Barriers in Entry. Sellers concentration indicates that how some firms acquire dominance in an industry, consequently the real competition between the firms is lessened or limited. If there are some barriers in the entry of new firms, then the prospective competition is also limited. The types of such barriers are as follows:

(i) Cost profit to the present firm which is not available to the new firms.

(ii) Legal barriers in entry.

(iii) Product difference and advertisement etc. cause the presence of strong preference among consumers for the products sold by the established firms.

(e) Other Elements. Apart from these main elements, there are some other elements to be considered. One of them is the growth rate of market demand. In this situation the firms are somewhat idle. On the contrary in a rapidly growing industry the firms also become more competitive. In the growing market every firm is struggling and striving for more demand.

If there is more elasticity of the price demand of a product, the firm will be motivated to lessen the price in order to increase ones portion in the total sale. In the condition of oligopoly when a firm decreases price other firms also do the same. Then all firms derive benefit in the condition of more elastic demand. If the product demand is inelastic no firm will tend to change price.

Market Performance

Market performance means the evaluation of the derivation of the behaviour of any industry when it behaves differently than the established superior laws of the market. It is assumed that in the position of the perfect competition only an industry can perform well. But when the market is derivated from the condition of perfect competition, then the market behaviour also changes.

Now the question arises, as to how a market performance can be evaluated in any industry? Certain acceptable indicators are as follows:

1. Profitability. As we already know all firms have an objective like profitability, profit maximisation or satisfactory level of profit. But profitability in any industry does not depend only upon the performance of the firm. It also depends upon monopolist power, product diversity, or inefficient use of resources etc. Economists have used the hypothesis of normal profit. It is the rate of profit which makes the firm not to leave the industry. The performance level affects the quantity of profit significantly.

2. Productivity. It is an index of production of per unit input used, if more production is possible by the same units then there is growth in productivity. Growth in production is an indicator of efficient performance of an industry. But this index is also not without practical shortcomings. Till we can not keep the other factors stable, it is difficult to measure productivity of certain means/ inputs, like labour on capital. Besides this the units of labour, capital, or land are heterogeneous, so when a change occurs in the quantity of an input, there is also a change in its quality. For example when we recruit more workers, first we recruit more skilled ones and then the less skilled.

3. Growth. Information about the performance of an industry can be derived from its growth rate also. The measure of growth rate of an industry can be known from the product, employment and wealth creation. But every index creates problems in measuring the performance. For example, it is possible that in an industry more and more people get employment, or there is a rapid rate of wealth accumulation. But it is also possible that the resources are not efficiently used. Likewise when the growth rate is high we do not have information of production cost, whether it is more or less.

4. Effect on Index. Now the question arises whether the market structure affects the indexes of market performance. Profitability is one of the many indicators of performance. For example in perfect competition, a firm earns normal profit in long term while in monopoly or market having monopolist power, the firm earns extra-normal profit in long term also. Excessive seller concentration, barriers in entry and product difference can make firm earn more profit in long term also. Likewise we take growth index. Both in monopoly and oligopoly markets firm produces less than its capacity or there is a position of extra capacity.

5. Ill Effect on firm Growth. Thus, the growth of the firm is affected adversely. Productivity and efficiency are associated with each other. In the position of monopoly and oligopoly a firm has extra capacity which means inefficient use of resources and low level of productivity. Lastly, the social performance of a firm is also affected by market structure. In monopoly and perfect competition, consumer and labour, both are exploited. Growth in competition decreases the power of exploitation of the producers.

6. Social Performance. The performance level of an industry can be evaluated in the item of many social bases. These social bases can be income redistribution or other indicators of social welfare. For example the social performance of the medicine industry can be measured by the decrease in the illness period or death rate. If the expansion/growth of any industry results in decrease of present inequalities of income in society, or it helps in reducing poverty or unemployment then the performance level of the industry can be called high.

Market Structure conduct Performance Interrelations

In micro economics the equilibrium of the firm and industry is studied. On the contrary industrial economics is more related to change in market structure, resulting in the changes of market behaviour or firms behaviour, which ultimately affect their market performance. So industrial economics can be studied with the help of structure conduct performance approach or model.

Complexity of Interrelations

According to the economists, the interrelations between the structure, conduct performance are sufficiently complex. To conclude it can be said that market structure affects the behaviour of a firm and behaviour of a firm affects its performance (profitability) in the market.

TYPES OF MARKETS

In common usage the word market designates a place where certain things are bought and sold. But when we talk about the word market in economics, we extend our concept of market well beyond the idea of single place to which the householder goes to buy something, For our present purpose, we define a market as an area over which buyers and sellers negotiate the exchange of a well-defined commodity. For a single market to exist, it must be possible for buyers and sellers to communicate with each other and to make meaningful deals over the whole market.

Several economists have attempted to define the term market as used in economics. Some of them are as under:

According to Curnot, "Economists understand by the term market not any particular market-place in which things are bought and sold, but the whole of any region in which buyers and sellers are in such free intercourse with one another that the price of the same goods tends to equality easily and quickly."

In the eyes of Prof. Chapman, "The term market refers not necessarily to a place but always to a commodity and the buyers and sellers who are in direct competition with one another ,"

In simple words, the term market refers to a structure in which the buyers and sellers of the commodity remain in close contact.

Features of the Market

On the basis above-mentioned definitions we can mention following main features of the market:

(i) Commodity. For the existence of market, a commodity essential which is to be bought and sold. There cannot be a market without commodity.

(ii) Buyers and Sellers. Buyers and sellers are also essential for market. Without buyers and sellers the sale-purchase activity cannot be conducted which is essential part of a market.

(iii) Area. There should be an area in which buyers and sellers of the commodity .live in. It is not essential that the buyers and sellers should come to a particular place to transact the business.

(iv) Close Contact. There should be close contact and communication between. buyers and sellers. This" communication may be established by any method. For example, in olden days this contact and communication was possible only when the buyers and sellers of a particular commodity could come at a particular place. But now with the developed means of communication physical presence of buyers and sellers at one particular place is not essential. They can contact with, each other through letters, telegrams, telephones, etc. In the boundary of a market we include only those buyers and sellers who can maintain regular close contacts. For instance, India's farmers (or sellers of grains) have no close contacts with the consumers (or buyers) of England, hence though they are the buyers and sellers of grains yet do not come under the purview of a market.

(v) Competition. There should be some competition among buyers and sellers of the commodity in a market.

THEORY OF THE FIRM

According to Prof. Samuelson a firm under perfect competition is "One, who can sell all its wishes at the going market price, but is unable, in any appreciable degree to raise or depress that market price." A firm is one more production units under the same ownership. The firm under perfect competition is price taker. It has no control over the price and thus has to adjust its production and sales policies to the given price in the market. Since the firm can sell all its wishes at the same price, its average revenue curve is perfectly elastic (horizontal to the base axis) and the marginal revenue curve coincides with the average revenue curve.

The basic postulates of the theory of the firm are:

1. The objective of the firm is to maximise net revenue in the face of given prices and technologically determined production function.
2. A price increase for a product raises its supply; a price increase for a factor reduces its demand.
3. The firm operates with perfect knowledge of all relevant variables involved in making a decision and it acts rationally while doing so.
4. The theory of the firm deals with the role of business firms in the resource allocation process. It uses aggregation as tactic and attempts to specify total market supply and demand curves.
5. Originally the theory assumed that the firm is operating within a perfectly competitive market. But it has now been extended to cover other market situations.

The theory has been criticized in as much as it has been contended that profit maximization is not the only objective of a firm. It has been suggested that long run survival is the primary motive of the entrepreneur. Again, while the importance of profit has not been denied, many economists have argued that profit maximization should be replaced with a goal of making satisfactory profits. So also, it is difficult to operate with full knowledge of the decision environment which is full of uncertainties.

However, there is a general consensus that the theory of the firm purpose to explain at a general level the way resources are allocated by the price system, profit being the main criterion used by the firms.

From the viewpoint of price analysis, it is very important for business management to gain a proper understanding of the nature and process of competition in the modern industrial society. Firstly, the management should understand the rationale of the free enterprise system within which its own business decisions have to be made and the purpose, aims and limitations of that system. Secondly, it must have full knowledge of the market and market situations in which its own business operates and of the policies appropriate to those market situations: Thirdly, it is necessary to have an understanding of the competitive process and how the variables in the process-price, product innovation and promotional activity-may be manipulated in enlarging the firm's market share. Fourthly, the firms having monopoly power should be familiar with the nature and the purpose of the law relating to monopoly and restrictive practices. What is more important, the management must also be allert and recognize when market conditions change. Although there is no substitute for the intimate knowledge of the ways of the competitors acquired by experienced executives, an understanding of the nature of competition can provide an insight into the probable behaviour patterns of the competitors. It will be useful to distinguish the following types of market situations to study how prices are determined:

1. Perfect competition.
2. Monopoly
3. Monopolistic competition.

4. Oligopoly and oligopsoly.

5. Duopoly

Industry. Under perfect competition the term industry implies all firms producing a uniform commodity. If a firm produces more than one commodity, it participates in more than one industry. Industry determines the price under perfect competition.

After understanding clearly the characteristics of perfect competition, firm and industry, we should recapitulate the features of short-run and long-run discussed in earlier lesson. Just to remind, short-run is one in which the firm cannot change its size whereas long-run makes such change possible.

Meaning of Perfect Competition

Economists have defined perfect competition in various ways. Some important definitions are as follows:

According to Prof. Marshall, "The more nearly perfect a market is the stronger is the tendency for the' same price to be paid for the same thing, at the same time is all parts of the market.

According to Prof. Benham, "A market is said to be perfect when all the potential sellers and buyers are promptly aware of the price at which transactions take place and all the offers made by other sellers and buyers, and when any buyer can purchase from any seller, and vice versa." Under such conditions the price of a commodity will tend to be the same (after allowing for costs of transport and Taxes) all over the market.

According to Mrs. John Robinson, "Perfect competition prevails when the demand for the output of each producer is perfectly elastic. This entails first, that the number of sellers is large, so that the output of any one seller is a negligible small proportion of the commodity and second, that buyers are all alike in respect of their choice between rival sellers so that the market is perfect."

These definitions explain that perfect competitions in a market situation where a large number of buyers and sellers gather to exchange identical products, they have full knowledge of the market conditions and the price tends to be equal all over the market.

Features or Characteristics of Perfect Competition

The following are the main characteristics of perfect competition:

1. Existence of Large Number of Buyers and Sellers. The number of buyers and sellers is so large that no individual buyer or seller can influence the market price and output by his independent action. Every buyer and seller purchase or sells a very insignificant amount of the total output. The individual firm must take the price as given. It is a 'price taker' not the 'price fixer .'

2. Homogeneous Products. A firm produces a product which is accepted by customers as homogeneous. The firm cannot differentiate among buyers. It will not earn profit or suffer loss by selling it's product to a particular buyer. An individual firm cannot change any other price more than that already prevailing in the market.

3. Free Entry and Exist or the Firms. Every firm is free to join or cave the industry. If the industry is making profits new firms can enter the market to share these profits. Similarly, if the industry suffers losses, the individual farm may decide to quit the market.

Distinction between Perfect and pure Competition

The market Distinction between perfect and pure competition which possesses these three conditions is termed as pure Competition Market by the economists. According to Stinger and Hague, pure competition market is a situation which is compity free from any monopoly elements. Some economists use the term Atomistic Competition' also for pure competition.

Besides these three conditions, when the following conditions also exist in the market it become perfect competition market.

The difference between perfect and pure competition is very thin and therefore the two terms are used in the same sense by economists. Existing firm cannot bar the entry of new firms and there are no legal prohibitions on entry or exit.

4. Perfect Knowledge. There is perfect and complete knowledge on the part of all buyers and sellers about the conditions in the market. For a market to be perfect it is essential that all buyers and sellers should be aware of what is happening in any part of the market.

5. Perfect Mobility. There is perfect mobility of factors of production geographically (*i.e.*,) from one place to the other) as well as occupationally (*i.e.*, from one job to the other).

6. No Transport Cost. It is necessary that the commodity of the perfect competition market should be capable of being easily transported from one part of the market to another. It is presumed that the transportation cost from one part of the market to another part is zero.

7. Horizontal AR = MR Curve. In a pure and perfect competition market the average revenue = Marginal revenue curve of the firm becomes a horizontal curve parallel to the x-axis which shows infinite elastic demand. It is shown in the diagram. The shape of the AR curve (or demand curve) suggests that a firm under perfect competition is price-taker arid not a price-maker. In other words, the market price will not be affected by the independent actions of a single firm. Different firms working under perfect competition market cannot have different prices, all firms have to keep the same price for the product.

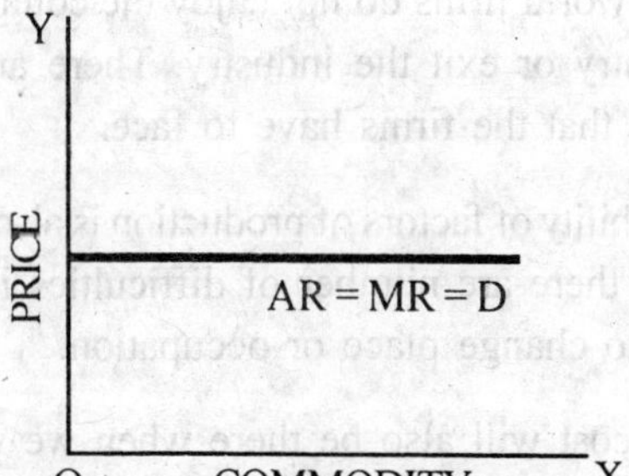

Thus, it becomes clear that perfect competition is a broader concept than pure competition. Pure competition means absence or monopoly power only while perfect competition includes some more features in it.

The Justification or Perfect Competition or Is Perfect Competition a Myth. Does perfect competition exist in the real world or is it a myth? Is it an important 'question to be probed ? Some economists have cited, agricultural commodity market, gold market and share market as the examples of perfect competition market. But when we adjudge these markets on the basis of the salient features of perfect competition market they also due not come to that level. In the real world we do not find any market to which we can term as perfect competition market. It is because of the following reasons:

(i) Real world markets do not have the number of buyers and sellers so large that no buyer .or seller can influence the market. Some buyers and sellers of the commodity are so big that they definitely influence the market.

(ii) There is no such thing as 'homogeneous product' in the real world situation which can be produced by all the firms in the market. For instance, if farmers produce wheat that does not imply that the wheat produced by all the farmers would be of the same quality.

(iii) Buyers and sellers cannot have the perfect knowledge regarding market conditions because of many reasons.

(iv) In the real world firms do not enjoy the complete freedom even in entry or exit the industry. There are number of difficulties that the firms have to face.

(v) Perfect mobility of factors of production is also not possible. Especially there are number of difficulties in the way of labourers to change place or occupation.

(vi) Transport cost will also be there when we will transport goods from one place to the other.

Thus out of the essential conditions of perfect competition, no condition is found in the real world situation. And that is why the concept of perfect competition is called an imaginary concept or a myth. If it is myth, why is it studied in economics ? The fact that perfect competition is not a real world situation does not reduce the usefulness of this model Though perfect competition is rare, we still study it for the following important reasons:

(i) **Simple Analysis.** It furnishes us a simple and logical analysis to understand the process of price determination.

(ii) **Ideal Situation.** The theory of perfect competition provides a norm against which the actual performance of the economy can be checked or evaluate perfect competition being considered the most efficient CX1C. For instance, price and output determined under perfect competition shall be ideal situations. Now by comparing the actual price and output of the country with this ideal we can find out the deviations from it and accordingly can plan policy formulations.

(iii) **Price Control.** The concept of perfect competition is also helpful to the government in its task of price-fixation and price-control. It will be difficult to fix price below the level of perfect competition price, hence it should be kept in mind while fixing the price by the government.

Thus, it is clear that in spite of the fact that perfect competition is not cent percent real world situation, it is an important and useful concept in economics. We can find a number of markets in the real world which are very close to the norms of perfect competition market. On the basis of empirical observations, Prof. Leftwitch, Stigler and many other economists are of the opinion that markets are gradually moving towards, perfect competition.

MONOPOLY

The market, form of monopoly is the opposite extreme from that perfect competition. It exists whenever an industry is in the hands of single of producer. In the case of perfect competition there are so many individual producers that no one of them has any power over the market and an; one firm can increase or diminish its production without affecting the market price. A monopoly, on the other hand, has power to influence the market price. By reducing its output, it can force the price up, and byincreasing its output it can force the price down.

The word MONOPOLY is made of two words; MONO +POLY. Here 'Mono' means one and 'Poly' implies the seller, thereby the literal meaning of the word Monopoly is one seller or one producer. Thus, pure monopoly refers to that form of market organisation wherein there is single firm (or producer) producing a commodity for which there are no good or close substitutes. According to Watson, "A monopolist is the only producer of a product that has no close substitutes." Changes in prices and outputs of other goods sold in the economy must leave the monopolist unaffected. Coversely, changes in the monopolist's price and output must leave the other producers of the economy unaffected.

Features of Monopoly

(i) Single Producer. There is a single firm producing the commodity in the market

(ii) No Close Substitutes. For the monopoly to exist single producer is the necessary condition but not a sufficient one. It is alsc essential that there should be no close substitute of the commodity in the market. This second condition would be even more difficult to fulfil than the first, since there are few things for which there is no substitute. For instance, Usha are produced by a single firm alone but there are close substitutes of Usha fans that are available in the market in the form of Relifans, Khaitan Ashoka, Crompton, etc. Hence, though the firm producing Usha fans is single yet it cannot be termed a monopoly firm. It is, therefore, essential for a monopoly to exist that there should by no close substitutes available in the market. This condition can be stated in other words as that the cross elasticity of demand for the output of the firm with respect to the price of every firm's product is zero.

(iii) Barriers to the Entry. The entry into the industry is completely barred or made impossible. If new firms are admitted into the industry, monopoly itself breaks down. This ban on entry may be legal, natural or institutional but it must essentially be there.

(iv) Firm and Industry. Since in monopoly there is single firm producing the commodity, hence the difference between firm and industry vanishes automatically.

(v) Downward Sloping AR and MR Curves. The monopoly firm is like an industry, and faces a downward sloping demand curve for its product; thus, it has to lower its price in order to sell more. For, it is this nature of demand curve that determines the nature of average and marginal revenue curves. Under perfect competition, We know, average revenue and marginal revenue curves coincide in a horizontal line. But that is not so under monopoly. With a monopoly, however, the average revenue curve, which is the same as the market demand curve, is downward sloping. Furthermore, the marginal revenue curve does not coincide with the average revenue curve rather, it remains below it. Thus, for a monopolist firm both AR and MR curve are downward sloping and MR remains below AR as shown in the diagram.

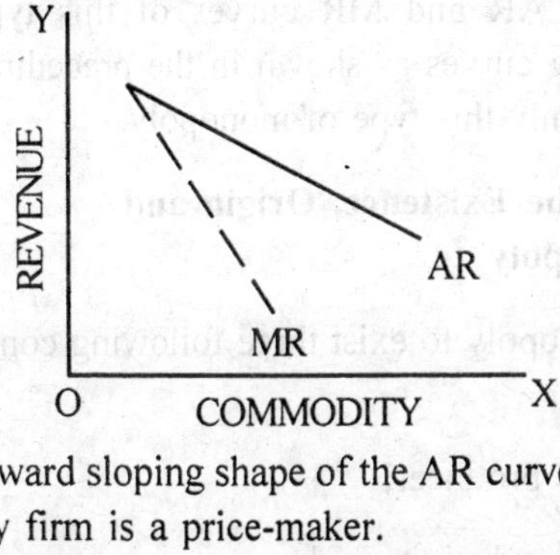

The downward sloping shape of the AR curve clearly indicates that a monopoly firm is a price-maker.

(vi) Price-discrimination is Possible. Under the conditions of monopoly price-discrimination is possible. It implies that a monopolist can sell its product at different prices to different customers. In short, monopoly depends basically on two factors:

(i) Absence of close substitutes; and

(ii) Restriction on competition.

PURE AND SIMPLE MONOPOLY

Economists, ordinarily, differentiate between two forms of monopoly. pure monopoly and simple monopoly. Pure monopoly is that market situation wherein there is only one producer of the commodity and the cross elasticity of demand is zero. In this situation total revenue at all levels of price and output remains the same. Hence the average revenue of the firm takes the shape of rectangular hyperbola. Here the monopolist is so powerful that he can extract the whole income from the consumers. In this situation producer would like to produce the minimum and he will fix the maximum price in order to intact its total revenue. But like perfect competition it is also an extreme and imaginary situation. It is not found in the real world situation.

On the other hand, simple monopoly is a market situation in which there is only one producer of the commodity and the cross elasticity of demand is not zero but small. In this situation firm can vary its price but its total revenue in all circumstances does not remain constant. AR and MR curves of this type of firm are downward sloping curves as shown in the preceding diagram. We ordinarily study only this type of monopoly.

Conditions for the Existence, Origin and Growth of Monopoly

For the monopoly to exist three following conditions must be fulfilled:

(i) Only one producer;

(ii) No close substitute and

(iii) Strong barriers to the entry into the industry.

The factors responsible for the origin and growth of monopoly are many and varied-natural, legal and institutional, technological, etc. Natural factors relate to the concentration of deposits of a particular mineral in a small area, as in the case of gold, copper ,salt, potash, diamonds, petroleum, etc..

In these days technological factors have become more important. In some industries requiring huge investment with long gestation period, the economies of large-scale production are so pronounced that the operation of market forces tend to lead to creation of monopoly, particularly when the size of the market is not very large.

Then there are legal monopolies, created by the state through "patent" laws and otherwise.

Distinction between Perfect Competition and Monopoly

A market wherein perfect competition between large number of buyers and large number of sellers of a homogeneous production is found, it is termed as perfect competition market.

A Market which has single producer of the commodity and no close substitutes is called monopoly market.

Perfect Competition	Monopoly
1. Large number of firms	1. Single firm.
2. A firm cannot adopt independent price policy. It is price-taker and not the price-maker.	2. Firm can have independence price policy. It is price-maker.
3. AR and MR curve are one and the same and parallel to the X-axis. AR = MR	3. AR and MR curves are down warld sloping curves and MR curve always remains below the AR curve MR < AR
4. Price-discrimination is not possible *i.e.*, a firm here charges the same price from all customers	4. Price-discrimination is possible

5. Full freedom to entry or exit.	5. Restriction on the entry.
6. Firm can get only normal profits in the long run.	6. Firm can earn supernormal profits in the long run.

Check on Monopolies

There are certain checks which always operate in the market. No monopoly, however strong its network may be, can escape the influence of those checks. These are:

1. Existence of Substitutes. Monopoly can control only few commodities, for which a market has been created. Every consumer will like that the commodity should continue to remain good, quality satisfactory, supply regular and prices reasonable. But once the monopoly tries to misbehave the consumer will try to find substitute for the commodity. The monopoly also knows that for every commodity there is a substitute and as such will not like that the taste of the consumer should in any way change.

2. Danger of State Intervention. The another check on the monopoly is that in case the monopoly does not behave properly the State may intervene. It may pass such laws, which will force the monopoly to properly behave. Such a behaviour will be more restrictive than the voluntary behaviour and the monopoly may be obliged to behave in a manner which it does not like.

3. Rise of Rivals. Monopoly is that it is always afraid that in case it does not keep pace with the wishes of the people, then it is just possible that some rival party may come in the market and successfully and easily capture that throwing them out of the market. Such a rival can have share in the profits and even control the whole market.

4. Nature of Product. Demand for the product can be both rigid as well as elastic. If monopoly is producing a product, for which demand is elastic, it will have to give the society many concessions. On the other hand if the demand is rigid, then it can behave to some extent, in the way it likes. So the nature of product also decides about the behaviour of the monopoly.

5. Price Consideration. The monopoly cannot arbitrarily fix price. It will have to take paying capacity of the customers into consideration. It will therefore, fix only such price which is considered reasonable by the society and not by the monopolist.

6. Fear of Boycott. Monopoly behaviour is also checked by the fear that the society might boycott the product, if the prices are fixed very high. The monopoly always should realise that customer can expect exploitation only to a limited extent. If the prices are kept high the consumers can well organise themselves and the industry might alienate the sympathies of the society. It is a very big check on the monopoly.

7. Taste of the People. Monopoly may be interested to produce such articles which can bring them heavy profits, but at the same time, it will have to keep the taste of the people and society into consideration. The monopoly will be forced to produce only what is required by the society no matter in that their margin, of profit is high or low.

MEASURES TO CONTROL MONOPOLIES

Monopoly is always in an advantageous position to fix the price of a commodity in a way it likes another exploit the society. It is very essential that the society should be saved from exploitation. This can be done only when the state interferes and for this some measures are always taken by the state. Some of important measures are:

(1) Anti Trust Legislation. One of the measures which is adopted by the monopoly is to form trusts. These trusts are of course voluntary, but all the evils of monopoly more or less creep into it, with the result that the State is forced to take legislative measures. In 1890 in the USA. Sherman Anti Trust Law was passed. Similarly in 1914 Olayton Anti Trust Law was passed. But many a time monopolists are very active. They try to undo the work of the state by either combining in another form or by reaching some informal understanding.

(2) Control over Prices. Monopoly will always try to fix the highest possible price which it can obtain from the customers, so as to earn minimum profit. The state can control the monopoly by fixing the profits and the prices and ensure that the industry does not earn undue profit. But it is also not very effective and cannot be put into actual practice. We know that it is very difficult to determine the cost of production, because the monopoly will never give a correct picture. Similarly, it will also,not like to leak out trade secrets. Then it is also difficult to have some margin of profit uniformly for all commodity, all over the country.

(3) Organised Consumer's Associations. The monopoly fixes high prices because it knows it fully well that the consumer is not well organised and will take time to organise himself and till then suffer. One effective method of checking and controlling monopoly is that the Government should help in the formation of consumers associations. It should give them some reasonable powers and patronage. It should be vested with the responsibility of bringing to the notice of the Government on the one hand and the society on the other, high handedness of the monopoly. But this proposal too is complex and complicated. The monopoly will always try to see that the consumers associations are not formed. They will always try to put many hurdles on the way. Even if the association comes up, the monopoly will see that it is not forceful and powerful. Then another difficulty is that the consumers are spread all over the country and it is usually very difficult to bring them nearer and closer to each other and that too in an effective manner.

(4) Effective Publicity. Monopoly works with some serious irregularities, which usually do not come to the notice of the people. It is therefore, desirable that proper publicity should be given to these defects. There should be provision for public supervision of monopoly houses. In the words of Prof. Pigou, "Under any form of state control over private monopoly a considerable gap between the ideal and the actual is likely to remain. The method of control whether positive or negative is in short, an exceedingly imperfect means of approximating industry towards the price level and output proper to simple competition. Moreover, it is apt to prove a costly method."

(5) Creating Fair Competitions. Monopoly can continue only as long as there is no real competition. This competition must be effective, if monopoly conditions are to be checked. But the difficulty is that the monopoly will never allow any competition, because that will mean sharing in profits on the one hand and check on arbitrary fixation of prices on the other.

Monopoly chěck competition in more than one way *e.g.*:

(a) It will see that those who come in competition are discouraged. Their resources of supply are cut, and the suppliers are bribed and so on.

(b) When the rivals come in the market, the prices of the commodity are drastically reduced in the name of efficiency and economic production and for benefiting the consumers, this will force the newly emerging competitors to go out of the market.

(c) The monopoly will try to set up new firms to compete the new rival at all levels. The firms will be allowed to suffer losses for sometime. These will be wound up only after the competitor has gone out of the market.

(d) The suppliers of raw material, distributors and dealers will be given better terms for sometime.

In this way the monopoly will make every effort to see that competitor goes out of the market.

(6) Nationalisation. The last resort of the Government is that it should nationalise the business, in which monopoly exists and which the society is not willing to tolerate. But again the difficulty with this system is that the Government has limited economic resources and can nationalise only a few industries. Similarly while nationalising it is to take into consideration nature of the commodity. If it is of public utility then it may go in for nationalisation immediately otherwise it may be forced to wait for nationalisation, till such time, as the resources are available.

Thus it is very difficult to really effectively either check or control the monopoly. The only effective method is creation of fair competitions. The task is quite difficult, but once that has been created, monopoly can be most effectively checked.

ANTI-MONOPOLY GOVERNMENT POLICY

Consequences of Industrial Concentration in Private Sector. Discussing the consequences of industrial concentration in a few industrial houses as described above, the Monolies Inquiry Commission was of the view that there was widespread distrust existing among the people about such concentration of industries in the hands of some private industrial houses or groups. There was hardly any goodwill for them in the minds of the common people. There was widespread feeling among the people that big industrial houses were eating into the very vitals of democratic machinery in the country. This belief was based on the consideration that big industrial houses were eating into the very vitals of democratic machinery in the country. This belief was based on the consideration, that big industrial houses had given considerable financial assistance to the ruling party, especially at the time of general elections. Big houses, according to the Commission, resorted to bribing public officials for some consideration in their favour.

Dynastic Control. The majority of the members of the Commission were of the opinion that though there were complaints of dynastic control over industrial establishments, big business houses had been able to supply, over a fairly long period of time a considerable amount of entrepreneurial skills and abilities of high quality. But a minority of members expressed the opinion that the dominance of big industrial houses had prevented the emergence and spread of entrepreneurial and managerial talents and skills among larger sections of population; it thus, was responsible for retarding the development of managerial skills on a broader basis in the country.

Vigilance. The Commission, therefore, recommended the setting up of a permanent body to exercise vigilance and prevent the evils of monopolistic and restrictive trade practices. The permanent body should have the powers to initiate an enquiry on its own or on receipt of a complaint from the Government or from the public. It should have the power to order the concerned party to desist or discontinue the practice against which a complaint is lodged with it.

Remedial Measures. The Monopolies Inquiry Commission was of the view that the dangers of economic concentration and of monopolistic and restrictive trade practices were genuine and existed on a fairly large-scale in the country. The Commission was of the view that the Government with the existing powers was not in a position to check and much less eliminate the evils of monopolistic and restrictive trade practices as practised at present in the country.

Non-Legislative Remedies. In addition to the above legislative measures, the Commission also made certain other non-legislative recommendations to curb the monopolistic and restrictive trade practices of big industrial houses. The Commission opined that political parties should stop accepting financial contributions from big industrial houses for election purposes and once the politicians freed themselves from the corrupting practices of industrial houses, it would be easy to deal with government officials dealing in corrupt practices in relation to big industrial houses.

The second recommendation of the Commission was that licensing policy of the Government should be liberalised so that it would be easier for new entrepreneurs to obtain industrial licenses which, therefore, would not get concentrated in the hands of a few big industrial houses.

Thirdly, in the matter of issuing of import licences either to established importers or to users, care should be taken to see that consumers are protected from exploitation by industrial establishments enjoying a monopolistic position.

Public Sector. Fourthly, the Commission was of the opinion that to counter the abuses of private industrial monopolies, there should be emphasis on the expansion of the public sector industrial establishments. But, at the same time, the Commission warned against the dangers of expanding public sector enterprises that they might work in an inefficient manner and prove expensive to the public and to tax-payers.

Small Scale Sector. Fifthly, the Commission opined that the establishment of small-scale industries and consumer cooperatives would help curb monopolistic and restrictive trade practices of private industrialists. One of the members of the Commission suggested that the Life Insurance Corporation and the Unit Trust of India and other public financial institutions which give financial assistance to industrial establishments should take greater interest in their policies and affairs, there was also the suggestion that the Companies Act be suitably amended to ensure that shareholdings of industrial establishments be thrown open to the public and that it be made more broad-based among the public rather than being concentrated in the hands of a few industrialists and their close associates and friends.

The Monopolies Inquiry Commission submitted its report and recommendations (in the form of a draft bill) in October, 1965.

On the basis of the draft, the Monopolies and Restrictive Trade Practices Bill was presented to the Parliament in August, 1967 and the Monopolies and Restrictive Trade Practices Act was passed in December, 1969.

Change in Government's Policy in Respect of Monopolies and Big Industrial Houses. Government of India started changing its attitude towards monopolies and big industrial houses since 1981 onwards.

The Industrial policy of July 1991 has for all practical purposes almost totally reversed hereto adopted policy in regard to monopolies and big industrial houses.

The Industrial policy of July 1991 made the following statement in regard to Monopolies and Restrictive Trade Practices Act (MRTP Act-1970). "The interference of the government through the MRTP Act in investment decisions of large companies has become deleterious in its effect on Indian industrial growth. The pre-entry scrutiny of investment decisions by so-called MRTP companies will no longer be required." Hereafter, the main business of the MRTP Commission will be to look after and try to control and regulate restrictie and unfair trade practices, rather than making it necessary for the large industrial houses to seek prior approval of the Central Government for their industrial expansion, establishment of new industrial undertakings, merger, amalgamation, or takeover of other industrial units.

The objective of the new Industrial Policy of July 1991 in respect of monopolies and big industrial houses is to increase their investments and accelerate industrial growth-rate in the country.

Industrial Policy of July 1991 and Monopolies and MRTP Act. The Industrial Policy of July 1991 states as follows in regard to the MRTP Act and Monopolies Commission and its functions. "The interference of the Government through the MRTP Act in investment decisions has become deleterious in its effects on Indian industrial growth. The pre-entry scrutiny of investment decision by so-called MRTP companies will no longer be required." This means that hereafter for establishing an industrial unit with any amount of investment, or for expanding productive capacity and production of existing industrial units, for mergers of existing big units and for their amalgamation, permission of the MRTP Commission will no longer be required.

Investigation. After 1991 the only function of the MRTP Commission will be "to initiate investigation on its own initiative or on the basis of complaints received from consumers or classes of consumers in regard to restrictive and unfair trade practices appears extremely doubtful, if past experience in this matter is taken into consideration. Large business houses have formed their own associations which are very powerful; these associations can create artificial scarcity and push up prices. These large industrial houses make huge contributions to political parties in the country as also to different trusts established by different political parties (not to speak of political party in power.)

MONOPOLISTIC COMPETITION

Economists found that perfect competition and pure monopoly were unrealistic market situations. The actual market situations are somewhere between perfect competition and pure monopoly. The theory of Monopolistic Competition was first propounded and popularised by an American economist E. H. Chamberlin. Sometimes monopolist competition is termed as Imperfect Competition also.

Meaning. Now let us understand the meaning of monopolistic competition. As Stonier and Hague put. "It means the large group or firms making very similar products. Here there is keen but not perfect competition between many firms making very similar products (products are not homogeneous as in perfect competition or remote substitutes as in monopoly, but they are differentiated)".

In the words of Dominick Salvatore, "Monopolistic competition refers to the market organisation in which there are many firms selling closely related but identical commodities."

Thus monopolistic competition refers to the market situation in which many firms producing differentiated products (closely related but no identical products) compete with each other for the sale of their products. So defined, monopolistic competition is a market situation with some elements of pure competition and some elements of pure monopoly. This explain the essential nature of monopolistic competition. It is competition between a large number of firms, each of them enjoying a measure of monopoly power. That is why, monopolistic competition is sometimes described as "Polypoly."

Features of Monopolistic Competition

(i) Many Sellers. There are large number of firms producing commodity in the market. Large number here implies that there are so many firms that the activities of one firm has no perceptible effect on the other firms in the industry. Each firm controls a very small or negligible share of the total output of the industry. The competitive element results from the fact that there are many firms in the market.

(ii) Freedom of Entry or Exit. Every firm is free to enter into the industry and come out from the industry as and when it wishes.

(iii) Product Differentiation. Product differentation is the most important feature of a monopolistic competition market. Under monopolistic competition products of different firm are neither completely homogeneous as in perfect competition nor entirely distinct as in monopoly. Here each firm produces a products that is somewhat different from the products of its competitors, but it is not entirely distinct, it is very close to the products of other firms. Products of two or more firms, are not exact substitutes but also are not entirely different. They are each other's close substitutes. But each firm is known for its own product, which has some distinction. For its product, the firm is a monopolist. But because of close substitutes, it faces competition with other firms. In fact, absence of differentiation would mean pure competition and perfect differentiation would mean pure monopoly. Partial differentiation, therefore, defines the nature of monopolitistic competition.

There might, for example, be a large number of competeting firms producing different brands of soap, all similar but by no means identical products. Each soap would differ in physical composition from competing soaps; it would also have different packing, and as the advertisers-say, a different 'brand image' from its competitors.

Thus, products may be differentiated in many ways, *e.g.* by changing in brand name, trademark, design, packing, colour, size, weight, measurement, etc. We are giving some examples of product differentiation below so that the term could be understood more clearly.

Cycle-Atlas, Estern Star, Hind, Hero, A-One etc.

—Sewing Machines-Usha, Luxmi, Singer, etc.

—Cigarettes-Wills, Gold Flake, Bristol, Taj, etc.

—Soap-Lux, Rexona, Hamam, Jai, Lifeboy, Pears, etc.

—Tea-Brooke Bond, Lipton, Modies, Tata, etc.

We can find a number of examples of such differentiated products. Cross elasticity of demand between such commodities is very high.

(iv) Each firm is a Monopolist for its Product. Every firm has a monopoly over the production of its product *i.e.*, no other firm can manufacture the product of this brand name. For instance no firm other that the Atlas Cycle Company can manufacture Atlas Cycle or no firm other than Hindustan Lever can manufacture Lux toilet soap.

(v) Consumer Exhibits Market Preference. In this market situation a consumer exhibits market preference for a particular product in the market. For instance, some consumers prefer Brooke Bond tea while others prefer Lipton.

Those who prefer a particular product would like to purchase it at even somewhat higher price.

(vi) Selling Costs. Selling costs have an important place in this market. Every firm seeks to modify consumers' preferences through advertisements and salesmanship. This gives rise to what is called selling costs. Thus there is non-price competition among firms under monopolistic competition.

(vii) Independent Price Policy and Downward Sloping of AR-MR Curves. A firm under monopolistic competition can have an independent price policy. It is price maker for its product. Hence the

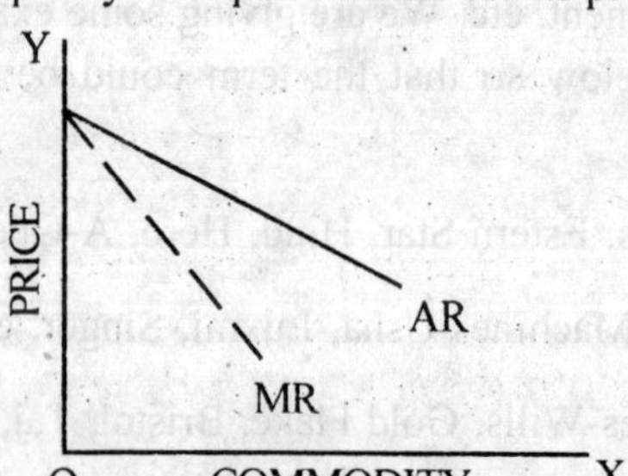

AR and MR curves facing a firm under monopolistic competition will be downward sloping similar to the monopoly. But there is an

important difference between the AR curves under monopoly and monopolistic competition. The AR curve under monopolistic competition is somewhat flatter than in the monopoly. AR and MR curves of a firm under monopolistic competition are illustrated in the diagram:

MONOPOLY AND ITS FORMS

Monopoly situations and conditions are prevailing in all economies, either in one form or the other. Though some of the nations are trying to check monopolies, yet the fact remains that these are rapidly increasing and not being checked, because the system has its own advantages.

Monopoly is a situation in which a group of persons is in a position to end competition in a particular commodity and control sale and supply of that commodity. That group is also in a position to influence its price. An extreme monopoly situation arises when a firm or group of closely connected and interested persons only begins to produce a particular commodity. In the words of Stonier and Hague, "The pure monopoly, as we may call it, will occur when a producer is so powerful that he is always able to take the whole of all the consumer's income whatever, be the level of his output." Similarly Liftwich has said that, "Pure monopoly is a market situation in which a single from sells a product for which there are no good substitutes."

Is Perfect Monopoly Possible? Perfect monopoly situation is not possible in the world. For production, distribution and pricing there must be some sort of competition, though in some cases it may be very tough, while in others only normal. It will be only an ideal situation in which competition can be completely eliminated.

Form of Monopoly

A monopoly situation provides the monopoliser with an advantage of fixing the price, or produce quality of goods or distribute them in the way he likes and as such every person or business house is in a position to have monopoly. This monopoly is created either by an individual with his own vast resources, or by combining together and thus pooling their resources or groups of industries coming together so that mutual competition is avoided and monopoly is created. The Monopolies may be classified as *(a)* Natural Monopoly; *(b)* Legal Monopoly; *(c)* Social Monopoly and *(d)* Voluntary Monopoly.

(a) Natural Monopoly. This is monopoly in which individual has... and nature has more role to play. In it nature blesses the nation with bounties in a particular commodity and that is available in that country, which can control that in the way that likes. Arab nations have oil monopolies and they can control the world economy in so far as oil and oil products are concerned.

(b) Legal Monopoly. In some cases, a product does not exist or if that exists that is comparatively less or unknown. An organisation or an individual works hard, carries out research, spends his life and is in a position to produce and market that. He feels that his product is being well received and does not wish that any individual or organisation should take advantage of his labour. He gets his trade mark and formula registered with the Government by paying fixed fees. After that has been accepted no one else can either use formula or trade mark. that then becomes his absolute monopoly. It is called legal monopoly.

(c) Social Monopoly. In every society there are certain civic amenities and facilities to be provided to the citizens. Therefore, an organisation may be allowed to provide those facilities *e.g.* in Delhi, electricity is supplied by Delhi Electric Supply Undertakings or water is supplied by Delhi Water and Sewerage Department and so on. This type of organisation which is solely responsible for the supply of a particular civic amenity, is stated to be enjoying a social monopoly in that commodity.

(d) Voluntary Monopoly. It is also known as combination. In it some of the producers dealing in the same commodity come nearer and closer to each and combine in one form or the other so as to avoid competition. There is no external force or compulsions to join or to combine, that is why it is called voluntary monopoly. Such a monopoly can be in the form of Trusts or Cartels. This voluntary monopoly can be both vertical or horizontal. A vertical combination is also known as integration. A horizontal combination can be in the form of pools, holding company and complete merger. All of these forms have already been discussed earlier.

Monopolies are not very much appreciated these days because it is felt that socially these are more harmful than useful to the society. Moreover, it is felt that monopolists exploit the situation to the greater disadvantage of the common man, resulting in his ruthless exploitation, and leaving him with little option or choice.

Advantages of Monopolies

Some of the advantages of the monopolies are as follows:

1. Economies of Large Scale Production. Monopolies can only successfully function, only when there is large scale production. In such a situation obviously advantages of scale economies accrue to the organisation or the individual. These include economies in buying, selling and savings in transportation and overhead charges. Then it becomes possible to employ qualified people at good salaries and drain in competent people from other organisations. Similarly we also find that it becomes easy to have an up to research laboratories and purchase latest machinery to modernise the industry. All these advantages of large scale economy make it possible to lower down the cost of production and sell the commodities at cheap rates in the market.

2. Elimination of Competition. Usually there is cut throat competition in the market. But when there is monopoly, there is no competition and a lot of money is saved, which can be advantageous to the society. The individual or the group can lower the price of the goods produced can sell them at cheap rates.

3. Essential in Public Utilities. Every society needs public utility services. Some of the services are really very costly and require huge capital, which one firm cannot spend. It is in the interest of the society itself that monopolies be created *e.g.*, electric supply, milk supply or water supply etc. Any competition in these services is bound to do more harm than good to the society. In such services only monopolies can serve the purpose.

4. Depression can be Faced. When there are depressions most of the small and uneconomical industries go out of the market. Only the monopolies, which have vast sound financial resources can not effectively survive and face the situation. Monopolies can afford to suffer losses, which fall in prices bring with them. In the face of losses, they can continue to produce and try to control the market.

5. Ability to Face Competition. Today there is keen competition, both in the local, national and international markets. It is usually difficult to face the competition, with the result that many small scale firms go out of the market, after suffering heavy losses. But when monopolies arise, obviously the monopolists try their best to face all competitions. Thus monopolies have always proved useful and effective in facing international competitions.

6. Efficient Production. Under monopolies uneconomical and in-efficient firms producing costly goods with out any research facilities go out of the market. On the other hand, the situation is quite different with monopolies, which have the advantages of economical and better production.

7. Necessary for Developing Countries. Monopolies are necessary for developing countries because these alone can produce goods at cheap rates. Moreover, the monopolies can produce better laboratories and well paid and qualified staff. Similarily, the developing countries need variety of goods and it is possible only by big industrialists and industries, which are controlled by monopolists to produce them.

8. Large Financial Resources. Monopolies usually have large financial resources which can go a long way in expansion of the programme of the firm, in introducing new items, in expansion of market and in providing better facilities and improved working conditions for the workers and the employees, who remain satisfied. With the help of financial resources raw material can be purchased, stored at the most appropriate time and thus the crisis in production hardly arise.

Disadvantages of Monopolies

Monopolies have their disadvantages as well. Some of the important disadvantages are as follows:

1. Leads to Exploitation of Workers. Onc of the important duties and responsibilities of the industry is to promote social welfare. But under monopolies usually there is exploitation of workers. The industry knows that the workers cannot go out because chances of employment, out of the firm have been reduced to the minimum. It does not care about their welfare, which cannot be justified on any ground.

2. Arbitrary Price Fixation. One of the characteristics of monopolies is that it can thus fix the price arbitrarily. Usually it is fixed on the vary high side. The consumer has no other alternative but to accept the price. In absence of competition, the consumer also cannot bargin as well. Thus this results in many serious problems for the society as a whole.

3. Control Over Output. In monopoly situation the producer decides what to produce when and in what quantity. Obviously he will like to produce only such commodities which give him maximum profit. While deciding about the output he may or may not care for social needs. Thereby creating social crisis at any time, by not producing sufficient quantities of the commodities needed by the society.

4. No Gain to the Consumer. There is no doubt that monopolies enjoy the benefits of large scale economies including production of goods at chcap ratcs, but monopoly is not prepared to share the gains of large scale economies with the consumers. It wants to keep the profit with itself. Therefore, consumer is least profited by the gains of large scale economies of monopolies.

5. Wrong Allocation of Economic Resources. Monopoly till try to have maximum control over the economic resources. This in itself a big distortion. Not only this, but in every industry, monopoly can provide employment to very limited number of persons. This has the advantage of new and well equipped machinery. It can place man be machine.

6. Political Corruption Encourages. In a country with democratic set up, chances of political corruption cannot be ruled out. The monopolists, in order to maintain and strengthen their monopoly will always try to corrupt politicians so that no legislation opposed to their interests is brought forward. They will always influence that political party as a whole, by giving financial support at the time of elections. The monopolies and industrialists will become members of these parties and try to occupy important posts and positions.

7. Concentration of Wealth. A monopoly situation can be created by those who are already economically strong and sound. Hence this situation has been created more money begins to flow in. It begins to go on concentrating in the hands of only few persons, who control, distribute and fix the price to suit their profit motives. Thus the rich grow richer and their capacity to exploit considerably increases which is good for healthy society.

8. Interests of Workers Not Cared for. In monopolies interests of the workers too are not cared for, while finalising the combinations or mergers. Those who are found surplus in the new arrangements are thrown out of job. Their respective positions are ignored and they are given new positions to suit the convenience and whims of the management.

9. Sacrifice of the Interests of Shareholders. One of the forms of monopoly is voluntary monopoly. Before combination however may bargains are struck and under hand-deals finalised. In these only individual interests are preserved. The interests of the shareholders are least cared and protected. It is unfortunate that those who invest money by spending in the shares are made scape goats, for protecting the interests of the few who control the firms. Thus the interests of a vast majority of the people are sacrificed.

10. Corrupt influence on Business. Monopolies try to corrupt whole business by using unfair means in the business. In order to eliminate local competitions, the monopolies fix different prices of the same commodity in different localities, thereby encouraging such economic offence and crimes as smuggling. In order to maintain their monopolies, they even fix prices below cost price in some cases, so that the rival is thrown out of market.

11. Apathy Towards Technical Progress. Still another drawback of the monopoly is that it shown an apathy towards technical progress. It is on account of two reasons. Firstly the monopoly feels that any technical progress or advancement is bound to create some dislocation, which will disturb status quo, for which the industry is least prepared under the monopolists. Then another problem is that the monopoly feels that when their products are already acceptable to the society, why should they spend money on research and technological advancement.

12. Economic Depressions and Cycles. It is very unfortunate that monopoly, which should have helped in maintaining prices has acted to the contrary. The investors are usually motivated more by personal rather than by social gains. They create depressions and economic cycles in the way they like. They make the whole economic market erratic, irritating not only the government, but also the consumer.

Growth of Monopoly

Monopoly exists in every society, and there are no effective checks for controlling monopoly. But monopoly grows and develops only under certain favourable circumstances, which may briefly be discussed as under:

1. Control over Raw Material. When monopoly gets control over the raw material it is bound to grow and develop. This control can be that the nature has helped in the process or that the industrialist himself has manipulated in getting the control. But availability of raw material with exclusive control is very much favorable for the growth of monopoly.

2. Legal Backing by the Government. The monopoly can flourish with legal backing. If the government is decided and determined to crush a monopoly, it is bound to face many complications and might not even survive. On the other hand, if the government supports, it will grow. The government can give backing by accepting its patent trade marks, by punishing those who violate them and by providing some financial and other facilities. The least it an do it that it shall not allow interference in the affairs of the monopoly.

3. Demand for the Product. If the product is of high quality and the society has appreciated that, then the monopoly will definitely grow. But on the other hand if the product is of sub-standard quality and the society is accepting that simply because it has no other alternative, then monopoly situation is not likely to last for long. As soon as the society finds an alternative, it will immediately go in for that and the monopoly will then receive a serious setback.

4. Behaviour of Monopoly. How the monopoly behaves, is another factor which decides about its growth. The society is bound to be influenced by the behaviour of the management, its personnel and salesman. In case monopoly behaviour is upto the expectations of the society, it will have social support, which will help in its growth. As soon as that support is lost, the monopoly will go on the path of retardation.

5. Healthy Combinations. Monopolies come into existence when some firms combine together. These combinations can be both healthy as well as unhealthy, fair or underhand means. When combinations arise out of fair and healthy means, it can be presumed that the monopoly was growing and developing. But when these combinations are based on unfair means, not only that the progress will be slow, but these will not grow.

6. Control over Essential Services. Then monopoly control over essential services goes a long way in deciding whether monopoly would grow or not. In case monopoly exercises control over such essential services as water, power, transport etc., then the monopoly may quickly grow. If these services are not under their influence and control, the pace of growth might be very slow.

7. Satisfaction of the Staff. Each monopoly would employ several hundred people, if not more. The people will fall under various categories. Broadly speaking there will be skilled, unskilled and semi-skilled people. Most of them might have conflicting interests. The greatest problem is to keep them satisfied. Growth of monopoly is linked with the satisfaction of the employees. Only satisfied employees can give better production and help manufacturing and controlling the market.

8. Providing Varieties. The people always want a change. A commodity which a society once accepts, will remain acceptable only for sometime and not for long. If monopoly can keep the customers satisfied by providing varieties, then well and good; otherwise the people will themselves try to search for variety, giving setback to the monopoly.

9. Flow of Finances. Each monopoly will need finances to grow. If the money is forthcoming quickly then the credit of monopoly in the market will increase and no project will ever receive any serious setback. On the other hand if the monopoly is short of finances, one day or the other it will receive set back.

10. Scope of the Market. What is the scope of the market in respect of the product, which it is producing. If the market is wide and there is scope for expansion then there is every chance to believe that the monopoly will grow. On the other hand, if the scope is limited, then it can be seen that one day rival will come and may wipe out the existing monopolists, by providing a touch competition. Moreover, if the scope of the market is limited, then at some stage a saturation point will reach, beyond which there will be expansion. The people may search for the alternatives.

INDUSTRIAL MERGERS

Industrial combinations or mergers are gaining ground these days. In fact these are outstanding feature of modern industrialisation. Behind each formation of industrial combination there are certain motivating forces and factors. There are certain causes responsible for the growth of combinations. Industrial combinations have both advantages as well as disadvantages. Not only this, but industrial combinations are of different types and there are different forms of industrial combinations.

Organisational Ability. Many combinations are formed because of the ambition of the industrialists. They are encouraged by favourable tariff policy and capital market etc.

Trade Cycles. Combinations are encouraged when in the country there are too many economic fluctuations and business cycles. During depressions many smaller as well as inefficient industrial units go out of market. These are then absorbed by the bigger units, which are comparatively more efficient and survive even under depressions. Therefore, there is desire on the part of smaller units to combine with bigger units. Economic fluctuations can also result in boom in the industry. It is at this stage that every industrialist will try to take maximum risk, so that it can earn. During boom period there is also desire for combination so that element of risk is reduced to the minimum. Since industrial cycles are inevitable, therefore, desire to have combination is bound to be there and that cannot be wiped out.

Rationalisation. Rationalisation can be effectively introduced when there is some sort of collective action. It demands that efficient and inefficient units must work and combine together. Similarly it is provided that big and small units must also combine with each other. It is with the help of combinations that stabilisation in industry becomes possible.

Technological Advancements. Modern technology has resulted in setting up of large size industries and specialisation. It has also resulted in the concentration of economic power in the hands of very few persons. All this has encouraged and is bound to encourage combination, because it is quite clear that advantages of modern technology cannot be fully derived unless there are industrial combinations. No small industrial unit can possibly face national or international competition.

Governmental Policies. Combination is also encouraged by the policies which the government follows. If governmental taxation policies are such which encourage combinations, obviously the industries will try to combine. Similarly, if these policies discourage big industries, obviously the industrialists will try to remain separate, rather than coming closer and nearer to each other. Thus governmental policies go a long way in encouraging or discouraging combinations.

Diversification in Industry

In the contemporary industrial world most firms produce more than one product. In other words, firms adopt the policy of diversification. Soveyer, Amey and Herid have found in the study of U.K. that nearly 14% 19% products were produced under the conditions of diversification. Hence it is natural to raise the question of measurement of the extent of diversification.

According to L.R. Amey "Diversification is the spreading of its operations by a business over dissimilar economic activities."

There are many theoretical and statistical problems to be faced in defining diversification. However, it can be defined as a position where a firm produces and/or supplies more than one products or services.

Measurement of Diversification

There are two approaches of measurement of diversification:

(i) Estimate of the ratio of other production activities of a diversified firm besides its main or primary productive activity.

(ii) Estimating the number of industries where diversified firms operate.

Under the first approach the following formula is used to measure the diversification.

$$D_p = \sum_{i=1}^{n} W_i P_i$$

D_p = Degree of diversification

i = Product or industry.

W_i = Weight given to each i product (here n is a number) where the firm operates its activities.

P_i = Share of i product in the operation activities of the firm.

In easy words, according to this approach the degree of diversification of a firm depends upon the share of different products produced by it and its relative share in different industries.

According to the second approach diversification is measured by using Govt. index, Beri index and Entripi index. According to C.H. Beri, degree of diversification can be measured with the help of Herfindahl index. This index is given below:

$$D_p = 1 - \sum_{i=1}^{n} (P_i)^2$$

where P = I is the ratio of total product or sale of a diversified firm.

where i = 1, 2, 3.... n

It is clear from the above explanation that in the situation of a single product firm it will be as follows:

$$\sum_{i=1}^{n} (P_i)^2 = 1$$

Hence value of Dr is zero. It means as the number of products produced by a firm grows it begins to operate into many industries. Consequently value of Dp reaches 1.

Extent of Diversification

The interest to know about the extent of diversification grew only around 1960, in the industrial countries. In 1962, W. Gort, tried first to study the extent of diversification in American industry. Then

Amie, Beri (1974) and Vitan (1977) made such studies. A broad conclusion can be drawn from these studies the diversification is an important and growing fact. It has become an important characteristic of the large firms. These economists have seen close relations between diversification and the size of the firm.

Determinants of Diversification

Now question arises as to why firms, especially the large ones emphasise on the diversification instead of specialisation in production. There are many determinants of diversification, such as:

(i) Profitability. In an industry firms try for diversification of products in order to increase profitability. The monopolist units operating separately are seen being combined as one firm when these products are closely substituted. Price policy of one will affect the sale of the other because the cross demand elasticity of the products of these firms is positive. Joint prices for both can be determined, while working as a single firm so that profits may be enhanced. Diversification causes economically more intensive use of stable factors of production which increases the profits of the firms.

(ii) Stability. Usually a trade operates under uncertainty and instability. The cyclical changes in demand, price, profitability etc. create an environment of instability. But these cyclical changes do not affect all profits equally. Firms attempt diversification to reduce the risk, created by such changes.

(iii) Tax Incentives. Some tax incentives are available for diversified firms. Hence they can attract capital on lesser cost. There is also a concession for some years in the initial stages of a new line of production. This causes people's attraction to purchase the shares of diversified companies. Companies/firms reduce their liabilities by allotting their inner funds for different lines of production.

Kinds of Combinations

Industrial combinations are of different forms. Some of these forms may be discussed as under:

Horizontal Combination. It is also called trade or paralleled or unit integration. It is a form of combination, in which combining industries are of a similar character and engaged in the same sphere of industrial activity. This type of combination is most popular and helps in effective external economies in buying, selling or research. When there is horizontal combination bulk purchasing, standardisation of materials and finished gods, specialisation use of by product etc. becomes possible. Under this sort of combination collective advertisement can be done and also it becomes easy to have research work done. By this sort of combination unhealthy competitions are avoided and technical knowledge of the combining firms can be combined usefully and purposefully. But this sort of combination has been criticised because that encourages monopolistic trends and tendencies. It also reduces number of competing firms.

Vertical Combination. Vertical combination is also known as industry or process combination. It is a type of combination which brings together a number of industrial units which are not identical. They have different successive stages in production and manufacture of the finished goods. In this combination usually finished goods of one industry become raw material for the other. Intermediary profits are eliminated.

Advantages. Vertical combinations help in reducing their cost of production by eliminating intermediate profits and it becomes possible to control supplies of raw materials. It becomes also possible to have better control of the products which he wants to sell. It is also believed that with this combination it becomes possible to accomplish economies of storage, selling, buying and transport of material between various processes. Usually there is greater efficiency in industry and available men, money and material is put to the best use.

Categories of Combination. Vertical Combinations can be of two types namely backward vertical integration and forward vertical integration. In the words of L.A. Joshi, "When the unit combines the processes which follow or precede that which is undertaken by it, it becomes respectively a case of forward and backward integration." Saviyya and Dass while explaining this have said that, "When a company manufacturing locomotives obtains control over an iron and steel company through the process of combination, it is known as backward vertical integration. When vice versa happens, it is forward vertical integration-say when iron and steel company combines with locomotive manufacturing company to get control over it."

Types of Industries which tend to get Integrated. There are certain types of industries which get easily vertically integrated. These being those where quality of product is important and finished product of one industry can easily be consumed by the other as its raw material. Then the industry where one process is complementary to the other and where balanced production is significant, are other types of industries, which tend to be vertically combined.

Disadvantages of Vertical Combination

1. Its effects can only be seen in large scale and not in small scale industries.
2. There is every chance that the industry may become inflexible.
3. There is every danger that in the case of dislocation of any single process, whole organisation may be thrown out of gears.
4. Such a combination does not help in reducing the risk of combination among units engaged in the same industrial sphere.
5. If a wrong decision is taken by one unit, then the whole industry suffers, which no nation can afford.
6. Usually sizes of the units which combine vary, but this type of combination can give best results when units do not vary, which of course is rare.
7. Such combination fails to reduce the risk of competition among the units engaged in the some industrial sphere.
8. Such accelerate the process of concentration.

Lateal or Allied Integration. This type of combination or integration is formed when the units which combine together are engaged in the manufacture of different kinds of products but at the same time they are allied also. Such an integration can be both convergent lateral integration and divergent lateral integration. In the case of convergent lateral integration there is combination of different industrial units which supply goods and services to help in the functioning of one major common undertaking. In such a combination finished products of many constitute raw material from one. A printing press can be an integration of number of units engaged in the manufacture of paper, ink etc. On the other divergent lateral integration involves such combination where different combining units draw the supply of their raw material from one common enterprise.

It is believed that convergent lateral combination brings with it the advantages of the economies of large scale production. Cost of production goes down and quality of goods produced is considerably improved. In so far as divergent lateral combination is concerned, it helps in having divergent market for an industrial undertaking.

Circular Combinations. Saviyya and Dass are of the view that "Circular combination is said to be present where economies producing allied goods or sometimes altogether different kinds of goods, *i.e.* goods belonging to same lines but different in nature and quality *e.g.*, radios, fans, heaters and other electrical goods, combine with one another for using the same process of production or the same channel of distribution with a view to secure managerial economies and also market economies." The firms which enter into such a combination might not essentially be competing firms but could probably be benefited by marketing the goods through the same outlets.

Diagonal Combinations. It is a type of combination in which ancillary goods are combined with the main process of production. Thus ancillary services are provided within the organisation itself. In some cases even producing firm combines with itself distribution of the goods produced as well.

Though integration and combinations have come to stay but all combinations cannot be a success. For successful combination it is essential that the industries must be geographically nearer and closer to each other. Those industries which are very far away cannot successfully combine with each other. Then another fact to be remembered is that integration is not an absolute, but only a relative term. In fact each industry in one way or the other is integrated with the other industry. In some cases this integration can be more, while in others it might be less.

Market Concentration and Effects

Concentration of Economic Power. To check concentration of economic power and diffuse and decentralise economic power has become the accepted goal of a modern economy. Concentration of power in a few hands is a negation of social justice since it leads to larger inequalities of income and wealth. In free enterprise economies and in mixed economies with an important role for the private sector there exists a tendency for the economic power to be concentrated in a few hands. In India a few big business houses each being controlled by members of a family or house wield large economic power. The economic power is manifested in the control by few big businessmen over the price of industrial products, the attempt and pattern of investment and the choices of technology and therefore over the creation of employment opportunities in the economy.

Evils of Concentration of Economic Power

1. Concentration of economic power is associated with monopolies and therefore with high prices and exploitation of consumers.

2. The small scale units are not in a position to compete with them without the development of small and cottage industries concentration of economic power can not be diffused.

3. The large profits made by the rich people are usually spent on luxurious consumption, this creates demonstration effect and as

a result propensity to consume of the other people is raised. This reduces the rate of saving.

4. The big businesses block the entry of new young entrepreneurs in the industrial field by the use of their advertising strength and large resources and influence.

5. Big businesses use their resources to corrupt officials and politicans. To quote the words of the commission appointed by the government of India, "We can not ignore the unfortunate reality that some big business houses do not hesitate to use their deep pockets to try to corrupt public officials in the attempt to continue and increase their industrial domain."

In view of the serious evils of concentration of economic power steps should be taken to check this concentration and ensure wider diffusion of economic power. Small scale industries, cooperative enterprises should be encouraged.

What is Industrial Concentration

Industrial concentration means sellers concentration. In other words, in a market some big firms have dominance over production and sales. The limit of this industrial concentration depends upon two main factors, firstly number of active firms in the given market, secondly, quantity of demand fulfilled by a firm out of the total market demand. If in a market number of firms is limited, the size of firms will be relatively big and a big firm will have the control over a large portion of total supply. This situation is known as high quantity of seller (or industrial) concentration. High class industrial concentration depends upon the market power of every firms. Market power means the capacity of a firm or seller to influence the price of a product or commodity. In the perfect competitive market situation this market power is zero, which means the industrial concentration is zero. But more we move towards the monopoly market more the industrial concentration.

Methods of Measurement of Seller Concentration

It is important to measure industrial concentration for many reasons. Firstly, one of the characteristics of the perfect competition is that there is large number of firms in the industry. Lesser the number of firms, more the concentration. For example in 1975, there were 50 firms in the Plastic and Synthetic Resin industry in U.K. Out of these 422 firms had a net production of 10% while the biggest firms had that of 40%. Hence the market power of such firms which are less in number but big in size, is more than those which are more in number but less in size. Secondly, it is necessary to measure industrial concentration because it indicates the ratio of concentration. For example Concentration Ratio (CR) 53.6% indicates that the biggest five firms produce more than 50% in this industry.

The methods of measurement of industrial concentration can be divided into two categories i.e. absolute and relative.

Absolute Measures of Concentration. The central point of the absolute measurement is the absolute number of firms and their share in the production, employment or wealth of the industry. Two absolute measurements are explained here as follows:

1. The Concentration Ratio (CR). In the concentration ratio, the share of production, sales, employment etc. of three, four or five biggest firms in the industry is measured. We take here only the analysis of production. For example production share of the biggest 10 firms is considered. Now we take an imaginary example of an industry where total number of firms is 40. Out of these, the biggest 5 firms have a shape of total production as follows:

Firm A	10,000 Units.
Firm B	12,000 Units.
Firm C	9,000 Units.
Firm D	15,000 Units.
Firm E	13,000 Units.
Total Production of the Five Biggest Firms	59,000 Units.

Total Production in Industry—1,10,000

Concentration Ratio of the

$$\text{Five firms} = \frac{59,000}{1,10,000} \times 100$$

$$= 53.64\%$$

Hence the industrial concentration of 5 firms is 53.64%

Concentration Ratio can also be shown in the geometrial form. In this situation a cumulative concentration curve is formed. In the following graph this work is shown on the basis of the above figures.

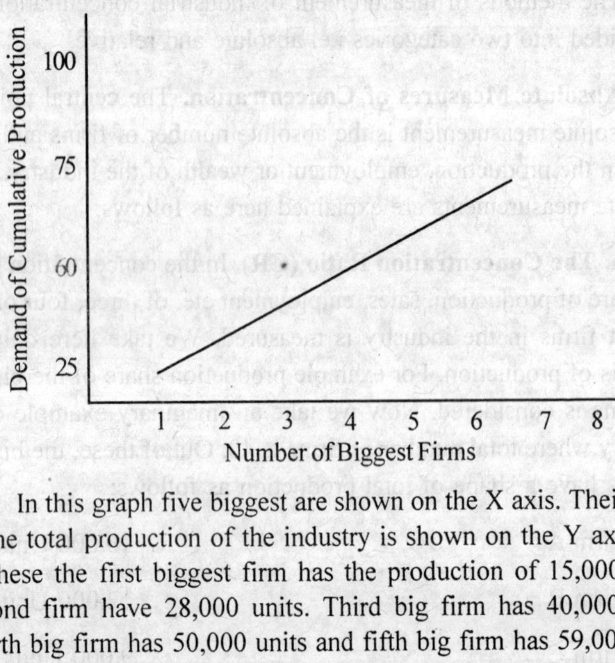

In this graph five biggest are shown on the X axis. Their share in the total production of the industry is shown on the Y axis. Out of these the first biggest firm has the production of 15,000 units, second firm have 28,000 units. Third big firm has 40,000 units, fourth big firm has 50,000 units and fifth big firm has 59,000 units production. When these concerned points are combined in the graph we get the cumulative concentration curve. Here D is notable that the height of concentration curve measures the degree of concentration. For example more the height of curve of the four firm more the concentration ratio of these four firms. The degree of concentration in two or more industries can be shown or measured with the help of the related concentration curve. We require the related figures from two or more industries. Different curves can be drawn from these figures, and conclusions can be drawn by comparing their heights.

The greatest difficulty in measuring the concentration ration, is the choice of n number of seller concentration. This choice is important but there is not any theoretical basis for this. Some traditions are followed in this context. For example in Britain concentration ratio of 3 to 5 firms is estimated, while in America concentration ratio of 4 firms is known.

The Herfindahl Index. This is an absolute measure of industrial concentration. Sometimes it is also known as Herfindahl Herschman index. Under this method instead of some big firms all the firms in the industry are considered. H-index can be defined as follows:

$$\text{Hi-index} = \sum_{i=1}^{n} \left[\frac{x_1}{T}\right]^2$$

where, n = Number of firms in industry.

x = Absolute degree of firm production.

T = Total production of the industry.

It is clear that in H index all the firms in the industry are included in calculation. The value of this index is between zero and one. When the number of firms of equal size is much more in any industry the value of this index is considered zero. On the contrary when there is only one firm in the industry, its value is 1.

H-index can be understood by a simple example. Suppose there are only 4 firms in an industry and production of every firm in the industry is 500, 350, 300 and 200 units. Hence the value of T is 1350, share of every firm in the total production of industry is $\left[\frac{x_1}{T}\right]^2$ means 0.37^2, 0.26^2, 0.22^2 and 0.15^2 so, the value of H index is 0.275. As this value is much near zero, it shows that the level of concentration is not more in the industry. This index is used to know the degree of concentration in different periods in the industry.

2. The Relative Measures of Concentration. In this measure the main stress is given on the inequality of firms. That means in a market firms of unequal sizes also have unequal degree of production. The relative measure of seller concentration can be measured by the help of Lorenze Curve. Its algebra synonym is Gini-coefficient of Gini concentration.

Gini Concentration Ratio. This is a statistical measure which is based on Lorenze Curve:

Gini coefficeint of inequality

$$= \frac{\text{Area between Lorenz Curve and Equality Line}}{\text{Dalta area below Line}}$$

the value of Gini co-efficient is between 0 and 1. If all firms are of equal size, the equality line and Lorenze Curve will be same. In this position the value of Gini coefficient will be zero. More he inequality grows, more the value of Gini co-efficient will grow.

Growth of Monopolies and Concentration of Economic Power in India

Monopoly Situation. Monopoly situation is s situation in whch a group of producers acts adn behaves in such a way that it begins to effectively control the supply of a particular commodity. Monopoly can be a different forms. Monopolies have their own advantages as well as disadvantages. These days there is an increasing demand that Monopolies should be checked and controlled, for which different steps and already of Monopolies and developing nations are taking particular steps for their control, so that the measses are not exploited and welfare of the people is not ignored.

Monopoly situations and conditions are prevailing in all economics, either in one form or the other. Though some of the nations are trying to check monopolies, yet the fact remains that these are rapidly incereasing and not being checked, because the system has its own advantages.

Monopoly Defined. Monopoly is a situation in which a group of persons is in a position to end competition in a particular commodity and control sale and supply of that commodity. That group is also in a position to influence its prince. An extreme Monopoly sitaution aries when a firm o group of closely connected and interested persons only begins to produce a particular commodity. In the words of Stonier and Hague. "The pure monopoly, as we may call it, will occur when a producer is so powerful that he is alwasy able to take the whole of all the consumer's income whatever, be the level of his output." Similarly Liftwich has said that, "Pure Monopoly is a Market situation in which a single form sells a product for which there are no good substitutes." From both these definitions it becomes clear that under monopolies there is sole right to supply the product or service thus collected.

In Perfect Monopoly Possible? Perfect monopoly situation is not possible in the world. For production, distribution and prncing there must be some sort of competition, though in some cases it may be very thugh, while in others only normal. It will be only an ideal situation in which competition can be completely eliminated.

Form of Monopoly. A monopoly situation provides the monopoliser with an advantage of fixing the price, or produce quality of goods or distribute them in the way he lakes and as such every person or business house is in a position to have monopoly. This monopoly is created either by a individual with his own vast resources, or by combining together and thus pooling their resource or groups of industries coming together so that mutual competition is avoided and monopoly is created. The monopolies may be classified as *(a)* Natural Monopoly; *(b)* Legal Monopoly; *(c)* Social Monopoly and *(d)* Voluntary Monopoly.

Natural Monopoly. This is monopoly in which individual has less and nature has more role to play. In its nature blesses the nation with bounties in a particular commodity and that is available in that country, which can control that in the way that likes. Arab nations oil monopolies and they can control the world economy is so far oil and oil products are concerned. In it the people have contributed less, whereas nation has contributed far more.

Legal Monopoly. In some cases, a product does not exist or if that exists that is comparatively less or unknown. An organisation an individual works hard, carries out research, spends his life and is in a position to produce and market that. He feels that his product is being well received and does not wish that any individual or organisation should take advantage of his labour. He gets his trade mark and formula registered with the Government by paving fixed fees. After that his been accepted no one else can either use formula or trade mark; that then becomes his absolute monopoly. It is called legal monopoly. We find that in every country patent marks are registered with the state.

Social Monopoly. In every society there are certain civic amenities and facilities to be provided to the citizens. Therefore, an organisation may be allowed to provide those facilities e.g., in Delhi, electricity is supplied by Delhi Electric supply undertakings or water is supplied Delhi Water and Sewerage Department and so on. This type of organisation which is solely responsible for the supply of a particular civic amenity, is stated to be enjoying a social monopoly in that commodity.

Voluntary Monopoly. It is also known as combination. In it some of the producers dealing in the same commodity come nearer and closer to each and combine in one form or the other so as to avoid competition. There is no external force or compulsions to join or to combine, that is why it is called voluntary monopoly. Such a monopoly can be in the form of Trusts or cartels. This voluntary monopoly can be both vertical or horizontal. A vertical combination is also known as integration. A horizontal combination can be in the form of pools, holding company and complete marger All of these forms have already been discussed earlier.

Monopolies are not very much appreciated these days because it is felt that socially these are harmful than useful to the society.

Monopoly and Concentration of Economic Power. Monopoly refers to the control on production or distribution of any commodity by any institution or firm. So, market power is essential for monopoly. State of monopoly can be found even in small scale industries. On the contrary concentration of economic power means centralisation of effective control over important economic activities (Industry, Agriculture, Transport etc.) to decide, to make jobs available and on the stream of income and wealth in the hands of some persons or groups.

In India concentration of economic power has been occurred through monopoly. Thus monopoly is the means through which concentration of economic power flourishes and its flourishing enhances the power of monopolistic institutions.

Extent of the Concentration of Economic Power in India

In a developing economy such concentration of economic power widens the gap of disparity in income and wealth, which is harmful to the development of the country. This malady is growing fast in India. Many committees were formed to study it and to suggest remedies.

1. Mahalanobis Committee (1960). According to this committee "the working system of the planned economy has encouraged the growth of big companies in Indian industries. These received financial assistance from Indian Industrial Finance Corporation, National Industrial Development Corporation etc. which are public institutions. These have derived more profit of tax reliefs and other facilities.

2. Monopoly Enquiry Commission (1964) has studied the extent, effect and causes of this concentration and conclude that, "Concentration has been promoted more by way of planned economy which was adopted for rapid industrialisation in the country." The main causes, according to the commission, are defective licensing system and discrimination in availability of institutional loans."

3. Other Committees. Hazari Committee Report (1966) and Batta Committee (1967) have also underlined that big houses had adopted corrupt means for getting licences. 8% big houses received 38% licences.

Extent of Concentration. According to the Mahalanobis Committee. "In 1960-61 86% companies (which have paid up capital less than Rs. 5 lakh) had only 14.6% of the total paid up capital in the country while Big Companies having paid up capital above 50 lakh, and which are only 1.6% in number had 58.1% of the total paid up capital of the corporate world in the country. Monopoly Enquiry Commission found out that there is high grade of concentration in 65 commodities, medium in 10, low in 8 and zero in 17, and 2259 goods under study. These are controlled by 82 Industrial houses.

According to the Sachhar Committee, "Top 20 houses had 89.4% growth in their asserts during 1972-78." They had assets of Rs. 648 crores in 1951, which were multiplied nine times up to 1978 (5795 crores).

Current Position. According to the Economic Times Research Beareau, in 1987-88, "There are 251 big companies in private sector in which 101 are considered Jiant' and 150 as mini Jiant. Rs 29,720 crore were invested in the Jiants' The Biggest in these is the Reliance Industries (which had 250,00 crore rupees assets in 1988). Next come Tata Steel, Larson & Tubro, Tata Engineering. J. K. Synthetics, and Southern Petro-Chemicals.

In 1987, Tata Group had the biggest assets. Then came Birlas and Reliance. Five Toppers out of 20, have increased their assets from 7312 crores in 1983 to 14311 crores in 1987, that is 95.7% growth during the period of 5 years. Also they controlled 58.4% of the total resources under the top 20. This means that the utmost concentration has been in these 5 toppers. Among these five Reliance stood first in the growth rate, *i.e.,* 259.2%. Among 20, Chidambaram Group had the most spectacular growth rate. During 4 years it had 910% growth in its assets, it has leaped up from the 47th position in 1983 to 9th in 1987.

Forms of Concentration of Economic Power. Monopoly Enquiry Commission has mentioned two forms of concentration in 1964:

1. Product-wise Concentration. When a production or distribution of any commodity or service is controlled by any person or group, it is called product-wise concentration. It is divided in three parts:

(a) High Concentration. On 75% or more by 3 main producers or distributors.

(b) Medium Concentration. On 60% to 75% by 3 main producers or distributors.

(c) Low Concentration. On 50% to 60% of production or distribution by 3 main producers. If the concentration is less than 50% it will not be considered as concentration.

2. Country-wise Concentration. If ownership or control of most enterprises engaged in production or distribution of different goods is in the hands of one person, family or industrial group it is called country-wise concentration.

Causes of Concentration of Economic Power in India

In a rapidly rising and growing economy like India some degree of inequality and concentration of economic power and wealth in a few hands is to be expected, but the disturbing things is that the degree of inequality and concentration is very much more that can be justified on an ground. The following are the major causes for concentration of wealth and economic power in few hands:

1. Government Policies. The Dutta Committee (1969), pointed out nearly that the Government of India never specified clearly to the licensing authority the objective of preventing concentration of economic power or monopoly.

2. Rule of Government Financial Institutions. The financial institutions contributed to the growth of concentration of wealth and economic power. The financial institutions were set up with the ideal of helping the private sector. But the large industrial houses managed to influence its lending policies of those institutions. The Dutta Committee found that about 56 per cent of the total assistance provided by the IFC, IDBI etc. had gone to the large industrial houses.

3. Guidelines of Large Industrial Houses. So, after independence the Government of India launched upon a programme of massive economic development. The government provided financial, tax benefits, etc. for the promotion of the private sector. The industrial houses which were already in the field saw the abundant chances for their growth and expansion. They took full advantage of the concessions.

4. Role of Commercial Banks. Before Bank nationalisation the large industrial houses controlled the banking system. The bank deposits coming from the general public were used exclusively for financing industries owned and managed by large industrial houses. Even after nationalisation in 1969 there was not much of a change in the lending policy of the nationalised banks.

5. Inter-Company Investments. Inter-company investment means, purchasing shares of a company by other company. Big companies or Industrial groups purchases stock of other companies on large scale and make them as their subsidiaries.

6. Technological Progress. Big firms can reduce the production cost through modern technology due to their sound financial condition. Thus they get large economies and become more powerful.

7. Managing Agency System. This system has greatly controlled in the development of big companies by providing financial assistance. These maintained their credit through inter company investments. Though the system was abolished in 1970, its dominance still remained upon industrial groups.

8. Monopolistic and Restrictive Trade Practices. Monopolistic firms adopt such practices as creating artificial shortage of goods, and get high prices, decide high distribution rates of goods, exploit the consumer by distributing market among themselves. Sell goods on different prices to different purchasers, rejecting sales to some buyers or by other producers etc.

9. Strict Import Policy. After independence the Government had given protection to various industries, and restricted imports. This resulted in imposing monopoly by some Indian producers upon the market.

10. Foreign Collaboration. After independence India has accepted foreign collaboration on large scale. Foreign industrialists prefer to collaborate with big firms. Thus their dominance got increased.

11. Taxation Policy. Government offers many concessions on starting new industries, such as relief in income tax and sales tax. Grants are also provided. Big industries derived utmost advantage from this.

Findings of the Monopolies Inquiry Commission

Causes of Economic Concentration. According to the Commission, the development of joint-stock companies and the economies of scale arising out of continual technological advancement that was taking place were the main causes of increasing concentration of economic power in the private corporate industrial sector. The Commission noted. "The evolution of the corporation has made it possible for captains of industry to use these economies of scale to their greatest advantage. "An industrialist holding a small percentage of share capital was in a position to collect through the scale of shares vast amounts of money and acquire control over the industrial establishments and the process went on in a snowballing manner—controlling other companies through the originally promoted company, a third company through the first and second company and so on.

Managing Agency System. Along with the joint-stock form of business organisation and economies of scale, the managing agency system played a vital role in bringing about industrial concentration in the private corporate industrial sector. Dearth of management skills in the country results in vesting enormous economic power in the hands of those who had the capital to function successfully as managing agents.

Acquiring shares of another industrial company by one company and continuation of this process gave enormous economic power to the managing agents, which led to increasing the number of companies in control of each managing agent.

Another device was inter-locking of directorships. The same boards of directors in several industrial establishments producing similar product or producing the needed raw materials and engaged in the production of allied products resulted in increasing economic concentration in a few hands or in a few industrial houses.

Also, large fortunes amassed during the Second World War (1939-45) helped entrepreneurs to promote new industrial companies when the country became independent in 1947 and the Five Year Plans with emphasis on rapid industrialisation began to the implemented since 1951 and especially with the commencement of the Second Five Year Plan (that is, after 1956).

Sale out of British Firms. Also, when the country became independent, many industrial houses in India managed to acquire industrial establishments of British and other foreign nationals who sold them and left India for good. This had the effect of accentuating economic concentration.

Licensing Policy. Further, acceleration of the concentration of economic power in the private corporate industrial sector took place because of the system of industrial licensing, control of capital issues and regulation of imports due to the difficult balance of payments position in the country.

The already well-established industrial companies could take advantage of their position in securing additional licences for expanding the already existing industrial units or starting new ones, and securing permission for additional capital issues, additional imports and so on.

Additional Funds. The big industrial houses were in a more favorable position to raise additional funds because of their well-established connections and past experience; licensing authorities preferred to give additional licences to companies already well-established than to some unknown industrial concerns; well-established companies could get additional licences because of their ability to manage to get foreign collaboration agreements, foreign companies naturally preferring already well-known industrial companies rather than entering into agreements with some unknown companies; new companies found the procedure for obtaining licenses extremely complicated and time-consuming and almost beyond their capacity.

❑

4

Price Determination and Policies

In order to formulate an appropriate princing procdure for the firm certain general steps are to be kept in view. As we know pricing of product is a very complex problem; infact it is twilight zone between business interest and pulbic good. A firm has to reconcile both these objectives. There cannot be a model process for pricing the products of each firm, however, following general considerations can be described as the gradual steps in this process.

The brief description of the steps is as follows:

1. Firm's Objectives. Pricing is a means to achieve the objectives of the firm. Thus the objectives of the firms are the objectives of pricing. Now the question is what are the possible objectives of a firm. Ordinarily, the broadest object of a firm is 'Survival' but to be specific a firm's objectives are related to rate of growth, market shares, maintenance of control or ownership and independence of operations and earning revenue. The above objectives are often in conflict. Therefore, it is necessary to prepare long range plans to reconcile them. The role of a price policy starts at this point and the firm has to decide how prices are to be used in the overall strategy.

2. Anticipating Competitive Situations. A firm may have to face different competitive situations. Different competitive situations require different pricing policies. Therefore, a good solution of pricing problems, needs a clear understanding of the firm's competitive environment. For instance, a firm faced with a pure competitive situation has pricing problems. Such a firm has no discretion, it has to sell or it may devoide not to sell at the price prevailing in the market. But when the firm is faced with imperfect competition, the price policy attains a real practical significance. The firm can use its discretion and sell its products inspite of disparities with its competitor's prices. The degree on prices discretion that a firm can have depends on the following conditions.

(i) Number of competitors.

(ii) Size of competitors.

(iii) Product line of competitors.

(iv) Likelihood of potential competition.

(v) The state of consumer acceptance of the product.

(vi) The degree of potential market segmentation and price discrimination.

(vii) Degree of physical distinction from competitor's product.

(viii) The extent of reputation of the product and service.

3. Product and Promotional and Distribution Policies. Though pricing is a very important but not the only aspect of market strategy. There are other important aspects like products and promotional aspects which must be considered by the firm along with pricing. If the product and promotional policies are faulty. it is no justification to change the price for better results. Various policies of company relating to products channel of distribution should be given proper

4. Nature of Price Sensitivity. There are man forces which tend to minimize the importance of price sensitivity which is often exaggerated by businessmen. The forces that create insensitivity to change in princes are flexibility in consumer behaviour, change in effectiveness of market effort, nature of the product, multiple dimensions of the quality of the product and importance of the service after sales.

5. Entry of Non-business Groups into the Consideration of Price. The government or trade unions controls price to prevent misuse of monopolistic power and collusion among businessmen. Therefore there is need of some policies even in price determination.

6. Estimation of Demand. First step in the pricing of product is the estimation of the total demand for the product. It will depend upon the expected price. Experienced wholesalers/retailers can evaluate our product. We can conduct regular survey of potential buyers. We can determine the expected price in a few test markets, by trying different prices in different test markets and comparing the results with a controlled market in which price is not altered. Once we know the expected prices, we can compute sales volume at special prices.

7. Determining Share of Market. Determining the share of market you expect at the expected 'price. Higher initial price may be fixed if you anticipate a smaller share whereas if you expect a much larger market share, you will have to prefer relatively lower prices. Proper pricing strategy is to be evolved to research the market target either through skimming price of through penetrate price or through a compromise.

8. Selecting a Suitable Price. The last step in the process of price determination is selecting a suitable price. The most appropriate method is the cost plus mark-up method, usually called cost-plus method. It is very suitable for wholesalers and retailers too. According to it:

Price of Product = Cost of Production + Operating Expenses + Profit Margin.

Yardsticks Used in Pricing a Product

There are number of factors affecting the price range of product.

(i) Cost of production and distribution.

(ii) Price of rival producers.

(iii) Consumer reaction response.

(iv) Middlemen's reactions.

(v) Prices of substitute products.

(vi) Government rules and regulations.

Price fixation is the right of one department or one manager only but it is the prerogative of top management to decide it. But a foresighted management should try to involve all the important functional executives in the process so that an integrated price policy for different products of the firm may be evolved. Adjustments and revision in the prices are very much essential as there is nothing static in a competitive economy, suggested is a foundation for such judgement based on facts with a realistic regard for the current position of the firm and an optimistic eye towards the future.

As mentioned earlier, pricing is a means for achieving the goods of business. There is no exact and infalible formula for pricing each firm's product and market situation have some unique features of its own type. Therefore, every situation should be explored on its own merit and the pricing policy should emerge from careful consideration of all the forces mentioned above. Pricing is a matter of judgement but to be effective it should be based on sound principles and all possible information. A price is always to trial in the market and is supposed to be successful and right if it attracts sufficient number of customers.

PRICE DISCRIMINATION OBJECTIVES & CONDITIONS

Generally a manufacturer charges one price for one product from all the customers but sometimes it happens that different prices are charged for the same product (or service) from different customers. This policy is commonly known as price differential or price discrimination policy.

Mrs. John Robinson has defined price discrimination as follows. "The act of selling the same article, produced under a single control at different prices to different buyers is known as price discrimination". According Prof. J.S. Bain, "Price discrimination refers strictly to the practice by a seller of simultaneously charging different prices to different buyers for the same goods."

According to Spencer and Siegleman. "Differential pricing may be defined as the practice by a seller or charging different prices to the same or to different buyers for the same goods without corresponding difference in cost."

Thus, price discrimination may be of various types such as individual price discrimination, geographical price diserimination use discrimination etc.

Motives Behind Price Discrimination. (Objectives)

From the seller's standpoint, the differential price that result from the application of various discount structures and from product-line pricing may serve several purpose. It is, therefore (desirable to look first at the company's structure of price discriminations in terms of its motives, which may be grouped follows.

1. Market Expansion. Differential pricing that is designed encourage new users or new customers is a common goal product-line pricing, but it also extends over various phases of discount structure, depending upon the circumstances of a purchase by a new user.

2. Market Segmentatlon. A major objective of price discrimination is to achieve profitable market segmentation when legal and competitive considerations permit discrimination. It permits the appropriation of the consumer's surplus so that it accrues to the producer rather than to the consumer.

3. Implementation or Marketing Strategy. The patterns of price differentials should implement the company's overall marketing strategy. These price differentials should efficiently geared with other elements in the marketing programme to reach of the sectors the market selected by strategy. In doing so the job of a particular structure of discounts may be quite specific.

4. Reduction of Production Costs. Differential prices can sometimes help solve problems of production. Seasonal or other forms of time-period discounts may be allowed partly for the purpose of regularising output changing the timing of sale. For example, since electricity cannot be stored, classification of electric rates are designed to encourage off season users and penalizing users that contributed to peak.

5. Competitive Adoptation. Differential prices are a major device for selective adjustment to the competitive environment. Discounts are often designed to match what competitors charge under comparable, conditions of purchase, in terms of net price to each customer class When products are homogeneous, competitive parity is a compelling consideration.

CONDITIONS OF PRICE DISCRIMINATION

Price discrimination needs some conditions in the market. They are as follows:

1. Existence or Monopoly. Discrimination is possible only if monopoly exists and there is no competitor in the market or when the producers enter into agreement among themselves to sell the products at agreed prices.

2. Division or the Markets into Sub-markets. The market is distinctly divisible into various parts among which the product cannot be exchanged; examples are a home and a foreign market separated by governmental restrictions or by a tariff wall and the market for hair-cuts or a surgeon's fees; in the former case domestic buyers cannot import the product at the low price and in the latter services are rendered to individuals personally.

3. Expenditure in sub-dividing the market should not be more than the expected profit increase from price discrimination. Sometimes a monopolist has to incur some expenditure on keeping the sub-markets separate so that he can fix different prices in different sub-markets and the consumers are restrained from transferring the product from one sub-market to the other.

4. Consumer's Ignorance. When the consumers of one market are ignorant of the prices prevailing in the other markets, price discrimination can be successful.

5. Difference in Consumer's Purchasing Power. Variance in the purchasing power of the customers also help in price discrimination. Non-price factors in such a situation pay to the producers.

6. Purchaser's Irrational Feeling. Some purchasers judge the quality of goods only by the high or low prices. There the policy of price discrimination can successfully be launched.

7. Geographical Distance and Tariff Walls. Between two distant markets where the transportation charges make differences in the cost of the product, price discrimination can be practised easily.

8. Nature or Goods and Service. Goods and services which are not transferable among buyers *e.g.*, charging more from rich and less from poor by a doctor can be easily subjected to price discrimination.

9. Sale on Orders. When the goods are produced on the specific instructions of the customers, price discrimination is possible. One customer does not know what is being charged from the other.

10. Product Differentiation. Sometimes a monopolist's market consists of rich and poor consumers. He takes advantage of the whirms of the rich and offers the same production in a de-luxe packing. Thereby he is able to charge a higher price from the richer section of consumers.

11. Govt. Sanction. Sometimes government also permits the public utility services like the railway to charge different prices from different consumers, and different prices for the use of electricity by Individual and domestic purposes.

Degrees or Price Discrimination

Price discrimination is done only when elasticity of demand for the product is different for different buyers, the amounts demanded of the product differ at the same price *i.e.*, the demand prices differ. Discrimination is designed to gain revenue by varying the price in term of the demand prices of the customers. On the basis of the limit to which a monopolist can go on charging different prices for his product from his customers, various degrees of discrimination were discussed by Professor A.C. Pigou.

(1) First-Degree Discrimination. In discrimination of the first degree the monopolist is supposed to know the maximum amount of money each consumer will pay for any quality. He then sets his prices accordingly and extracts from each consumer the entire amount of the consumer's surplus. Such a monopolist, in Mrs. Robinson's phrase, is a 'perfect' discriminator. This is 'perfect' price discrimination because it is an extreme limiting case of the same. In practice, few monopolists can and actually do that. An example of limited discrimination of the type is to be found in the practice of doctors of varying the charges on their customers according to their income status. A breeder of horses dealing individually with various buyers in different parts of the country, with a highly imperfect market and absence of knowledge on the part of each buyer of the prices being charged from other buyers, may be able to carry on perfect discrimination to a limited extent. Obviously, perfect discrimination is useful only in theory as a concept.

(2) Second Degree Discrimination. It occurs where a monopolist sets different prices for different customers but does not fully exploit their potential demand prices; the monopolist captures only parts of his customer's consumer's surpluses. The schedules of rates typically charged by public utilities like railways can be regarded as form of second-degree discrimination.

(3) Third Degree Discrimination. It means that the monopolist divides his customers into two or more classes or groups on the basis of the elasticity of their demand for the product, and charging a different price to each class of buyers. Each group is a separate market. In discrimination, of the third degree, the monopolist makes some attempt to benefit from the differences in the elasticity of demand for the product on the part the different groups of buyers.

This is the only type ordinarily possible and therefore we address ourselves to this type of discrimination in detail and study the price and output determination of such a monopolist.

Desirability of Price Discrimination

Price discrimination is generally hatred as an unpopular idea because justice is supposed to go with the concept of equality and similar treatment among all customers. Therefore, it is considered as anti-social, undesirable and unprofitable act. But, now-a-days, it has become essential for the seller to create market for the goods taking into consideration the various factors such as economics, social, geographical location, availability of goods, available alternatives etc. Price discrimination is not anti-social, infact, it means charging reasonable prices from all sections of the buyers according to their capacity, status, elasticity of demand, etc. Such differentiation helps the manufacturer in not only increasing the sale but serving the maximum members of the society. In the following circumstances, price discrimination is very well justified.

(1) When Community's Welfare is the Main Aim. There are many public services which would not be available to the poor if there was no price discrimination. For example, electricity, water, doctor, education may be cited here.

(2) Operation of Public Utility Services. Such public utilities as railways, electric supply companies and water supply companies must be allowed to have price discrimination. This is because the price of the service has to be kept low. For example, electric supply rates have to be low for industrial concerns and agricultural operations if we want to encourage industrilisation and agricultural development. This necessitates charging higher price from consumers who can pay, otherwise, costs will not be covered.

Is Price Discrimination Anti-social?

In the following circumstances, the price discrimination will be treated as anti-social:

(i) When it is based on customer's ignorance,

(ii) When its main purpose is to earn maximum profits,

(iii) When it is instrumental in eliminating the small scale enterprises.

Price discrimination is regarded now-a-days as essential for the seller to create market for the goods taking into consideration the various factors such as economic, social, geographical location, availability of goods and alternatives etc., and this can not be regarded as anti-social. But if the intention of the seller is to make capital due to economic "difficulties of the people and to charge higher prices from any group of buyers more than what he should, in that case it is certainly an anti-social practice. Price discrimination should mean charging reasonable price from all sections of the buyers. It may also mean charging even lower price from groups of buyers or individual buyers to a certain period to create taste to the goods and to establish market.

PUBLIC UTILITY

In every state there are public utility services which provide to the citizens. These services include supply of water, electricity, telephone, transport and communication etc. Obviously while deciding pricing policy of these services, profit cannot be the sole motive. But before we actually discuss pricing policy in this regard, we must not forget that these services have certain peculiarities. These are:

Peculiarities of Public Services

(i) Public utility services may either be services or product of services and as such it is essential that their supply be regular to avoid serious dislocation for the society as a whole.

(ii) Being 'Service' in nature these can't be stored. Either the service must be provided to the society, or the service will go waste. In case any attempt is made to store the services that 'will be so costly that the society will not be in a position to afford that and also their storage might create instability in the market.

(iii) The demand for these services can increase and decrease according to time, season and occasion. A transport service may be under heavy pressures at the time of festivals; postal departments during Christmas or Diwali or when news about election results are to be communicated and so on.

(iv) Essential public utility services *e.g.*, water, gas, railways etc. are needed for all the 24 hours of the day. Their disruption at any hour can result in many problems particularly in hospitals, factories etc.

(v) There can be no variation in the supply of services to different customers in the same areas Thus the water must flow from the same pipe line and serve the locality uniformally, whether in that the people having different political ideology or economic status and standard are living and using that.

(vi) The service supplied. by a publiç utility organisation is not transferable.

(vii) Since public utility services are to be uniformally supplied and it is to be ensured that these are available during all the 24 hours of the day, these are to be supplied under monopoly situations. This monopoly may either emerge of its own or might be encouraged by the State. Thus there can be deliberate attempt for encouraging monopoly. Any competition in the supply of these services is bound to create many problems.

(viii) Since the services are provided under monopoly conditions, sometimes, the cost to be paid is higher and the services may not to be available according to the satisfaction of the consumer. The quality of the services, in some cases may also come down.

Public Utility, Price Policy

Obviously when question of price policy in respect of public utility services arises, that cannot be on commercial lines and care will have to be taken that state is responsible for providing these essential services to the society.

While fixing price another consideration always is that there are both large and small consumer or services. Obviously the water and electricity to be consumed will be much more in the factories where the people living in the platial buildings than by the hut dwellers.

Still another consideration is that there are some kinds of services which exclusively are used of a section by society *e.g.* telephones. This is a service which is used only by well to do and not the poor people. Then we find that transport facilities for transporting goods from one place to the other either by rail or by road are used by business community.

Therefore, there is strong and powerful section of the society which believes that there must be some discrimination between the rates to be charged by those who are bulk consumer of services, and by those who are not. Their main line of argument is that since out of the capital which is invested for providing these services, major benefit is taken by the bulk users, they must pay higher price. On the other hand there is equally a powerful section which argues out that there should be no discrimination, According to them, it is the duty and responsibility of the state to provide these services. The state is to invest in any way. It is for the society to see that it takes advantage of the facility being provided to the consumer. In case a section of the society does not taken advantage of the facility, why should the other section, suffer or pay heavy charges for that. This controversy is still continuing.

Accordingly for price fixation different principles have been suggested, which may briefly be discussed as under :

Cost Service Principle

According to this principle, it is believed that the price of a service should be fixed in proportion to the cost. In other words, if the cost is more then the price should be higher and if less, it should be low. But this principle has its own difficulties *e.g.*,

(a) The services which will be supplied at difficult approaches *e.g.* the hills or deserts, will definitely be costlier, as compared with the plains, Obviously there people will be required to pay more. In actual practice and reasonably these people should be required to pay less, on the principle of social welfare. but if this principle is adopted, they will be expected to pay more.

(b) If cost principle is to be taken into accounts then some of the social utility services, will become so costly that common man may not be in a position to afford. Milk and vegetables as well as fruit to metropolitan cities are brought from far off distances and that too in air conditioned coaches etc. In case cost principle is applied here, then their cost of transportation will go up so high that common man may not be in a position to purchase the goods.

(c) Then another difficulty is that under this principle cost will have to be linked with the capital, investments and dead stocks. To be just and fair, depreciation will have to be taken into account, but in actual practice, it is difficult to take all these factors into consideration.

(d) In case this principle' is accepted then the price for the same service will differ from one place to the other, which will mean price discrimination, which socially may not be justified.

(e) Reasonably, on this principle the cost of service depreciation and investment should broadly, be divided into two parts namely the one for those who are bulk or frequent users and the one those who are the usual or not bulk users.

The Value of Service Principle

According to this principle each class of consumer is charged a price that it is able to pay according to its demands for the service. Thus if it requires a better service, it will have to pay higher price. We find that in the railways the passengers interested in travelling in first class or by air conditioned coach are required to pay higher rates than the passengers, who travel by second class. Similarly, the passengers travelling by Delux Bus Coach will pay higher rates, as compared with the passengers travelling by ordinary bus. We also find that the business men using electricity for commercial purposes are required to pay more as compared with those who want electricity for domestic use. In actual practice highest price for a service is charged where the elasticity of demand is the lowest. Obviously under this principle there are two major conditions; firstly paying capacity of the consumer and secondly the availability of substitutes. In so far as first consideration is concerned, it is believed by the society that since, the person or section of society wants to have better service therefore he or they have the capacity to pay. As regard, second consideration the agencies responsible for fixing the price are to see that the price is fixed after taking into consideration the availability of alternatives. In case the alternatives are available at cheap rates the people will switch over to the alternatives. Then in this case the authorities also will have to take into consideration the rates of the peak hours and off hours. We find that the rates of telegrams and trunk calls are different between the peak hous and off hours. During peak hours, if the consumer is to contact party on trunk a rates payable will be higher, as compared off hours.

Problems of Public Utility Price Policy

We have already said that in public utility price policy, the most serious problem is whether the price should be fixed to earn profits or to provide service. But it is not the only problem. There are many other problems. Sometimes an attempt is to be deliberately made to charge higher rates, while at other times lower rates are to be deliberately charged. When the service it to be given at peak-hours, where there is little capacity, deliberately an attempt is made to charge high rates, so that the people are discouraged to use that service and there is no extra loading. At other times an attempt is made to charge low rates because the service is to be promoted and the people are to be approached. At places railways charge much less than they should ordinarily charge because it is believed by the state, that the people of that region are to be approached. These are to be linked with other parts of the country. Some times as we find that fare and travel concessions are given to the public to encourage them to go on excursions, pilgrimages and attend certain functions. Similarly the students are given travelling concessions to go and see the country and those parts of the land, which ordinarily they will not like to visit. In some colonies water is supplied at most lower cost and in some cases only nominal fixed annual rates are charged. In some cases public hydrants are provided and the public is not at all charged for that. Similarly we find that while fixing rateable value of a house, locality and paying capacity of the people is always taken into consideration and so is the case while allocating market cities to the people. At places the markets are provided at very low rates to protect the interests of weaker sections of society.

Is Price Discrimination Inevitable?

All societies must have both the weaker as well as rich sections in it. The weaker sections must be provided concessions and charged at lower rates, as compared with the strong who must pay at higher rates. The rich and the poor cannot be charged at the same rates and as such while fixing prices for public utility services price discrimination will have to be maintained and in fact that is a must.

PUBLIC UTILITY PRICES TRIBUNALS

Public utility services must be provided by each state. It is another matter that in some cases the state provides more, while in others less. In modern times more and more pressure is being exerted on each state to provide better public utility services. Since these are provided under monopoly conditions it is essential that effective measures should be taken to ensure that there is no exploitation of the consumers.

Public Utility Prices Tribunals. The aim and object of Public Utility Prices Tribunals primarily is to suggest to the Government and the agencies responsible for providing services, such reasonable prices of the services that the consumer is not exploited and at the same time the service does not become a heavy and unreasonable liability on the tax payer. The task is a cobweb of difficulties and problems.

Problems of Public Utility Prices Tribunals. Had it been simply a profit and loss statement and assessing the price of the goods after taking into consideration depreciation, it would not have been a very difficult task. But the problems are many. Some of the serious problems which a tribunal is likely to face, or which it usually faces are as under:

(1) The basic idea of providing a service is that the consumer should not be exploited and at the same time, there should be a marginal profit, so that the tax payer is not heavily over-burdened. Now question arise as to what is reasonable margin of profit and whether in calculating such a margin original investment of capital or the book value of the goods at the time, when the service is to be provided should be taken into consideration. In case the prices of the material have fallen down and the consumer is required to pay according to original investments, then he will be sufferer and that will mean his exploitation. On the other hand if value of the goods used has fallen down and the consumer is required to pay low prices, then the agency providing services will suffer serious losses.

(2) Still another difficulty with these tribunals is that the servicing agencies will never provide a correct picture of the cost or service. These agencies will always show higher costs. This is done through many ways. There can be on paper high cost of purchase or heavy depreciation charges, costly transport charges, losses in transit and so on and so forth. Though the tribunals may try to assess the figures on the low side, keeping margin for the higher costs which the industry may show, yet it cannot be sure of the extent to which the costs on, the higher side have been shown.

(3) Then another difficulty for tribunals is that the prices proposed cannot be uniform all the year round. There can be good years when the services may not be under any strains and affected or influenced by the upheavals. On the

other hand there may be bad years, when the services may come under heavy strains.

(4) In price fixation process human element is also involved. The agencies loaded with the responsibility of providing service will always try to corrupt the members or the tribunal. In case the members get bribes or sccumb to other temptations, then the price is sure to be fixed on the high side.

(5) Prices can reasonably be fixed only when there is correct assessment of the margin of profit. No agency will provide correct figures about profits, and there is no other alternative to that. Unless correct assessment of profit is available, there cannot be any realistic price fixation.

(6) Still another difficulty is that these tribunals, are required to fix the price of the same commodity differently for different consumers. Thus they are to see that a section of the society pays according to its paying capacity and also keeping in view the extent of the services which the society is otherwise obliged to provide. We know that in India water supply to the urban people living in big cities, is provided after making them pay something, but it is considered social responsibility of the state to provide immediately drinking water to the tribunals living in remote corners of the country. The pricing policy of the two obviously cannot be the same. These tribunals are to go into the system of both and decide the price to be charged.

SENSITIVITY ANALYSIS OF INVESTMENT

Investment Decision Methods. An entrepreneur adopts the various methods of evaluating the investment while making the decision. These methods can be classified into two major categories.

(i) Conventional investment approaches.

(ii) Modern investment approach.

Traditional Approaches. The traditional methods of investment evaluation are based on three main assumptions:

(i) the profit making is the only objective of the firm,

(ii) The investors take decisions about investment in the atmosphere of full certainty. In other words the entrepreneur knows fully about the present and future of cost, demand, degree of competition etc. and

(iii) A firm is free to make decisions. Its decisions are not affected by the central authority decisions.

When an entrepreneur establishes any industrial undertaking he adopts any one of the following methods in order to evaluate his investment:

(i) The Payback Method. It is a relatively easy but less scientific method of evaluating the investment proposal. Under this method the investor chosses a certain period, which is called payback period, at his sweet will, when he would regain the primary investment within a certain time limit.

The characteristics of this method are. The calculation in this method is easy and rational. It is a direct method in which the objective of the firm is to get back its investment. as soon as possible. Thus the firm minimises its risks, because longer the time period, greater will be the risk.

The main drawbacks of this method are:

(a) In this method there is no discount on the future income.

(b) The assumption of maximising profit is impractical. In this method the period after payback is neglected. and

(c) This method says nothing about getting a definite rate of profitability on the proposed investment.

(ii) The Book of Accounting Rate of Return. The book of accounting rate of return is the ratio of average annual profit on the primary capital. To calculate this ratio; gross profit and gross investment expenditure or as an alternative, average profit and average capital is taken into account. There are different methods of defining capital in different countries. Likewise the profit is defined variably in various projects of the same country.

(iii) The Net Present Value Method. To main drawback of above method is that to know total net income or profit the returns of different years are added. This is not appropriate from the point of view of economics. Because the value of money received at present and that of money be received in future is not the same. Money has also a time value. The value of sum received in the present is relatively more than that of a certain sum to be received in future. For example if we give 100 Rs. for an year on loan, we will receive Rs. 110 at the interest rate of 10%. Hence the present value of the income is calculated by discounting the future income from a project, time is an important factor of the every aspect of the project. Every project has an economic life which begins with the first year of production and ends with the project itself. This life totally depends on future, while designing and evaluating it. This means, the inputs, output, their prices, direct costs and profits of the project are all things of future. The outline of the project is a future chronology of the input, output, cost and profit of the lifetime of the project.

(iv) The Internal Rate of Return or the Marginal Efficiency of Capital Method. The present value of investment profit and profit-cost ratios of any project, can be estimated only when we know the appropriate, rates of discount. If in any case the social rates of discount are not given, the only alternative left for the project investors to go on decreasing the zero ascending discount rates in the chronological order of social cost and profit. The sum of the present value of profit on every rate and its difference with the sum of present value of cost should be calculated that means the present value of net profit. If the present value of net profit is positive on certain discount rate, then the present positive value of net profit should be calculated again on the next higher discount rate. This process should be repeated till we reach the discount rate where net profits present value equals to zero. This discount rate is termed as the internal return rate of the project. It is called internal because it is derived from the cost profit figures of the project and requires no outward help. It is called the rate of return for in reality it is a per unit return on investment cost of any project.

Shortcomings. According to the extra return rate standard, an early profit bearing project should be chosen, for it bears a high internal return rate. But this choice proves to be wrong. If the project is selected on the basis of the standard of profit-cost ratio of the present value of the net profit. Apart from these shortcomings it does not provide any perfect decision-making law about the selection of internal return rate. Because it requires some standard of comparison, some pre-determined private or social interest rate on which the investment fund is loaned or made available.

Modern Approaches of Investment Decisions. Some new techniques are discovered to evaluate the investment in the economic planning in the underdeveloped countries. Some economists like Mission, Morglin, Haberger, Organisation of Economic Commission for Development (OECD) and United Nations Industrial Development Organisations have developed some useful techniques of social evaluation of industrial projects.

The OECD Approach. This approach technique is developed by Little and Missless. In this approach a legitimate criteria is given in order to evaluate the social cost-profit of a project. It was followed by another approach called the UNIDO approach in 1965.

UNIDO Approach. The United Nations Industrial Development Organisation. UNIDO started its work in 1965 to develop the techniques and processes of evaluation of industrial projects through national profit-cost analysis. The most important work in this context was the study, captioned as 'Guidelines for Project Evaluation'. It was prepared by Portuo Das Gupta. Amartya Sen (now a Nobel Lauriette) and Stephen Marglin. In this study those projects were selected which help in achieving the ultimate objectives of the under developed countries. It produced the guidelines for government projects. Thus these guidelines provide a basis for social cost-profit analysis. The Objective of this analysis is to maximize the net social profit. Net profit of a society is the difference between the gross social profit derived from a project and the total social cost.

Social-Cost Profit. Which items should be included in the social cost and social profit while doing a practical evaluation of a project? According to the guidelines the difference between profit and cost is of sign only. A profit derived from a project becomes cost in the context of other project. For example a project produces extra consumption goods for society. In this situation it will be considered as a social profit. But in case, some other project is selected in place of the first, we have to make sacrifice of this extra consumption and this will become the cost of another project.

National Objectives. *(i)* Objective of total consumption, *(ii)* Objective of income redistribution, *(iii)* Objective of reduction of unemployment, *(iv)* Objective of self-dependence, *(v)* Social goods (Female education etc.) objective. After determining the social objectives, the next problem is to transform these objectives into profits and then to change them into single, gross measure.

Social Cost Profit Analysis. In a social cost profit analysis social costs are also evaluated. UNIDO considers the opportunity cost as the measure of social cost. An opportunity cost of a project is defined as the maximum alternative benefits foregone. If to select X project, Y and Z project profits (prospective) are to be abandoned, then the maximum profit derived from these projects will be the legitimate social cost of the X project.

Hence it is clear that the total profits of a project are the social profits while foregone profits are social costs. The profit of a project includes net product. Net product refers to the quantity of available goods and services in the economy, which would not have been derived in absence of that project. Likewise net inputs are included in the cost of a project.

Indirect Profit Cost. We have discussed the direct profits and costs of a project in the analysis so far. But we have to consider also the indirect profit and costs while evaluating the investment. Generally these are included in the item of external effects. As these external effects cannot be measured easily the UNIDO approach includes only those indirect effects or external effects which can be identified and measured easily. These are the net profit of society which can not be measured with the product, of title project. For example a road built for any specific project can be utilised by other also. In this situation, it is not possible to measure the indirect or external profits. Likewise there are indirect costs of a project. These indirect costs cause net loss for a society. For example, the climate is polluted after starting any industrial project. This is the indirect external effect which puts the society to loss.

UNIDO Method of Evaluation of Risk and Uncertainty. Apart from the two methods, mentioned in the previous question, there is a third method to evaluate the investment having risk and uncertainty, developed by UNIDO. It calculates, is such position the 'Expected Present Value (EPV). A1ternative results cannot be pre-estimated in the condition of uncertainity and there can be many consequences in future. UNIDO method considers many possibilities in evaluation to solve uncertainty in the performance of the project. For example different probabilities in the prices of future for the product under the industrial project are taken into consideration. Impossible situations, which cannot happen are excluded but of these probabilities. Remaining various results on the basis of their probably prospects are kept for consideration. In this context help may be taken from the past experience.

COST PLUS METHOD

Price is the value of a product denoted in terms of money. It is the amount paid by a buyer to a seller for buying a unit of that product or service. A firm may adopt various price methods for the product being produced by it. These various methods can be grouped in two major groups.

A. Princing Methods based on Cost

1. Full-Cost or Cost plus Method.

It is the most common method utilised for pricing. In this method, price is adjusted to cover costs (of material, labour and overhead) and a pre-determined percentage for profit. Management works out the cost of goods manufactured or purchased for resale and adds a percentage of profit to determine the selling price. This percentage is never alike among various units within the industry and even products of the same concern. It is because of the rate differences in competitive intensity, differences in cost base and turnover rate with risk exist. It shows some vague idea of just profit.

Limitations of the Cost Plus Method

(i) **Demand is Ignored.** There is no reciprocity between cost and demand for the goods. Demand is totally ignored in pricing.

(ii) **Failure to Show the Forces of Competition.** It fails to reflect the forces of competition fully.

(iii) **Exaggeration of the Precision of Allocated Costs.** It exaggerates the precision of allocated costs.

(iv) **Based on Cost Concept.** It is based on concept of cost that may not be relevent for the decision of the price.

The cost-plus pricing method is suitable in the following cases:

(i) **Ideal Method.** It is an ideal, fair and just method of pricing. Prices can be fixed very easily and with speed. Prices are more defensible on moral grounds."

(ii) **Uncertainity of Demand.** In practice, firms are very uncertain of the demand of their product and the probable response to any price change. The method is then a fool-proof method.

(iii) **Stability.** The firms which prefer stability can get it from full cost pricing due to uncertain market and incomplete knowledge. In such cases where costs of getting information are high with process of trial and error, they stick to it so that the cost of decision making is reduced to the minimum.

(iv) Management tends to know more about product costs than other factors relevant to pricing.

(v) **Major Uncertainty in Cost Setting.** Rivals prices could not be known hence, it is difficult to set the price accordingly. Cost plus pricing only can live stability to set a price by which the profits could be acceptable to other members of the trade.

(vi) **Product Tailoring.** When the selling price is predetermined, the products design can be determined very easily.

(vii) Other advantages of cost plus pricing are.

(a) ***Pricing or products when they are manufactured on the orders of a single buyer as per specifications.*** Pricing is determined cost plus gross margin.

(b) ***Monopoly Buying.*** Buyers know of the suppliers' costs. If they do not get the product to the price of their satisfaction, they will prepare the product themselves at relevant costs.

(c) ***Public Utility Pricing.*** According to cost plus formula, if one expects decline in industry, he must increase price. This price policy is useful in times of depression. Cost plus is a pricing scheme based on arbitrary costs and arbitrary make up. It is taken into consideration as it is simpler to apply.

2. Going Rate Pricing. Here we are more concerned with the market price and' cost is not given any consideration. The firm adusts its own price policy to the general pricing-structure in the industry. Where costs are particularly difficult to measure this may seem to be the topical step in a rational pricing policy. Here price leadership policy fits in well. Here the rates are fixed according to the competitors' prices and this is the safest way. The risks of price fixation are saved. It is no more costly and no calculations are needed.

This process is adopted in the world markets. The firm has enough power to set its own prices and can be a price maker if it likes to face all the consequences.

3. Marginal Cost Pricing or Incremental Cost Pricing. All traditional theories of pricing behaviour fall under the heading of marginalism. They assume an entrepreneur who weighs the penalties and rewards of price decisions.. He compares the additional gain and additional cost of. increasing output or charging price. He works at a point where gain and loss (cost) are equal. These theories are based on the recognition that both demand and cost condition influence pricing. The firm adjusts to changes in the market force revising price as demands shift or costs change.

The traditional theory has certain limitations. They are as under.

(a) **Assumption or Profit Maximisation.** The theory rests on profit maximisation objective of the firm. Although profit maximisation is the primary objective there are other objectives as well that guide the entrepreneur. Maximising sales of increasing the market share interest the manager more than profit at times. The trusteeship principle of social responsibility sometime becomes more important than profit maximisation.

(b) **Inadequate dealing with Dynamics or Pricing.** The traditional theory does not distinguish clearly between the long-run and short-run effects of changes in prices. It does not indicate the effect of today's price on future Profits. It considers the present marginal revenue curve and the present marginal costs curve only.

(c) **Assumption on a Single Product.** In practice firm products not one but several products which are inter-dependent both in sales and in production.

(d) **Problem of Uncertainty.** The traditional theory assumes full knowledge of firm's demand cost functions to the manager. In real world this is hardly true. Uncertainty does exist and the manager must take it into account while pricing.

Under this method, prices are fixed on the basis of variable costs or direct costs of the products. This method is available when a new product is to be introduced in the market by existing firms. During depression period also this method is workable. But it is only a short-term phenomenon.

4. No-loss No-profit Price Policy. It is a price equal to total costs per unit or where sales revenue is equal to .total costs, total costs include fixed costs as well as variable costs. This method is suitable during depression periods, when there is acute competition in the market, when a special order is to be supplied or when a new product is to be introduced in the market by an existing firm.

5. Rate of Return Pricing Policy. Many firms follow the policy of rate of return on their investments. Under this method, a price is fixed by manufacturer or distributor as to give him a fixed return on his total investment in the process. This method is more suitable for distributors and for the products which can be sold in bulk quantity and that have a quick, turnover of capital.

B. Pricing Methods Based on Market Conditions

1. Established Price. Sometimes, long-term prices of a product are established or stablized in the market. It is its normal price or long-term price and the sport price or market, price or-short-term price of that product revolves around it. So, whenever any producer brings as new product in the market, he will have to fix the price of his product near about that price.

2. Leadership Prices. In some industries, one or two large business units control the lion's share or the market. This business unit acts as a price leader. Small firms in such a situation have no alternative except to follow the leader. The prices charged by these firms are identical to those charged by the leader firm. They make changes in price at the time and to the extent as are made by the industry leader. Such a policy is adopted by a firm when it funds that undercutting of prices is dangerous and over-changing is not possible because it may be difficult to sell products at a price higher than the one charged by the industry leader. There is no price competition among the firms in the industry.

3. Penetration Pricing. A firm may adopt the strategy of charging low price to obtain a larger share of the market and to develop brand preference. This is also used to obtain the advantage of economies scale because charging a lower price may be used to prevent the entry of new firms by keeping the margin of profit low. The flrm adopting this policy benefits in the long-run because of the brand preference developed in the introductory stage.

4. Skimming the Cream Policy. This policy if adopted in the case of speciality goods, a manufacturer may keep the price very high to recover the amount invested by him quickly. It is also adopted to make quick profits because of fear of competition at a later stage. Such a policy is possible to be adopted in the case of those products which are drastically departing from the available products. This policy is desirable in the following circumstances.

(i) It may be used to avoid the loss resulting from competition specially when the entry in that line of business is easy.

(ii) When manufacturers may be interested in keeping the price high to earn a higher initial profit to be ploughed back in the business to meet the increased demand.

(iii) The initial cost of product is generally high. It is, therefore logical to charge a higher initial price.

5. Charging what the Traffic will Bear. This policy is adopted by the persons and institutions engaged in rendering some personal service, Doctors, dentists, lawyers, for example, charge the prices for the services rendered by them on the basis of the customer's ability to pay. This policy, obviously. takes into account the needs and resources of the customers. Cost factor does not dominate this pricing policy. This policy is specially useful when the product of a unique type capable of creating a fad. This policy. however, does not find a wide recognition in the market because customers do not look with favour on a business unit following a policy of charging what the traffic will bear.

6. Psychological Pricing. Psychological pricing is the practice of setting prices at odd amount such as Rs. 9.95 Rs. 13 or Rs. 39. It is known as odd pricing. it was originally introduced to check the honesty of sales clerks by forcing them to make changes more frequently in accepting payments from the customers. Today, it is used to secure a positive buying behaviour from the customers. It is thought that odd pricing succeeds in inducing a buyer to some extent to make purchases. The reason for this expectation can be easily understood if we compare a price of Rs. 6.95 with price of Rs. 7. Although there is a marginal difference between these two price, yet a price of Rs. 6.95 appears to be over Rs. 6 rather then almost Rs.7". Similarly, a car priced at Rs. 15998 suggests the price to be over Rs, 15,000 rather than almost Rs. 16000. Not only this, price of Rs. 15998 suggests to a buyer that the price is reasonable and he is not being over-charged. These two factors secure a positive buyer behaviour. There is, however, little evidence to suggest the importance of psychological pricing in increasing the sales volume of a business concern. Yet a casual glance at prices indicates that psychological pricing dominates pricing particularly in the case of consumer goods.

PRICING POLICIES

Pricing Policies of Public Enterprises in India. What pricing policy should a Public Enterprise (PE) adopt? It is a complex problem and is not possible to lay down, general principle of pricing that should be followed by all the PEs. The complexity of pricing problem arises because of the fact that some PEs are industrial and commercial undertakings; some PEs are promotional and developmental; and some PEs provide basic and essential infrastructure facilities. A1so, competitive environment—domestic and international—has got to be taken into account in the case of goods produced by some PEs. There is also to be considered the need for financial resources for investment purposes in a developing country like India. From all these considerations; it should follow that there cannot be just a single, principle of guiding of pricing that can be prescribed for or that should be followed by all PEs.

The following are some of the important principles of pricing which are suggested in the case of PEs.

1. Marginal Cost Basis. Marginal cost is the cost of producing an additional unit of a product. The reasoning behind the 'marginal cost basis' of pricing policy, is that, if a consumer is willing to pay for an extra unit of a product, welfare of the community gets maximised when that extra or additional unit of product is made available to him. It is argued that if a consumer is not willing to pay the cost of the additional unit (*i.e.* marginal cost), that additional unit should not be produced in the interest of maximising welfare of the community. It is also argued that if marginal cost basis is followed in pricing policy of PEs, resources of the community will automatically be allocated to the production of different goods that will lead to maximisation of the welfare of the community.

Marginal Cost. While considering 'marginal cost' in the short run, capital cost is fixed and only variable cost is taken into consideration therefore, called 'short-term marginal cost'. In the case of long-term marginal cost, even fixed capital becomes variable capital and marginal cost has in that case to take note of both fixed capital cost and variable cost.

Criticism. One criticism against the marginal cost principle of pricing of products of PEs is that, if strictly applied, it would result in deficit in the case of industries experiencing increasing returns or decreasing costs. Such deficits may have to be met by imposing taxes on other consumers who are not purchasing that commodity and this could reduce their welfare.

Surplus Revenue. The principle of marginal cost would mean, in the case of industries which are functioning under conditions of decreasing costs, an increase in the price of commondity with every increase in production of that commodity. This would result in a large surplus revenue. This surplus revenue, apart from inviting public protests, migh also result in a demand for a rise in wages and bonus by workers in that unit of the PE.

Practical Difficulties. The marginal cost principle may also be found unworkable because of the practical difficulties of calculating, with any degree of accuracy, the marginal cost in public utilities such as electricity, State transport services, post and telegraph and so on.

2. Pricing on the Basis of Average Cost. 'Average cost pricing principle' refers to fixing the price of a commodity on the basis of the average cost of population of the commodity. In the case of average cost pricing, total revenue obtained by selling a certain amount of commodity will be equal to its total cost of production. Thus, average cost pricing principle ensures that the entire cost of production is absorbed in to the price of the commodity.

It may be noticed that while calculating total cost of production, alongwith various other costs, normal profits is also included. On account of this, the price of a commodity is a little higher than the price based on the principle of 'No profit, No loss'.

Calculation Problem. It is claimed that it is easy to calculate total costs and therefore, also the average cost of a commodity, whereas it is not always possible to accurately calculate marginal cost, and sometime it is even impossible to-do that. Thus, in the case of railways, electricity and other public utilities it is possible to calculate total costs and therefore, also the average cost of production of a commodity or service whercas it is not possible in their cases to calculate marginal cost.

Merits. The following merits are claimed for the principle of average cost pricing of commodities or services of PEs.

1. Every consumer pays the entire cost of production of a commodity that he is consuming instead of only its marginal cost. This appears reasonable.
2. Since nobody pays more than the average cost of production of a commodity or what it has cost the commodity to be

produced and no more, there is no question of any body being exploited (by changing a price that is higher than what on an average the commodity has cost).

3. 'No Profit, No Loss' or 'Break-Even' Principle. 'No profit, No loss' or 'Break-even' principle of pricing of products or services of PEs maintains that the price should be fixed in such a way that there will be neither any profit, nor any loss for the concerned PE. In simple terms, price should just-cover all costs of production.

Marginal Cost Pricing. It is noted that in the case of marginal cost pricing, in the case of decreasing cost condition, the concerned_PE will suffer a loss which will have to be subsidized by taxing people to the extent of the deficit suffered by the PE. There is thus cross subsidization. In the case of 'No profit, No loss' principle of pricing of products of PEs there is no question of any loss and, therefore, no subsidizing the PE out of the government treasury or by taxing the people. This means that when 'No profit, No loss' principle of pricing is adopted by a PE non-consumers of the commodity in question are not forced directly or indirectly to bear a 'burden for the benefit of those who consume the product.

Arthur Lewis has advocated this principle of 'No Profit, No loss' on the ground that the principle will prevent either over-expansion or under-expansion of a PE and will thus help avoid either inflationary or deflationary tendencies.

In India, the Damodar Valley Corporation, (DVC) follows the principle of 'No profit, No loss' in pricing. Other PEs which follow this principle of pricing are Hindustan Antibiotics, Hindustan Insecticides, Export Guarantee Corporation, etc.

4. Profit-making Principle of Pricing. Profit-making principle of pricing of the products or services of PEs maintains that the price charged should be such as to get for the concerned PE some surplus after absorbing all the cost elements, including normal profit. It is maintained that in developing countries like India, PEs are expected to generate as much surplus as possible so that these surplus funds can be further invested in developmental projects.

In Developing Countries. In many developing countries like India. PEs have been occupying a prominent place in the economy. Huge amounts (amounting to more than Rs. 1,13,234 crores on Central Government projects) have come to be invested in PEs. In developing countries, people being poor with an extremely low per capital income, there is limited scope for both direct and indirect taxation. If the rates are raised abnormally, the yields might decline and people may also develop tax-resistances. It is, therefore, suggested that PEs should generate as much surpluses or profits as possible which will augment government's financial resources which can be invested for further development purposes. In countries, where PEs have come to occupy a commanding position, it would be easier and also practicable that the country's financial resources for developmental purposes should be augmented by this way than by raising financial resources by taxation or deficit financing or borrowing from the public.

Pronouncements. We observe the pronouncements of politicians and economists in India in favour of this principle of pricing of the products of PEs. Thus, Mrs. Indira Gandhi, then the Prime Minister of India, pronounced that Government advocated expanding the public sector so that the PEs can "provide surpluses with which to finance further economic development". Mr. T.A. Pai (once Union Minister for Industries) argued that 12 per cent return on investment in the public sector should be regarded as equitable Dr. V.K.R.V. Rao maintained that the pricing policy of PEs "should be such as to promote the growth of national income... public enterprises must make profit and the larger the share of public enterprises in all enterprises, the greater is the need for their making profits. Profits constitute the surplus available for savings and investments, on the one hand, and contribution to national social welfare programmes, on the other, and if public enterprises do not make profits, the national surplus available for stepping up the rate of investment and the increase of social welfare will suffer a corresponding reduction.

Taxation Committees Report. The Taxation Enquiry Committee (1952) observed. "...in certain age where the State has made substantial investment a policy of regulating prices so as to secure an adequate return on the capital invested is not only unobjectionable but may indeed be desirable. This is particularly so, where public enterprise itself, fostered at State expense, may in turn play a role in financing the country's development."

The Industrial Policy Statement of 1948 observed. "It is to be expected that public enterprises will augment revenues of the State and provide resources for further development to fresh fields."

Plans. India's Five Year Plans have also advocated the same principle. Thus, the Third Five Year Plan maintained. "Substantial investments have been made in the public sector over the last ten years and every effort must be made to ensure that they yield an adequate surplus on the basis of which to plan further advance.

The Sixth Plan Observed. "Almost all the Central and State enterprises would need to adopt appropriate pricing policies in order to achieve an adequate rate of return on capital employed."

It is thus maintained that according to this princple, while particular PEs, such as Hindustan Insecticides and the Hindustan Antibiotics may operate on the principle of 'No profit, No loss.' PEs which are essentially industrial or commercial in nature (and not concerned with matters like education, research, public health and so on) should generate surpluses and augment the pool of investment funds.

Comment on Profit-making Principle of Pricing for PEs

The following points of criticism are brought against the profit making principle of pricing for PEs.

1. It should be noted that a reasonable return on investment in a PE is not the same thing as making maximum profit or mopping up Maximum resources for further investment purposes. If PEs as a whole are considered, there is ground for argument that on the whole, the public sector should yield a 'reasonable rate of return' on investment by which we may say what a similar investment in the private sector yields.

Adverse Effect. But if the Government aims at a higher than reasonable rate of return or profit, the State having an absolute monopoly in some of the essential services and commodities, the State can do that; but that will have an extremely adverse effect on the welfare of the people (as in the case of railway travel and electricity) and on other sectors of production, because many of the commodities produced by PEs (*e.g.* coal, electricity, iron and steel, chemicals, fertilizers, etc.) happen to be important inputs of some other industries.

2. Reasonable Rate. In the case of PEs in India, it is possible to raise objection even against the principle of reasonable rate of profit on the basis of investment. In India, most PEs have an extremely long gestation period and that resulted in the escalation of costs and amount of investment. All this was often due to faulty project planning, wrong location of a project under political pressure, employing too many workers again due to political reasons, etc. To expect the PEs to cover a reasonable rate of profit on this unnecessary heavy investment would only mean covering up inefficiency of the PEs. The reasonable rate of profit should be based on the efficient running of PEs.

3. Welfare point of view. In some cases like fertilizers, antibiotics, milk for poor school children and mothers, etc., from the welfare point of view, it is necessary to subsidise their prices.

4. And therefore, the principle under discussion cannot be a general criterion for all types of PEs.

5. Pricing Policies of Some of the PEs in India. The PEs in India follow a number of practices while fixing prices of their products or services. Following some of the important practices adopted by PEs in India.

(a) Administered Prices. Administered prices or controlled prices are fixed by the Government, as in the case of steel, electricity, railways, cement, sugar, etc. While fixing their prices, the Government may follow any principles mentioned above, namely reasonable rate of return. 'No profit, No loss', subsidised prices and so on.

(b) ***Subsidised Prices.*** As a matter of policy, some of the prices of products of the PEs charged by the government are below their cost of production, the Subsidy being paid by the Government. Government may do this to specially help a certain section of the community. Thus, in India, fertilisers are subsidised to boost agricultural production; similarly certain sections of society are provided loans at lower rates of interest by nationalised commercial banks as they are too poor to pay the normal rate of interest charged for the public. With a view to reduce the birth-rate in India, prices of contraceptives produced by the Hindustan Latex are subsidised.

(c) ***Parity Prices.*** In the case of products of some of the PEs that have to face competition in the open market with imported goods of similar types or close substitutes, party with the landed cost of the imported commodity is made the basis of fixing the prices. In India, this happens in the case of the Hindustan Shipyard which has a monopoly in shipbuilding. In this case, parity with prices of similar goods imported from the United Kingdom is aimed at.

(d) ***Cost-plus Prices.*** Cost-plus prices is the price fixed by the Government in the case of the products of certain PEs on the basis cost of production incurred plus a margin (around 10 per cent for profit) in addition to that. In India this is done in the case of PEs like the Indian Telephone Industry, Hindustan Aircrafts and Bharat Electronics Limited, which fix prices on thc 'cost-plus basis.

The danger in following this principle is that since a margin over cost of production is permitted, this may breed inefficiency in the PEs leaving no incentive to increase efficiency and reduce cost of production.

In India, captive producers like Hindustan Aeronautics, Hindustan Cables, Bharat Dynamics, etc., follow this principle.

(e) ***Discriminatory Prices.*** In the case of discriminatory prices, the PEs charge different prices for the same product of the PEs for different sections of the community. Thus, nationalised commercial banks in India charge different rates of interest in the case of the very poor, the agriculturists with small landholdings and big industrialists.

(f) ***Following the Leaders.*** In this case, prices are fixed by PEs taking into consideration the prices of similar goods fixed by a leading undertaking in the same line of production. For example, Kerala Soaps and Oils, while fixing the price of its product, takes into account the prices fixed by Hindustan Lever, Tata Soap, and Mysore Sandal, etc.

(g) ***Trade Association Pricing.*** In India, the Air India International fixes the price (*i.e.* airfares) on the basis of the recommendation, of the international Air Transport Association; and the Shipping Corporation of India fixes prices or rates of its shipping services on the basis of the recommendations of the Shipping Conference which is an international organisation.

(h) ***Competitive Prices.*** In India, certain PEs like the Ashok Hotel fix their prices on the basis of competition Prevailing in the market (that is, prices or rates charged by other similar Five Star Hotels in the private sector).

(i) ***Dual Pricing Policy.*** In the case of 'Dual Pricing Policy, a public sector enterprise charges one price for some sector of the economy and another price for other sectors of the economy. The dual pricing policy may be illustrated by the public sector steel units. In the case of public sector steel units, the Government has been following a dual pricing policy since 15th October,1977. According to this policy, steel is sold to priority sectors at a lower price, and

In order to compensate for this loss Involved, the public sector steel plants are empowered to sell the balance of their production at higher prices to other sectors of the economy.

Machinery for Price Fixation. By a resolution, Government setup in January 1970, the Bureau of Industrial Costs and Prices, (BICP) on the, recommendation of the Administrative Reforms Commission. The BICP undertakes investigations, if and where necessary, regarding prices to be charged by PEs and gives its advice in the matter. In this work, the BICP is assisted by the Bureau of Public Enterprises (BPE).

The principles and practices adopted for pricing their products or services would be different in the case of the following different categories of public sector undertakings.

1. PEs engaged in the production of public utilities and services;
2. PEs engaged in trading activities; and
3. PEs which are public financial institutions.

Guidelines on Pricing of PEs by the Bueau of Public Enterprises

The Bureau of Public Enterprises (BPE) is intimately concerned with problems of pricing by PEs. The BPE has issued in this connection the following guidelines:

1. In case PEs produce goods in competition with private enterprise, it is the normal market forces of demand that should govern prices of such products of PEs.

2. Government should invariably puchase goods from PEs, if available, to meet their requirements. Price preference not exceeding 10 per cent will be admissible to PEs. But this cannot be permanent or taken for granted. Every effort should be made to reduce the cost of production and prices to a competitive level.

3. In case PEs operate under monopolistic or semi-monopolistic conditions, the landed cost of comparable imported goods should be the ceiling limit. Within this limit PEs should fix prices at a suitable level. If the landed cost of similar goods that are imported is found to be artificially low, the matter of pricing under such circumstances should be referred to the Administrative Ministry, the PBE and the Ministry of Finance.

ROLE OF COST IN PRICING

In the price setting process, cost data are most important element. Hence, cost must be relevant to the pricing decision and under-estimation and exaggeration must be avoided. Besides costs, there are also other factors that require consideration. An increase in the demand may make an increase in prices possible even without an increase in costs. Pricing is like a tripod having three legs. In addition to costs there are other two legs if market demand and competition. As we cannot say definitely which of the legs supports the tripod, similarly, we cannot assert which of the above three factors determines the price. Demand is at times more important than even cost. If cost is increased, the price is to increase even if the demand does not permit to do so.

It is Price that Determines Cost that may be Incurred. The product ultimately goes to the public and their capacity to pay is known. Given the price we arrive at the cost working backwards from the price, consumer can afford to pay. If the quality of the product is to be improved this may be possible only when customers are willing to pay higher price because cost will naturally go up.

If Costs were to Determine Price. Why do so many factories report losses? Different producers have different costs of production. But in the market, prices are close together for a somewhat similar product. Therefore costs are not the determining factor for the pricing. Again it is also difficult to measure costs accurately as they are apportioned. Costs are affected by volume and volume is affected by price. The management has to assume some desired price and volume relationship for determining costs.

The above discussion does not purport to indicate that costs should be ignored altogether while setting prices. Costs have to be taken into consideration like many other factors. In the long run if costs are not covered manufacturers will withdraw themselves from the market and the supply will be curtailed and prices will be raised. All this goes to show that cost is not the only factor in setting prices.

Relevant Costs. For managerial decisions in the short run, direct costs are more relevant. In a single product firm all costs are direct. The management would try to cover all the costs. But problems are more complex in a multi-product firm. Relevant costs are those costs, that are directly traceable to an individual product. Selling price must cover all direct costs variable and fixed that are attributable to the product. In addition, it must include some profit. But in short period of time, it is tolerable if the price of a product has to do no more than cover its direct costs only (only the direct variable costs).

Example. During recession, a firm manufacturing a certain component was operating at 50% of its capacity. A foreign importer offered to purchase 5,000 units of the component at Rs. 5 per unit. The average cost of the product is Rs. 6. The question was whether the order should be accepted. The cost data were as follows:

Total capacity	20,000 components
Actual output	10,000
Direct materials	Rs. 10,000
Direct labour	Rs. 10,000
Fixed expenses	Rs. 40,000
Total cost	Rs. 60,000
Average cost	Rs. 6 (per unit)

On analysis of the above data, we find the additional cost of producing 5,000 units would be only Rs. 10,000 (Rs. 5,000 for material and Rs. 5,000 for labour). The incremental revenue would be Rs. 25,000 and the firm would gain Rs. 15,000 by accepting this order.

In the same way, while making quotation for tenders in and highly competitive situation the more important is that at least the direct costs must be covered. But before accepting this order considerations have to be made. If other customers learn that the component is being sold at a lower price they may also demand a similar price cut or else threaten to cancel their orders. What is essential for the firm is that the acceptance of this order should be kept a guarded secret.

In the long run the aggregate revenues from all products must cover not only the direct costs but also contribute towards common costs. Ideally, each product should make a significant constitution to common cost bot it is not possible to state any general rule for determining satisfactory or unsatisfactory contributions.

If a competitive price does cover direct cost and yields some contribution to common cost, the question arises how high must that contribution be to justify the long run continuance of a particular product in a company's product line? If the product is discontinued, will any other product be substituted for it. What effect will the discontinuance of the product have on the demand for the other products in the line? Product pricing decisions should be made with a view to maximise company's profits in the long run.

Another problem that has to be faced is "How can the common costs be covered, if individual prices are set in consideration of, direct cost only?" The point is that covering of direct costs is only a starting point in the pricing decision. Factors of supply and demand and competition may allow price that will give very substantial contribution to common costs.

If the economic determinants of price are such that the combined price for all of a company's products are not sufficient to cover common costs in the long run the conclusion is not that the individual prices are wrong but rather that the firm is economically inefficient. Such a firm must either improve its working efficiency or cease working and wind up.

Demand Elasticity and Price Policy. The price policy of a firm will depend upon elasticity of demand as well. If the demand is inelastic, it will not be profitable for the firm to reduce its prices. But, if the demand of the product is less elastic then the firm should take care not to fix very high price. In that case a policy of price rise would not pay. If the demand is elastic, it is a policy of price reduction rather than the policy of price increase. These price strategies are illustrated by the following example relating to two products A and B, former having a very little elastic demand and the latter a highly elastic demand.

Effect or Price Reduction with Elastic and Inelastic Demand

	Price	A	B
Rs.	2.20 Number of units sold	5,000	5,000
	Total Sales	Rs. 11,000	Rs. 11,000
	Total Expenses	Rs. 9000 Rs.	9,000
	Net Profit	Rs. 2,000	Rs. 2,000
Rs. 1.95	Number of units sold	5,500	10,000
	Total Sales	Rs. 10,725	Rs. 19,500
	Total Expenses	Rs. 9,900	Rs. 18,000
Net Profit		Rs. 825	Rs. 15,000

From the above it is quite clear that price reduction for expanding sale would be profitable for product B with highly elastic demand and not for product A with little elastic demand.

Cost Reduction, Elasticity or Demand and Price Policy. A firm able to reduce its costs will have to decide if the prices are to be reduced or not. We have to note here the elasticity of demand. If the demand is elastic, a reduction in price will be less profitable than the maintenance of the price itself. This become clear from table given above.

FACTORS AFFECT PRICE POLICY

A manufacturer should pay adequate attention to the following factors while taking any decisions relating to price of his products:

1. Objectives of Business. First of all, the management must review the objectives of the firm as they are the real deciding factors. A firm may have alternative objectives such as a suitable return on the capital employed, maximisation of sales, capturing market from competitors, etc.

2. Cost or Goods. It is a simple proposition that prices charged must be such as will enable the manufacturer to recover his cost. *i.e.* the average total unit cost and earn a reasonable profit. No business can continue for long if the price of product falls short of the average total unit cost and thus results in a loss.

3. Market Position. The next factor in pricing policies is the study of nature of market, *i.e.* the nature of prospective buyers of the product concerned. The management should attempt to find out the composition of their market, that is they should consider such questions as follows. Is the market of their product composed of industrial users or commercial houses or individual consumers of householders? Does their market consist of individual consumers, and whether they are rich, middle or poor class? Is the product meant for young men or for grown-ups ? Is it to be used by males or females? What motives do impel them to buy the product? What is the relative utility of the product to the consumers? What is their elasticity of demand? All such questions will guide the management in fixing correct prices.

4. Competitior's Price. It is a prescriptive approach factor in deciding upon the prices of its own product by a firm. The competitor's price policy for similar merchandise, and the effect of one's own price policy upon the price polices of the competitors, upon the sales of the merchandise in question and upon one's reputation in the community must be considered. No sales manager can afford to ignore the prices charged by other suppliers of identical products. A price higher than the one charged by others will wean customers away from him. But a very much lower price may create a suspicion in their minds about the quality of the product and may not increase sales.

5. The marketing policies pursued by the sales organisation. The first important consideration here is of the channel of distribution selected to market the products. Normally, the longer the chain of distribution the higher is the margin added to cost in fixing the price. Secondly, warranties and after-sale service facilities attached to a sale will also have a bearing on the pricing of goods. Finally, proper adjustment should also be made for regular or irregular rebates, concessions, cuts on other reductions in prices; allowed to customers as an incentive to promote sales.

6. Social and ethical Consideration. These include the following:

(i) **Public Policy.** Sometimes, the Government may announce a general policy about pricing of goods (as these days in India Government is averse to any rise in prices of necessities of life) or may specifically fix and control prices of goods as in the case of iron and steel, cement, coal, sugar, etc. Under such circumstances the sales manager has little or no control over the prices, and he has to fall in line with the public policy.

(ii) **Reasonable Price.** There has been a business ethics to charge reasonable and just prices for their products. Though the canons of 'What the traffic will bear' and 'what competition will allow' has been popular, the principle of reasonableness has also guided the prices.

(iii) **Attitude of Labour Leaders.** It is also a guiding factor in pricing decisions. If prices are Fixed high; workers also demand more wages and more bonus, etc.

(iv) **Consumer's Reactions to Rising Prices.** It should also be taken into account.

7. Price Elasticity or Demand. Price elasticity refers to consequential change in demand due to change in price of the commodity. As there is an inverse relationship between price and demand, the demand will in crease with the fall in prices or vice versa. So, a high price may be fixed for inelastic goods and, on the other hand, price of elastic goods cannot be fixed at a higher level. A price reduction policy may suit the highly elastic goods.

8. Product Differentiation. In a non-price sensitive market. The price depends more on the differentiation of the product in its size, colour, quality etc. In such markets different characteristics are added to the products in order to attract the customers and high prices may be charged. Customers may happily pay higher prices for new style, fashion, quality or packaging etc.

9. Product's Stage in the Life Cycle. Pricing policy may be different in different stages or product's own life cycle. In the introductory stages prices are fixed lower to increase the demand or the product of higher to earn the maximum profit, considering the competitive situations in the market. The policy may then, lead to slow reduction of prices with a view to expand the market. In the maturity stage, penoetrating pricing may be followed.

10. Buying Patterns or Consumers. Buying petterns, of consumers also affect the pricing' decision of the concern. If the purchase frequency of the product is higher, lower prices should be fixed to have a low profit margin resulting in higher total profits of the firm. All consumer items of daily use have high purchase frequency. Low purchase frequency items may be sold at high price. Durable consumer products like T.V. and refrigerators are, therefore, priced higher.

11. Government Policy. Price discretion is seriously hit by the government price control decision in order to arrest the inflationary trend in prices of certain commodities. The producer of such items will have to fix as per the directives of the Government. If the producer charges higher prices, the government may think of nationalising the concern or it may take legal action. Sometimes

Government starts selling those items fair shops or starts production. So, the prices cannot be fixed higher.

12. Economic Environment. In recession, prices are reduced to a sizeable extent to maintain the level of turnover. On the other hand, prices are charged higher in boom period to cover the increasing cost of production and distribution.

INVESTMENT DECISION AND SIZE OF FIRM

Problem of decision making for investment is closely related with the size of firm, and maximisation of profit.

What should be the optimum size of the firm is problem with which our present day industry is faced. A.G. Robinson while discussing optimum size of the firm has said that "It is a firm in which existing condition of technique and organising ability has lowest average cost of produciton per unit, when all those costs which must be covered in the long run are included." Prof. Kuchhal is of the view that "The optimum firm is likely to result from the ordinary play of economic forces where the market is perfect and sufficient to maintain a single firm of optimum size". Thus in an ideal situation all firms will try to grow up upto a stage where they are in a position to most economically use their productive resources at most economical cost.

Criticism of the Concept. While discussing and adjudging the concept of optimum size of the firm, one basic factor is ideal situaiton and condition of perfect competition. But in actual practice we know that it is difficult to obtain conditions of perfect competition. Moreover, 'perfect competition' in itself is a very vague term and in actual practice it is difficult to measure that. Moreover, it is usually not possible to find out as to what is the optimum size of a firm in various industries.

Factors Determining Optimum Size of a Firm. There are five factors which might help in determining optimum size of a firm. All five factors in some cases, may lead to approximately similar optimum size. In the words of Robinson, "The equilibrium may be similar either to the tug of war rope, which is motionless because no one is yet pulling in either direciton, or to the tug of war rope which is motionless because two teams are for the moment, equally matched".

Technical Factors. Every firm increase its productivity by specialisation and no less by division of labour. Technical specialisation can result in replacement of old methods by the new ones and division of labour is primarily responsible for attaining perfection and quality speedily and without many complications. But the difficulty with this is that upto a particular stage both technical specialisaiton and divison of labour can help in attaining productivity at economical costs, but beyond that instead of being economical, the process becomes costly.

Managerial Forces. In the words of Sivayya and Das, "The managerial optimum is the result of the economies and diseconomies associated with the division of labour and integration of processes in the managerial functions". A large firm instead of concentrating the task of management in the hands of a person, divides that into many parts and each part is then given to a specialised person in the field. In this way rare abilities are not wasted on attending routine work. This divison of labour at management level enables the firm to put persons to the jobs, who have aptitude for the nature of work and specialists are created from within.

The management factor has its own limitation. Though to certain extent it helps in productivity, yet an optimum size reaches beyond which it becomes either impossible or unprofitable for a management to be productive or useful Elaborate division is bound to result in the serious problem of coordination. In the words of Prof. Kuchhal, "Moreover, the difficulties of coordination beyond a certain size lay down on upper limit to the size of the optimum managerial unit. How big a firm can successfully grow will depend upon how it solves the problem of coordinating the various departments and specialists".

Financial Factors. Optimum size of a firm is dependent on the capacity of the firm to raise capital for running its activities, including borrowing capacity of the firm. The capital influences size and structure of the firm as well. Nature of industry of course influence its financial structure and one finds that some firms and industries start with small capital and gradually develop and grow. In actual practice we find that large and well known firms are in better position to raise funds as compared with firms which are either small in size or are less known. Even banks and other government agencies are always inclined to give financial assistance liberally to well known firms.

Marketing Factors. We are all aware that success of an industry is directly linked with its marketing efficiency. In marketing price of raw material which an industry pays, plays a big role becuase final price of a finished product is related to the cost of raw material. Moreover, a large firm can purchase in bulk, is in a better bargaining position and can use the waste than any small industry. A big concern is in an advantageous position because on the average it is required to spend less on advertisement per person and having its own efficient sales organisation can avoid intermediaries. Robinson is of the view that first as a large machine requires a large establishment so that it can keep that running with full capacity, similarly an irreducible sales and buying organisation requires a large undertaking so that cost per unit of the output is kept at barest minimum. In other words optimum marketing unit is the outcome of economies and diseconomies which are available because large scale buying and selling.

Risk Factors. Every entrepreneur will take into consideration fluctuations in demand. Changes in demand result in uncertainty and risk and thus to some extent effect optimum size of the firm. Every firm is thus supposed to be ready to face unexpected declines. The changes which come in the industries can be of four types namely. *(a)* Permanent; *(b)* Cyclic; *(c)* Seasonal and *(d)* Erratic. Permanent changes come in the industry when there is change in habit of the people, in so far as their product is concerned or radical techniques in production have some. The strongest firm is one which can face problems created by such changes.

As regards cyclical changes, these come and occur due to the existence of trade cycles. During economic depressions demand for every commodity goes down though that may vary from commodity to commodity. It will obviously vary in respect of consumer goods, for which demand can temporarily be postponed and for goods for which are to be used for further productive purposes.

Then come seasonal changes. In come cases demand for some commodities is only seasonal. In such a firm is required to see that only those goods are produced which are either in immediate demand or which can be stored without any deterioration. In order to avoid losses a firm which has a capacity produces a seasonal commodity with another seasonal commodity whose period of maximum consumption corresponds to the minimum period of the first commodity.

Then come erratic fluctuations in the demand. These usually come in the industries which do not manufacture goods on standardised pattern but to individual orders or designs. In such cases sometimes there are considerable risks and in order to avoid them non-standardised goods are manufactured in combination with standardised goods at secondary level, in which not too much of skill is required.

External Economics. External economies which influence optimum size of firm arise due to growth of subsidiary activities, port and shipping facilities. A Beachman in "Economics of Industrial Organisation' has tried to clearly distinguish between internal and external economies by saying, "The main difference between internal and external factors affecting the size of a firm is that the force of the latter varies from firm to firm, whereas the former will effect the size of all firms in the industry or group to approximately the same extent."

There are six important factors which help in determining optimum size of a firm. But all the above factors almost never lead to same optimum output. Therefore, a problem arises as to how to reconcile these factors in order to make decision for investment.

Vertical Disintegration. In order to solve the problem sometimes vertical disintegration is adopted. When in the firm there is only one technical unit which needs to be large, not because all the processes require to be on a large scale, but because one process only needs to be on a large scale, in the words of Robinson, "that process tends to be separated off and performed for the main industry by another subsidiary industry". He further writes that, "Even the Ford works which has long prided itself on its self-sufficiency, has recently adopted the policy of buying many parts from outside specialist firms".

Variations in Size. These variaitons are not because of one reason but many and some of these are:

(a) A variation can arise due to difference in the optimum of the various factors.

(b) Concept of optimum size is not absolute but only relative.

(c) In efficient units need be eliminated and that is done on the basis of perfect competition but in actual practice there cannot be perfect competition. It is imperfect competition which exists and leads to the existence of units of inefficient size by the side of optimum ones.

(d) Degree of integration of an industry and its age also varies.

Conclusion. In this way one finds that the problem of reconciliation of different factors is not easy. The differences and variations are bound to exist and as long as there is no perfect competition, variations cannot be avoided. We know that in actual practice perfect competition is impossible and variations unavoidable. This should be considered at the time of investment decision making.

Risk and Uncertainty. The decision making person should consider the expected income factor cost, extra employment and consumption etc., resulting after the establishment of industry. In this we assume the perfect certainty. But the real world is full of risk and uncertainties. As we cannot estimate and assess about the full life time of a project with perfect discretion. We have to keep in view these uncertainties while evaluating the project. But what is this risk and uncertainty after all? In simple words, risk means those knows damaging effects which can be measured. For example, it is said about the Indian monsoon, that it has a five years cycle. Two years average raining and two years less than average raining, one year more than average raining. In this position we know the alternate consequences.

Element of Uncertainty. Different economists have included the element of uncertainty in the evaluaiton of investment. According to the first method the rate of discount is more where the results of the project are uncertain, so that net present value can be lessened. According to other method, in such project more stress is given on the future cost and less on expected profits. Thus the projects of uncertain results are penalised in comparison to the projects of certain results.

Causes of Low Profatibility

The performance of any private industrial and commercial undertaking can be best judged from the index of its profitability. However, to come to any conclusions about the performance of any public sector undertaking solely on the basis of its profitability would be erroneous and misleading. This is so because whereas a private enterprise has the sole objective of providing adequate return to those who have invested their capital in it, the public sector enterprises have many more objectives such as to create necessary infrastructure for rapid industrial development, to promote redistribution of income and wealth, to promote balanced regional development, to create substantial employment potential, to ensure efficient allocation of productive resources, etc., Thus, the public enterprises, which are financed not from the private sources, but are funded by the Government, have certain degree of social responsibility and are, thus, not purely profit making undertakings.

However, it is now being increasingly felt that even the public enterprises, while discharging their social obligations, must also pay their way, so that their efficiency is not eroded in the guise of fulfilling their social responsibilities. Since the public enterprises are the pillars of economic development, they must generate sufficient surpluses to finance programmes of socio-economic development. It is neither in the interest of these enterprises nor of the society at large, that these industrial and commercial giants should be accumulating losses and thus be a burden on the exchequer and through that on the tax payers. Judged from this criterion of generating adequate surpluses (profits) the performance of public enterprises in India has been rather dismal.

Profitability Profile of Public Enterprises

The public enterprises, even though not to be commercially profit-oriented ventures like the private enterprises, are also expected to give an adequate or reasonable return on investment made on them. The profitability, for evaluating the performance of public enterprises, can be viewed from various angles. Gross margin, which does not take into account the elements of depreciation (the wear and tear cost of the capital asset) and interest (financial cost of the capital), is generally regarded by the economists as a reasonable measure of the return on investment to the national economy. The accountants, on the other hand, lay greater emphasis on the gross profit concept which takes note of depreciation but overlooks the charge on account of interest. The tax collector looks at the profit from his own viewpoint as a source of revenue and hence is more concerned with pre-tax profits. Pre-tax profits assume greater importance as a yardstick for judging the operational efficiency of management since the level of tax rate, at any given point of time is determined by the Government and, therefore, constitutes an extraneous factor beyond the control of the management.

In absolute terms, the gross profits of public enterprises have increased substantially from a low figure of Rs. 1420 crores in 1980-81 to Rs. 11102 crores in 1990-91 and then further to Rs. 30570 crores in 1996-97. However, since these enterprises have mainly financed their investments through borrowing rather than equity participation, the interests paid out by them have been quite large. Consequently, the next pre-tax profits which were almost insignificant amounting to barely Rs. 19 crores in 1980-81 have shown improvement since 1990-91 onwards and have increased from Rs. 3500 crores in that year to Rs. 15400 crores in 1996-97.

If we analyse group/sector-wise figures, we find that only four such industrial, groups viz., petroleum, power, minerals and metals and engineering industries (both light and heavy engineering goods industries) have shown some reasonable profits over the past few years. And of these, the largest share of profits is accounted for by the Oil and Natural Gas Commission. Other important sectors such as steel coal, fertilizers, pharmaceuticals, transport equipment etc., have either shown persistent losses or have only recently started earning some insignificant profits.

The performance of the public sector enterprises as judged from the rate of return on investment, has not been satisfactory. The gross rate of return (gross profits as a percentage of capital investment) has been very low. For example, during 1970-71 the gross rate of return (before tax) was 4.2 per cent. There was some increase in profitability of these enterprises in 1980-81, when the gross rate of return went up to 7.8 per cent. In 1990-91, the gross rate of profit was 10.9 per cent which increased to 15.8 per cent in 1995-96. It marginally dropped to 15.1 per cent in 1996-97.

Net profit (after tax) for these enterprises presents a very dismal picture. For number of years it was negative showing losses to most of these concerns. However, in 1981-82 and 1982-83, these enterprises recorded some net profits, and the rate of return (after tax) has turned positive though still very low at only 2.0 per cent and has varied between 2 and 4 per cent ever since then. The rate of return on investment is thus very disappointing from commercial point of view.

Causes of Low Profitability

First, the location of many of the public sector industries has been determined not by economic and technical factors but by the political pulls and pushes. This has resulted in a higher cost of production.

Secondly, the interference of the political bosses into the affairs of these enterprises, which are superficial autonomous bodies, has led to much of inefficiency.

Thirdly, there is a lack of co-ordination between different departments of the government with which these enterprises have to deal. Red-tapism breeds inefficiency and corruption.

Fourthly, senior positions in the public sector undertakings ore held by government officials who are more armchair bases than shrewd entrepreneurs. Consequently, the industry is bound to suffer.

Fifthly, management in the public sector undertakings has not the same control over its employees as in the private sector. In the private companies, promotions depend upon efficiency and dismissal from service is the result of inefficiency. But in public sector undertakings promotion goes by seniority and no harm can be done to those who do not work.

Sixthly, many of the projects have suffered inordinate delays in their completion due to insufficient planning and faulty implementation. As a result the cost of the projects went up considerably and the actual investment in them was much larger than the investment initially planned for. The benefits from the project were not only realised quite late but was also less than contemplated.

Seventhly, many public sector units run below capacity. For example, most of the public sector steel plants run on around to per cent capacity compared to near 100 per cent capacity utilisation in TISCO. Same is true of heavy electricals, heavy engineering units as well. This naturally means more average fixed cost and the consequently low rate of return.

Eighthly, in public sector generally speaking, accountability is largely missing as no one is specifically held responsible for failure to achieve targets. Even precise targets of production are not laid down and no yardstick for assessing performance is prescribed. It is only recently that a beginning has been made towards assessing performance in the form of Memorandum of Understanding (MoU) under which management undertakes to achieve certain targets for which it is given full autonomy in working.

Ninthly, most of the public sector industrial units are over capitalised in the sense that their fixed investment (in plant and machinery) bears a large proportion to their total investment. This accounts for a high fixed cost per unit of output. Further, since most of such investment is financed through borrowed capital (as against equity capital) a greater part of the earnings of these enterprises goes to meet interest costs.

And finally, the public sector undertakings usually enjoy a monopolistic position. There is no chance for them to access the performance *vis-a-vis* any rival competitors. Hence, they become lethargic and inefficient.

Besides above reasons these overstaffed public enterprises also spend a great deal on welfare of their employees in the form of provision for housing, medical and educational facilities, etc. These also add to cost and hence cause lower returns. But such facilities are also given to their staff by private sector enterprises such as TISCO) yet they make more profits due to their inherent efficiency better management bestowed with initiative and drive. Public sector singularly lacks in these qualities.

But all these defects which have been pointed out above can be removed if the government follows a sound policy. Further, with the gaining of experience, many of the problems would be automatically solved. We hope that very soon the public sector industries will become successful and profitable.

Autonomy Versus Public Accountability

The question of autonomy versus public accountability assumes special significance in context or the public sector enterprises which are owned by the Government and managed either by the Government itself or by any other agency appointed by the Government for their management. Autonomy means independence to take decisions for timely and quick action. Public accountability implies that these enterprises should be responsible to some public authority be it the Department of the Government or the Parliament of the country; and through them to the scrutiny of the public in general.

The need for autonomy arises on account of the fact that the activities of the public enterprises, whether it is production, sale, purchase, inventories, etc. are essentially the business type activities which require quick decisions, timely action and immense initiative on the part of the management. If the management of a public enterprise does not have the powers to take quick decisions, *i.e.* if their decisions are to be approved by the complex bureaucratic machinery, which is inflicted by red-tape and delays, before these could be implemented, these enterprises are bound to suffer vis-a-vis the private sector competitive enterprises which are more business-like and autonomous. Thus, autonomy is the essence of success at the Government department or even the Parliament cannot take quick and timely decisions. It is therefore necessary that the process decision-making and responsibility must be vested in the Board of Management of Public Enterprises.

The need for public accountability of the public enterprises, on the other hand, arises from the peculiar nature of their ownership and management. The profits or losses of public enterprises accrue to the Government who have invested public funds in them. The management of these enterprises is in the hands of persons who have hardly any stake in them, since they are paid Government or semi-Government servants or bureaucrats, who have nothing much to do with the profits or losses of these enterprises and whose appointment to the Board of Management as well as promotions largely depends upon their seniority or political push and pulls rather than on their efficiency and skill. Thus, absence of any personal involvement in the business of enterprises may lead to inefficient handling, incompetent management and perpetual losses to the exchequer. It is therefore necessary that the managers of public enterprises should be made accountable to the public authorities who could closely scrutinise their work and policies and take suitable action in the interest of efficient functioning of these enterprises. Further, public accountability is also necessary so that these enterprises move in line with the planned programme of economic development and fulfil their social obligations. Too much autonomy without accountability may lead to endangering the very objectives for the attainment of which public enterprises have been set up.

Thus, to be efficient, public enterprises must be given autonomy, but too much autonomy without public accountability may lead to many distortions and inefficiencies. On the other hand, complete or too much of public accountability, which may manifest itself in excessive interference by the Government and complete control of decision-making is unhealthy for the growth and efficient working of public enterprises. Hence, a reasonable balance has to be struck between autonomy and public accountability. This can be best done through a clear division of functions between the Government which is the owner of the public enterprises and the Board of Management which is responsible for the efficient running of these enterprises. The Government should concern itself mainly with laying down the policy guidelines, taking or approving major investment decisions, appointment top level management personnel, appraisal of working of the enterprises and issuing of necessary directions in accordance with the overall policies and programmes that it seeks to implement. Within these parameters, the management of the enterprises should be given a free hand in carrying the out day-to-day administration and in the matters regarding production, management, purchase and stores policy, marketing and sales and other activities allied to their business.

Lately, there is some move towards privatisation of some public enterprises with a view to improve their efficiency and reducing burden on the exchequer due to their perpetual losses. The New Industrial Policy of July 1991 gives these enterprises only a promotional role as against the earlier policy wherein public enterprises were regarded as agents of development. The move towards privatisation of public enterprises has gathered support because in spite of its best efforts the Government has not been able to make these enterprises efficient and viable units of industrial growth.

POLICY OF PROFIT

Public enterprises, as already pointed out are, those enterprises which are set up by the state for the welfare of people. Sometimes, these are set up to fill gaps which are created by the the private enterprises for one reason or the other, usually with profit motive. Sometimes these enterprises are set up because the state feels that it should not entirely depend on the private enterprise and must regulate its behaviour. Sometimes these enterprises are set up because the capital costs are heavy and a private enterprise is not in a position to invest in that. There can be also another reason namely that public enterprise can have better facilities, as compared with the private one, and as such the state may be tempted to start an enterprise, which private enterpriser may decline. But a basic problem which has been raised is whether a private enterprise should not earn profits. Should it run on profit and loss basis or the basis of 'No Profit, No Loss.' Similarly the problem is, if it is to earn profits then to which extent and if not why not.

1. Welfare of the People. Those who argue that public enterprises may earn profit argue that the profit. will be used for welfare of the public. The public will be benefited either by 1 of reduction in cost or by depositing amount in the public funds. In both the cases it is desirable that the public enterprises should earn profit.

2. Expansion Becomes Possible. In case it is desired that public enterprise should expand, it is most desirable that it should try to become self-generating and self-supporting. It should not always depend on the government both for maintenance as well as expansion. It can do so only when it is earning profit. Even if it is running on 'No Profit, No Loss Basis' it cannot think of expansion.

3. Suited to Poor Countries. In poor countries national economy is also under heavy strains. The government is required to deal with many priority programmes and each programme in its own turn is a pressing and immediate. In case each enterprise begins to depend on the government, then financial difficulties for the state will increase many fold. It is, therefore, essential that the enterprises should be run on profit and loss basis, so that each enterprise becomes self-supporting and gradually becomes in a position to set up subsidiary undertakings.

4. Relief in Taxation. In public enterprises begin to run on profits, then the tax payer will get some tax relief. In case it is not earning profits, then the tax payer will be required to pay for maintenance and expansion. The amount saved can be used for other purposes and to that extent also the tax payer will be saved and less burdened.

5 Encouragement in Nationalisation. There is a general feeling that as far as possible industries and enterprises should be nationalised, so that the consumer is saved from exploitation. But if the public enterprises begin to fun in loss or just maintain themselves, then tax payer will grumble and the whole process of nationalisation will receive a serious setback. For the promotion nationalisation it is essential that the public enterprises should be run on 'Profit and Loss' basis.

6. Essential for Labour Welfare. Usually there is a charge against the private sector that it squeezes the blood of the workers. It is expected of public sector enterprise that it will steps for labour welfare. But facilities can only be provided when adequate funds are available. For providing better facilities introducing welfare schemes it is essential that the enterprise should show positive gains.

7. Expansion of Employment Opportunities. Public enterprises provide employment opportunities. If these are earning profits and expanding, then these shall be in a position to absorb more and more people. In case these run into losses, then there will be a widespread demand that there should be retrenchment and shrinking. Therefore it is profit alone which can help in providing employment opportunities to the workers and can prove socially useful and advantageous.

8. Indication of Efficiency. In an enterprise, profit is a safe yard stick of measuring efficiency both of the managerial staff and also that of the workers and their sense of involvement in the work.

In case the enterprise is incurring losses, it can be presumed that the managerial staff is inefficient and has not been in a position to win the co-operation of the lower staff or the enterprise is not giving production to its capacity or that the workers have no sense of involvement. This can also lead to the conclusion that there is some drainage on the resources of enterprise, which are either being misused or used for personal interests and so on. Profits can thus be used as a measuring yard stick of the efficiency of a public enterprise.

9. Provision of Social Securities. Every public enterprise by law is required to provide certain social securities. These include age pension, disability pension, provident fund benefits, medical benefits to the employees and also the members of their families. Though old age pension and provident contributions etc. are deferred payments, yet ultimately the enterprise is to pay amounts to the workers.

Case Against Earning Profits

We have already said that there is a section of the society which strongly feels that public enterprises should not at all earn profits. At the most these should be run on 'No profit, No Loss Basis'. They have their own lines of arguments. Some of the arguments which can be advanced in this regard are all under:

(a) **No Real Relief to Tax payers.** One of the arguments which is advanced in favour of profit earning of private enterprises is that it will provide relief to the tax payer. But in actual practice it does not so happen. What happens is that when the enterprise is in profit, the workers begin to put forth demands for additional wages and other facilities. Since the enterprise is in a position to pay the demands are accepted without much inconvenience.

(b) **Continuance of Exploitation.** Public enterprises are set up so that the consumers are saved from exploitation of the private enterprises. If these enterprises also begin to earn profit and exploit the workers, then the exploitation of the workers will continue as it was. Simply hitherto he was being exploited by the private enterprise and now he will be victim of exploitation of public enterprise. Thus no profit can be justified in so far as exploitation is concerned.

(c) **Defeat of the Purpose.** Basic purpose of setting up public enterprises is that gaps which are created by private sector enterprises should be filled. With the private sector these gaps remain unfilled up simply because either there is no profit or the margin of profit is so low that a private enterpriser does not feel tempted to invest. In case public enterprise is also guided by profit motives, then the basic idea and purpose of setting up a private enterprise will be defeated.

(d) **Slow Development of Industries.** In case public enterprises run on 'profit and loss' basis, then these will also be guided by profit motives. Like private sector enterprise these sectors will also produce only few commodities in limited quantity which can give them better results. In many cases there are certain subsidiary industries which are dependent on the material produced in a public enterprise. In case in a bid to earn profits, public sector enterprises restrict supply of some material, then subsidiary industries will receive a serious setback. This attitude and policy will very much retard economic progress of the country.

(e) **Power to Discriminate.** In public enterprises monopoly situation prevails and in that situation it is possible to discriminate. When profit is the motive, then discrimination becomes guiding force and factor, which no society can afford.

Whether public sector enterprises should or should not be guided by profit motives is of course a controversial issue, but the fact remains that every society will like that there should be no losses, so that the society is not forced to bear for the inefficiency of the workers, or the managerial staff, which is loaded with the responsibility of running the enterprise.

PROFIT MAXIMISATION IN INDUSTRY

Every nation has both large scale and small scale industries. These industries are run both under private and public sectors. In both these sectors, it is usually believed that profit maximization is the basic motive and idea, more particularly, the industries which are set up in the private sector. Some of the economists have, however, disputed this well established view and according to them it is not the maximization of profit, but that of satisfaction, which the industrialist will like to have. This has raised a controversy.

Prof. Ruths Child's View. It is good to start, according to him with the presumption that the desire to earn and have maximum profits is always there and also that the businessmen strive hard to earn maximum profits. But in spite of this desire, no businessman is prepared to openly come out with a statement that he wants to earn maximum profit or squeeze blood of the customers to the extent possible. According to Ruths Child businessman wishes to have maximumisation of profit at a particular time or for a particular period of time. Instead it will always be his endeavour and desire that there should be steady flow of profits for longtime. In his own words, "Profit maximization has uptil now served as a wonderful master key that opened all the doors leading to an understanding of the enterpreneur's behaviour's .... But there is another motive which cannot be so slightly dismissed and which is probably similar order of magnitude as the desire for maximum profits. The desire for secure profits."

Prof. Watson's Views. Prof. Watson is of the view that let us presume that a firm does not wish to have maximum profits, but only satisfactory profit. A question therefore arises, as to what is satisfactory profit. The term satisfactory as we know has neither definite nor rigid meaning. For one firm it may mean in flow of capital from outside, while for the other it may mean provision and scope for normal expansion, while for another firm which is under serious competition, a little profit may be satisfactory.

Prof. Baumal's Views. Prof. Baumal has come up with the idea that it is not the maximisation of profit, but only maximisation of sales, which is the aim of a good firm. In his own words, "The firm tries to promote sales not merely as a means to further its other objectives, namely operational efficiency and profit, but for a businessman sales have become an end in themselves". Not only this. but any good businessman will like to have more sales output and will be satisfied as long as there is reasonable return on the investment. To quote him again, "So long as profits are high enough to keep shareholders satisfied and contribute adequately to the financing of company's growth, the management will lend its efforts to the augmentation of sales revenues rather than to further increase in profits.

Scitovskys' Views. Economists like Scitovsky have given the idea of utility maximization as the aim of enterpreneur. According to him the profits will be limited in case the industry only wants to earn profit and if the profits and not linked with leisure. He therefore wants that the profit should be linked with leisure and as such the aim of the business should not be profit maximisation. In his view Scitovsky has been supported by Prof. Higgines, who also does not believe in the idea that profit maximisation as the aim of every entrepreneur. According to him an entrepreneur is very much guided by the sense of satisfaction, rather than that of the profit. It fact, according to him when there is imperfect competition, there cannot be a successful conception or profit maximisation. He is of the view that desires for non-profit maximisation can be those which lead an enterprises to produce at point below the profit maximising output *e.g.*, choice of some leisure.

Full Cost Principle. Hall and Hitch, on the basis of a study conducted by them, have come to the conclusion that by and large the enterpriser is not interested in he maximisation of his profits. According to their study an enterprisr will be satisfied as long as he gets the prices which cover his average cost, including his normal profits. This principle is also known as Full Cost Principle. the study has also brought them to the conclusion that no entrepreneur is interested in getting abnormal profits becuase, if abnormal prices are charged, then the rival firm may get in the market and throw the existing enterpriser out of the market.

In this way we find that usually a wrong notion is held that an enterprises is interested in earning abnormal profits. He wants to have profits, but at the same time there are many other considerations which weigh with him and those are usually so heavy that profit earning motive is subordinated to them.

Role, Rationale and Objectives of Public Sector in India

Public sector in the Indian economy has registered a phenomenal growth since Independence. The number of public enterprises under the Central Government was only 5 at the beginning of First Five-Year Plan in 1951. Not much of industrial development took place during the first Plan. The expansion of public sector started from the Second Plan (1956) onwards. Rapid expansion of public sector undertakings under the Central Government stood at 236 with an investment of Rs. 202000 crores.

Public sector has to play an important role in India. It is through the expansion of public sector that the state can assume commanding heights of the economy and give practical shape to its socio-economic policies designed at economic development with social justice. Public sector is important due to the following reasons :

1. Accelerated Economic Growth. To ensure a high rate of economic growth it is necessary that the state must actively participate in the programmes of economic development. The direct investment by the government in new industrial undertakings would lead to a rapid pace of industrialisation. Therefore, the government has stepped up the rate of investment in the economy and consequently much expansion is witnessed in the public sector enterprises.

2. Socialist Pattern of Society. Achieving a socialist pattern of society has been accepted as the ultimate object of economic policy in India. The attainment of this objective involves the setting up of more and more industries in the public sector. The sphere of private industry must contract and that of the government enterprises must expand if the State has to exercise a greater control over the economic activity in the country.

3. More Equitable Distribution of Economic Power. The expansion public sector was also thought to be desirable because it ensures a more equitable distribution of economic power. If industry is left entirely in the private hands, it leads to monopolistic tendencies which are against the interests of the masses. Therefore, to avoid exploitation by the capitalists, the economic power must not be allowed to concentrate in a few hands. The public enterprises, either by replacing or by offering competition to the private industries, can serve the best interests of the consumers.

4. Balanced Regional Growth. The expansion of public sector Industries is also necessary to ensure a balanced regional growth. While industries concentrate in certain parts of the country the others parts may remain backward in this field because of a number of economic and non-economic factors. Therefore, the state must start new industries in those regions which have so far remained neglected.

5. Foreign Aid. One of the reasons for the expansion of the public sector industries is the aid for industrial development given to the government by the foreign countries. The Socialist countries give aid to the public sector industries only, while other countries also think it feasible to deal with the government rather than with the individual entrepreneurs. Therefore, many of the public sector industries have come up because of the foreign aid to such industries.

6. Nature of Investment. Public sector industries have been considerably expanded because some of these industries are such that they can be started only by the government. For example, major irrigation projects, steel, plants or heavy industries require a huge investment which may be beyond the capacity of the private people. Further, such investment does not give quick returns while the private people want to maximise profits within the shortest possible period of time.

7. Ploughing Back of Resources. Expansion of public sector industries may also be partly attributed to the ploughing bock of the profits by such industries. While, in the private sector, most of the profits are distributed by way of higher dividends, in the public sector industries they are invested for further expansion. However, in India, only a few public sector industries have shown any significant amount of profits. Many of them are actually running at a loss. Therefore, ploughing back of profits does not constitute any major factor responsible for the expansion of public sector.

The public sector has thus been designed to play a significant role in India's socio-economic development. It is through the public sector that the government can help, promote, guide and control the economy to attain its social and economic goals.

Objectives of Public Enterprises

The public enterprises comprise all those industrial and commercial undertakings whose ownership belongs to the government and whose management is done either by the government itself or by any other agency appointed by the government for this purpose. All the industrial and commercial undertakings established and run by Central Government, the State Governments and by the Municipal Committees or Corporation come under the category of the Public Enterprises.

Public ownership and management of industries is not something unknown to India. Even before Independence, railways, post and telegraph, broadcasting and irrigation works were owned and managed by the government. But, barring a few exceptions, the government generally followed a policy of non-interference in economic matters. However, after independence, the government had to assume direct control of a large number of industrial and commercial enterprises for accelerating the rate of economic growth and for achieving the object of setting up a socialist pattern of society. It was realised that to lay down a healthy industrial foundation in the country, the government must play an active part in its Industrial development.

The major objectives of public enterprises could be summarised as follows:

(i) to help in the rapid economic growth and industrialisation of the country and create the necessary infrastructure for economic development;

(ii) to earn return on investment and thus generate resources for development;

(iii) to promote balanced regional development;

(iv) to assist the development of small-scale and ancillary industries;

(v) to promote redistribution of income and wealth;

(vi) to create employment opportunities; and

(vii) to promote import substitution, save and earn foreign exchange for the economy.

Organisation and Management

From the point of view of management, the public sector undertakings in India can be classified into three categories.

(1) Departmental Undertakings. The departmental undertakings include those enterprises whose management is done by a department of the government itself. The minister incharge of that department is the chief executive of these enterprises. The budget of these undertakings is discussed and passed by the Parliament of India and all their revenue receipts are deposited with the government treasury. The Indian Railways, the Chittaranjan Locomotive Works, etc. are the examples of departmental undertakings in India.

(2) Public Corporations. The Public Corporations are established by special Acts of Parliament to run the corporate form of public undertakings. These corporations are those organisations of public enterprises whose ownership belong to the Government but whose management is given in the hands of a Board appointed by the government under an Act of the Parliament. Even though these corporations are fully accountable to Parliament, the government however does not much interfere in their day-to-day working, as is the case with the departmental undertakings. Indian Airlines Corporation, Life Insurance Corporation and the Industrial Finance Corporation of India are some of the examples of public corporations.

(3) Joint Stock Companies. One of the important forms of public sector undertakings in India is the Joint Stock Companies. These companies are established under the Indian Companies Act and are organised like any other private sector companies wherein the individuals or the business houses contribute to the stock of capital and have a share in profits and management. However, in the case of Public Sector Joint Stock Companies, the entire stock of the company may be contributed by the government and consequently, all the Directors are appointed by the government. This represents the full ownership and complete control of government and are thus, known as fully owned government companies. Sometimes, the government may subscribe only to a major share of the company's capital (by purchasing not less than 51 per cent of the company's share capital) and thus gain the control of the company's working, while the private individuals contribute the remaining part capital of the company. This type of company is known as a company of mixed ownership. The main advantage of this form of undertaking is that here the government can gain a major share in the control and management of the company, and can also avail of the private domestic capital, foreign capital and foreign expertise in the field of industry.

Difficulties in the Management of Public Enterprises

The management of public enterprises in India has posed a number of problems. In most of the cases such establishments have been running Inefficiently. Very often the have been incurring heavy losses. The inefficiency in the management of public enterprises can be attributed to the following reasons.

(a) The persons incharge of public enterprises are the civil servants who do not have the experience of running commercial establishments. More often they follow a timid policy and are under the constant fear of being censured by the superiors and the political bosses.

(b) The civil servants in charge of the public enterprises have no incentive to work hard because their promotion depends upon their seniority and not on their work. Further, the sense of security in the public service makes them all the more lethargic.

(c) The private sector enterprises attract the best of the talent by offering salaries which are many times higher than those offered by the government. There is a general dearth of management personnel in the public sector industries.

(d) Red-Tapism and delay is a most common evil of public enterprises because the managers of such establishments are subject to a number of checks and controls from their superiors. Much of the time is lost in the movement of files. No on-the-spot decision can be made. This naturally results in inefficiency.

(e) A constant interference by the politicians into the affairs of public enterprises poses a big obstacle in their efficiency.

OLIGOPOLIES

Oligopoly refers to a market situation with a few (but more than two) sellers. Under oligopoly, the industry is dominated by a few firms who are producing an identical product or producing close substitutes but not perfect substitutes. Oligopoly has been variously called as limited competition, incomplete monopoly or multiple monopoly etc. But these days the term oligopoly is used popularly to refer competition among the few. An oligopoly situation may emerge in any industry when.

(a) Economies of scale or advantages of large scale production exit as a result, a few firms are able to supply all or much of the total industry output (steel industry, automobiles, cement, petroleum industries in India are good examples).

(b) Superior entrepreneurs reduce the large number of firms into a few, through mergers and holding companies.

(c) The exclusive ownership of patents and other rights by a few firms or exploitation of the advantages of product differentiation creates oligopoly market.

(d) The controlling power of a few firms over the available national resources reduces competition only to a few firms.

(e) The need for heavy investment of capital in some industries prevents the entry of larger number of firms.

Generally in an oligopoly market, there are a few well established firms with products well-known in the market. It might be really different for a new entrant to popularise its new product against the already established product.

Classification of Oligopolies

Oligopolies have been classified into various types:

(a) On the basis of competitors into the industry oligopoly may be closed or open one. Open oligopoly permits free and easy entry of new firms while closed oligopoly does not allow entry of new firms and the industry is closely controlled by a few well entrenched firms.

(b) On the basis of the nature of the product produced and marketed oligopolies are distinguished between pure and differentiated. Pure oligopoly refers to the situation where all the rival firms are producing an indentical or homogeneous product, while differentiated oligopoly refers to market situation in which each rival is producing a different variety of a product. Petroleum industry is an example of the former and the soap industry is an example of the latter.

(c) Partial and Full Oligopoly. Depending upon the dominance by a few or a large number of firms.

(d) Collusive and Non-collusive Oligopolies. Depending upon whether the competing firms are combining through some agreement or collusion between them or not.

(e) Organised and Unorganised Oligopolies. On the basis of whether they work on the basis of some agreement on prices, output quotas, sharing of the markets etc.

Features of Oligopoly

The following prominent features of oligopoly will enable us to distinguish oligopoly easily from other market situations such as perfect, competitions, monopoly etc.

(i) First, every firm under oligopoly has to be conscious of the reactions of the rivals. After all there are only a few firms and what one firm does will definitely influence the others.

As the number of firms is few, any change in output produced by one firm will have a direct effect on the other who naturally, retaliate by changing their own prices, output, products etc. Each firm will have to estimate, as best as it can, the nature of its rival's reactions to its product, price and output policies. This is not so under perfect competition and monopoly.

(ii) Secondly, the oligopoly is characterised by indeterminateness. A firm does not know for certain whether its decisions regarding price and output will affect its competitors favourably or adversely. It does not know whether its competitors will approve or disapprove of its decisions and in what way, their reactions will be known. Hence the oligopoly firm's demand curve for the product is clearly indeterminate since the traditional assumption of "other things being equal" does not apply here.

(iii) Oligopoly firms may show Conflicting attitudes to one another. On the one side, they may appear to realise the disadvantage of competition and rivalry and may work out some policy of collusion or they may continuously come in conflict with one another as each is interested in maximising its share of profits. One result of this conflict is the uncertainty in the minds of sellers.

(iv) Oligopoly firms resort to various aggressive or defensive marketing methods to increase their share of the market or to prevent a decline in their share of market. They resort to extensive advertisement and sales promotion. In fact there is competitive advertisement and sales promotion between them. Aggressive sales promotion by some provokes others to do the same.

(v) An oligopoly seller has some monopoly power over the product it produces (brand, name patent etc.) but it does not acquire monopoly control of the market. This is the basic difference between oligopoly and monopoly. At the same time, oligopoly restricts competition, as there are only a few sellers, under perfect competition, the number of Sellers is too many. Besides, the oligopoly producer has to be fully conscious of the reactions of his rivals. But the firm under perfect competition receives the price from the market and does not bother what the rivals think or act.

PRICE DETERMINATION UNDER OLIGOPOLY

Generally, models of oligopoly and duopoly are based on the usual assumption of profit maximisation. In practice, however, oligopoly firms may have difficulties in attaining maximum profits. It may be remembered that maximum profit is related to the concepts of demand and cost. But under oligopoly conditions, firms lack information about the market prices and costs. Further an oligopoly firm may have consideration such as not disturbing the market conditions through constant adjustment of price and output with the idea of maximising profits or invite government interference and regulation of potential competition. Finally, the oligopoly itself may place certain restraints on firms maximising profits. These restraints may be considerations of safety; desire for stable profits and the conservative policy of large corporation which follow the principle of "live and let live".

There is no system of pricing in an oligopoly market. We have already referred to indeterminancy of oligopoly, demand and the uncertainty about the reaction patterns of rivals. Naturally, it is not easy to analyses the price system under oligopoly. Economists distinguish between these different kinds of pricing under oligopoly viz., independent pricing, pricing under collusion, and pricing under price leadership. These are in addition to the duopoly models we have already discussed and which are used to explain oligopoly pricing.

Kinds of Pricing Under Oligopoly

1. Independent Pricing. Every firm under oligopoly may estimate the reaction and calculations of its rivals and then fix its own price and output. On the one extreme, each firm may fix a price—a monopoly price-assuming its product to be completely different from the products of all its rivals. On the other hand, if all firms are producing more or less identical products, they will fix a common or identical price for the product. In practice, however, this may not be so, as firms produce different varieties of product, have different costs of production and enjoy different shares of the market. Independent pricing, under these conditions, will lead to price wars between rivals; the ultimate result may be either price instability and continuous price wars or price stability when a satisfactory price has been found. There is bound to be antagonism, uncertainty and insecurity among the rivals and therefore, a constant tendency to come together. But in general, belief among economists is that independent pricing cannot last long and it is bound to lead to either price leadership by the leading firm or some type of collusion between the rival firms.

Generally business firms follow the "cost plus pricing." system of fixing the selling price of products. For instance, a firm may calculate its average cost of production and then add say 20 or 30 per cent when a firm produces multiple products, it may calculate only the AVC and add say 50 or 60 per cent to take care of overhead costs (AFC) and profits.

2. Pricing under Collusion. Collusion implies "to pay together." When competing firms cooperate in pricing they are said to collude. Collusion may be of various types. Open or explicit collusion is generally sanctioned by the government or tacit or implicit collusion is normally secret. Collusion may be based on agreements either oral or written. Collusion may be based on written agreements between rival producers on prices, output, divisions of sales territories etc. and creates what is known as cartels.

The cartel agreement may estimate the price to be fixed, the quantity to be produced, the allocation of markets and the sharing of markets. In case there are too many units in the industry, cartel agreement may specify the closing down of inefficient plants temporarily or permanently. In precise perfect cartel may not be practicable because.

(a) It is possible that some of the firms in the industry may not join the cartel organization.

(b) Even if all the firms are members of the cartel agreement it is possible that new rivals may not become a party to such an agreement.

(c) The distribution of profits among members may be source of dissatisfaction and may result in the dissolution of the cartel.

(d) The collusive price may be secretly under-cut by members through special concessions, discounts and rebates.

Thus perfect collusion may not be possible in practice. Instead some form of imperfect collusion between rival oligopoly firms may be agreed upon.

□

5

Small Scale and Cottage Industries

The basis of distinction between the large-scale, medium-scale and small-scalle industries is generally the size, capital resources and labour force of the the individual unit. The differences between the small-scale and cottage industries are basically two: *(i)* while small-scale industries are mainly located in urban centres as separate establishment, the cottage industries are generally associated with agriculture and provide subsidiary employment in urual areas; and *(ii)* while small-scale industries produce goods with partially or wholly mechanised equipment employing outside labour, the cottage industries involve operations mostly by hand which are carried on primarily with the help of the members of the family. The basis for this distinction between the small-scale and cottage industries was laid down by the Fiscal Commission in 1950 when it stated that. "A cottage industry is thus one which is carried on wholly or primarily with the help of members of the family either as a whole or a part-time occupation. A small-scale industry, on the other hand, is one which is operated mainly with the hired labour, usually 10 to 50 hands".

Probably it was this definition that prompted the industries (Developoment and Regulation) Act, 1951, to exempt units employing less than 50 workers with power, and less than 100 workers without power, from registration. This exempted sector came to be known as the small scale sector.

Another criterion for differentiating small-scale and village industries from the large-scale industries has also been adopted. This relates to the 'fixed capital investment in a unit'. Prior to 1975, the village and small indutries sector covered undertakings having investment in fixed assets in plant and machinery not exceeding Rs. 7.5 lakhs and in the case of ancillary units Rs. 10 lakhs. This limit has continuously been raised upwards. In 1975 it was raised to Rs. 10 lakhs for small scale units and Rs. 15 lakhs for ancillary units. In 1980 these limits were raised to Rs. 20 Lakhs and Rs. 25 lakhs respectively; and in 1985 to Rs. 35 lakhs and Rs. 45 lakhs respectivcly. The investment limit was raised further to Rs. 60 lakhs for small-scale units and Rs. 75 lakhs for ancillary units in April 1991. In Addition, a tiny sector has also been defined. This includes units having investment limit of less than Rs. 5 Lakhs (prior to August 1991 the limit was Rs. 2 lakhs.)

Industrial units included under the 'small-scale and village industries' by virtue of fulfilling the above capital investment requirement are a 'hybrid' of units of various type ranging from the age-old household industries to modern mechanised small-scale units. Broadly speaking, we can divide them into the following two categories: *(i)* traditional industries based on traditional skills and techniques, and *(ii)* modern small-scale industries making use of modern technology as well as artisans' workshops engaged in activities such as repairing of various implements, machinery, vehicles etc. The traditional industries can be further subdivided into two categories—*(i)* handicrafts producing highly sellective goods of high-skill workmanship (wood and ivory carving, carpet making, metal works, etc.) and *(ii)* village and household industries producing comman consumer goods and other utilitarian products predominantly by hand or using simple tools (pottery, leather products, handwoven taxtiles, silk materials etc.)

Growth of Small Scale Industries

The result of the second All-India Census of registered small-scale units conducted by the Small Industries Development Organisation (SIDO) in 1987-88 were published in August 1992. Using the Data presented in this Census and the data presented in the first Census (conducted for the year 1972 and published in 1977), one can from some idea regarding the growth and structural change in modern small industry over the 15-year period, 1972 to 1987-88.

There has been a substantial growth of small-scale units over the 15-years period, 1972 to 1987-88. As shown in column (4) the number of units in the frame of the census reports increased by 282 per cent. Investment in fixed assets rose by 267 per cent, production by 420 per cent and net value added by 284 per cent (1972-73 prices), and employment by 122 per cent.

Productivity of capital and labour also increased in varying measures between 1972 and 1987-88. For instance, the ratio of net value added to fixed assets increased from 1.06 to 1.10 or by 38 per cent, and net value added per person employed from Rs. 5.09 thousand to Rs. 8.81 thousand or by 73 per cent. However, captial inensity also rose considerably from Rs. 48.19 thousand to Rs. 79.83 thousand or by two-third. In other words, "a lakh of rupees investment in field assets which employed 21 person in 1972 employed only 13 person in 1987-88, showing a decline of 40 per cent."

According to the Economic Survey, 1995-96, the number of small-scale units stood at 25.71 in 1994-95—indicating increase of 7.8 per cent over the previous year. The value of output of the SSI sector in 1994-95, at current prices is estimated at Rs. 2,93,990 crores—about 21.7 per cent higher than the output in 1993-94. However, adjusted for inflation, the real growth of output of the sector in 1994-95 was 10.1 per cent. Estimated employment in the SSI sector rose from 139.38 lakh in 1993-94 to 146.56 lakh in 1994-95, an increase of 5.2 per cent.

The Role of Cottage and Small-Scale Industries in Indian Economy

The important role being played by the small-scale sector in Indian economy would be clear from the fact this sector presently accounts for around 40 per cent of he gross turnover in the manufacturing sector, 6.9 per cent of the net domestic product and 34 per cent of the country's exports. The Second Plan emphasized the role of small scale and village industries on the following five grounds : *(1)* generation of employment opportunities; *(2)* an equitable distribution of national income; *(3)* mobilisation of capital; *(4)* mobilisation of entrepreneurial skills; and *(5)* regional dispersal of industries. Let us now discuss these arguments in favour of small-scale and village industries in some details.

1. Employment Generation. After agriculture, small-scale and cottage industries provide employment to the largest number of people. Given the acute unemployment problem in India with backlog of unemployment estimated at around 17 million in 1992, creation of employment opportunities will depend crucially on the development of small-scale and cottage industries. This would be clear from the fact that while employment in the factory sector as a whole (large scale, medium scale and small scale) increased by only 2.21 per cent per annum over the period 1972 to 1987-88, employment in small-scale sector grew at the rate of 5.45 per cent per annum. Thus small-scale sector was able to generate employment opportunities for about 2 million people over the period 1972 to 1987-88. As far as future prospects are concerned, the rural non-farm sector accounting for about 22 per cent of rural employment can play a crucial role in the further expansion of employment opportunities in the rural areas. An important constituent of this sector is the manufacturing activity consisting mainly of textile-based and agro-based products and units producting construction materials. In the urban areas employment potential seems to be the largest in the non-household, tiny sector segment of the manufacturing sector.

2. Efficiency of Small-scale Industries. A controversy has raged in this country over the issue of efficiency in the small-scale industries vis-a-vis large-scale industries. While some studies have pointed out that small-scale industries are more efficient, others point out that large-scale industries are more efficient. Thus no clear-cut answer can be given to the question "which is more efficient—small-scale industry or large-scale industry?' The fact is that the debate has been coloured by the ideological commitments of the participants.

One of the earliest studies on the relative efficiency of small-scale industries in India was undertaken by Dhar and Lydall. They concluded that modern small-scale industry is fairly capital intensive; that is, these units do not generate more employment per units of capital than large-scale industry. Similar findings were reported in the studies of Hajra and Sandesara. Hajra used the Census of Manufacturing Industries (CMI) data for 17 industries for 1955 and 1958 and reached the following two conclusions: *(i)* both labour and capital productivity are low in small-scale industries, and *(ii)* the ratio of material cost to value added is high in small-scale industries (suggesting, thereby, inefficient use of material input). Sandesara used CMI data for 28 industries for the period 1953-58 and reached the conclusion that, for given volume of investment, small-scale units neither generate more employment nor produce more output compared to large-scale units.

In his paper published in 1988, Bishwanath Goldar compares for 37 industries at the three-digit level the technical efficiency of small-scale and large-scale industries for the year 1976-77. He found that the SSIs (compared to the large-scale industries) generally have low labour poductivity, high capial productivity, low capital intensity (measured as capital per employee) and low total factor productivity. He inferred that the modern small-scale sector is inefficient relative to the large sector in a large number of industries. He also found that the relative efficiency of the SSIs varies directly with capital intensity, so that the SSIs cannot be relied upon as a source of efficient employment generation.

The above analysis suggests that large-scale units are more efficient than the small-scale units. However, the evidence that the small-scale industries are relatively more efficient is equally strong. Using data presented in Annual Survey of industries for 1960, 1963, 1964 and 1965, Ramsingh K Asher showed that the small-scale sector is more efficient. After the study the table showed that the small-scale factory combined the largest number of workers with a ruppee's worth of fixed capital; that a rupee worth of fixed assets produced almost seven times an output in small as compared to large industries and that the value added by a rupee worth fixed investment in small factories was at least three times as large as that for a large factory.

Two All India Sample Surveys of small-scale industries conducted by the Reserve Bank of India in 1976-77 and the National Small Industries Corporation (NSIC) in 1979 corroborate the above conclusion. They show that the smaller units use capital more efficiently. Morevoer, the profitability of the small-scale sector is greater than the profitability of the large-scale sector. For instance, the RBI Survey found that profit after tax was 43,72 in the small-scale sector whereas it was 34 90 in the corporate sector. Profit after tax as per cent of net worth was 21.05 for the small-scale sector whereas it was only 7.90 for the corporate sector. According to R.N. Nagaraj, the plausible reasons for the relatively higher profitability in small-scale sector seem to be the lower wage and greater exploitation of labour on the one hand and fiscal concessions on the other.

After all this discussion on the efficiency of the small-scale industries vis-a-vis the large-scale industries what emerges is a totally confusing picture. While some studies show that large-scale industries are more efficient, others show that small-scale industries are more efficient. Therefore we cannot give any firm conclusion. However, what we must add in the end is that factor endownments of a country must not be lost sight of. Since India is a labour surplus economy and since small sector (particularly village and cottage industries and traditional handicrafts) has a high employment potential, the problem of unemployment (and underemployment) can be tackled only when small-scale and cottage industries are promoted on an extensive scale.

3. Equitable distribution of national income. One of the main arguments put forward in support of the small-scale and cottage indutries is that they ensure a more equitable distribution of national income and wealth. This is accomplished because of the following two considerations *(i)* the ownership of small-scale industries is more widespread than the ownership of large-scale industries, and *(ii)* they posses a much larger employment potential as compared to the large industries.

Dhar and Lydall have pointed out that this argument is wrong. According to them, workers in small-scale and village industries are unorganised and cannot fight for their rights. As such, wages paid to them are much less than the wages paid to workers in large industries (for instance, wages in small-scale industries in India are just about half the wages paid in large-scale industries). In all countries including England. USA, West Germany, Japan and India, small industries have failed to achieve the objective of equitable distribution of income and decentralization of economic power.

This argument cannot be defined since is misses point (ii) made above. We must not forget that the small-scale indsutries have a high employment potential and consequently they enable a vast majority of people to share the fruits of economic development. In their absence, the only option before these people would be to remain unemployed or seek still less remunerative jobs.

4. Mobilisation of Capital and Entrepreneurial Skill. The small-scale industries are at a distinct advantage as far as the mobilisation of capital and entrepreneurial skill is concerned. A number of entrepreneurs are spread over small towns and villages of the country. Obviously, large-scale industries cannot utilize them as effectively as the small-scale and village industries distributed over the entire length and breadth of the country. Similarly, large-scale industries cannot mobilise the savings done by people in areas far flung from the urban centres. But this task can be effecively accomplished by setting up a network of small-scale and cottage industries. In addition, a large number of other resources spread over the country can be put to an effective use by the small-scale and cottage industries. The rapid development of small-scale industries in the post-Independence period is a proof that given the neccessary credit, power and technical knowledge a large quantity of latent resources of the economy can be mobilised for purpose of industrial development.

5. Less Industrial Disputes. Supports of small-scale industries frequently argue that large-scale industries are ridden with more industrial disputes than the small-scale industries. Because of the 'tensions' in the relations between workers of large-scale industries and the millowners, such industries frequently face srikes and lockouts.

Against this, the small-scale industries are free from such hazards and there is consequently less loss of output. However, this viewpoint is not totally correct. In capitalistic form of production whether the unit is small or large, the millowner does exploit the workers. This does lead to tensions and conflicts. However, whereas the labourers working in large-scale industries are organised and resort to collective action (in the form of strike), workers in small-scale industries are not organised and have no way of expressing their resentment. Any worker who gives a vocal expression to his resentment is immediately thrown out. Therefore, apparently the relations between the employers and employees in a small-scale unit seem to be harmonious while actually they are not.

6. Contribution to Export. With the establishment of a large number of modern small-scale industries in the post-Independence period, the contribution of the small-scale sector in export earnings has increased by leaps and bounds. What is heartening to observe is that the bulk of the exports of the small-scale industries (in fact, around 93 per cent) consists of such non-traditional items like ready-made garments, sports-goods, finished leather, leather products, woollen garments and knitwear, processed foods, chemical and allied products, and a large number of engineering goods. The total exports of the small-scale industry products increased form Rs. 155 corres during 1971-72 to Rs. 28,000 crores in 1994-95.

GROWTH OF SMALL SCALE INDUSTRIES

Cottage and small scale industries all over the world have survived, becaues in many respects these have an egde over big industries *e.g.*,

1. In large scale industries, there is no personal contact between the employer and the employees. On the other hand here the contact is personal and each one knows every other person quite well and puts his heart and soul in the work for maintaining its quality etc.

2. In small scale and cottage industries there is always a direct touch with the consumer or what were call as customer. If the buyer wants some changes those too can be introduced. On the other hand

in large scale in industries there is no direct contact. Contact can be maintained only with the help of marketing manager, advertising manager etc. In case any changes are needed, these cannot be very quickly introduced, because many complications arise in changing a set pattern.

3. Then another edge is that in small scale and cottage industries there are no over head charges. In large scale industries, these charges are very heavy and at times even strain the industry and reulst in increase in prices for which the society is the sufferer.

4. Then another edge is, that it is always possible to have supervision in the case of former, whereas in the case of later, it is not at all possible, because the number of employees in former case is very low and secondly because employer in the later case is to depend on the intermediary staff. Moreover in small scale industries the producer is always in a position to examine even minute details and there can be no wastage of material. He can check every leakage of material and ensures that every labourer is giving output and supervision that a worker finds it difficult to cheat.

5. Much of time, money and energy in a big industry is wasted in red tapism which is involved in taking a decision. But small scale and cottage industries have an edge in this regard because there is no red tapism involved in it. The decisions are taken immediately and on the spot by the employer and are also immediately implemented.

6.Then comes 'Labour Problem'. In this regard too, small scale and cottage industries have an edge over large scale industries. In large scale industries labour problems are really very serious and result in frequent lock outs strikes, in loss of man hours and also in lowering down of production. But there is no such problem in so. far as small scale and cottage industries are concerned. There are very few labour problems and loss of man hour.

7. Still another edge is that in the case of heavy industries there is top heavy management. But in the case of small and cottage industries there is no such problem. The management is not at all heavy, there are no problems of maintaining an accounts branch for keeping accounts.

8. In the field of non exploitation too small scale and cottage industries have an edge over large scale industries. In the later case there is ruthless exploitation of the workers. The indusrialist pays them some move and rest he keeps with himself as his profit. He goes on setting up new industries and further exploitation starts. But in small scale and cottage industries there is no question of exploitation. The workers are either family members or work as a members of a big family. They are aware of the profit and loss and become equal participants in that.

9. Still another edge is that in cottage and small scale industries producer has dignity of labour. He is not subordinate to any one. The workers work as colleagues. All take initiatives and try to of that of a superior and inferior, improve the quality of goods. All combined together push the sale. But in so far as large scale industries are concerned there is no digntity of labour . The workers come to earn their livelihood. They have no concern with the product, but are concerned only with the wages. Not only this, but each product is to pass through so many stags before becoming marketable, so that no worker can claim that that has been produced by him.

10. Last but not least important point is that in the case of small scale industries decision makers take decisions on the spot and can change trade policies according to changing times, therefore, as compared with large scale industries, there is more adaptability to changes, which obviously is good for the industry as well as the society.

CIRCUMSTANCES WHICH FAVOUR SMALL SCALE OR COTTAGE INDUSTRIES

There are certain situations under which small scale industries can find favourable atmosphere. The first consideration in this regard is the market. It is to be seen as to what type of commodities are demanded in the market. In case the types of good are such that the demand for them is uncertain then, there is no fun in producing the goods in bulk. In large scale industries, bulk production is inevitable, but if goods of fluctuating nature are produced in bulk, then that will be more wastage and even small scale and cottage industries can be most suitable. Then another favouable circumstances can be when the nature of job is such that no division of labour is needed. Still another favourable condition can be when the capital is short and scare and it is not easy to install large scale industries and at the same time the needs of the people are urgent and pressing. Another favourable condition can be when the nature of work is such that it cannot be put to routine and needs care and constant vigilence, on the spot action and so on. This can be the case with agriculture, where the cultivator is to see whether the time for harvesting watering and reaping is appropriate or not and he is to take on the spot and quick decision.,

PROBLEMS OF SMALL SCALE AND COTTAGE INDUSTRIES

The small-scale and cottage industries are palgued by a number of problems which often force these units to close down. The second all-India census of registered small-scale industrial units conducted in 1987-88 (results published in August 1992) showed that of the 9.87 lakh registered units as on March 31, 1988, 3.05 lakh units constituting about 31 per cent of total registered units had closed down. Thus almost one-third of SSI units had closed down. Of these, 1.49 lakh units (*i.e.* one-half) had closed within five years of commencement of operations. Not only this. A large number of small-scale units are sick. As we shall note in the chapter on 'Industrial Sickness, 'about 2.33 lakh small-scale units were sick as at the end of September 1992 (this constituted 99 per cent of the total sick units). Let us now consider the main problems that the small-scale units have to face.

1. Finance and Credit. The scarcity of finance and cradit is the main obstacle in the development of small-scale units. The position of cottage and village industries in this regard is even worse. The capital base of the small industrial units is usually very weak since they generally have partnership or single ownership. The artisans or craftsmen running cottage industries either run their business with whatever littel capital they possess or take credit from the mahajans or the traders who supply raw material to them. In many cases such credit is obtaind on a very high rate of interest and is thus exploitative in character. The small-scale industries are somewhat better placed. However, the profit earned by them is often not enough for investment purposes.

The main institutional sources for small industries are the following ; State directorate of industries, State Financial Coporations, Public Sector Banks and other banks. Ever since the introduction of the social control of banks in 1967, the commercial banks have liberalised their policy of granting credit to small-scale and cottage industries. After the nationalisation of banks in 1969, the situation has improved still further. The change in attitude of banks would be clear from the fact that whereas the amount of credit outstanding (of public sector banks) to small-scale industries stood at only Rs. 251 crores in June 1969 it rose to Rs. 21,440 crores in March 1994.

2. Raw Material Availability. The majority of the small-scale and cottage industries depend on local sources for their raw material requirements. The handloom industry depends for its requirement of cotton on local traders. These traders often supply cotton on the condition that the weavers would sell the cloth only to them when it is ready. Thus the weavers are subjected to double exploitation at the hands of the traders. The traders sell cotton to them at high prices and purchase the ready cloth at low prices.

Earlier the small industries mostly produced items dependent on local raw materials. Hence there was no significant problem in obtaining the necessary raw material. However, ever since the modern small-scale industries have appeared on the industrial horizon manufacturing a lot of sophisticated and new products, the raw material constrant as emerged as a significant constraint on their production efforts. Many small-scale industries used imported raw material. Whenever there was a difficulty in obtaining this raw material either on account of the foreign exchange crisis or some other reason, these industries had to suffer a severe setback.

(3) Under-utilization of Capacity. Data presented in the second-all India Census point to considerable under-utilisation of capacity in the small-scale sector. For instance, in 1987-88, capacity utilisation was only 41 per cent in electrical mechaniery and parts, 58 per cent in leather products, 60 per cent in transport equipment and parts. 30 per cent in miscellaneous manufacturing industries and 32 per cent in metal products. For small-scale units as a whole, capacity utilisation was merely 48 per cent. This shows that half of the capacity of small-scale units is not utilised.

(4) Machines and Other Equipments. Machinery and other equipments in many small industries has grown obsolescent. On account of this reason while their costs of production are high, the quality is inferior as compared to the large-scale units. Moreover, the small-scale units often do not care about the changing tastes and fashions of the people. Accordingly, modernisation and rationalisation are urgently required in small-scale industries.

This task can be accomplished only by a network of technical assistance. Improved technology can help in increasing the productive efficiency of small-scale units and encourage new product lines in respose to the change in attitudes and fashions of the people.

5. Problems of Marketing. One of the main problems faced by the small-scale units is in the field of marketing. These units often do not possess any marketing organization and consequently their products compare unfavourably with the quality of the products of the large-scale industries. Therefore, their suffer form a competitive disavantage vis-a-vis large-scale. Because of the shortage of capital and financial resources, these units do not have adequate 'staying capacity' and are often forced to sell their products at unremunerative prices.

To save small-scale units from competition from large-scale units the government has reserved certain items for the small-scale sctor. The list of reserved items has continuously expanded from 77 to 124 in the Fourth Plan to 500 in 1977 and subsequently to 836. The Trade Development Authority and the State Trading Corporation help the small-scale industries in organising their sales.

6. Other Problems. In addition to the problems enumerated above, the small-scale industries face a number of other problems like inefficient management non-availability of cheap power, unchanging and unresponsive production pattern, burden of local taxes, competition from large-scale industries, ete.

Data given by the second-all India Census of registered small-scale industrial units shows that of the 3.05 lakh units closed down as on March 31, 1988, 1.48 lakh units (*i.e.*, one-half of closed units) were closed because of finance and marketing problems. According to the Seventh Five Year Plan, growth of the small-scale and village industries has been constrained by a number of factors "including technological obsolescence, inadequate and irregular supply of raw materials, lack of organised market channels, imperfect knowlegde of market conditions, unorganised nature of operations, inadequate avalability of credit, constraint of infrastructure facilities including power etc. and deficient managerial and technical skills. There has been lack of effective co-ordination among the various support organisations set up over the period for the promotion and development of these industries. Quality consciousness has not been generated to the desired level despite various measures taken in this regard. Some of the fiscal policies pursued have resulted in unitended splitting up of these capacities into uneconomic operations and have inhabited their smooth transfer to the medium sector.

IMPORTANCE & ROLE OF INDUSTRIES

Cottage and small-scale industries occupy an important place in Indian Economy. These industries are contributing half of the total industrial production in India and provide gainful economic activity to more than five times the number of people employed in the large and medium sized industries in the country. Their contribution to India's export earnings has reached significant proportions during the past few years.

The development of cottage and small-scale industries holds solution to many side problem of Indian economy. The economy reeling under excessive population pressure, on agriculture subject to the vagaries of nature, a people oppressed by massive unemployment and the consequent misery and a nation struggling to stand up and build its economy, has much to gain from the development of cottage and small-scale industries.

Increase in Employment Opportunities : The Employment Argument. Unemployment, both in the rural and urban areas of the country, has assumed alarming proportion and it continues to mount up despite our efforts at creating more and more job opportunities under the plans for economic development. Establishment of cottage and small-scale industries on a very wide scale can contribute a great deal in removing much of this unemployment prevailing in the country at the present time. With the limited amount of capital resources, the small-scale industrial sector holds promise of creating greater employment opportunities. This is so because the cottage and small-scale industries are more labour intensive *i.e.*, they employ more labour per units of capital than the large scale industries.

This argument is not acceptable to many economists. Dhar and Lydall believe that employment should not be created only for the sake of employment. Technically speaking, we need more employment to create more output and therefore any employment which does not result in increased output can not have an economic justification. Thus, employment must be productive *i.e.*, it makes sufficient addition to output. Interpreted in these terms, the employment argument is essentially an output argument which entails that scarce resources must be put to best possible uses so as to result in maximisation of output. In other words, we must establish those enterprises which have a high output capital ratio *i.e.*, which give more output per unit of capital employed or to say the same thing differently, use less capital per unit of output. From their studies, Dhar and Lydall found out that large scale industries produced a large amount of output per unit of capital than the smaller enterprises. This is because the large industrial units, though capital intensive in nature, turn out much larger volume of output by working in two or three shifts each day with the same given amount of capital equipment, machinery and plant.

However, many other economists do not agree with the analysis of Dhar and Lydall. R. Venkataraman from his studies found out that employment generating capacity of the small industries was about eight times higher than the large scale industry sector. Even the output capital ratio (*i.e.*, output per unit of capital employed) was about four time higher in the small industries as compared to large industries. Thus, Venkataraman makes a strong case for small scale industries on the basis of employment argument because both employment and ouput, according to his findings, are higher per unit of capital employed in the small-scale sector.

Economy in the Use of Capital : The Capital Scarcity Argument. India is not as lucky in the matters of capital resources as has been the case of the industrially advanced nations. In fact, acute scarcity of capital has been one of the major causes of our economic and industrial backwardness over the past centuries. Therefore, there is a greater need for judiciously utilising this scarce factor so as to achieve largest possible output and a quicker pace of economic development. Thus, we need to establish those industries which use a small amount of capital per unit of output, or to say, in other words, which generate larger output per unit of capital. The ratio of output to capital (output-capital ratio) should be maximised or the ratio of capital to output (capital-output ratio) should be minimised. It has been generally observed that modern large-scale industry is highly capital intensive or that it uses more of capital per unit of output. On the other hand, the small-scale industry produces a much larger volume of output with a smaller amount of fixed capital equipment.

The argument that the small-scale industries require smaller amount of capital, and in view of the capital scarcity in less developed countries like India, they must be given a high priority in the programme of industrial development, is only a static argument *i.e.*, it does not take into consideration the impact of such industries in the growth rate of capital formation and availability of capital for investment in future. Dahr and Lydall argue that such industries will unfavourably affect the growth rate of captial formation and thus reduce future availability of capital. This is because, those industries being labour intensive, wage bill or labour income will constitute a major share in the total value of output or sales revenue of these industries. Since labour has a very high marginal propensity to consume (MPC) all labour incomes will be use for consumption and so there will not be any significant flow of savings. Capital has a lower income share in the output, and even with low MPC, would no be able to contribute much to the national savings. Thus, overall saving rate would be reduced thereby adversely affecting future rate of growth of investment, output and employment.

This argument would thus make a case for development of large scale rather than small scale industries. The implicit assumption here is that labour would consume all wages while the capitalist would automatically save a larger portion of their income. If however, through proper policy measures, technological upgradation and modernisation programme labour productivity and income are raised in the small scale sector, their savings would also come out of labour incomes and add to the stream of capital formation. It is also not true that capitalists save most of their income and use it for reinvestment. In the modern society, conspicuous luxury consumption is rampant and much of the profit income is used for this purpose. Therefore, a proper policy of encouraging small scale industries would serve the interest of present employment as well as future growth by encouraging saving, investment and capital formation.

A Means to Achieve More Equitable Distribution of national Income: The Equality Argument. The development of cottage and small-scale industries ensures a equitable distribution of income and wealth. The ownership of small and cottage industries is much more diffused and is spread over millions of people, while the large-scale industries are owned by only a few big industrial houses. Thus, while large-scale industries lead to concentration of income and wealth in a few hands, the small-scale industries help a wide dispersal of income and thus ensure a more equitable distribution. Further, since the smaller industries have a much bigger employment potential, they naturally distribute incomes among a much larger labour force, which further assures a better distribution of income in the society. Thus, the development of cottage and small-scale industries, on the one side, helps in reducing the concentration of income, wealth and economic power, on the other hand they ensure that largest number of working people obtain the gains of industrialisation and economic development.

The development and spread of small-scale and cottage industries helps in reducing income inequalities and securing a more just disribution of income in a number of ways. Firstly, the small-scale enterprises employ a large number of workers. Therefore, the wage bill or the share of labour in the output is much higher than that of capitalist incomes. This reduces functional inequalities between the capitalist and the labour incomes. Secondly, the total wage bill is distributed among a very large number of workers. Thus, each worker has a comparatively equal share in the total labour income. This creates greater equality of income among the workers. Thirdly, each worker's income is used for meeting this consumption and other needs of the dependents and family members.

Whereas the objective of income equality may be laudable, it is bound to create problems with regard to growth of income, output and employment in future. Setting up labour intensive small-scale industries would, no doubt, give a greater share of income to labour; but it would also reduce future rate of investment thereby bringing down rate of growth of output and employment. It will therefore result in smaller avenues of employment for workers in future, increase unemployment and social unrest. There would then be greater inequalities between those who get jobs and those who fail to do so. Thus, greater equality now may result in more inequality in future. More jobs today may mean less jobs in times to come.

Using Unutilised Captial and Skill : The Latent Resource Argument. A strong argument in favour of the small small-scale industries is that their establishment would make use of the latent resources which are lying idle. Establishment of village and small scale industries would lead to utilisation of hoarded wealth, family labour, local skills of artisan and craftsman, etc. It would also lead to development and use of native entrepreneurship. These resources and capabilities being spread over the entire country and its far flung areas, can not be made use of by the large-scale industries. But the spread of village and small-scale industries can harness these resources, make them a vehicle of country's socio-economic transformation. In fact, over the past few years the development of such industries have indeed contributed a lot in utilising the rural savings and the skills of craftsmen, artisans and the rual entrepreneurs.

Cottage Industries—A Source of Rural Prosperity: Rural Development Argument. Cottage and village industries can contribute a lot towards rural prosperity and the economic well-being of the village people. Development of such industries can provide part-time occupation to the people engage in agriculture and a whole-time job to the village artisans and craftsmen. It is a known fact that more than seventy-five per cent of India's population lives in villages and nearly seventy per cent of country's work force are directly engaged in agriculture. Now, agriculture being a seasonal occupation, cannot provide full-time employment throughout the year. Besides, excessive pressure of population on agriculture has given rise to the perpetual problems of under-employment and disguised employment. Spread of village industries offers a viable solution to all these problems of rural unemployment, poverty and economic oppression. By creating more job opportunities in non-agricultural activities within the villages, industries can contribute a great deal to relieve the excessive pressure of population on land, thereby paving the way for the mechanisation and modernisation of agriculture. Thus, the development of cottage industries, not only provides additional job opportunities and income to the village people, but also assures improvement in agricultural productivity and enhance village prosperity.

Checks Large-Scale Migration of Population to the Urban Centres. The development of cottage and small-scale industries in the countryside can effectively check the migration of rural population to the already overgrown and congested urban areas. The rural masses steeped in poverty and unemployment due to law productivity in agriculture, are attracted to the urban centres with a view to making better living. However, because of the slow pace of growth, in the industrial and commercial activity in the urban areas, most of them who come here, fail to find out adequate job opportunities and thus only add to the urban unemployment and overcrowding in the cities. The establishment of cottage and small-scale industries in the rural areas will help in providing jobs to the rural unemployed and thus prevent the migration of rural population.

Export Potential. The cottage and small-scale industries contain a huge export potential. As is evident from recent trends, contribution of such industries have increased manifold during the past years, they contribute nearly one-fourth to the total export earnings of the country. With the further development of these industries, this share is bound to go up rapidly in the near future. Hence, to reduce the tremendous strain on our balance of payments, development of cottage and small-scale industries need to be developed faster.

Industrial Decentralisation. Cottage industries will help in achieving the much-needed decentralisation of industries in India. This is very essential from military, social and econmic point of view. There is also the problem of industrially over-congested and depressed areas in the country. There is industrial concentration in a few big cities while the rural areas have so far remained practically shunned off from any industrial activity. Cottage industries can prove to be the most apt insturment for bringing about a balance regional development of the country.

Critics of cottage industries contend that the cost of production in respect of these industries is so high that they can never compete with the large-scale industries. It may, however, be observed in this connection that social cost in respect of cottage industries is comparatively low. Cottage industries do not give rise to evils of large-scale production like labour-capital disputes, over-crowding, immorality, etc. Besides, it is wrong to assume that money costs in cottage industries are necessarily high. The experience of China and Japan bears testimony to the fact that with the use of power and small machinery the money costs can be considerably reduced even in cottage industries.

In view of the above consideration, we may safely assert that cottage industries from the very backbone of economic life in our country. They must, therefore, be given a vital place in any scheme of economic planning.

❒

6

Industrial Finance and Foreign Capital

INDUSTRIAL FINANCE

It is really difficult to depend on any one source for Industrial financing and as such different sources must be tackled. Some of the important sources of financing industries in India being as under:

1. Sale of Shares. Each industry floats shares for financing its programmes. These are offered to the public. The money raised through shares is quite substantial and if the industry has established a credit, it can raise any amount for financing its projects.

2. Voluntary Deposits. When the industries establish their credit worthiness, the individuals, who have surplus money deposit their amounts with the industry. In this way also sufficient amounts are raised.

3. By Borrowing Money on Interest. When the money raised is still needed the industry approaches big financiers or houses to loan them money on interest. This amount is raised only when the industry feels that the investment is sure to have returns. Usually the rate of interest paid is much higher than the bank rate and this attracts the people to loan surplus money to the industry rather than depositing that with the banks.

4. Industrial Financial Corporations and Banks. Government of India has set up many financial corporations such as Industrial Financial Corporation of India, Industrial Credit and Investment Corporation of India, Industrial Credit and Investment Corporation of

India, Industrial Reconstruction Corporation of India and Industrial Development Bank of India. All these agencies and bodies are quite prepared to finance the industries in the country, so that industrial progress of the nation in any way does not retard. These will be discussed in detail separately.

5. Financial Assistance from the Bank. With the nationalisation of banks commercial banks are liberally coming forward to help the industries, both small scale as well as large scale, to finance their projects. These banks are of considerable assistance when the industry is in financial difficulty or when it is facing serious financial crisis.

6. Managing Agency System. Managing agencies also invest capital in the industry with the result that these provide finances for the industries. similarly funds are also raised through debentures as well. But these methods have their own drawbacks with the result that these are not in common use in so far as funding of industries is concerned.

SOURCES OF FINANCE

Capital requirements of the industry on the basis of their use can be divided into two categories, viz., *(a)* fixed capital, and *(b)* working capital.

Fixed capital is used to provide the necessary means of production to the industrial units, like land and buildings, plant and machinery, furniture and fixtures, tools and equipment, etc.

Working capital provides all the expenses that are necessary in order to manufacture and sell the product or service offered. It is either invested in strocks of raw materials, stores and finished products, loose tools and spare parts or is needed for granting credit to customers or for meeting day-to-day administrative and other expenses.

On the basis of time, the capital requirements of industry are classified into:

(a) short-term capital, *(b)* medium-term capital, and *(c)* long-term capital.

Short-term capital is required for a period ranging up to one year; medium- term capital is required for a period ranging from one to five years; and long-term capital is required for a period exceeding five years.

Sources of Industrial Finance. Industrial units raise finance to meet their capital requirements from different sources, the important among these are as follows:

1. Shares and Debentures. A company's owned capital is split into a large number of equal parts, each part being called a share. The company invites members of the public to buy as many shares as they like. (Note: Now, no restrictions have been imposed on the quantum of shares being purchased by the Non-Resident Indians). The share capital of a company is ideal for meeting the long-term requirements.

A debenture is an acknowledgement under seal of debt or loan. Uniform parts of loan are called debentures. Debentures carry a fixed rate of interest to the holders and used to finance long and medium-term requirements of the industry.

2. Public Deposits. The system of public deposits has been the only source of working capital for some industries in some regions of the country in the past.

On account of the malpracties of the borrowing units, the system came in for much disrepute. The system has, however, been rehabilitated by the Reserve Bank after making suitable amendments of the Companies Act.

3. Ploughing Back of Profits. This source, in fact, is the indicator of the inner strength and stability of any enterprise. Companies can use their reinvestible surplus to finance the expansion and modernisation of existing plants and establishment of the new ones.

4. Bank Loans. The commercial banks provide short-term or working capital to industries. They feel hesitant to finance fixed capital needs of industries because of the risky nature of the shares. Banks also do not subscribe to debentures because it is very difficult to dispose them of at a time when they are very much in need of funds.

In short, however, it should be noted that during the last 20 years bank advances to industry have shown remarkable progress. Outstanding advances of the scheduled commercial banks to industries—large, medium and small-scale—have increased from Rs.2,068 crores in March 1968 to Rs. 1,02,963 crores in March, 1995. In percentage terms, however, the share of bank advances to industry in total advances declined from 67.5 per cent to 53.2 per cent during the same period.

5. Foreign Capital. Foreign capital is also an important source of medium-term and long-term finance to industry. Foreign capital is available to the industries, both in the from of loans and equity participation. The sources of foreign capital comprise international institutions like International Bank for Reconstruction and Development, the International Finance Corporation, foreign governments and private investors.

6. Specialised Financial Institutions. The most important sources of long-term finance to industry are the various financial institutions that have been specially set up to meet the credit needs of industry. Among these institutions mention may be made of the Industrial Finance Corporation of India, the Industrial Credit and Investment Corporaiton of India, the Industrial Development Bank of India, the Unit Trust of India and the Industrial Reconstruction Bank of India.

In brief, there are both internal and external sources of industrial finance. In the recent past, the specialised financial institution are playing a dominant role in industrial financing.

Soundness of the Financing Agencies. It is a matter of debate whether the present financial structure is sound enough to sustain the pressure of growing industrialisation of the country. Among all the financing agencies, the most effective and reliable source of finance are the specialised institutions or the development banks. These institutions not only provide loans but also offer technological know-how and expert guidance to industries. The finncial strength of these institutions, however, is not sound enough to meet all the credit requirements of industries.

Foreign capital is again an important source of industrial finance but it has its own limitations. Foreign capital is the most unreliable source of finance. Its availability depends upon the political ties with the lender countries. Moreover, certain political strings are attached with the foreign capital. In some cases, only project-tied capital is offered by the lending countries.

Nationalised banks are playing a useful role in the various development programmes by making finance available for different projects. But in the sphere of industrial activities, they have not been able to provide term loans to industries.

To sum up, the present financial structure is not strong enough to meet the challenges of growing industrialisation.

Importance and Functions of Development Banks

Development banks are the financial intermediaries which cater to the capital requirements of industries. A development bank is not merely a lending institution, it has to ensure effective and proper utilisation of the financial help which it renders to industrial units. It can formulate its lending policy in such a manner so as to promote balanced regional development of industries by creation of income and employment in the relatively backward regions of the country.

Functions of a Development Bank. Within the framework of the traditional lending activities, a development bank can promote industrial development of the country in the following ways:

(i) optimising the use of scarce resources;

(ii) achieving a socially desirable product mix;

(iii) promoting industrialisation in the hitherto backward regions through dispersal of industries;

(iv) providing technological know-how and expert guidance to the entrepreneurs; and

(v) promoting the growth of small new and technician-entrepreneurs in the country.

(vi) preventive concentration of economic power by influencing pattern of ownership of the means of production.

In brief, a development bank performs a variety of functions for promoting the industrial development of the country.

Role of Development Banking

(1) Development banks extend credit facilities to industries in two forms: *(a)* loans, and *(b)* underwriting and direct subscription. Loans are extended both in the from of rupee and foreign currency loans.

Loans constitute about three-fourths of the total assistance provided to industries. Development banks also assist industries by underwriting of new issues, subscription to share capital and debentures, rediscounting of bills and refinancing industrial loans granted by eligible financial institutions.

(2) The share of development bank in financing industrial investment is well over 35 per cent. The total disbursement of assistance amounted to Rs. 31,850 crores in 1994-95.

(3) The development banks have granted loans to both consumer goods and capital goods industries. More than 25 per cent of assistance sanctioned by these banks has gone to the machine manufacturing industry. Textiles and food manufacturing accounted for an assistance of about 18 per cent and 17 per cent respectively in 1994-95.

(4) Although the development banks have extended financial assistance of industries in both public and private sectors but the

major thrust to their activities has been financing the capital needs of the private sector. About two-thirds of the total assistance disbursed by these banks has gone to the private sector.

(5) The development banks have given assistance for the establishment of new projects, expansion of the existing projects, modernisation, diversification, etc. A large portion of the total assistance has, however, been provided for the establishment of new projects.

Growth and Constituent of Development Banks

In response to the varied and growing needs of the industry, the Government took the initiative to set up development banks immediately after Independence, Today, there are 60 development banks, the important among these are as follows:

1. The Industrial Finance Corporation of India (IFCI) established in 1948.
2. The State Financial Corporations (SFCs), which came into effect in 1952.
3. The National Small Industries Corporation Ltd. (NSIC) established in 1955.
4. The industrial Credit and investment Corporation of India, Ltd. (ICICI) established in 1955.
5. The Industrial Development Bank of India (IDBI) established in 1964.
6. The Industrial Investment Bank of India (IIBI) established in 1971.

In addition to these institutions, the Unit Trust of India, the Life Insurance Corporation of India, the General Insurance Corporation of India also meet the financial requirements of the industry.

Weaknesses of the Development Banks. Notwithstanding the significant role played by these development banks in the country's industrial development, these banks suffer from certain shortcomings which are as follows:

1. The IFCI and the ICICI have promoted the concentration of the economic power by assisting the development of large and medium-large projects.
2. The SFCs have given assistance mostly to medium and small-medium projects, requiring a fairly large investment by way or promoters' capital.
3. The development banks did not go for intensive technological survey of the borrowing industries which has led to a very high rate of default.
4. Backward regions have been neglected by the financial institutions. As a result, the regional imbalances have further increased.
5. Due to lack of proper co-ordination between different institutions there has been over-financing in the case of some industries.
6. Most of the financial institutions have shown undue interest in the direct market purchase of shares than providing underwriting facilities to the companies.
7. The development banks have not shown adequate interest in the promotion of few entrepreneurial class.
8. The rate of interest charged by the development banks is very high. High cost of credit has retarded the growth of small enterprises.

INDUSTRIAL FINANCE CORPORATION OF INDIA

In India the capital is very shy and the financiers feel that in case their hidden capital comes out, they may be penalised for evading taxes. Accordingly they are not prepared to come out with their hidden wealth. Moreover, those who were prepared to invest have very limited capacity and the amount spared is for long term investment and usually it becomes difficult for the individual or the organisation to withdraw the amount once spent.

In India there is also no organised market which can always come forward with the money needed either for the expansion of an industry or to save that from financial difficulties or crisis. The result is that the industry gets into problems as soon as the question of raising additional funds arises.

Still another reason for setting up Industrial Finance Corporations in the country is that in India process of capital formation is slow. In case the present rate of slow capital formation is continued the result will be that the nation will take a very long time to become self sufficient and have an honourable place and position in the family of nations.

Commercial banks, which could finance the projects were not found interested to lock up heavy amounts in the industry and that too for a very long time and as such industry could not expect much for that source as well.

Setting up the Corporation. Due to the difficulties enumerated above, it was found essential that the Government may set up industrial financial corporations in the country to solve long term financial problems of the industry. In fact attention of the government to this important aspect of the problem had been drawn by such important bodies as Industrial Commission (1916-18); the External Capital Committee (1925) and the Central Banking Enquiry Committee (1929-31), Second World War made it amply clear that there was dire need and necessity of setting up an industrial corporation. Accordingly on July, 1948, Industrial Finance Corporation of India was set up with the main object of making medium and long term credits available to the industrial concerns in India.

Functions of the Corporation. The Corporation is responsible for under-writing the shares, bonds, debentures of industrial enterprises provided these are disposed of by the Corporation within 7 years of the date of acquisition. It grants loans or advances to industrial undertakings on long term basis and also provides guarantees for these undertakings for the loan raised from the scheduled or States Co-operative Banks. It can also directly subscribe to stocks or shares of any industrial concern.

Objectives of the Corporation. The Corporation was set up with the clear objective of providing finances, both medium and long term to large scale industries, engaged in manufacturing, preservation or processing of goods, mining, generation, distribution of electric power etc. Nationalised industries are also eligible for receiving financial assistance from the Corporation.

Financial Resources of the Corporation. The authorised share capital of the Corporation is Rs. 20 crores, which is divided into 40,000 shares of Rs. 500 each. The shares of the Corporation are guaranteed by the Government as to the repayment of principal as well as the dividend. The minimum rate of dividend that the Corporation can declare is 5%. On 30th June, 1974 the authorised capital of the Corporation stood at Rs. 20 crores and issued, subscribed and paid up capital stood at Rs. 10 crores. 50% shares were held by IDBI; 20% by the scheduled banks, 22% by Insurance Companies and remaining 8% by Cooperative Banks. The Corporation has been empowered to borrow from the Reserve bank of India for a period not exceeding 90 days. It frequently borrows from the Central Government and is also authorised to accept deposits from the public, State Government and local authorities.

Management of the Corporation. The management of the Corporation is carried out by a Board of Directors, consisting of 4 Directors to be nominated by the Development Bank, 2 by the Central Government and 6 to be elected by the share holders. The Chairman of the Board is to be nominated by the Government of India.

Procedure for Granting Financial Assistance. While giving financial assistance, the Corporation is to take following facts into consideration:

1. That the industry is included in the priority category in the Five Year Plan.

2. That assistance will promote regional dispersal of industries.
3. That industrial cooperatives and new entrepreneurs will get encouragement.
4. That due regard is being paid to the interests of the industry, commerce of the general Public.
5. That the cost proposed in the scheme is feasiblc.
6. That the industry can provide strong security.
7. That the industry is of national importance.
8. That the product is greatly needed by the country.
9. That the concern has adequate supply of technical personnel and raw material; and also that it has compctent management.

Each request received by the Corporation is properly examined by an advisory committee. The Board of Directors sanctions financial assistance on the recommendations of the advisory committee. After the loan has been sanctioned a letter of intent is issued in which main terms and conditions for the loan sanctioned are mentioned. The party which is sanctioned loan is required to send regular progress report. Where the amount sanctioned is quite substantial, the Corporation has a right to nominate one representative of its own on the Board of Directors of that concern.

Advisory Committees of the Corporation. The Corporation has six important advisory committees, one each dealing with textile, sugar, chemicals, engineering, Jute and miscellaneous. An advisory committee is required to deal with a request falling within its scope.

Repayment of Loan. The loans are granted against mortgagc of fixed assets and not against raw material or finished goods. Usually a borrowing concern will not declare a dividend of more than 6%. Though the duration of loan is 25 years, yet the average period of repayment does not exceed 12 years. The repayment of loan starts after second or third year.

The Rate of Interest. The effective rate of interest on rupee loan is 10.25% p.a. and 10.75% p.a. on sub loans in foreign currencies. The rate of interest charged from the industries located in the notified or less developed areas is 8.5% p.a.

Working of the Corporation Upto July 1948, the net cumulative assistance sanctioned by the company was Rs.439.82 crores, whereas upto June 30, 1974 the total amount disbursed was Rs. 404 crores and the outstanding was 224 crores and net sanctions amounted to Rs. 474 crores. By 1978-79 the corporation sanctioned Rs. 907 crores and disbursed Rs. 676.13 crores. As many as 671 industrial projects were financed by the Corporation. Assistance was sanctioned to 604 concerns. About 35% of the total assistance was for modernisation and diversification of industries; 42% of the total loans sanctioned went to Tamil Nadu, Maharashtra and West Bengal. The Corporation sanctioned 367 applications for under-writing of equity and preference shares. Industry-wise distribution of net financial assistance, as on 30.6.73 shows that 22.7% went to sugar; 18.3% to chemical; textiles 12.0%; non-ferrous metals 7.3%; Paper and paper products 6.5% nd so on. In Madhya Pradesh 137; in West Bengal 77; in Tamil Nadu 67; and in U.P. 53 projects were sanctioned.

Criticism of the Working of the Corporation

1. It is said that financial policy of the Corporation is such that economic power gets concentrated only in few hands. This defect was also brought to light by Dutt Committee as well.

2. Due to nepotism and favoritism the Corporation has become a big financial racket and a handmaid of only few persons.

3. Corporation has failed to develop industrially backward areas and the wealth is getting concentrated in such areas which are already industrially advanced.

4. Overhead charges incurred by the Corporation are very high, but on the other hand efficiency is low.

5. The procedure followed by the Corporation in granting the loans is very cumbersome and lengthy.
6. A very long time is taken by the Corporation for initiating action against industries which do not pay back the loan once taken.
7. The Corporation has ignored the interests of small scale and medium industries.
8. While granting loans consumer goods industries were more benefited as compared with basic and capital goods industries.
9. Corporations did not properly supervise the industries granted loan. In many cases loans were given to profit earning industries which could otherwise raise loans.
10. There was no standardised from of application in which information about each industry could be sought on a uniform pattern.

Inspite of the shortcomings of the Corporation, it cannot be denied that it has helped in developing managerial talents. Not only this, but it has also helped in bringing members of different institutions closer and nearer to each other. It has also played an important role in so far as exchange of views and ideas was concerned.

WORKING OF STATE FINANCIAL INDUSTRIAL

It was in 1951 that State Financial Corporations Act was passed. In accordance with he provisions of the Act, first Corporation by Punjab Government was set up in 1953. At present there are 18 such corporations.

Capital of the State Corporations. Each corporation can have a maximum authorised capital of Rs. 5 crores. The shares of the corporation can be purchased by the general public as well. The State Government concerned guarantees a minimum dividend of 3½ per cent on the share capital. The dividend however, cannot exceed 5 per cent on the share capital. The corporations can augment their resources by floating bonds and debentures. By the end of March 1974, the corporations had issued bonds amounting to Rs. 116 crores. The corporations can borrow from the Reserve Bank of India as well as from the State Governments.

Functions of the Corporations. State Finance Corporations provide financial assistance either by way of granting loans or advances or subscribing to debentures of industrial concerns, or by guaranteeing loans raised by industrial concerns or by underwriting the stocks, shares, bonds and debentures. The corporation can assist private limited concerns and partnership firms as well. The loans are granted against mortgaged assets and technical soundness of the project is given foremost consideration while granting loans.

The management of the corporation is run by a Board of Directors. The Managing Director is always appointed by the State Government concerned. State financial institutions are represented by three Directors on the Corporation. The Corporation has advisory committees to assist the Board of Directors for arriving at a decision.

Working of the Corporations. The total effective loans disbursed by the Corporations since their inception to the end of 1972-73 amounted to Rs. 37,115 lakhs. In 1973-74 Corporations combined together sanctioned loans amounting to Rs. 99.7 crores. The Corporations had outstanding loans amounting to Rs. 215.3 crores at the end of March 31, 1974. Since then both the sanctions as well as outstanding loans are increasing. Textiles, food products, chemicals, fertilisers and metal Industries received maximum loans. Medium industries were more benefited than small scale industries in grant of loans. The Corporations have played really an important role in meeting medium term financial needs of medium sized industrial concerns. The Corporations have formulated special schemes for assisting technician entrepreneurs during the course of last few years. They charge a minimum of 7.5% rate of interest on the loans advanced.

Critical Review of the Working of the Corporations. Though in each state financial Corporation has its own problems, yet on the whole the industry is not satisfied with its working. The Corporations have not done much in underwriting and guaranteeing operations. The management are weak. The cost of borrowing is very high and rate of interest charged not very high but and in fact prohibitive.

Problems of the Corporations

1. The default in repayment of loans is very high with the result that the ability to roll over the funds is considerably restricted.

2. Most of the small business units which get loan from the Corporations do not follow accepted principles and practices of accountancy. Thus it becomes difficult to keep watch over the expenditure.

3. While granting loans to small scale industries, peculiar problem faced is that in these industries individuals very much count. An industry which might be running quite efficiently under one man, might become inefficient after the death of the same man. Thus continuity of efficient management can hardly be assured. This enhances the difficulties of the Corporations.

4. While granting loans proper securities should be available, but in many cases there are not with the result that Corporations find it difficult to safely advance loans.

5. In order to ensure the return of loan, the Corporation is required to observe certain rules and regulations, but the difficulty is that the industries which approach for getting loans do not appreciate these difficulties and create many problems for the management.

6. The Corporations have no adequately trained staff to provide advisory service to the industry, when a request for financial assistance is received. In case permanent staff is maintained for processing each type of request that will be too costly for the Corporation and ad hoc staff cannot be depended upon.

7. The Corporation lack self-sufficient organisational set up and also specialised trained staff, thus there is no continuity in policy formulation and execution.

8. The Corporations have very limited financial resources, keeping in view the fact that new industries are coming up and more and more requests are being received from these industries for financial assistance.

9. The Corporation has no adequate provision, resources and arrangements to survey backward areas, which have potentialities for growth with the result that their growth suffers.

10. There is overlapping in the activities of state financial Corporations and commercial banks resulting in competition rather than cooperation. The competition creates many complex problems.

11. It is said that same set of rules is applied both in the case of long term as well as short term loans, applied by small scale industries which is unjust.

12. Due to many reasons many industrial units which come forward for loans, are not prepared to give complete information about their actual output and programmes of development, and thus the Corporations find it impossible to have correct assessment of repayment capacity of the industry.

Suggestions for the Improvement of Working

1. Due place and consideration should be given to the integrity and honesty of the persons applying for the loan, instead of rigid observance of the rules.

2. Conferences of representatives of the Corporations should be periodically convened to exchange ideas on points of common interest and also to enable each Corporation to get benefit of the experience of the others.

3. State governments should provide interest free loans to the Corporations to augment their financial resources.

4. Wastages of money and resources should be located and avoided.

5. Repayment schedule should be so arranged that at the time of repayment small scale and medium industries do not get burdened.

6. More concessions should be given to small scale industries, while granting loans.

7. Dividend requirements should be waived for some time, till Corporations financial resources get augmented.

Reserve Bank of India Working Group Recommendations

It appears that the State Governments are quite conscious of the difficulties of small scale and cottage industries. The problems have been discussed at the conference of the representatives of the State Financial Corporations. International development Financial Association has promised a $25 million credit in foreign exchange to these Corporations. The Reserve Bank of India also set up in 1970 a working group to review the working of these Corporations and report of group was made available to the Bank in 1972. The working group recommended augmentation of financial resources of the Corporation and also suggested that scope of assistance of these Corporations should be enlarged. In the opinion of the group management of the Corporation should be strengthened, cost of resources lowered and recovery of loans quickened. The working group came out with the recommendation that at least 2/3 of the assistance disbursed by the Corporations should go to small units and that dividend obligations should be waived for sometime. In 1972 State Financial Corporations Act was amended to enable the Corporations to widen their functional role and to extend geographical coverage.

INDUSTRIAL CREDIT AND INVESTMENT CORPORATION OF INDIA

Functions of the Corporation. The Corporation was set up in January, 1955 with its headquarters at Bombay. The main objects and functions of the Corporation were as under:

1. To assist the industrial enterprises within the private sector which can be in the from of creation, expansion and modernisation of enterprises.

2. To provide finances in the from of medium or long term loans.
3. To make funds available for reinvestment.
4. To provide managerial, technical and administrative advice.
5. To sponsor or underwrite new shares or securities.
6. To guarantee loans from other private investment sources.

The Corporation helps the industry in getting land, building and machinery. It makes direct subscription to industrial securities and guarantees payment of loans made by others. The Corporation provides loan to any limited liability company, but not partnership and proprietary firms. It helps the industry in the planning and execution of investments. It also provides risk capital through direct participation in share capital issues.

Resources of the Corporation. Initial resources of the Corporation were of the order of Rs. 17.5 crores, but gradually these went upto Rs. 365 crores. The Corporation borrowed Rs. 271 crores from the World Bank and other international agencies. The resources position of the Corporation some time back being:

Share capital	Rs.	10.00 crores
Reserves	Rs.	11.00 crores
Debentures	Rs.	18.00 crores
Loans from Government of India	Rs.	27.00 crores
Advances from IDBI	Rs.	15.00 crores
Credit from World Bank	Rs.	187.00 crores
Credit from other international Bodies	Rs.	30.00 crores

Operations of the Corporation. Total net operations of the Corporation some time back amounted to Rs. 445 crores for 856 enterprises, of these 285 were new undertakings. Of the total assistance Rs. 259 crores were in the from of foreign assistance and Rs. 17

crores by way of direct subscription to 62 enterprises. By the end of December 1973, the Corporation had disbursed a total amount of Rs. 309 crores. Maximum grant was given to chemicals and Petro-chemical industries, followed by basic metal products, machinery manufacturing industry and textiles. Maharashtra, Gujarat, Tamil Nadu and West Bengal have been most benefited by the Corporation. By June 1978, the Corporation had sanctioned about Rs. 1220 crores and disbursed Rs. 882 crores.

Management. The Corporation is managed by a Board of Directors consisting of not less than 5 and not more than 15 members. In addition the government can also appoint a Director. If there is any dispute between the Government of India and the Corporation, that will be settled by arbitration.

Appraisal and Impact. The Corporation has helped in fostering growth of a healthy capital market in the country. It is working in close cooperation with other financial organisations. The Corporation is playing a useful role as a supplier of foreign credit to the industry in India, thereby it has been augmenting available foreign exchange resources of the country. For promoting and encouraging private foreign capital, it has succeeded in setting up an investment centre. It has succeeded in building up a large folio of projects in diverse industries, mainly non-traditional. It has also taken active part in carrying out surveys to determine industrial potential in various states.

A criticism levied against Corporation however, is that it is helping only those states and industries which are otherwise considerably advanced. In order to remove this criticism, it has started giving loans to industries in backward areas at low rate of interest. For better coordination, it has set up regional offices for more assistance to backward areas and small units in different regions.

Outlook for the Future. On the whole it can be said that the Corporation has done a good job. It has been giving considerably high dividend (10%) and is paying special and particular attention for setting up of industries in the backward areas. looking at the performance of the past, it can be said that the Corporation has good future.

ROLE OF UTI

Unit Trust of India was set up on 1st july, 1974 with a view to providing small investors an opportunity to purchase shares of small amounts and thus to participate in the development and growth of national economy of the country. The Trust was created with an initial capital of 5 crores. Shares worth Rs. 2.50 crores were purchased by the RBI, Rs. 0.75 crores by LIC, Rs. 0.75 Crores by SBI and its subsidiaries. Scheduled Banks and other financial institutions purchased shares worth Rs. 100 crores. Each unit of the trust is worth Rs. 10 only, but is to be sold at a price which suits the Trust.

Functions of the Trust. The Trust is expected to sell as many units as possibly it can so as to involve maximum number of small investors in the industrial development of the country. It is also expected of the Trust to invest in, acquire, hold or dispose of securities and also to keep money on deposit with the scheduled banks.

Management of Trust. Management of the Trust is run by a Board of Trustees, which are nominated as follows:

5 trustees, including Chairman by	RBI
One Trustee	LIC
One Trustee	SBI

2 Trustees to be elected by other contributing agencies.

Investment of the Fund. While investing great care is taken to see that the money invested in one company is not more than 5% of the value of total investible funds of the Trust and also that net more than 5% of the investible funds should be invested in the initial issues of the new industrial undertakings.

Progress of U.T.I. Almost all investible funds of U.T.I. have been invested in private corporate sector. Even a decade back total investment amounted to Rs. 142 crores. Textile industry accounted for 14.5%, engineering for 14.30%; for electricity generation electricity 12.2% and cement industry attracted about 7% of the total amount available to the industrial sector. The Unit has also been helping small scale units. It has three different schemes through which it works. But the working of the Unit Trust has come under criticism. Trust efforts in pooling savings are not much impressive and 94% of the total assistance has been made available to large scale industrial units. It is also said that administrative charges of the Trust are very high and that there is scope for savings in the expenditure.

WORKINGS AND PROGRESS OF IDBI

Industrial Development Bank of India was set up by an Act of Parliament in 1964, with the following objects:

Objects of the Bank

1. To finance industrial concerns on its own either by granting financial accommodation for export of capital goods or other commodities or by granting loans or by subscribing the shares or debentures of industrial concerns or by guaranteeing deferred payments or by underwriting new issues of industrial concerns.

2. To provide financial and administrative assistance to any industrial enterprise for promotion, management or expansion.

3. To locate and fill up the gaps in the industrial structure.

4. It can refinance term advances of 3–25 years maturity made to industrial concerns by financial institutions.

5. To undertake surveys and make investment research.

Resources of the Bank. The authorised capital of the bank is Rs. 50 crores, but this amount can be raised to Rs. 100 crores as well. The Central Government has advanced a loan of Rs. 10 crores. The Bank can get loan from the R.B.I. The Bank is also empowered to raise loan in foreign exchange from any financial institution in any foreign country. By June, 1972, the Bank had borrowed Rs. 142 crores from the Government of India. By this time the paid up capital of the Bank was Rs. 40 crores. By June 1974, the Bank had sanctioned direct assistance aggregating Rs. 366 crores to 265 projects. It has also sanctioned 86 schemes of expansion. By 30.6.79 the Bank had sanctioned financial assistance of about Rs. 4130 crores and disbursed Rs. 2770 crores.

Management of the Bank. The management of the Bank is in the hands of Board of Directors. The Directors are nominated by the Government. The Bank has its own Chairman and Vice-Chairman. The Bank can also set up its own executive committee. Since 1976 it has been delinked from the R.B.I.

Progress of the Bank. By the end of the June 1973 the Bank had granted assistance to the tune of Rs. 736.2 crores which rose to Rs. 4130 crores in June 1979. According to Bank's report even a decade back, 32% of the total grant went to machinery, 13% to basic metal industry and 11% to fertilisers. The Bank report also points out that 60% of the total assistance was sanctioned to basic and capital goods industries. The Bank gave Rs. 243 crores by way of direct loans; Rs. 48.8 crores by subscription to shares and under-writings, Rs. 185.00 by way of recounting of bills and Rs. 27.4 crores by refinancing of export credits. The Bank also advanced Rs. 51.1 crores by way of direct loans for exports. In order to tackle the problem of imbalance in development between States, the Bank completed industrial potential surveys of all the States. It has promoted the establishment of Industrial Reconstruction Corporation of India and started Kerala Industrial and Technical Consultancy Organisation. A similar consultancy service was started at Gauhati. The Bank is also providing financial assistance to public sector undertakings for purposes of expansion or diversification of production. It has started Machinery Bill Re-discounting Scheme to assist the machinery manufacturers to market their products at easy credit terms. Now the scheme is providing substantial assistance to small and medium sized industries in modernising and expanding their equipments.

In order to stream line its working the Bank has opened regional offices at Delhi, Calcutta and Madras. It has also opened 12 branch offices in different states. It is struggling hard to bring about regional balances by promoting industries in less developed regions. It is also improving its appraisal methodology and now every project is referred to a committee of technical and financial experts before it is sanctioned. Since the Bank is required by which Bank's share of indirect assistance has been considerably to fill financial gaps, therefore, a healthy trend has now emerged improving and going up. The share of assistance to industrially backward areas has gone up by 30.3%. Similarly share of small scale sector in refinance assistance has gone up by 65%. During the last decade the Bank provided assistance to 27 large projects, amounting to Rs. 928 crores. It has provided direct assistance aggregating to Rs. 366 crores to 256 projects and indirect assistance of Rs. 484 crores. The Bank has also helped in the development and growth of indigenous technology and gave encouragement to new entreprcneurs.

Steps for the Improvement of Activities. If the Bank is to diversify its activities, it is essential that it must improve its working. Some of the steps which have been taken in this regard are:

1. In consultation and collaboration with other financial institutions the bank is setting up consultancy services at state levels.
2. Legal and financial procedures are being simplified for the borrowers and greater flexibility in terms and conditions of getting loans is being introduced.
3. In order to promote and finance export of goods, the Bank is establishing its export departments and giving wide publicity to export schemes. It is also providing assistance to exporters.
4. In order to provide better service to small scale and medium industries the Bank is improving its relations with commercial Banks.
5. The bank is setting up both branch as well as regional offices to provide better service to the industry.

FEATURES OF CAPITAL MARKET

Capital market is the type of market, which provides funds for industrial and commercial enterprises in the country on long term basis. It is dependent on savings both individual, public and corporate. The demands on the capital market can come from agriculture, industry and trade and the sources of income can be individuals as well as the government. In an ideal capital market finance is used as a hand maid to serve the needs of industry. For a rapid economic growth of the country capital market is not only essential but inevitable.

Capital Market and Money Market. Both capital and money markets are quite different from each other though both are interdependent. It is only in the narrow sense that both can be differentiated from each other. It is in that sense alone that money market is concerned with floating or liquid balances and their short term employment in trade and industry through the banking system.

Categories of Capital Market. Capital market can broadly be divided into two categories namely *(a)* organised capital market and *(b)* unorganised capital market. In an organised sector of capital market demand for long term capital comes from corporate enterprises, government and semi-government institutions requiring funds for various development activities. On the other hand an unorganised capital market consists of local bankers in the towns and money lenders in the villages. In the organised sector demand for capital is always heavy, as compared with the supply, with the result that the rate of interest charged is always heavy.

Why Organised Capital market? It is felt that organised capital market is most essentially and vitally needed for the growth of economy. There are various reasons for this. For all the private capital can never be in a position to meet ever increasing demands of industries, where heavy capitals are needed. Still another reason is that the rate of interest charged by the unorganised sector of capital market is so heavy that it is usually impossible for the industry to bear it. Moreover, it is easy to contact and convince well established financial institutions, rather than unorganised capital market people.

Why Unorganised Capital Market in India? It is realised everywhere that for industrial development and advancement of the country, it is essential that the country should have a well organised capital market. It is with this end in view that financial institutions like the Industrial Development Bank, Unit Trust of India, National Development Industrial Corporation, Industrial Corporation of India etc. have been set up. It is also realised that there is a very close relationship of industrial growth with the capital market because industries are the main source of demand of capital in the country. As the industry grows with that the demand on capital market also increases. But in spite of this in India capital market is ill-organised and ill-developed. For this there are various reasons:

1. Agriculture, constituting the main occupation, did not lend itself to the flotation of securities.
2. Growth of securities was hampered because foreign business linked itself with the foreign and not with the Indian market.
3. Managing agency system also contributed in the ill-development and growth of capital market in the country.
4. The investment habits of the individuals and the restrictions imposed on the investment patterns of the various financial institutions circumscribed to the capital market.

Growth of Capital Market in India. Capital market is largely influenced by the saving capacity of the people. In the initial stages of industrial development of industries good capital market plays a big role. In a country like ours, capital market is considerably influenced by the saving capacity of the people, because the masses have very poor per-capita income and in case small saving resources are mobilised, particularly in the rural areas, the capital market in the organised sector can have sufficient economic resources. Rate of savings is slow and small savers are even heavily taxed with the result that whatsoever they save that goes out in taxes and little money is left for small savings.

Defects of Capital Market in India

1. Government securities though negotiable, are seldom in the hands of common people.

2. Taxation rate has been increasingly very fast thus whatsoever can be saved by the people goes away by way of taxes. This has resulted in the starvation of capital market.

3. Unorganised sector of capital market is also contributing in its own way in the development and growth of organised capital market.

4. Public on the whole is not quite aware of the importance of well-developed and properly organised capital market even those who are interested in the system of organised capital market cannot properly contribute in that direction.

5. In India there is serious lack of investment advisory bodies and also there is dearth of industrial houses.

Steps Taken for Removing Defects of Capital Market

1. An elaborate legislative code has been adopted by the Government to protect the investors interests. These measures include the Companies Act 1956. The Capital Issues Act, The Securities Contracts (Regulations) Act, 1956 and Monopolies and Restrictive Trade Practices Act (1970).

2. In the country many sound financial institutions have been set up, which have huge capitals and can provide short and long term advances for industrial advancement and growth of the country.

3. During recent years underwriting activities of many financial institutions have made satisfactory progress. This has given sufficient encouragement to business activity in the country.

4. Commercial Banks have encouraged growth of capital market by granting more advances against shares and debentures. These banks also make their funds available to finance Corporations by purchasing their shares and debentures.

5. The formation of Industrial Development Bank and Unit Trust of India have also contributed a lot in the capital market of India and in its proper organisation.

6. Another important cause which has helped in the growth of capital market in the country is growth of joint stock business. In the words of Prof. Kuchhal. "The growth of joint stock from of business, the expanding role of Reserve Bank in the sphere of rural credit, the establishment of various finance Corporations, the extension of banking into the interior the diversification of the function of commercial banks, and the government assistance to industry have all been the contributive factors to this integration."

COMPONENTS OF FOREIGN CAPITAL

Foreign capital can be obtained either in the from of concessional assistance or non-concessional flows or foreign investment. Concessional assistance includes grants and loans obtained at low rates of interest with long maturity period. Such assistance is provided generally on bilateral basis (government to government) or through multilateral agencies like the World Bank, International Development Association etc. Loans have generally to be repaid in terms of foreign currency but in certain cases the donour may allow the recipient country to repay in terms of its own currency. For instance, the U.S. Government allowed the Government of India to repay loans under PL 480 in terms of rupees. Grants do not carry any obligation of repayment and are mostly made available to meet some temporary crisis. Non-concessional assistance includes mainly external commercial borrowings, loans from other governments/multilateral agencies on market terms and deposits obtained from non-residents. Foreign investment is generally in the from of private foreign participation in certain sectors of the domestic economy. The main advantage of this from of assistance is that generally the foreign investor also brings with him technical expertise, machines, capital goods, etc., which are scarce in underdeveloped countries. The disadvantage is that a large part of the profits are repatriated to the foreign investor. If the underdeveloped country in question chooses to depend too much on private foreign investment, it would be risking too much interference in the conduct of its affairs. This would be against the long-term interests of the country.

In addition to these forms of assistance, the underdeveloped country can also receive direct supplies of agricultural commodities (foodgrains etc.) or industrial raw materials to face temporary shortages in the economy.

Need for Foreign Capital

Following arguments are advanced in favour of foreign capital:

1. Sustaining a High Level of Investment. Since the underdeveloped countries want to industrialise themselves within a short period of time, it becomes necessary to raise the level of investment substantially. This requires, in turn, a high level of savings. However, because of general poverty of masses, the savings are often very low. Hence emerges a resource gap between investment and savings. This gap has to be filled up through foreign capital.

2. The Technological Gap. The underdeveloped countries have very low level of technology as compared to the advanced countries. However, they possess a strong urge for industrialisation to develop their economies and to wriggle out of the low level equilibrium trap in which they are caught. This raises the necessity for importing technology from the developed countries. Such technology usually comes with foreign capital when it assumes the from of private foreign investment or foreign collaboration. In the Indian case, technical assistance received from abroad has helped in filling up the technological gap through the following three ways: *(a)* provision of expert services; *(b)* training of Indian personnel; and *(c)* educational, research and training institutions in the country.

3. Undertaking the Initial Risk. Many underdeveloped countries suffer from acute scarcity of private entrepreneurs. This creates obstacles in the programmes of industrialisation. An argument advanced in favour of the foreign capital is that it undertakes the 'risk' of investment in the host countries and thus provides the much needed impetus to the process of industrialisation. Once the programme of industrialisation gets started with the initiative of foreign capital, domestic industrial activity starts picking up as more and more people of the host country enter the industrial field.

4. Exploitation of Natural Resources. A number of underdeveloped countries possess huge mineral resources which await exploitation. These countries themselves do not possess the required technical skill and expertise to accomplish this task. As a consequence, they have to depend upon foreign capital to undertake the exploitation of their mineral wealth.

5. Development of Basic Economic Infrastructure. It has been observed that the domestic capital of the underdeveloped countries is often too inadequate to build up the economic infrastrucutre on its own. Thus these countries require the assistance of foreign capital to undertake this task. In the latter half of the twentieth century especially during the last three-four decades, international financial institutions and many governments of advanced countries have made substantial capital available to the underdeveloped countries to develop their system of transport and communications, generation and distribution of electricity, development of irrigation facilities, etc.

6. Improvement in the Balance of Payments Position. In the initial phase of their economic development, the underdeveloped countries need much larger imports (in the from of machinery, capital goods, industrial raw materials, spares and components) than they can possibly export. As a result, the balance of payments generally turns adverse. This creates a gap between the earnings and expenditure of foreign exchange. Foreign capital presents a short-run solution to the problem.

This shows that the economic development of an underdeveloped country should obviously receive a boost as a result of foreign capital. Accordingly, if foreign capital is obtained on easy terms and without any 'strings', it should be welcomed.

Supporters of private foreign investment argue that it brings with it new technology, better management and organisation, superior marketing and sometimes cheaper finance. The academic arguments in favour of private foreign investment are the following:

(i) Foreign investment constitutes a net addition to investible resources in host countries, and as such raises their rates of growth;

(ii) Foreign investment results in a pattern of growth which is desirable from the point of view of underdeveloped countries since new products are introduced and marketed; new tastes are created, and specific needs of the host economy are met; and

(ii) Free flow of capital is conducive both to total world welfare and to the welfare of each individual country. The operations of foreign firms, especially of modern multinational firms, knit countries together and closer into the web of international commerce, both by (vertical and horizontal) economic integration and by the transmission of tastes, designs, ideas and technology.

Indian Governments Policy Towards Foreign Capital

At the time of Independence, the attitude towards foreign capital was one of fear and suspicion. This was natural on account of the previous exploitative role played by it in 'draining away' resources from this country. The suspicion and hostility found expression in the Industrial policy of 1948 which, though recognizing the role of private foreign investment in the country, emphasized that its regulation was necessary in the national interest. Because of this attitude expressed in the 1948 Resolution, foreign capitalists got dissatisfied and as a result, the flow of imports of capitals goods got obstructed. As a result, the Prime Minister had to give following assurances to the foreign capitalists in 1949:

1. No Discrimination between Foreign and Indian Capital. The Government of India will not differentiate between the foreign and Indian capital. The implication was that the government would not place any restrictions or impose any conditions on foreign enterprise which were not applicable to similar Indian enterprise.

2. Full Opportunities to Earn Profits. The foreign interests operating in India would be permitted to earn profits without subjecting them to undue controls. Only such restrictions would be imposed which also apply to the Indian enterprise.

3. Guarantee of Compensation. If and when foreign enterprises are compulsorily acquired, compensation will be paid on a fair and equitable basis as already announced in government's statement of policy.

Though the Prime Minister stated that the major interest in ownership and effective control of an undertaking should be in Indian hands, he gave assurance that there would be "no hard and fast rule in this matter".

Despite the above assurances, foreign capital in the requisite quantity did now flow into India during the period of the First Plan. The atmosphere of suspicion had not changed substantially. However, the policy statement of the Prime Minister issued in 1949 and continued practically unchanged in the 1956 Industrial policy Resolution, had opened up immense fields to foreign participation. In addition, the trends towards liberalization grew slowly and gradually more strong and the role of foreign investment grew more and more important. The government relaxed its policy concerning majority ownership in several cases and granted several tax concessions for foreign personnel. Substantial liberalisation was announced in the New Industrial policy declared by the government in July, 1991 and doors of several industries have been opened up for foreign investment. Prior to this policy, foreign capital was generally permitted (as a matter of policy) only in those industries where Indian capital was scarce and was not normally permitted in trading activities, plantations, banking and financial institutions. It was not permitted in those industries which had received government protection or which are of basic and/or strategic importance to the country. The declared policy of the government was to discourage foreign capital in certain 'inessential' consumer goods and service industries. However, this provision as frequently violated as a number of foreign collaborations even in respect of cosmetics, toothpaste, lipstick etc. were allowed by the government. It was also stated that foreign capital should help in promoting exports or substituting imports. The government also laid down that in all those industries where foreign capital investment is allowed, the major interest in ownership and effective control should always be in Indian hands (this condition was also often relaxed). The foreign capital investments and technical collaborations were required to be so regulated as to fit into the overall framework of the plans. In those industries where foreign technicians and managers were allowed to operate as Indians with requisite skills and experience were not available, vital importance was to be accorded to the training and employment of Indians in the quickest possible manner.

In a bid to attract foreign capital and investments from Non-Resident Indians (NRIs), the government has in recent years announced a number of tax concessions, lower rates of taxation for certain designated priority industries, tax holiday on profits for a certain period to new industrial undertakings etc. NRIs investing in India were allowed higher investment limits, priority allotment of items in short supply, permission to buy shares in Indian companies etc. However, the real 'opening up' came with the announcement of the new industrial policy in July 1991. The important measures announced in July, 1991 and afterwards are as follows:

1. The government has prepared a specified list of high-technology and high-investment priority industries wherein automatic permission will be available for direct foreign investment up to 51 per cent foreign equity. Annexure III contains a list of 35 priority industries divided into the following areas: *(i)* metallurgical industries, *(ii)* boilers and steam generating plants, *(iii)* electrical equipment, *(iv)* telecommunication equipments, *(v)* transportation, *(vi)* industrial machinery, *(vii)* agricultural machinery, *(viii)* industrial instruments, and *(ix)* chemicals (other than fertilisers). This facility of 51 per cent foreign equity participation will be available to those firms which are able to finance their capital equipment imports through their foreign equity.

2. A special empowered board has been constituted to negotiate with a number of large international firms and approve direct foreign investment in select areas. This would be a special programme to attract substantial investment that would provide access to high technology and world markets. The investment programmes of such firms would be considered in totality, free from pre-determined parameters or procedures.

3. Prior to 1991 the government generally discouraged foreign equity holdings in service areas except for hotels. The 1991 policy has invited foreign equity holdings upto 51 per cent by international trading companies. In addition to hotels, 51 per cent equity will also be welcomed in other tourist related areas.

4. The new industrial policy provides for automatic approval to foreign technology agreements in the case of the 35 priority industries listed in Annexure III within certain guidelines. For the present, these guidelines will allow royalty up to 5 per cent of domestic sales and 8 per cent of export sales, alongwith lumpsum technology payments of up to Rs. 1 crore. This automatic permission would be available to other industries also if the payments can be made without resort to free foreign exchange resources.

5. To hasten the progress in the ailing power sector, the government (in a policy decision announced on July 31, 1991) has allowed 100 per cent foreign equity participation for setting up power plants in the country. Hundred per cent foreign equity participation allows free repatriation of profits and other incentives. Besides, it will help foreign parties to set up power plants without delays which considerably escalate the cost.

6. Hiring of foreign technicians and testing of indigeneously developed technology abroad earlier required case-by-case approval by the government. This involved unavoidable

delay. Henceforth, no permission will be necessary for these purposes.

7. NRIs and Overseas Corporate Bodies (OCBs) predominantly owned by them, were allowed in 1992-93 to invest upto 100 per cent equity in high-priority industries with repatriability of capital and income. NRI investment upto 100 per cent of equity is also allowed in export houses, trading houses, star trading houses, hospitals, EOUs, sick industries, hotels, etc. Foreign citizens of Indian origin are now permitted to acquire house property without the permission of the Reserve Bank of India.

8. Provisions of the Foreign Exchange Regulation Act (FERA) have been liberalised through on Ordinance dated January 9, 1993 as a result of which companies with more than 40 per cent of foreign equity are also now treated on par with fully Indian owned companies.

9. Foreign companies have been allowed to use their trade marks on domestic sales from May 14, 1992.

10. The government has allowed reputed Foreign Institutional Investors (FIIs) including pension funds, mutual funds, asset management companies, investment trusts, nominee companies and incorporated or institutional portfolio managers to invest in the Indian capital market subject to the condition that they register with the Securities and Exchange Board of India (SEBI) and obtain RBI approval under FERA. Portfolio investment by the FIIs in the primary and secondary markets are subject to an overall ceiling of 24 per cent of the issued share capital in any company.

11. Disinvestment of equity by foreign investors no longer needs to be at prices determined by the Reserve Bank. It has been allowed at market rates on stock exchanges from September 15, 1992 with permission to repatriate the proceeds of such disinvestment.

12. Foreign investors can invest in Indian companies through the Global Depository Receipts (GDR) route without any lock-in-period. These Receipts can be listed on any of the overseas stock exchanges and denominated in any convertible foreign currency.

Foreign Aid to India

Amount of Foreign Aid. In absolute terms India has been the biggest recipient of foreign aid for development purposes during the past four decades. However, its position is not enviable if we consider the amount of aid in relation to its population. During the First Plan period India had received on an average an external assistance of Rs. 40 crores per annum. This was certainly a modest amount by any standards. Thereafter, for more than a decade there was a steady increase in external assistance. During the Third Plan period this country received, on an average, an external assistance of Rs. 573.3 crores per annum, which was 3.2 per cent of national income. After the Third Plan was over, the long-term planning was suspended for three years. As the country's economy was in a bad shape in this period and it was not easy to raise adequate resources from domestic sources, reliance on foreign aid increased during the three years of Annual Plans. However, the Fourth Plan marked a distinct change in the pattern of finance. This change was induced basically by two reasons: *(i)* the USA cut down aid to India drastically as the latter refused to tow its lines on a number of political issues, and *(ii)* because of the increasing uncertainty of aid and the rising debt servicing charges, the Government of India opted for a policy of increasing self-reliance. Under the Fifth Five Year Plan, self-reliance was again accorded a high priority and thus the aid received for the plan in percentage terms was approximately on the same scale as under the Fourth Plan. The Sixth Plan envisaged a net inflow of foreign resources of Rs. 9,929 crores (Rs.5,889 crores as net aid and Rs. 4,040 crores as other inflows from abroad). This was about 10.2 per cent of the total public sector plan outlay of Rs. 97,500 crores. The Seventh Plan envisaged net capital inflow from abroad of Rs. 18,000 crores which was again 10 per cent of the public sector plan outlay of Rs. 1,80,000 crores.

These data show that utilisation of foreign aid in India has been considerably less than the authorisation. For instance, the total authorisation of foreign aid upto the end of Fourth Plan was Rs. 13,056 crores while utilisation was merely Rs. 11,922 crores. The shortfall has been particularly marked during the period of the Sixth and Seventh Plans. Another important conclusion that emerges from the table is that the authorisation of foreign aid has increased considerably during the last decade. In fact, the authorisation of foreign aid during the Sixth Plan was Rs. 16,761 crores which rose by more than two and a half times to Rs. 44,971 crores in the Seventh Plan.

Though authorisation of assistance has registered a perceptible increase in recent years, utilisation has risen at a much slower rate as can be seen from Table 1. in percentage terms, utilisation was 65 per cent of authorisation in the Sixth Plan and only 50 per cent in the Seventh Plan. However, during the period 1990-91 to 1994-95 utilisation was 83 per cent of the authorisation (Rs. 51,963 crores out of Rs. 62,419 crores).

Forms of Foreign Aid

India has received three forms of foreign aid-loans, grants, and PL 480/665 etc., assistance repayable in rupees and/or in convertible currency. Loans are meant to help the country in meeting the shortages of resources to carry out its development plans. However, if not utilised properly in the long period, they become a burden on the economy as substantial proportion of foreign exchange earnings is used up for servicing them (as amortisation and interest payments). Grants carry no such burden of repayment and are therefore better on this account. A substantial part received under PL 480/665 from USA till 1967-68 was repaybale in rupees. However, after this year, the USA expressed its willingness to grant assistance under this head only in convertible currency. Aid under PL 480/665 was completely stopped after 1977-78.

Total authorised foreign aid upto the end of the Fourth Plan was Rs. 13,056 crores of which the share of loans was Rs.9,665 crores (*i.e.* 74%) and the share of grants was Rs. 753 crores (*i.e.* 6%). The remaining Rs. 2,638 crores (*i.e.* 20%) was the share of assistance received under PL 480/665.' During the Fifth Plan period, total authorised foreign aid was Rs. 9,844 crores of which the share of loans was Rs. 7,913 crores (*i.e.* 80%) and the share of grants was Rs. 1,795 crores (*i.e.* 18%). Assistance under PL 480/665 was a negligible Rs. 136 crores. During the Sixth Plan period, the share of loans and grants comes out to be around 90 per cent and 10 per cent respectively. During the Seventh Plan, the share of loans rose further to 93.9 per cent. Taking the period of planning as a whole, total authorised foreign aid to India amounted to Rs. 1,48,556 crores of which the share of loans was Rs. 1,32,439 crores (*i.e.* 89%) while the share of grants was Rs. 13,343 crores (*i.e.* 8.9%). The remaining Rs. 2,744 crores (*i.e.* 2%) was the share of assistance received under PL 480/665.

External assistance is often classified as tied aid and untied aid. To prevent the misuse of assistance, the lending countries and international financial institutions generally prefer to give aid for particular projects. Since this assistance can be utilised for specific purposes only, it is called tied aid. A country receiving tied aid thus does not have the freedom to use it for other purposes. From the point of view of the borrowing countries united aid is better, as there is always some flexibility in its utilisation.

Foreign Aid and Capital Formation

For evaluating the role of external assistance in the capital formation in the public sector during planning period we must consider the ratio of aid to overall investment in this sector. During the Second and Third Plan periods the external assistance had accounted for 25 per cent of the total investment in the public sector. Subsequently, under the three Annual Plans contribution of external assistance to investment in the public sector rose to 40 per cent. Thereafter the relative importance of external assistance in Indian plans declined. Between 1955-56 and 1967-68 the ratio of aid to import surplus was also high which implied that a major part of aid was spent on meeting this deficit. During the Fourth Plan period, on account of recession in the industrial sector, investment activity did not reflect buoyancy. Hence the country did not require aid on the same scale as under the Third Five Year Plan and the three Annual Plans. Further, a major part of the aid received in this period was spent on financing the imports and thus its contribution to domestic capital formation was at best marginal. Under the Fifth Plan external assistance did not rise in percentage terms, yet the absolute amount of aid was considerably larger than the under the Fourth Plan. According to the original scheme of financing of the Sixth Plan the government hoped to raise approximately one-tenth of the resources through external assistance. However, in practice, external assistance contributed only 7.7 per cent of total resources. The Seventh Plan also expected to raise 10 per cent of resources from external assistance. In practice, 9.1 per cent of resources were raised through external assistance.

External Commercial Borrowings

As stated in the Chapter on 'India's Balance of Payments Problem', India had to rely heavily on external commercial borrowings and NRI deposits to meet the balance of payments deficits in the eighties as there was an increasing shortage of concessional assistance. Thus our dependence on high cost methods of financing increased. As far as external commercial borrowings are concerned, they were used extensively in the latter half of eighties to finance the current account deficit. In fact, in this period, external commercial borrowings accounted for more than 25 per cent of the total capital flows into the economy. In 1986-87, their share in capital inflows was almost half (to be exact, 48.1%). India started initially with the conventional syndicated loans, managed by American, European and Japanese banks and then started raising funds in the international bond market. Financial institutions and public sector undertakings together accounted for about 90 per cent of the approvals of external commercial borrowings. The government now realises the high cost nature of external commercial borrowings and their burden on the economy. Accordingly, it has tried to reduce its dependence on this source of financing the current account deficit. As a result, the share of external commercial borrowings in total net capital flows has been brought down from 34.4 per cent in 1989-90 and 30.6 per cent in 1991-92 to 12.4 per cent in 1993-94 and 14.6 per cent in 1994-95.

External commercial borrowings were modest before 1980-81. In 1980-81 they stood at Rs.1,038 crores. Over the entire period of the Sixth Plan (1980-81 to 1984-85), approvals of external commercial borrowings stood at Rs.7,259 crores. However, there was a substantial inflow of external commercial borrowings in the period of the Seventh Plan as authorisations were as high as $ 10.8 billion and disbursements were of $ 10.48 billion. However, net transfer comes to only $ 3.58 billion as a substantial amount of money was paid back in terms of debt service payments. Interest payments alone accounted for $ 3,49 billion. The last year of the Seventh Plan 1989-90 registered a substantial inflow of $ 3.29 billion. However, there was a steep decline in the availability of commercial credit to India in 1990-91. According to the Economic Survey, 1991-92, the reasons for this decline were as under: *(i)* fall in the overall availability of international credit due to capital adequacy requirements of the Bank for International Settlements; *(ii)* the Gulf crisis which created an atmosphere of uncertainty in the international capital market; and *(iii)* the downgrading of India's credit rating for long-term funds by international rating agencies. In fact, they years 1990-91 and 1991-92 even saw a net capital transfer abroad as gross disbursements minus debt service payments were negative in these years. Net capital transfer abroad was $ 530 million in 1990-91 which rose to $ 1,080 million in 1991-92. The year 1991-92 even saw a capital outflow of $ 70 million. In fact, against the gross disbursements of $ 1.10 billion in 1991-92, interest payments alone stood at $ 1.01 billion (which comes to as much as 92 per cent of the gross disbursements). These figures clearly show the high cost nature of external commercial borrowings.

The above trends continued in 1992-93 also. In this year gross disbursements of $ 1.2 billion were short of repayment resulting in an outflow of $ 358 million. However, things changed thereafter. Gross disbursements of external commercial borrowings rose to

$ 2.9 billion in 1993-94 and further to $ 3.84 billion in 1994-95. In net terms, external commercial borrowings during 1993-94 and 1994-95 amounted to $ 1,252 million and $ 1,029 million respectively. External commercial borrowings are permitted by the government as an important source of finance for Indian firms for the expansion of existing capacity and also for new investments. There was a large demand for such borrowing in 1995-96 on account of revival of investments in 1994-95 and opening up of infrastructure sectors like power for increasing participation by the private sector.

Before we conclude this section, two more observations made by Bimal Jalan need to be pointed out. The first observation relates to the delays in implementing the large public sector projects and the consequent debt servicing problem. According to Jalan, most long-term commercial loans have to be repaid in 5 to 8 years. The gestation period of most of the large public sector projects is at least 4 to 5 years. In fact, these projects are often delayed further due to a number of reasons. This implies that the government has to cover the entire repayment liability before any financial or other benefit is available from the project. Even after going into commercial production, these projects add very little to exports, and this further compounds the debt servicing problem.

Jalan's second observation relates to the risk of depending too much on short-term borrowings. During 1987-91 India borrowed Rs.6,000-7,000 crores by way of short-term loans (of a maturity of less than one year). This was in addition to the accretions of Rs.10,000 crores of non-resident foreign currency deposits (with a maturity of three years or less). These short-term loans required continuous 're-rolling' in order to reduce the burden of repayment. However, with the fall in India's credit rating, the renewal of the short-term loans became difficult. By March 1991, India's credit rating slipped to the bottom of the investment grade and India had to make large repayment of short-term commercial loans. These short-term obligations created serious problems and India was pushed to the brink of default in 1991 - first time in its post-Independence history.

The above discussion shows that too much dependence on external commercial borrowings, in addition to a high cost method of raising resources, is fraught with serious risks. This is particularly true of short-term commercial loans. As noted by Jalan, "Banks are extremely susceptible to adverse developments in any sphere and can quickly withdraw support with or without adequate cause. in good times, international banks compete fiercdely with each other for business. In hard times, they act in unison. The withdrawal of support by a single bank can trigger off a chain reaction among all other banks." Therefore, it would be a wise policy for India to try to reduce the short-term debt in future.

FOREIGN INVESTMENT POLICY

Before independence, India was treated as the colony of British empire. Foreign goods in the Indian market were dumped thereby killing indigenous industries. The foreigners invested heavily in tea, coffee, rubber, mining etc. The conditions were so miserable that External Capital Committee, in 1925 recommended that while allowing the inflow of foreign capital interests of Indian industries should not be altogether ignored. The Committee also recommended that definite rules should be made regarding exploitation of natural resources of the country for commercial purposes, by the foreigners. The Committee recommended that, "In the case of public companies the company should be registered under the Indian Companies Act, with a share capital expressed in rupees and such proportion of the directors as government may prescribe should consist of Indians. Where the concession is granted to exploit a wasting asset, such as mineral rights, no definite rule can be prescribed."

In 1914 foreign capital in India amounted to \$ 298.4 millions and according to some estimates between two world wars this amount went upto \$ 1000 millions. It is now accepted almost by every impartial reviewer that the Britishers during their stay in India, did not make efforts to industrialise India.

Foreign Collaboration After Independence. India became independent in 1947 and was immediately faced with the problems created by the partition of the country. Moreover, being a backward nation, she needed foreign capital and collaboration for economic development and for having a sound industrial structure. There was absolute lack of technical personnel in the capacity. The people were economically poor with low saving capacity. The process of capital formation was very slow, with the result nation had no other alternative but to depend on foreign capital. Therefore, the Government of India followed the policy of allowing foreign capital to come to India, provided it was prepared to follow national policies. Loans were obtained at Government to Government levels, from wherever these could be. By June, 1948 foreign capital investment in India amounted to Rs. 3204 mn of which 62% was supplied by U.K. By 1953 this amount rose to Rs. 4530 mn. and India's long term foreign liabilities rose to Rs. 10353 mn. Net foreign exchange investment in 1969 in private sector increased by Rs. 1530 mn. from Rs. 4561 mn. in 1955 to Rs. 6107 mn. in 1959. At the end of 1974, foreign capital in India was 1482 crores, direct investment being Rs. 800 crores.

Foreign Assistance Under the Plans. After the partition of the country, India decided to progress through plans. In the First Five Year Plan of the total investment int he public sector the foreign aid was Rs. 2930 mn. which was 10.1% of the total outlay. In the Second Plan the total investment in the public sector was Rs. 46000 mn., out of which foreign aid was Rs. 11000 which amounted to 21.7%. In the Third Plan the total investment in the public sector was Rs. 75000 mn. and foreign exchange component was Rs. 22000 mn. which was 29.3% of the total outlay. In the Fourth Five Year Plan, whereas total investment in the public sector was Rs. 159020 mn.; the foreign aid amounted to Rs. 39960 *i.e.* 25.9% of the total outlay Net foreign aid during the Fifth Plan period worked out to only 3.1% of total investment and 4.6% of public sector investment.

Government's Policy Towards Foreign Capital In April 1949, the Government of India made it clear that the general industrial policy of the Government of India will make no discrimination between foreign and Indian enterprisers and also that reasonable facilities will be granted to the foreign investors for the remittances of profits and repatriation of capital. The Government then also assured all foreign investors that as and when there was nationalisation of an industry, proper compensation will be paid for that. The result was that inflow of foreign capital in the country considerably increased. In 1959, the Government of India again made it clear that foreign capital in the country will be a welcome and continues to be so. Due to stable political and economic conditions in the country, the flow of foreign capital continued both from the private and governmental agencies. The World Bank also came forward with liberal foreign aid. During the Second Five Year Plan, of the total foreign aid of Rs. 14840 mn., 57.7% came from the U.S.A. and World Bank extended loan amounting to Rs. 3150 mn. of which 1/2 came from private sector.

Foreign Investment Board. In order to streamline procedures relating to foreign investment in India and to avoid delays, in 1968, Foreign Investment Board was set up by the government. The Board is empowered to deal with all matters relating to private foreign investments and collaboration in cases where total equity capital does not exceed Rs. 2 crores and where the foreign investment does not exceed 40% of the issued equity capital. The cases which are not covered under these categories, will be cleared by the cabinet. In order to facilitate the things the Government of India has drawn up list of industries where foreign capital investment will be permitted or where that will not be permitted. The Government also decided that foreign collaboration will be resorted only for meeting critical gap and where maximum utilisation of domestic know how and services was not inhibited. In sophisticated industries know-how from abroad will be encouraged but in the case of consumer goods industries, investment was to be discouraged. In 1971-72 India signed 208 collaborative agreements which rose to 335 in 1973-74, the number being 256 in 1972-73. During 1971-72 the total value of consents granted by the controller of capital Issues to Joint Stock Companies for non resident participation amounted to Rs. 56 crores. The total value of consents to joint stock companies for non-resident participation amounted to Rs. 26.5 crores during the years 1973-74 as compared to Rs. 14.3 crores during 1972-73. Regarding nationalisation of foreign concerns in 1972 the Government of India decided that companies with foreign direct holdings exceeding 75% will have to raise 40% of the estimated cost of expansion-representing the cost of land building, plants and machinery by issue of additional capital to Indians. In 1973, a Committee set up by the Government of India recommended that foreign equity participation should not be permitted unless it was unavoidable and that the only mode left for requiring technology is through foreign equity participation. In spite of all these precautions and steps taken by the Government to ensure that foreign capital does not exploit Indians, unfortunately India's experience with foreign capital has not been very happy. The foreign nations were usually not prepared to part with their know how and wanted to increase the period of dependency. The role of private foreign capital in the country in quantitative terms has been very marginal and growth of foreign investment has been mainly through the process of reinvestment.

Policy of Indianisation. The Government of India has been constantly trying to reduce dependence on foreign collaboration and to Indianise industries to the extent possible. It is evident from the percentage of non Indian employed in foreign owned/controlled companies on salaries of Rs. 2000 and more per month where the total employment has registered a steady and sharp decline from 74.8% in 1960 to 36.1% in 1965 and to 13.4% in 1970 and is still further going down.

Under present conditions, India will have to depend on foreign collaboration as without that process of economic development and advancement on the one hand and that of capital formation on the other and will be slow. But at the same time India is quite conscious that process of Indianisation in the industrial and economic fields must be hastened.

FOREIGN CAPITAL AND COLLABORATION

For quite sometime India remained under foreign domination and control with the result that foreign capital poured into the country in large quantities. When India became free, it was amply clear that without active foreign collaboration, it might be impossible to make rapid progress in the economic field. Therefore efforts were made to attract foreign capital. Some of the main reasons as to why foreign capital was allowed to pour in the country were as under:

1. Low Saving Capacity. After independence, India needed heavy capital for industrial progress. But the people had low saving capacity. The country had no self-generating economy and rate of capital formation was slow and continues to be so even now. If currency is allowed to circulate then the problem of inflation arises, otherwise capital formation becomes impossible.

2. Essential for Technical Advancement. India is a poor country and technologically backward. It was more so when she got independence about 3 decades back. This technical know-how can come to a technically backward country like India, when foreign collaboration from technically advanced countries of the world is available. India in this way also needed foreign collaboration.

3. Essential for Strengthening Industrial Structure. Industrial structure of India can only be strengthened when capital goods and equipments are available in large quantities. But in India these are very much in short supply, because we have limited economic resources. India can import capital goods with foreign assistance and collaboration alone.

4. Essential for Getting Benefits of Research. In India research in scientific fields cannot be carried out to the extent to which it is carried out in industrially advanced countries. It is due to various reasons *e.g.*, research involves heavy funds which India has not got. Similarly there is shortage of competent people and nation cannot wait till the results of the research are available. If India is to take advantage of the research already carried out in other countries of the world, foreign assistance is unavoidable.

5. Inflationary Tendencies can be Checked. In India, economic inflation had posed and can pose serious problems at any time. It is because the tasks before the nation are too many and economic resources very limited. If India is to check inflationary tendencies and adopt effective measures to check the flow of the currency, it is essential that foreign assistance must be sought and obtained.

Why should Advance Nations Invest? A question arises, as to why at all should an advance country invest in a poor country. The reasons for this are quite obvious. Firstly advanced countries have economic and material resources. In case commodities produced, due to industrialisation, are not dumped in the under-developed countries, these are sure to pose serious economic problems for the producing country itself, resulting in the dislocation of the economy. Then another reason is that these countries have spare available technical personnel, who can get good jobs in these developing countries, thereby reducing pressure on their own resources. Again it is this collaboration which brings developed and developing countries closer and nearer to each other and helps in establishing contacts. Still another good reason can be that a developed country cannot have good bargains, with another developed country, in respect of surplus goods produced by it.

In our modern times, in order to have their influence and control, and to have markets for their commodities, advanced countries of the world are trying to have maximum harmonious contacts with the developing countries like India. Since independence many countries of the world have been showing more and more interest in extending collaboration to India. It is primarily because, the conditions in the country are quite conducive for that.

Mudialar Committee and its Findings. It was in 1966 that Government of India set up a Committee under the chairmanship of Rama Swami Mudaliar to find out to which extent import of technical know how could be dispensed with and indigenous know-how could be deemed to be capable of commercial exploitation. The Committee was also to give general guidelines regarding the types of the cases for allowing foreign collaboration.

Why Favourable Climate of Investments in India? In India, since independence, there has been remarkable political stability.

It has repeatedly been announced that foreign capital is welcome in the country, provided it accepts rules and laws of the land in operation and those to be enforced in future. Similarly all the foreign investors have been assured of return of the capital, if the investor behaves in the desired manner. Being free economy in India, the investor can expect reasonable returns. Due to these reasons, foreign capital always finds an attraction in India.

Recommendations of the Committee. The Committee's recommendations were available in 1967. In the view of the Committee only in such cases collaboration should be encouraged where substantial import of capital goods was involved to a considerable extent and Government policy allowed foreign capital collaboration. The Committee felt that only then the foreign collaborator will be directly interested in the success of the venture. Committee recommended that liberal approach should be adopted towards foreign capital in the case of substantially export oriented industries. The Committee was convinced that it was wrong to believe that foreign collaboration had killed indigenous initiative nor that due to foreign collaboration, India had been put at the mercy of advanced nations of the world, either for raw material or for components.

In this way India has not been depending on foreign collaboration, but the country is welcoming only that type of assistance, which in the ultimate analysis is likely to reduce her dependence on the countries, which are today extending their cooperation, so that the nation becomes self-sufficient.

ADVANTAGES AND DISADVANTAGES OF FOREIGN CAPITAL

Poor nations need foreign capital to improve their economy. But this investment too has its problems. But foreign capital has certain adverse effects on the economy of poor nations as well. Advantages and disadvantages of investment of foreign capital on the economy of foreign nations, many briefly be discussed as under:

Advantages of Foreign Capital

To Meet Foreign Exchange Needs. In a poor country there is always shortage of resources. It is also always in a hurry to industrialise itself. But till the needs of the people cannot be deferred, these can be met by importing goods from various countries, where these are available. For this foreign exchange is needed. No poor nation has enough foreign exchange resources to meet these demands, with the result that these nations are always dependent upon the rich ones for meeting their foreign exchange needs, for which foreign assistance is unavoidable.

2. Need for Supplementary Resources. Poor nations have very limited resources. In many cases, these are so limited that these can not meet even minimum basic needs of the people. At the same time, these nations cannot hope to raise funds from internal resources, due to low paying capacity of the people. These nations therefore, needs additional capital, by which these can supplement their resources. These supplementary resources can be available only from the foreign capital.

3. Necessary for Meeting Domestic Needs. Poor nations are always in a vicious circle. These want to industrialise themselves, and to become self-sufficient. But for that money is needed which these cannot raise. In this way a never ending circle goes on. In order to break it, it is essential that the poor nations should have sufficient assistance from abroad and needless to say that foreign capital can go a long way in breaking the circle.

4. Better Mobilisation of Domestic Resources. Usually it is seen that in poor countries the capital is shy and the masses wish to avoid payment of taxes, mostly because they are poor and have no paying capacity. But when foreign capital is prepared to invest in the country, on the condition that domestic capital is also available, then national capital begins to come forward. Not only this but the government makes every effort to see that national resources are mobilised and made available to the foreign investor, so that economic growth of the country does not suffer. Thus foreign capital helps in Mobilisation of economic resources.

5. Helps in Completing National Projects. For economic development of a nation, it is essential that the nation should undertake projects which can accelerate economic growth. These projects can be setting up of new industries, modernising of existing industries, thereby increasing output and making them work to the fullest capacity and so on. These projects can accelerate economic growth of the nation But usually each project for its installation and completion will need foreign exchange. In its absence, not only this that economic growth will slow down, but the projects may even not be completed.

6. Multipurpose Schemes can be Undertaken. A poor nation may take up short term and single purpose schemes; but at the same time may give up costly multipurpose schemes, on the plea that these are beyond nation's reach. It may abandon them clearly knowing that if executed, these can help solving nation's many problems very easily and quickly. These schemes might also be abandoned simply because their completion will take very long item and the nation may not be in a position to strain resources for such long periods. Accordingly the nation might feel discouraged to take such projects on hand. But once foreign assistance and capital is available, the nation will definitely feel encouraged and tempted to undertake those projects.

7. Helps Maintaining Consumption Level. Consumption level of the population in poor countries is very low. The masses have very poor income and as such cannot spend on anything and everything. Their purchasing power is very low. In case out of this limited income they are required to pay heavy taxes, their spending vis-a-vis consumption capacity will very much go down. When foreign capital is available, the people are not taxed heavily and as such they can maintain their minimum consumption standard.

8. Helps in Providing Employment. One of the most serious problems of the poor countries is that of un-employment. Due to non-industrialisation, there are limited employment opportunities. The state is not in a position to provide employment by undertaking any multi-purpose long term costly project. The nation is not in a position to provide any employment even to very competent and qualified people. The result of all this is that discontentment and dissatisfaction among the people increases. But when the foreign capital is available, new industries and projects can be started. The nation goes fast on the path of industrialisation. With this employment opportunities are bound to increase.

9. Help in Maintaining Financial Stability. When a poor nation has limited economic resources and heavy demands by the people, one of the methods adopted is that of issuing paper currency without taking proper measures for checking inflationary tendencies. The result is that the value of the currency considerably goes down. The nation is forced to devalue its currency in the international market, creating many more problems for the people. Purchasing capacity of the people still more goes down. There is great economic stability in the country. The only way out to solve the problem is that of getting assistance from the foreign countries. With the aid of advanced countries, it becomes possible to meet demands of the people without much straining nation's resources.

10. Exploitation of Resources. Nature has blessed each country with some resources. These are very useful for the development of a country, if properly exploited. Rich countries have enough capital and technical know how to exploit those resources whereas poor nations have neither technical personnel, nor economic resources nor other facilities to exploit the resources. The result of all this is that poor nations cannot make their proper use. These remain buried where these are. In case foreign capital is available and these resources can be properly exploited, then many economic problems of a poor nation can be solved.

11. Helps in Proper Utilisation of Man Power. In developing countries usually there is population explosion and surplus manpower, which creates many social and economic problems instead of solving them. In case foreign capital is available, services of the surplus manpower-skilled, semi-skilled and unskilled, can be used for constructive purposes, instead of destructive ones, as is the case in many poor nations these days.

12. New Techniques of Management. Under developed or undeveloped nations usually do not have much knowledge about new and latest management techniques, with the result that even if foreign capital is made available to them, these might not be in a position to efficiently use that. But when a nation provides some assistance to another, usually new management techniques are discussed and even arrangements are made for providing sufficient training for new management techniques.

13. Helps in Research. Research in all walks of life is a very costly affair. When poor nations cannot afford. But unless research is done, it is difficult to find out new avenues for development. Therefore, a situation is created in which without research there is no advancement and without money there is no research. This problem can best be solved if foreign assistance is available, either in the from of capital grant or necessary research facilities are made available to the nation.

14. Helps in Creating Permanent Assets. Many new projects are undertaken with the help of foreign capital. These include construction of roads, bridges, dams, railways etc. etc. The foreign agency which constructs them, can not take these capital projects back after agreements providing financial assistance are over. These become permanent assets of the country, which can be used for all subsequent programmes of development. Had foreign capital not come to the aid of the poor countries, they would not have been in a position to build up these assets and their whole programme would have come to a standstill for quite sometime.

Foreign capital plays a very big and important role in the growth and development of economy of a poor nation. In many cases it even does pioneering work, in the sense that the money is spent in those projects, in which native capital is shy feeling that the money might not sink. The risk of loss is thus boldly borne by the nations which advance loan and importance of this aspect cannot be under-estimated in any manner.

Disadvantages of Foreign Capital Investment

1. Makes the Nation Dependent. It is said that when foreign capital is available, the nation becomes dependent. The people themselves become lazy and lethargic. They do not work hard, since they know that for completing their projects, some country or the other will come forward with financial assistance. They would otherwise have worked hard and tried to ensure that with their own labour, their programme should be completed and targets achieved.

2. Opposed to Self Sufficiency. Then another disadvantage is that this type of aid is opposed to idea of self sufficiency. When foreign aid is available then poor nations become slow in achieving self sufficiency. These are in no hurry to set up machinery or acquire technical know how very speedily or readily.

3. Encourages Inflationary Tendencies. Each nation has its own economic policies and programmes, which must keep pace with its economic resources. Budgets are prepared and finalised on the basis of those estimates. But when foreign money pours in, particularly unexpectedly, then more money become available. It gets circulated and upsets the whole economy. Inflationary tendencies get encouragement. In this way poor nations are faced with the serious problem of inflation. We know that once this circle starts it becomes difficult to check that.

4. Sudden Burden on the Nation. In order to meet the demands of the people or to gain popularity, the government of the day goes on borrowing. But after sometime the question of repayment of the loan comes. At that time the nation is forced to save out of its limited resources. The result is that there is sudden burden on national economy, which many poor nations cannot afford. The result is that economies of many recipient nations is shaken from the very foundations.

5. Politically Unhealthy Effects. Powerful and economically well off, almost always try financial aid to have direct or indirect strings attached to aid In case there are no such visible strings, the expectations always are that the recipient nation will depend on the powerful nation. In this way foreign aid upsets, political behaivour of the poor nations and makes them politically dependent on the powerful nations.

6. Heavy Cost of Foreign Capital. Usually foreign capital is invested in an industry in which there are chances of quick returns and heavy profits. In fact when foreign capital is invested, share is demanded in profits and the investor is given some dividend. The capital also charges some interest. Thus usually interest, dividend and profit comes to about 40% of the total return. Thus 40% of the total income is drained out and only 60% is left for the labour of the natives. This drainage of 40% is obviously not reasonable or justifiable.

7. Undependable in Difficulties. Foreign capital has always a tendency to earn maximum profit. This tendency becomes still more visible when the economy of the recipient nations begins to totter down. At this stage foreign investment should Sick firmly to the aid of the poor country. But it is at this stage that it begins to withdraw itself.

8. Money Cannot be invested in Key Sectors. Maximum investment is needed in key sector industries and it is in the development of these sectors *e.g.* manufacture of defence material, installation of steel factories etc. that every nation is most interested. But it is unfortunate that money cannot be spent in these sectors because that would mean leakage of national secrets, which can harm any nation, particularly when hostilities break out.

9. Exploitation of Natural Resources. With the foreign capital there is always ruthless exploitation of natural resources resulting in unbalanced economic development. While spending, foreign nations always keep their interests before the interest of the recipient nations.

10. Natives Denied Responsible Jobs. After the capital has been invested the loaning nation is very keen that it should preserve its interests and the capital. This is done by keeping all the key posts with itself. In this way their own incompetent people are preferred over competent natives. Thus all important jobs are denied to the natives and also they are not given proper training, so that they can deal with their own affairs in a most competent manner, after the foreign power has left the land.

Of course, inflow of foreign capital has its bad effects and influences on the economy of a poor nation and even sometimes may do considerable harm, yet no poor nation can ever think of disowning it. If the people are courageous, determined and decided to end dependence quickly, all that they can do is that with their efforts, and proper use of foreign capital they can reduce the period of dependence and nothing beyond that.

PRIVATE FOREIGN CAPITAL

Foreign capital refers to that part of total capital stock of a country whose ownership belongs to the foreigners. In other words, this represents the foreign investments in a country in its various spheres of economy. Since these investments are made by the foreigners in their private capacity (as against the loans and grants given by the foreign governments), it is called Private Foreign Capital. And, further, these investments are made directly in various business activities, industry or trade, this is also known as Direct Business Investment.

Advantages of Foreign Capital. Foreign capital confers certain distinct important benefits on the receiving country. First, we know that the rate of growth of an economy depends crucially on the growth rate of capital accumulation. Thus, for economic and industrial development the country must possess adequate supply of capital. But, unfortunately, the domestic sources cannot provide all the capital requirements required for the planned growth of the less developed countries. Consequently, there is a gap of capital resources, which must somehow be filled up if the economy has to achieve the planned rate of growth. Foreign capital can be used to fill up this gap, by supplementing the domestic capital supply it enables the underdeveloped countries to plan and achieve a higher growth rate of the economy.

Secondly, foreign capital ensures the best possible use of foreign funds. The private profit motive of the foreigners guide them to make investments in such a manner as to assure the maximum possible rate of return. The self interest of the foreign investors thus prevents the flow of capital into unproductive and wasteful activities.

Thirdly, as we know, in the less developed countries there are many unexplored fields and unexploited resources. Investments in these areas may be risky; they may yield fruit or not. Drilling for oil is one such example where many of the wells, where drilling is made, turn out to be unprofitable, use of scarce domestic capital resources in such fields may be full of risks. However, if foreign capital is used in these sectors, the risk is entirely borne by the foreigners and the country has nothing to lose.

Fourthly, foreign capital also helps in development and adoption of modern technology and efficient management techniques. Foreigners not only bring their capital, but also along with it, their techniques, engineers and technicians, management personnel and other specialists in various branches of business. Working with them, the natives too learn new techniques, better ways of organisation, new knowledge, modern work ethics, all of which can then be fruitfully utilized in other various spheres of industry and trade.

Lastly, perhaps the biggest advantage of foreign capital is that this type of investment does not pose any problems that are associated with foreign loans viz., repayment of loans and the interest on them. This is because this capital has been invested by the foreigners voluntarily and of their own risk. It is not a borrowed money which has to be paid back with interest. This foreign capital does not create balance of payments difficulties.

Disadvantages of Foreign Capital. From the above discussion, it can be concluded that foreign capital is a thing of extremely great help in the economic development of underdeveloped countries; it accelerates the process of economic and industrial development by supplementing the meagre domestic capital resources. But as our experience with foreign capital has shown, it is not an unmixed blessing. There are a number of arguments that can be put forward against foreign capital.

Firstly, it can be said that foreign capital, instead of helping the process of a more harmonious growth of the economy as a whole, creates further imbalances and distortions in the economy of the underdeveloped countries. Experience shows that most of the foreign investments have remained concentrated in extractive industries like exploitation of mineral wealth or in plantations like tea, rubber or in industries like jute or crops like cotton cultivation, all of which were meant not for the domestic market but for the more lucrative export markets. Such investments generally deplete the precious natural resources of the country only for the benefit of the foreign investors. They having nothing to do with the development of the economy of the country where these investments are made.

Secondly, it has been made out that foreign capital brings with it most modern technology, knowledge and experience, from which the local people can learn a lot and use it in other spheres of activity. But it is doubtful whether the foreign capitalists, in any way, help in the spread of modern technical knowledge in the underdeveloped countries. More often than not, such knowledge is kept as a closely guarded secret. In fact, there is always a great degree of discrimination against the local people who are never given higher positions in such foreign enterprises.

Thirdly, foreign capital may lead to excessive dependence of our economy on the foreign countries from where the capital has come in or the multinational firms which control foreign investments in the country. The MNCs are the big industrial giants with their headquarters in an advanced capitalist country and its branches and subsidiaries spread over many other countries. All these branches of the MNCs work with the sole purpose of maximising their global profits. These firms are so big that their sales turnover sometimes exceeds the GNP of many of the less developed countries. Then, by their sheer influence or domination in various sectors of an underdeveloped economy, and by corrupting the political machinery of a country, they may render a country entirely dependent on their mercy. This dominance-dependence relationship is highly prejudicial to the national interest of any country; it prevents the country from chalking out its own policies and programme best suited to its requirements; it makes our political set-up and political leadership a mere pawn in the hands of the foreigners; and it distorts consumption patterns of our population, retards domestic savings and capital formation and slackens the process of economic development.

Foreign Capital in India. Prior to Independence, there was substantial amount of foreign investments in India. Much of this capital was engaged in plantations and extractive industries. Almost the entire tea plantations, most of the jute mills, petroleum sector, rubber industries and many of the consumer goods industries were owned by the foreign capitalists. Largest share of foreign investments in India belonged to the United Kingdom followed by the USA. The other important countries who had made investments in India were Japan, Holland, France, West Germany and Canada. However, after Independence, the policy of the Government of India laid emphasis on accepting foreign investments with the majority participation of the Indian nationals. Further many of the foreign enterprises, particularly those in the petroleum sector were nationalised. Equity capital of many others was diluted to give major share of ownership, management and control to the Indians. Consequently, the flow of foreign investments declined and became almost a trickle in the past few decades. Consequently, the Government adopted a more liberal policy towards foreign investments.

UTILISATION OF FOREIGN CAPITAL

It is abundantly clear that no poor nation can make progress and go on the path of prosperity, unless capital from outside pours in. This leads us to another question, namely what is proper utilisation of foreign capital.

Some of the important methods which can be suggested in this regard are:

1. Use for Self Generation of Economy. Foreign capital should be used for self generating economy. When the capital is being used for setting up machines and industrialising the country, there will be growth in the economy. The capital spent will help in the generation of further capital. In this way dependency will reduce and economy will generate itself.

2. Should be Treated Supplementary and not Substitute. Foreign capital should always be treated as supplementary to the national capital and not substitute for it. In case it is considered as substitute, then there will be lethargy and slackness. The natives will feel that they have a substitute for their labour. If on the other hand it is considered as supplementary, then the intention will be that unless capital from national resources is available, foreign capital will have no meaning. It would mean equally hard work for creating capital form internal resources.

3. Should be used for creating Permanent Assets. It is most essential that the capital should be used for creating permanent assets. Once these assets have been created then the nation will continue enjoy the benefits of these assets; no matter whether the loaning nation continues to extend financial support or not. Obviously after the creation of the assets, the nation which extended financial assistance cannot take them back.

4. Should be Used for Priority Projects. Loan is not a charity. It is to be repaid with profit and interest. it is therefore, just burdening coming generations. Therefore, it should be spent only on priority projects. If the loan is being made available for low priority projects the nation may not even accept that. Therefore, only such loans should be obtained and utilized for the purpose for which the nation has fixed a priority.

5. Least Spent on Consumable Goods. Usually there is tendency on the part of the poor nations that these spend heavily on the import of consumption goods, just to meet immediate demands of the people. The money spent on the import of consumption goods as cosmetics, stationery goods etc. is merely a waste and a costly luxury, which the nation can not afford because money spent on the import of these goods is not better than the money wasted and this wastage should be saved for proper utilisation of foreign capital.

6. Should be invested in Collaborative Projects. One of the methods, which can be suggested for proper utilisation of foreign capital is that it should be invested in collaborative projects. Before the start of the project the loaning nation must clearly indicate its commitments and the recipient nation has clear idea about its responsibilities. In this way there is a joint effort to complete the project. But as already said the poor nation should clearly understand that the project is covered under the priority areas and not that a secondary project is getting priority over the primary project simply because foreign loan for the former is available.

7. Should be spent under National Management. Foreign capital can be better utilised, if it is spent under national management. It can be properly utilised, if it is considered as a training ground for the local people and their managerial capital capacity is best developed and they are made to learn how best are the alternatives available to the nation, for spending available foreign capital.

8. Used for Producing Finished Goods. A nation can only earn, if it can produce finished goods. If it goes on producing only raw material, then that will have to be taken out of the country normally at low rates of payment It will be turned into finished goods and sold in the same country which supplied raw material, at higher rates and the profit will be kept by the nation which turned material into finished goods. It will be proper and scientific use of foreign capital, if that is used for producing finished goods, instead of simply producing some raw material in rude or refine from and so on.

9. Improvement of Quality. It is seen that some of the poor nations produce a commodity, which is of poor quality. Due to lack of sophisticated equipments of production, the goods cannot be produced in bulk, with the result that the cost also cannot come down. The outcome of this is that goods cannot compete international market. Not only this, but the problem is that local people also do not accept low quality goods and they prefer foreign goods over the locally manufactured goods. They do not patronise local industry which at first suffers losses and then closure. The Government is forced to spend heavily on the import of better quality goods from outside. If the foreign capital is available, one of its best use will be to use that for the improvement of quality of the goods already being produced, so that, these are acceptable to the society on the one hand, and can face international competition on the other.

These are some of the suggestions which can be made for proper utilisation of foreign capital. But it must be remembered that the conditions of economy differ from nation to nation and those who are on the spot can best decide about proper utilisation of available foreign capital. on thing however, all the nations take into consideration is that inflow of foreign capital, does not strain national economy, by creating inflationary tendencies and trends.

INVESTMENT IN DEVELOPING ECONOMY

Industrial growth is essential for economic development of a nation, but at the same time it is also essential that national resources should be so distributed that all sectors of national life take proper advantage of nation's resources. In other words there should be investment in a planned way. There is no single criteria of investment in a planned economy. Some of the important criteria which have so far been discussed however, are as under:

1. Capital Output Criteria. According to this there should be close relationship between the capital invested and the output, which the investment would give to the society. The lower is the capital output ratio, the higher would be the rate of growth of the economy. This ratio helps in finding out the productivity of capital in various sectors of economy at a given point of time. Then the idea underlying is that projects in which money is to be spent are complete substitutes of each other. But this criteria has been put to several criticisms. Some of the important points of criticism are:

The criteria proceeds on the assumption that in the economic world, there is substitutability, but that is not actually so. There can be projects which may be supplementary to each other and not their substitutes *e.g.* industrial and agricultural projects. Then another criticism advanced is that, it is believed that output at a given point of time is the indication of development, but that is not so because the real indication of proper investment is rate of growth over a period of time and not development. Capital output ratio might be influenced by political and social considerations. The criteria proceeds on the presumption that capital output criteria is the sole one for determining output ratio, but that is not so. It can be only one of the criterion. There can be considerations about labour investment ratio, employment and distribution of wealth considerations as well.

2. Marginal Social Productivity Criteria. This has been given by Prof. Kahn. According to him, "The correct criterion for obtaining the maximum return from limited resources is marginal productivity or from the point of view of society as a whole, social marginal productivity." According to this criteria investment should be made in such projects in which social marginal productivity is the highest. According to them the investment should be so made that it maximises the ratio of current output to investment on the one hand and that of labour to investment on the other. Investment should also be made in the projects which might help in improving the real income and which help in producing such goods, which meet basic needs of the society. While investing care should be taken to see that the projects should be such which help in promoting external economies and in which maximum use is made that of domestic raw material.

3. Rate of Turnover Criteria. This criteria has been given by Polak and as such it is known as Polak's Rate of Turnover Criterion. According to this criteria the basic principle of investment should be that the capital should be invested in such projects which yield the highest value of output, as compared with investment. Turnover is likely to be higher in consumer rather than capital goods industries. But again this criteria has been put to criticism. If this criteria is accepted then maximum investment will have to be made in consumer goods industries, which may appear attractive for the present, but cannot, be termed as safe policy for the future development of the nation. Thus by this criteria of investment, rate of growth for the future will receive a serious set back. Then another criticism is that if investment is linked with turnover, then in some cases it may happen that high turn over may be owing to high rate of depreciations, but actually the net rate of output may not be high.

4. Employment Absorption Criteria. This is another criteria which is considered more appropriate for the poor countries. According to this criteria, capital should be invested in such projects where more labour and less capital is needed. It is because the poor countries are faced with the serious problem of unemployment and surplus man power. This criteria may not be very appropriate for the countries, which are not faced with the problems of surplus man power. But this criteria has also been put to certain criticisms. If this criteria is applied, then one cannot be sure whether that would maximise output. It is just possible that some techniques which require some capital and less labour may give better output, but may not be applied because the criteria requires less capital and more labour. Then another criticism advanced is that it makes labour employment an end in itself, rather than means to an end. In fact investment is made for the purposes of output. Thus output is end in itself, whereas employment is means to an end. Then it is also said that if this criteria is adopted in actual practice that would mean perpetuation of low labour productivity, which no nation can ever afford.

5. Local Community Works Criteria. Almost all underdeveloped and undeveloped countries have agricultural economy. Usually land needs much more man power than what it needs. The result is that though apparently the people may appear to be engaged on work, yet in actual practice, they are unemployed. This type of unemployment is also known as disguised unemployment. The criteria of local community works starts on the premise that there are many projects at the local community level, which can be undertaken by the society and turned as permanent assets. These projects though minor, can provide employment to the local people. These include construction of a school building or road of the village or a community centre. But this criteria has been considered as very limited and narrow, particularly int he sense, that it is bound to localise the capital and will surely not help in productivity. Of course a part of the investment can be diverted in this direction, but not the whole of it.

6. Balance of Payment Criteria. Underdeveloped and undeveloped nations always have unfavourable balance of payment. It is primarily beçause, these nations are to depend on developed nations for meeting most of their requirements. Many nations even import consumption goods. The loans which are taken by the poor nations are a liability for the future generations. This criteria of investment provides that amount should be so invested that unfavourable balance of payment is reduced. it means that the nation should spend and invest in such projects which help making the nation self-sufficient and less dependent on other nations.

Of course, it is a very good criteria of investment and no one can deny that each nation should make an attempt to become as much self-sufficient, as possibly it can. But at the same time it cannot be denied that no nation can spend all the resources on simply financing those projects on which it is to depend on other nations.

7. Time Lag Criteria. This is another criteria which has been suggested for investment of capital. Every nation is required to spend in two types of projects. One project is of the types which is likely to take long time for its completion. the nation will be required to spend heavily on that and it will have to wait for a very long time, till the project has been completed, and the nation can reap the fruit of investment. Then on the other hand there are short term projects. These do not need heavy investment. Much time is also not needed for their completion and nation begins to reap the fruit after sometime. Underdeveloped and undeveloped countries cannot afford to invest on long term projects, though that is a permanent investment. It is simply because the capital is short and priority needs many. The desire of the people is to meet needs as quickly as possible. If the nation is taxed for reaping fruit after a very long time, the result will be that the people will get dissatisfied. They are likely to feel that they are not being rewarded for what they are paying.

Of course the criteria is good, particularly for the poor nations, where the people are usually impatient for the results. But at the same time no nation can afford ignoring long time projects. Take the example of agriculture. Every nation which has agricultural economy, must undertake major irrigation projects on hand and try to complete as quickly as possibly it can, if in the agricultural field it wants to become self-sufficient. If the nation goes on postponing that then in practice, it will be postponing self-sufficiency. We also find that construction of dams and railway lines etc., are long term investments, but the question is whether can any nation afford to ignore them. Infact there might be situations in which investment on long term projects may get priority over investment on short term projects.

8. Market Demand Criteria. Then it is said that the money should be invested in such projects, which have ready market. That market can be both at the national and international level. This would mean immediate return for the money invested. It will also mean that the nation will not have to wait till the market is created and the goods are accepted by the society. Obviously when there is ready market for the goods, money gets into circulation very quickly and becomes available to the nation for reinvestment. This criteria is considered very useful for nations which have scarce money and short and shy capital. These nations obviously cannot wait till market for their products is created. This becomes particularly difficult in so far as international market is concerned, where competition is tough and the nations which are already in the market, may not allow entry to other nations. Of course, it is a good criteria, but greatest limitations of this in that in case investment is made only on such projects, where ready market is available, then the nation can never go on the path of progress. It will never be in a position to explore market for the commodities which have potentialities of growth. in the international market it will remain backward.

9. Criteria of External Economies. Some of the economists have come forward with the idea that the money should be invested in such projects which give benefits of external economies. According to them while investing particular care should be taken to see that investment is made in such industries, which give encouragement to the setting up of other industries. According to them, if this criteria is accepted then a chain of new industries will come up which will make the nation self-sufficient quickly and speedily.

Again in favour of this criteria, it can be said that it is good in so far as coming up of new industries is concerned. It must be accepted and appreciated that sooner new industries set up, better will it be for the nation, to get itself industrialise and become self-sufficient. Quicker industrialisation is bound to enhance the prestige of the nation. But at the same time it must be accepted that it is not always essential that only those industries which give the benefit of external economies to the nation are good. There can be and always are many industries which must be expanded, maintained and strengthened simply because these are priority areas, no matter whether the benefits of extra economies are available to the nation or not.

10. Technique Intensive Industries Criteria. Setting up of every industry needs certain techniques. These techniques can be of two types namely (a) managerial techniques and (b) machine techniques. From managerial techniques we understand that the top level persons or supervisory personnel in good number are available to run the industry and to put the capital to maximum use. In case competent persons are not available, then the industry will suffer. Similarly machine needs competent people to run it, this aspect becomes particularly important when more and more sophisticated machines are set up. A machine might be costly and prepared for giving extensive output, but in case there are no competent people to run that, then the same machine, instead of becoming an asset will become a liability.

The importance of this criteria is fully well realised and appreciated but for the poor countries, this is also loaded with some serious problems. First important serious problem is that what should be the policy of a poor nation in so far as labour intensive and machine intensive techniques are concerned. Poor nations are always faced with the problem of utilisation of surplus man power. In case machine intensive techniques are adopted then in practice that will mean replacing man by machine. It will also mean rendering the people surplus and instead of solving the problems of unemployment, it will mean creation of unemployment problem. If investment means creation of unemployment, then it cannot be a wise policy and no nation will ever cherish that. Then another difficulty with these nations is whether they should lay stress on techniques oriented or labour oriented investment. In case it is technique oriented, then the problem of employing labour will come to the front.

11. Leading Sectors Criteria. This criteria has been given by Prof. Rostow. According to him sectors of economy can be divided into three categories. According to the exponents of this criteria, if investment is concentrated in a limited number of such leading sectors, which generate growth in multiple ways, then the investment will be most useful. But this criteria too has been subjected to criticism and is being discussed separately.

12. Reinvestment Criteria. This criteria has been given by Walter Galenson and Harvey Leibenstein. It says that allocation of resources will be optimum when the marginal per-capita reinvestment quotient of capital is equalised in its various alternative uses. But this criteria has also been criticised. This is being discussed separately with some details.

13. Balanced Development Criteria. Many economists have come forward with the idea that it is wrong to think that there are certain more priority whereas others are less priority areas. For the advancement of a nation, all the areas should be given full and proper attention. They feel that it is difficult for the nation to decide whether industry or agriculture should fall in the priority category. Similarly, it is difficult for any nation to decide whether producer goods should have priority over consumer goods or vice versa. Therefore,, according to these economists, every nation should invest in the projects without taking into consideration priorities. According to them it is only then that balanced development will be possible.

But again this criteria is loaded with difficulties. As we know that no nation in actual practice can forget that there are some priority and other non-priority projects. How can a nation suppose that all are priority projects. In case scarce resources are also utilised for non-priority projects, then the nation will not be in a position to have proper returns for the investment made and on the whole it will be the sufferer.

❐

7

Public Sector and Policies

GROWTH OF PUBLIC SECTOR UNDERTAKINGS IN INDIA

In India, before independence, there were limited public sector undertakings. Except Post and Telegraphs and Railways, there were practically no public sector undertakings, though in some States and Provinces very small undertakings had been set up. Even after independence, for sometime no attempt was made to set by industries in the public sector, because the Government had no clear policy and attitude in this regard. It was in Industrial Policy Resolution of 1948, that the Government decided that there were some vital sectors of economy in which industries will be set up in the public sector. Public Sector became, however, more important in 1954, when Indian Parliament accepted and adopted a resolution to the effect that socialistic pattern of economy was the future development of India's economy. In 1956, when new Industrial Policy Resolution was adopted, it was made clear that all basic and key industries will be set up in the public rather than private sector, with the result that the State accepted direct responsibility for setting up of new industries. The result of this clear Policy has been that over the years the government has been setting up more and more industries in key and important sectors of national economy, including fertilisers, steel, electronics, machine tools, heavy engineering goods etc.

Classification of Public Sector Enterprises. Public sector enterprises can broadly be classified as *(a)* Those under construction, *(b)* Running concerns, *(c)* Promotional and development and *(d)* financial institutions. What amount of money should be spent on each category of industry is of course, dependent on stage at which the industry is and the amount available with the government. In fact stress has been changing both from year to year and plan to plan. But one thing is certain that the investment has been increasing from year to year. At the time of commencement of the first Five Year Plan the total investment was Rs. 29 crores, which rose to 81 crores when second plan started. At the commencement of Third Plan this figure rose to Rs. 95 crores, whereas in March 1973, the investment was of Rs. 5426 crores. At the end of March, 1972, total amount invested, in some of the important industries in the public sector was Hindustan Steel Ltd. (Rs. 1038 crores); Bokaro Steel Ltd. (Rs. 656 crores); Shipping Corporation of India Ltd. (Rs. 129 crores); Fertilisers Corporation of India (Rs. 252 crores) and National Coal Development Corporation Ltd (Rs. 209 crores). At the end of 1973-74, there were as many as 122 undertakings under construction and in the running stage, which where directly under the moneylenders of the Central Government whereas in 1971-72 this number was 101 and it stood at 113 in 1972-73. Total investment in 1971-72 was Rs. 5052 crores; in 1972-73 it was Rs. 5571 crores and in 1973-74 investment stood at Rs. 6237 crores. The percentage rate of annual growth was 8, 10 and 12% respectively. At the end of 1977-78 amount invested in the sector was Rs. 12,851 crores.

Parliamentary Control. In India, working of Public sector undertakings is subject to parliamentary control. It is however, admitted that the Parliamentary control should be only in respect of policy matters and nothing beyond that. For the purpose the Parliament has also set up a separate committee on Public Undertakings.

Objectives of the Public Sector Undertakings. A very interesting question arises is whether the undertakings should or not be run on profit and loss basis. Today it is, however, believed that public sector undertakings should be run on 'profit and loss' basis, though there should be no exploitation of the society. Some of the main objectives of public sector undertakings in India are that:

1. Rate of economic growth should be maximised.
2. Sound economic foundations should be laid down, so that the people are in a position to have gainful employment.

3. Living conditions and standards of the workers should be improved.
4. Disparity of income and wealth, which is created by private sector, should be reduced to the minimum.
5. Growth of private monopolies and concentration of economic power in the hands of only few persons should be checked and protected.
6. To properly channalise small savings, to wide as well and deepen its scope.

But all these objectives are to be achieved with some considerations namely that there is maximisation of output, quality of goods produced, creation of funds needed for reinvestment, maintenance of labor efficiency and operation of the whole undertaking in such a fashion that the society feels the utility of the undertaking as a whole.

Role of Public & Private Sector

In every society private and public sectors go hand in hand in the economic field. Till the close of 19th century the role of public sector in the development of industries was almost negligible. It was because till then the concept of laissez fair or free trade was catching the imagination of the people. It was believed that each industry must face the competition and let there be survival of the fittest. The idea of laissez faire when put into practical be however, resulted in many evils. It was responsible for the exploitation of the workers who were paid very low wages. There was also concentration of wealth in the hands of very few people. On the whole the outcome was that in the industries where the workers toiled and laboured from morning till evening, they got not enough to maintain themselves. There was therefore a great demand that the state must step in to save the workers from exploitation and more industries should be set up by the government, so that the workers could be provided adequate amenities and facilities and their ruthless exploitation could be effectively checked. Soon after when welfare states began to emerge the concept of police state gave way to that.

Private Sector Defined. Industry needs money and capital. It also requires man power, initiative and risk. When the money is invested by a person or by only few persons who are very closely related to each other and have personal interests only, that is called private sector. In such a system responsibility for taking initiative, vests with that person or group of persons. They formulate, and execute all policies and all appointments etc. are made by the investors of the money. All the losses suffered by the industry are borne by them. Similarly they pocket all the profits earned by the industry. The industry is then not responsible to the public for its doings and activities.

Public Sector Defined. As against private sector, there is public sector. In this sector all the money spent in setting up an industry is spent from the public exchequer. The management is responsible to the Parliament/Legislature for all its failures as well as achievements. In this sector, it is not the profit which is major consideration, but important consideration is need and necessity of the people. The demand of the society is considered paramount. Profit and losses are shared by the tax payers.

Advantages of Public Sector. Public and private sectors have their own advantages and disadvantages. In fact advantages of one are the disadvantages of the other and vice-versa. Advantages of Public Sector are as under.

1. Possible to Spend Heavy Amounts. There are some industries which need heavy investment. A private sector may not have enough resources to raise capital with the result that industry will either be completely ignored, or not flourish. On the other hand, the state has sufficient resources. Once it is felt that there is need for setting up the industry the state will find finances and see that the industry is set up. In this category one can quote instances of heavy amounts required for setting up steel or shipping industry etc.

2. Easy to Raise Loans. In case the finances are needed for setting up of an industry public sector which is backed by the state, will have much more credit than the private sector. The result will be that it will be easy for the public sector to raise loans as compared with the private sector which will obviously face many difficulties in raising loans for setting up an industry.

3. No Desire for Quick Returns. Even if the private sector has enough capital, it will like to have quick returns. Every capitalist will therefore, be tempted to spend in such projects which are of short duration and likely to repay money. On the other hand in so far as public sector is concerned, there is no such consideration. The amount spent is primarily for meeting social needs, rather than expecting quick returns.

4. Non Shyness of Capital. Capital with the investor is always shy. It will not easily come out in the market. Private industrialist will think several times before spending. But in so far as public sector is concerned, the capital is not shy. It is always ready to make up any gap.

5. Availability of Better Skills. For running each good industry, it is essential that well qualified and trained staff should be available. It is also essential that there should be adequate research and training facilities. All these are costly affair and not possible for the private industrialists. But in so far as public sector is concerned state will be in a position to spend.

6. Mass Production Possible. In so far as production is concerned private sector will be guided by many factors. The greatest restraint is the capital. Though in some cases, this sector may like to produce large quantities of goods, but by and large it may not be in a position to do so, for want to finances or machinery or trained staff etc. But in so far as public sector is concerned, with its vast resources, it is possible for the Government to produce at large scale, once it is convinced that such a production is badly needed.

7. Better Control Over Marketing. Private Sector with limited resources cannot have that effective control over the market, as that is enjoyed by the public sector. The later has more distribution facilities. It can approach the customers with ease and provide better utility services, as compared with the private sector, which would provide them comparatively costly good with less dependency. Moreover, private sector will be in a position to cover a limited market.

8. Social Utility of Profits. Industry is run with a view to earning profits. But when the profits are available to private sector then these are used for their personal advancement. On the other hand, when these are available to the public sector, these are used for the welfare of the society as a whole. Thus whereas in the private sector the profits become a source of exploitation, in public the same profit becomes source of public service.

9. Money Becomes Available for Priority Development Areas. In every society the sources are scarce and limited as compared with the needs of the society which are always unlimited. The State has therefore, no other alternative, but to fix priorities. When the industry is in private sector, there is no such consideration. On the other hand when it is in public sector, then alone such priority areas are located. If the industry in other areas is earning profits, the amounts available can be spent on the development of priority areas, resulting in over all development of the national economy.

10. Easy Availability of Resources. In every society there are always shortages. The state is but to regulate great able resources. This is done by issuing licences etc. But when the industry is in the public sector, then many of the problems which ordinarily arise and are considered hurdles by the private sector, do not come on the way at all. The state arranges raw material as a matter of responsibility and ensures that production does not go down simply because the supplies in one form or the other were not available.

11. Sense of Confidence. When a commodity is being manufactured in a private sector, the consumer can not sure about standards. He thus remains under the impression that he is being cheated and paying more. On the other hand when the articles are being manufactured in the public sector, there is confidence that the goods manufactured will be of high standard. There is also a sense of confidence that there will be no unreasonable margin of profit.

12. Foreign Loans can be Obtained. For setting up many industries foreign exchange is badly needed in many cases. In fact there can be industries in which foreign exchange component can be very high. It is essential to arrange for foreign loan to proceed with the work. But at the same time it cannot be expected that the industry will immediately start repaying the loans. The loan will therefore, have to be arranged on long term basis.

13. Foreign Collaboration becomes Available. There are many projects which need foreign collaboration. This collaboration can be both for longer as well as shorter period. This can be in the form of technical know how on in the shape of financial assistance. Such a collaboration can be in term of lending the experts for planning and execution of the industrial programmes. Without such collaboration, it may even not be possible to set up highly technical or sophisticated industries. Obviously a private sector industrialist cannot manage to have successful international collaboration. He will have to look to the Government to arrange for the people and machine from abroad. On the other hand, when industry is proposed to be set up in the public sector, or it has already started working and its expansion is needed, then foreign collaboration in any form can easily be managed.

14. Attraction for Foreign Investment. Most of the developing countries, both in the public and private sectors, do not have enough economic resources. Inspite of their best efforts the nation cannot have rapid economic development for want of finances. The result is that either industrial advancement should be slowed down or foreign capital should be attracted. If foreign capital is allowed to set up industry in the private sector, then one day or the other this sector might possibly control the nation's industrial advancement and exploit the situation. We find that in many developing countries, the Governments had to terminate the agreements with the foreign investors, as soon as their term of the contract was over. The only other alternative is to attract them to spend money in the public sector.

15. Sense of Guarantee to the Investor. The investor has a sense of guarantee that the money which he is loaning will be rapid to him after the prescribed date. He therefore, is quite willing to advance money to the public sector undertaking even to low rate of interest. We find that when the loans are floated by the Government, these are subscribed by the people very quickly and the amount is paid much before the closing date and that too when the rate of interests is not very attractive. Thus public sector industries can get loans at low rate of interest as compared with private sector enterprise.

16. Checking Economic Fluctuations. When the industry is controlled by the private sector, then national economy becomes dependent on that and it exploits the situation. In order to earn maximum profits, the industry creates artificial or man made scarcities and shortages. There are many economic fluctuations in the market. Black marketing and smuggling is encouraged. Not only this, but price discrimination is maintained. The effective and positive reply is that the industries should be set up in the public sector as well, so that as son as the industry in the private sector begins to misbehave public sector industry steps in and checks as well as controls the situation.

17. Desire for Nationalisation. In many countries of the world, particularly in the developing countries, as well as the countries which have won their freedom very recently, there is a desire that industries should be nationalised, so that the masses are saved form the capitalists. Then a great advantage of the public sector undertaking is that it meets the aspiration of the people and their demand for nationalisation, which is quite powerful these days among newly emerging nations of the world.

18. Effective Check on Monopoly. In private sector the industries will try to combine with each other and in one form or the other will make an attempt to create monopoly conditions, sc that the market goes under their control and they can regulate that in the way they like. One of the most effective checks to check monopoly situation is to set up industries in the public sector. Thus one important gain of public sector industrial set up is that it can check monopoly and no one can under-estimate this important advantage to the society.

19. Defence and other needs are adequately met. National defence is always paramount for every country. The defence requires many equipments which are quite costly and their manufacturing involves highly technical knowledge and expertise. It is also essential that the supplies should be very regular and quality of goods provided precise and specific. All this cannot be done by the private sector. In fact it will not like to undertake production of defence material usually because the profit is not in keeping with their aspirations.

DISADVANTAGES OF PSUS

Public sector undertakings are becoming very popular in developing countries because of the advantages which that give to the society. But alongwith the advantages there are many equally serious disadvantages of system. Few such disadvantages are as under:

1. No Body's Concern. As industry can successful run when the industrialist pays proper care and attention to every detail of the work. In private sector those who own the industry devote their maximum time and attention. In so far as public sector undertaking is concerned in it no body considers that industry is his own. This psychology prevails from top to bottom.

2. Un-economical Buying. Since no body pays due attention and care, the result is that no body cares to buy the raw-material and machinery at economical rates. The result of all this is that when costly raw material is purchased, finished goods become costly. This will not happen in the case of private sector undertaking. The industrialist will ensure that he is purchasing cheap and good quality goods to maintain both his reputation as well as profit.

3. Top Heavy Administrative Expenditure. Usually in the public sector undertakings expenditure is top heavy. The undertaking employs Managers, Deputy Managers, Chief Engineers, Shift Engineers and what not. It has also staff to complete many formalities.

The result of all this is that the amount which is required to be paid on the salaries of the personnel becomes a burden on the undertaking. Coupled with uneconomical purchasing cost of production goes up very much and the consumer is required to pay a higher price for the same commodity, which he would have paid, had he purchased form the private sector.

4. Shirking Responsibility. In this sector everybody shirks responsibility. In fact the man at the lower status will pass the bulk to his next superior and that one to his still next senior officer. When no body is prepared to take responsibility, naturally the industry will suffer for want of decision taking authority and clear cut policy.

5. Non-Clearness of Objective. A private sector undertaking works with the objective of earning profits and all its activities are directed towards profit making. But in public sector undertakings there are no clear objectives. In case the undertaking takes social welfare into consideration, then it will incur losses and these are bound to be burden on the exchequer. Not only this, but there is bound to be public criticism as well. In case it works with profit motive, then a criticism is bound to be there that like a private industrialist, the government is also exploiting the consumer and so on.

6. Too much Political Interference. In this sector there is usually too much interference from political leaders. They wish to run the industry in such a way that suits their political ends. Change in political power brings change in the public undertaking as well. Accordingly too much political interference very much spoils the image and economic position of the public sector undertakings.

7. Difficult to Adjust Conflicting Interests. In public sector undertakings there are many conflicting interests. On the one hand are workers and labourers who organize themselves into trade unions and wish to bargain with the management. Then are the interests of the technical staff, secretariat staff, who all organise themselves into trade union. Usually the interests are very conflicting and it becomes difficult to adjust. Not only this, but there is serious problem of discipline due to conflicting interests. On the one hand is the problem of maintaining discipline, in which government and management is interested, whereas on the other is the strong trade union system, which feels that demands can be effectively met by creating indiscipline and such problems as strike, work to rule, mass leave and so on.

8. Inconsistency due to Transfers. In a private sector undertaking the enterpriser, after deciding the policy follows that. There is no question of his transfer from one place to the other. Accordingly, there is always consistency in the policy. On the other hand in public sector undertakings there cannot be consistency in policy. Officers at higher levels, who are required to implement policy decisions and execute programmes, get transferred quite frequently. With the transfer of one officer, there is always change, both in policy as well as its implementation.

9. Influence of Civil Servants. In many public undertakings, management is headed by civil servants. These people are trained in a particular manner. They have administration oriented training. When put in a commercial undertaking, they find themselves as complete misfit. They lay more stress on administration rather than on economic aspect of the problem. Moreover, mostly the civil servants are not enterprising. They fear that in case their initiative does not succeed, it is just possible that they may invite the wrath of the superiors.

10. Corruption and Nepotism. A private sector undertaking will never tolerate that incompetent persons should in any way occupy any positions high or low. On the other hand in so far as public sector undertakings are concerned, usually many appointments are made on the basis of patronage and influences. Corruption and nepotism in making appointments, giving contracts, supply of raw material, giving distributing agencies is quite common. It is due to this that competent people do not occupy senior positions. Due to their incompetency goods get stocked, wishes of people are not properly assessed, opportunists manage to plot scandals and make away with public funds and so on. Due to their appointments and favours the staff gets discontented and there are grudges and grumbles.

11. Red Tapism and Routine. No private undertaking will ever think of red tapism and routine to the extent that it delays their whole process and programme of production, purchase and distribution. But in public sector undertakings usually there is red tapism and routine. In fact the whole system becomes so much burdened with red tapism and routines that it becomes almost impossible to come out of the rut. The result is that the things set delayed and the undertaking always suffers for want of policies, decisions and quick disposal of the issues.

MAJOR PROBLEMS OF PSUS

Before we actually discuss the problems of public sector undertakings, it must be remembered that forms of organisation of these industries very widely differ. Some of the industries have been set up and organised as Private Limited Companies which include Fertilisers and Chemicals Ltd.; Hindustan Air Craft Ltd. and Hindustan Ship Yard Ltd. etc. But this form of organisation has been criticised on the plea that in such a set up the company can evade the constitutional responsibilities, which a state owned enterprise owes to the Parliament. It is also said that in such a form of organisation the law regulating limited companies becomes a mere fiction. The problem was examined by the Administrative Reforms Commission in all its forms and in 1967, the Commission came to the conclusion that the form of a statutory corporation should in general be adopted for public sector projects in the industrial field.

The Estimates Committee also made some other important recommendations in respect of public sector undertakings in the country. The Committee was of the view that there was no need of organising a new company or corporation for each new enterprise. There should be only small number of operating corporations and each in command of a considerable and increasing number of enterprises. It is only then that the Government and the Parliament can effectively deal with them. The Administrative Reforms

Commission in 1967, supported this view point while giving the idea of Sector Corporations.

In addition to the patterns of organisation available in Hindustan Aircraft Ltd. in India we also have the pattern of a holding company as well. In 1973 a holding company for steel was set up known as the Steel Authority of India Ltd. commonly known as SAIL, which has been loaded with the overall responsibility of steel development in the private and public sectors and also to exercise control over steel input industries.

Problem of Public Sector Enterprises. In India public sector enterprises are being organised and have been organised on different patterns. This in itself is on less a serious problem, because in the absence of a uniform pattern of organisation, it becomes difficult for the government to adopt a uniform policy and pattern of management.

There has been a common complaint that the Boards of Directors on these enterprises are not playing their role properly. Mostly, Government nominated members do not devote proper time and attention to this part of the job. Attention to this serious problem was drawn by the Estimate Committee in its 16th Report and also by the Krishna Menon Committee, which came to the conclusion that Chairmanship of the Board should not be a kind of berth for a retiring civil servant or other who are appointed, as a part of reward for the services rendered to a political party. No public man should be on the Board of Directors. The Government considered the proposal of the Committee and in May 1968, it decided that normally the Chairman cum Managing Director of a company shall be appointed on whole time basis.

In our traditional administrative system a top civil servant, though absolutely non-specialist, is considered quite competent to deal with highly technical and commercial matters of a public enterprise.

Then there is another serious problem, namely that the controlling ministries too much interfere in the working of public enterprises. Estimates Committee has come to the conclusion that public enterprises should be given maximum autonomy to run on commercial patterns. In this regard, the most serious problem, which India has always been facing is how to maintain proper and healthy link between autonomy of the enterprise on the one hand and control of ministry, which is ultimately responsible to the Government on the other.

Still another problem is that of lack of trained personnel. In India, the number of public enterprises is very rapidly increasing, but at the same time no attempt has been made to produce competent people to run the jobs. The result is that even after an enterprise has been set up there are no competent people to run and manage that. No only this but in many public sector undertaking there is no proper assessment of man power requirements and also there is no co-ordinated approach for getting the people properly trained, so that there is no proper in built system of getting trained people.

Usually employer-employee relations in these undertakings are not satisfactory. The workers have due to various reasons, not been given due share in the running of the management. The leadership of the trade unions of the workers is in the hands of political to restrict leadership to the workers, who actually work in the enterprise.

All public sector enterprises are required to be run on commercial pattern,which can successfully be run only when there is increased output. This needs incentive. What form of incentive should it be, to which extent should it be given and at what level is the incentive needed, are some of the problems connected with efficient working of public enterprises.

In most of the cases public sector industries run into many odds. No proper care is taken to see how can be these run on commercial pattern. Usually detailed feasibility is not studied for its commercial viability. Usually these industries are over capitalised with the result that there is unfavourable input output ratio which invites public criticism of the whole project. Since public sector undertaking is no individual's responsibility, therefore, there are many avoidable wastages even at construction and planning stages.

How far should there by public participation in share capital of the public undertakings is another problem. Krishna Menon Committee recommended public participation in share capital, as early as in 1959. Similar recommendations were made by a study group set up by the Planning Commission for the purpose. Mr. T.A. Pai, Minister for Industries and Civil Supplies even put forth a concrete proposal in this regard for the consideration of the House. Public participation in share capital of public undertakings has been allowed in Scooter India Ltd. But the public sector undertakings are still faced with this serious problem, of public participation.

Problem of effective ministerial control is then another problem. Only few members are interested in indepth study of problems of public sector undertakings. Thus whatever comes to their notice is brought to the Minister and many omissions thus do not come to the notice of the Minister at all. In so far as Minister himself is concerned, the Management will always try to conceal omissions and as such it is not an easy task to dig out omissions.

The capital for running the industry is raised by the Government from the public at low rate of interest. Inspite of all the facilities which are provided to the project, for quite some time, these run into losses. But both the workers and managerial staff demand bonus. If no incentives or bonus are given then the production goes down and if these are allowed, then there is no justification and in doing so on justice is done with the public.

Pricing Policy of a public sector undertaking is really a very serious problem to be tackled and considered. If the prices of the commodities are kept at very low rate then, there may be heavy losses which poor tax payer in India may not like to afford. On the other hand, if a public sector is allowed to fix price of a commodity in the manner he likes, then being almost in monopoly situation, he may fix high price, resulting in artificial profits, having no relevancy with efficiency.

The Government and the public feel that these sectors are having vast autonomy. On the other hand these undertakings feel that

Government control is too heavy and the enterprises in India are not being allowed to work smoothly. There is too much interference by the controlling ministry and so on. But the experience of a common Indian, with the working of public enterprises is not very happy. In fact the losses which such an enterprise incurs are always an eyesore with the public, who then considers such an enterprise a liability rather than a national pride.

GROWTH OF PSUS

Public Sector Undertakings in India have their own serious problems. But inspite of these difficulties, public sector undertakings are rapidly growing. We find that at the beginning of First Five Year Plan there were only five units in this sector, with total investment of Rs. 29 crores. This number rose to 21 at beginning of second plan, to 48 in Third Plan and at the beginning of Fourth Plan, the number rose to 85. On March 31, 1973, the number of public sector undertakings was 113. Similarly there was increase in total investment made in these undertakings. At the end of Second Five Year Plan, total investment made was Rs. 81 crores whereas at the end of third plan, this investment rose to Rs. 953 crores. According to information collected by the Government the amount invested as on 31st March, 1973 was Rs.5671 crores. Since then investment in this sector has been very rapidly increasing. Some of the important causes may briefly be discussed as under:

Causes Responsible for Rapid Growth of Public Enterprises in India

1. Defence and Public Industries. Private sector was least prepared to spend heavy amounts on setting up industries which produce defence material. Even if it was prepared to do so, it was not safe to depend on it. It was therefore imperative need of the hour that industries connected with production of defence material should be set up in the public rather than private sector.

2. Socialistic Pattern of Society. India has adopted socialistic pattern of society as its goal and ultimate objective. It was, therefore, essential that the state should step in the industrial field and up industries in key sector of economy, particularly where heavy investment and no returns.

3. Essential for Rapid Economic Growth. In India it was felt that if industries were left to the case of private sector alone then the nation could not hope to have rapid economic growth. Whereas private sector should be allowed to contribute, the major part should be played by the public sector for industrial development of the country. This attitude of the Government also resulted in rapid growth of public sector enterprises in the country.

4. Equal Distribution of Wealth. In India it was decided that benefits of industrial growth and development must be shared by the society as a whole. This was possible only when industries were in the public and not in the private sector.

5. Essential for Capital Formation. Private sector is always interested in producing consumer goods, where the investments are not heavy and returns very good. In India, the Government was always keen in capital formation industries. Accordingly these industries could be set up only in public sector.

6. Misbehaviour of Private Sector. Unfortunately in India, private sector has not properly behaved. It has always tried exploit to the masses created artificial scarcity, encouraged smuggling and black marketing and used the profits thus earned in creating parallel economy, thereby under-valuing rupee value of the country. In order to check all these evils, it as most essential that public sector should be encouraged.

7. Essential for the Growth of Industrial Research. The work of industrial research cannot make any significant headway unless proper time and care is taken. Private sector will obviously not be interested in making this kind of investment. It can be done only in the public sector and for this reason too public sector is receiving encouragement.

8. Foreign Aid Collaboration. Most of the major projects and industries can be started only when foreign exchange component is available. Foreign collaboration can easily be obtained for public sector enterprises and not private sector undertakings, where investment is not considered safe.

9. Essential for the Welfare of the Workers. The workers in the private sector are simply exploited ruthlessly. One of the reasons for the rapid expansion of public sector in India is favourable climate which the workers find in the public sector.

10. Essential for Balanced Regional Growth. In India there are industrially both backward, and forward regions. But for balanced growth of the country it is essential that there should be development of industrially backward areas. This can be done in India, in case industries in the public sector are set up.

11. Nature of Investment. There are many projects in every country where nature of investment is such that only public sector can step in and private sector will be least interested to invest *e.g.*, construction of irrigation projects, roads, railways, dams etc. Since in India these are priority projects, therefore, public sector is becoming increasingly popular.

Role of Public Sector in the Indian Economy

Public sector in India has been criticized vehemently by a number of supporters of the private sector who have chosen to shut their eyes towards the achievements of the public sector. Following description should be sufficient to convince one that public sector has played a definite positive role in the economy.

Public Sector and Capital Formation. The role of public sector in collecting savings and investing them during the planning era has been very important. During the First and Second Plans, of the total investment, 54 per cent was in the public sector and the remaining in the private sector. The share of public sector rose to 60 per cent in the Third Plan. The Fourth, Fifth and Sixth Plans envisaged respectively 59 per cent, 57.6 per cent and 53 per cent share of public sector in plan investment. However, for the first time since the advent of planning, the Seventh Plan reduced the share of the public sector investment below 50 per cent; it was kept at 47.8 per cent for the public sector as compared to 52.2 per cent for the private sector. The Eighth Plan has reduced this further to 45.2 per cent (this reflects the increasing importance that is now being accorded to the private sector). The nationalized banks, State Bank of India, Industrial Development Bank of India, Industrial Finance Corporation of India, State Financial Corporations, LIC, UTI etc. have played an important role in collecting savings and mobilization of resources.

However, savings in the public sector itself are not much. In fact, there has been a precipitous fall in the share of public sector in gross domestic savings during the last decade and a half; it was 16.2 per cent in 1980-81, 7.3 per cent in 1992-93 and 6.9 per cent in 1994-95. During the period of Sixth Plan as a whole, public saving was 18.6 per cent of total domestic saving and this fell to 10.8 per cent during the period of the Seventh Plan. This sordid state of affairs is due to the fact that, although the non-departmental enterprises have been augmenting gross internal resources (in fact, the savings of public enterprises have increased steadily from 1.7 per cent of GDP in 1980-81 to about 4 per cent of GDP in 1989-90), massive negative contributions of the administrative departments have depressed the overall public savings.

Development of Infrastructure. The primary condition of economic development in any underdeveloped country is that the infrastructure should develop at a rapid pace. Without a sufficient expansion of irrigation facilities and power and energy, one cannot even conceive of agricultural development. In the same way without an adequate development of transportation and communication facilities, fuel and energy, and basic and heavy industries, the process of industrialisation cannot be sustained. India had inherited an undeveloped basic infrastructure from the colonial period. After Independence, the private sector neither showed any inclination to develop it nor did it have any resources to make this possible. It was comparatively weak both financially and technically, and was incapable of establishing a heavy industry immediately. These factors made the

State's participation in industrialization essential since only the government could enforce a large-scale mobilization of capital, the coordination of industrial construction, and training of technicians. The government has not only improved the road, rail, air and sea transport system, it has also expanded them manifold. Thus the public sector has enabled the economy to develop a strong infrastructure for the future economic growth.

Strong Industrial Base. The share of the industrial sector (comprising manufacturing, construction, electricity, gas and water supply) in Gross Domestic Product at factor cost has not increased much during the period of planning. It was 18.74 per cent in 1960-61, 22.35 per cent in 1970-71 and 27.5 per cent in 1994-95 (at 1980-81 prices). This shows that the contribution of industries to national income has grown at a snail's pace. However, there is no denying the fact that the industrial base of the Indian economy is now much stronger than what it was in 1950-51. There has been significant growth in the defence industries and industries of strategic importance. The government has strengthened the industrial base considerably by placing due emphasis on the setting up of industries in the following fields—iron and steel, heavy engineering, coal, heavy electrical machinery, petroleum and natural gas, chemicals and drugs, fertilizers, etc. Because of their low profitability potential in the short run, these industries do not find favour with the private sector. However, unless these industries are set up, the consumer goods industries cannot progress at a sufficiently rapid pace. Therefore, the production of consumer goods industries in the private sector is also likely to suffer if the State does not invest in heavy and basic industries. As noted by A.H. Hanson, "Even the view that it is the function of the State to provide only basic 'services' leaves room for a great deal of public enterprise in manufacturing industry, as well as in power, transport, communications, etc. For consumer-goods industries, which are usually capable of attracting some private capital, depend on the 'services' of the producer-goods industries in which private capital is—at least initially—less interested.

Economies of Scale. In the case of those industries where for technological reasons, the plants have to be large requiring huge investments, setting up of these industries in the public sector can prevent the concentration of economic and industrial power in private hands. It is a known fact that in the presence of significant economies of scale, the free market does not produce the best results. Accordingly, considerations of economic efficiency require some form of government regulation or public ownership. Even in the U.S.A. firms in electric power, natural gas, telephone and some other industries are being regulated by Federal and State regulatory commissions. Countries like France and the United Kingdom have explicitly preferred public ownership in the fields.

Removal of Regional Disparities. The government in India has sought to use its power of setting up of industries as a means of removing regional disparities in industrial development. In the pre-Independence period, most of the industrial progress of the country was limited in and around the port towns of Bombay, Calcutta and Madras. Other parts of the country lagged far behind. After the initiation of the planning process in the country in 1951, the government has paid particular attention to the problem and has set up industries in a number of areas hitherto neglected by the private sector. Thus a major proportion of public sector investment has been directed towards backward States and backward regions of these States. For example, all the four major steel plants in the public sector—Bhilai Steel Plant, Rourkela Steel Plant, Durgapur Steel Plant and Bokaro Steel Plant—were set up in the backward States. It was believed that the setting up of large scale public sector projects in the backward areas would unleash a propulsive mechanism in them and cause economic development of the hinterland.

Import Substitution and Export Promotion. The foreign exchange problem often emerges as a serious constraint on the programme of industrialization in a developing economy. This constraint appeared in a rather strong way in India during the Second Plan and the subsequent plans. Because of these considerations, all such industries that help in import substitution are of crucial importance for the economy. Bharat Heavy Electricals Limited, Bharat Electronics Ltd., Hindustan Antibiotics Ltd., Indian Oil Corporation, Oil and

Natural Gas Commission, etc., in the public sector are of special importance form this point of view.

Several public sector enterprises have also played an important role in expanding the exports of the country. Specific reference of Hindustan Steel Limited, Hindustan Machine Tools Limited, Bharat Electronics Ltd., State Trading Corporation and Metals and Minerals Trading Corporation can be made in this context.

Check Over Concentration of Economic Power. In a capitalist economy where the public sector is practically non-existent or is of a very small size, economic power gets increasingly concentrated in a few hands and inequalities of income and wealth increase. During the four decades of planning in this country, it has been said time and again that the expansion of public sector will help in putting a brake on the tendency towards concentration of wealth and economic power in the private sector.

Public sector can help in reducing inequalities in the economy in a number of ways. For instance *(i)* profits of the public sector can be used directly by the government on the welfare programmes of the poorer sections of community; *(ii)* public sector can adopt a discriminatory policy by supplying materials to small industrialists at low prices and big industrialists at high prices; *(iii)* public sector can give better wages to the lower staff as compared to the private sector and can also implement programmes of labour welfare, construction of colonies and townships for labourers, slum clearance, etc.; and *(iv)* public sector can orient production machinery towards the production of mass consumption goods.

Performance of the Public Sector

It is usual to judge the performance of private sector units by the yardstick of net profit or loss since in their case, maximization of profit is the sole aim. This yardstick fails miserably in the case of public sector undertakings. Such units are frequently started in those sectors where profitability is low and gestation period long. For instance, investment in infrastructure and basic industries is not likely to yield early returns and, accordingly, profits in the beginning are likely to be very low and in some instances, may even be negative. Yet these investments serve important ends since they create the basis for expansion of industrial activities in the future. Investments made by the public sector in the steel industry, fertilizers, power projects, mining, etc., come under this category. Then, in some cases, public sector provides inputs to the private sector (for example, iron and steel to machine building, tools, automobile industry, etc.) It is very easy for it to earn huge profits by merely hiking the prices of its output. However, this is likely to have an adverse impact on the industrial activity in the private sector on the one hand, and push up prices on the other. Accordingly, prices are intentionally kept low even though this cuts into the profits of the public sector seriously. Also, as noted by Hazari and Oza, private sector has invested mostly in consumer and lighter goods which have been granted far greater protection against external competition as compared to capital goods which were mostly produced by the public sector and which faced stiff competition from imports financed by aid and foreign private investment. Another point that needs specific mention is that the public sector is not merely capital-intensive and characterised by longer gestation periods; in steel, which accounts for the bulk of investment, it is also material intensive, and to that extent its value added component is smaller than in items like, say, chemicals.

Because of considerations such as these, it is often maintained that the performance of the public sector units should not be judged by what they earn in the form of profits but by the total additions they make to the flow of goods and services in the economy. Thus, instead of profits, the yardstick should be the total value of the sales of an enterprise. For instance, if an iron and steel plant produces steel worth Rs. 500 crores in a certain specified period but makes no profit because it aim is to provide steel at low prices to the industries using steel as an input, it would be wrong to say that its performance is disappointing on this count alone. What is important from the point of view the industrial development of the country is the fact that this plant has added steel worth Rs. 500 crores to the social pool of goods and services obtaining in the country.

Expansion of the Public Sector and its Sharein National Production

Public enterprises in India constitute a major National capability in terms of their scale of operations, coverage of the national economy, technological capabilities, and stock of human capital. There are over a thousand public enterprises, about 700 of which are owned by the States. The rest are in the Central Sector. These include departmental undertakings (*e.g.* railways, post and telecommunications, financial institutions, and non departmental enterprises or government companies or corporations which are either incorporated under the Company Law (*e.g.* the Steel Authority of India and the Indian Petrochemical Corporation Ltd.) or statutorily created by Acts of Parliament (*e.g.*, Coal India, Air India, Indian Airlines and the National Thermal Power Corporation).

There were only 5 central public sector enterprises at the commencement of the first Plan with investment amounting to only Rs. 29 crores. As on March 31, 1994, the number had risen to 240. Total capital employed in these enterprises, amounted to staggering Rs. 1,59,307 crores. Gross sales of public enterprises rose from Rs. 1,17,623 crores in 1990-91 to Rs. 1,33,268 crores in 1991-92. Value added rose from Rs. 31,922 crores to Rs. 35,312 crores over the same period. As far as the share in national production is concerned, public sector enterprises play a pivotal role in the production of fuels, basic metal industries, non-ferrous metal industries, fertilisers and communication equipment. They contribute the entire output in the case of petroleum, lignite, copper and primary lead; about 98 per cent of zinc; well over 90 per cent of coal; more than half of steel and aluminium and about one-third of fertilisers.

The Question of Profitability. Though we have pointed out earlier that profits are not the criterion for examining the performance of public sector enterprises, their financial performance is of wide interest and concern as they are set up at a huge cost to the national exchequer. Gross profit of these enterprises rose from Rs. 2,654 crores in 1980-81 to Rs. 18,438 crores in 1993-94. In the same period, net profits increased from Rs. 445 crores to Rs. 4,435 crores. This shows that the profitability of public sector enterprises is not all that bad as many critics seem to suggest. However, the Economic Survey, 1994-95 notes that the profitability of public sector enterprises in terms of ratios of gross margins and gross profits to capital employed has not improved over the last ten years. For instance, the ratio of gross margin to capital employed declined from 18.29 per cent in 1980-81 to 17.33 per cent in 1993-94 while gross profit as a proportion of capital employed declined from 12.10 per cent to 11.5 per cent over the same period. However, the ratio of net profit to capital employed which was 2.03 per cent in 1980-81 rose to 2.78 per cent in 1993-94.

In a study published recently, R.Nagaraj has calculated self financing ratios for the public sector and the private sector for the period 1960-61 to 1988-89. Self financing ratio has been defined as gross saving as a proportion of gross capital formation and thus indicates the share of internal resource generation in financing investment. This ratio for the public sector enterprises shows generally an upward trend, especially in the 1980s while that for the private sector shows a downward trend, with the two ratios converging to more or less similar levels of around 40 per cent towards the end of 1980s.

Employment and Labour Welfare. As far as this criterion of the performance is concerned, the public sector seems to have done exceedingly well. It has contributed to a significant extent in improving the overall employment situation in the country and has acted as a model employer by providing the worker with better wages and other facilities as compared to the private sector. The number of persons employed in the public sector enterprises stood at 23.05 lakhs as on March 31, 1991. The industrial sectors which have a sizable number of employees in the public sector include coal, steel, textiles, heavy engineering, and medium and light engineering.

The public sector enterprises have also spent a considerable amount on the development of townships around them. These townships were provided with facilities like schools, hospitals, shopping complexes, etc. A substantial sum of money is spent annually on the maintenance and administration of these townships and social overheads. The employees of the public sector enterprises also enjoy medical amenities, subsidized canteen facilities, transport and educational facilities, etc.

Performance of Public Sector Enterprises

The economic and social responsibility of the State has led to the progressive enlargement of the public sector in India. The number of Centre's public enterprises has increased from 5 in 1951 to 246 as at the end of 1995-96. The investment during the same period has increased from Rs. 29 crores to Rs. 1,75,000 crores. The share of public enterprises in national income has increased from 10.66 per cent in 1960-61 to 26.0 per cent in 1995-96. Similarly, the employment in the public enterprises has gone up to 30.0 lakhs in March, 1995. In brief, the public enterprises occupy an important place in the Indian economy.

Performance of Public Sector Enterprises

As on March 31, 1996, there were 246 Central public Sector Enterprises (PSEs) owned by the Government of India. Out of these, 237 were operational enterprises with an employed capital of Rs. 1,56,000 crores and employed strength of 22.0 lakhs. Of these, 13 enterprises earned an overall net profit of Rs. 7,346 crores during 1995-96, 104 enterprises suffered net loss of Rs. 3,951 crores, and the remaining one enterprise making neither profit nor loss.

The performance of the operational PSEs could be assessed by considering their achievements in respect of the following:

1. Gross Margin. Gross margin of PSEs which was only Rs., 2401 crores in 1980-81 went are Rs. 26,137 crores in 1993-94.

2. Percentage of Gross. Margin to Capital Employed. The percentage of gross margin to capital employed which stood at 13.19 per cent in 1980-81 went up to 17.3 per cent in 1993-94.

3. Depreciation and Deferred Revenue Expenditure. The depreciation and deferred revenue expenditure went up from Rs. 903 crores in 1980-81 to over Rs. 9,000 crores in 1993-94.

4. Gross Profit. The gross profit of the PSEs went up from Rs. 4,418 crores in 1980-81 to Rs. 19,000 crores in 1993-94.

5. Percentage of Gross Profit to Capital Employed. PSEs have not been able to achieve high percentage of gross profit to capital employed. In 1980-81, this percentage stood at 7.79 and went up marginally to 11.82 per cent in 1993-94.

6. Net Profit. In 1993-94, net profit of 240 PSEs are estimated at Rs. 3,396 crores as against net profit of Rs. 3,396 crores in the preceeding year.

7. Non-monetary Performance. Public sector enterprises are not guided purely by monetary considerations. Their objective is to promote public welfare at large. It is, therefore, suggested that the performance of the public enterprises should be assessed in terms of welfare criteria which involves the following considerations;

(i) Whether public enterprises have promoted welfare by providing essential goods and services at reasonable prices;

(ii) Whether public enterprises have generated additional employment opportunities;

(iii) Whether public enterprises have helped in the development of small-scale and ancillary industries;

(iv) Whether public enterprises have promoted balanced regional development; and

(v) Whether public enterprises have created the necessary infrastructure for the speedy growth of industries.

Non-monetary performance of the public enterprises has been very encouraging. The enterprises have created a base for industrialisation, regional development and promotion of public welfare. However, the rate of growth and the performance could have been better.

Reasons for the Poor Performance of Public Enterprises. The following reasons account for the poor performance of the public enterprises:

(1) Underutilisation of Capacity. A large number of public enterprises function at a capacity far below the rated capacity. Because of the underutilisation of the plant capacity, there is wastage of material and manpower resources which leads to escalation of the cost of production. According to the 1994-95 Public Enterprises Survey conducted by the Bureau of Public Enterprises, capacity utilisation in 20 per cent units was between 50 and 75 per cent, and 20 per cent units showing capacity utilisation less than 50 per cent.

(2) Over-capitalisation. Input-output ratio obtaining in many public enterprises is unfavorable. Factors like bad location of project, inadequate planning, delays in the completion of project, surplus plant capacity, expensive turnkey projects, etc., lead to over-capitalisation of the public enterprises.

(3) Administrative Inefficiency. Public enterprises lack the strong cadre of professional managers. In most of the public enterprises the common practice is to use bureaucrats as chairman, managing directors and managers, no matter how much inefficient or incompetent they may be to manage these enterprises.

(4) Price Policy. The pricing policy of the public enterprises is not guided solely by profit motive but social consideration as well. Public enterprises have to keep the prices of their products low even when costs and prices have been rising Now, it is being gradually realised that profit should be recognised as an index of efficiency.

(5) Take over of Sick Units. Public sector has taken over the management and control of several units declared sick in the private sector. Most of the loss making units in the public sector are the sick enterprises taken over by the government from the private sector.

(6) Less Remunerative Enterprises. Most of the public sector enterprises are set up in these areas of production which have a very low rate of return on investment. These enterprises employ large capital and the gestation period is also too large. These enterprises are generally established in relatively backward areas, and this adversely affects their profitability.

(7) Higher Social Cost. Public enterprises have to incur huge expenditure on social overheads like construction of labour colonies, development of townships, construction of roads, bridges, etc. Excessive expenditure on social overheads causes increase in total cost.

(8) Ministerial Interference. The Parliamentary Committees and the Government do not allow the public enterprises to function independently. Purely political considerations have sometimes led to overstaffing, mismanagement and other inefficiencies. political interference also leads to unbalanced regional development of industries.

Suggestions for Improving the Performance of Public Sector Enterprises

The following measures can be suggested for improving the performance of public sector undertakings in India:

(1) Managing of these undertakings should be entrusted to the trained and skilful personnel.

(2) the price policy of the public sector undertakings should aim at improving the profitability of the public undertakings. These profits can later on be used for the establishment of new enterprises, expansion and modernisation of the existing units.

(3) All-out efforts should be made to make fuller utilisation of the capacity in different enterprises. Possibilities of export promotion should also be explored.

(4) Public sector units should be allowed to raise larger deposits from the public. In fact, they have been allowed to raise public deposits up to 35 per cent of their share capital.

(5) Establishment of public enterprises be based purely on economic and social welfare consideration rather than political pressures.

(6) Disinvestment of a part of Government holdings in the share capital of selected public sector enterprises in order to provide

market discipline and to improve the performance of the public enterprises.

(7) Sick public sector units should be merged together to make them economically viable units. There should also be restructuring of loss-making enterprises.

(8) Before the installation of these enterpirses, pre-investment surveys should be conducted thoroughly. Delays in the installation of units should be avoided.

(9) The Sick Industrial Companies Act (SICA) has been amended to bring PSUs under its purview.

Strategy in the Eighth Plan

In the framework of the New Economic policy, public sector enterprises have to play an important role as autonomous, competitive and efficient units to provide essential infrastructure, goods and services development of natural resources and areas of strategic concern. The initiative will consist of the following integrated strategies:

(1) Restructing involving modernisation, rationalisation of capacity, product-mix changes, selective exit and privatisation to make PSEs viable, efficient and competitive.

(2) Introduction of new technology to improve competitiveness and efficiency.

(3) Establishment of new institutional set-up that is responsive to environmental change.

(4) Increase in autonomy and performance accountability of public enterprises.

(5) Changes in management practices of specific enterprises level to promote efficiency and resourcefulness.

In order to improve the performance of the PSEs, the following measures have been suggested:

(i) The public sector should make investment in those areas where investment is of an infrastructural nature which is necessary for the facilitating growth and development;

(ii) The public sector may withdraw from the areas where no public purpose is served by its presence;

(iii) The products of the PSEs, unless these satisfy the needs of the poorest in the society, should be priced as per cost and costing with full efficiency in operations;

(iv) Policy for sick public enterprises to be same as that for the private sector;

(v) Improving performance through the performance contract or Memorandum of Understanding (MoU) system by which management are to be granted greater autonomy and held accountable for results.

(vi) Disinvestment of shares in PSEs to raise resources and encourage wider participation of general public and workers in the ownership of the PSEs.

❐

8

Role of Multinational Corporations

Multinational Corporations (MNCs) are huge industrial organisations which extend their industrial and marketing operations through a network of their branches or their Majority Owned Foreign Affiliates (MOFAs). MNCs are also known as Transactional Corporations (TNCs). Instead of aiming for maximization of their profits from one or two products, the MNCs operate in a number of fields and from this point of view, their business strategy extends over a number of products and over a number of countries. At the onset of the 1990s, there were 37,000 TNCs whose tentacles straddled the international economy through 1,70,000 overseas affiliates. They possess staggering resources as would be clear form the fact that the revenue of 200 top corporations stood at $ 3,046 billion in 1982 which rose further to $ 5,862 billion in 1992. Their share in world GPD rose from 24.2 per cent to 26.8 per cent over at the same period. Their aggregate profits stand at a mammoth $ 73.4 billion. Of this, the share of the largest 10 corporations is as much as $ 34.8 billion—a towering 47 per cent of the profits of the 200 mega corporations.

The above data show the massive control exercised by the MNCs on the world economy. In fact, because of their huge capital resources, latest technology and worldwide goodwill, MNCs are in a position to sell whatever product they choose to manufacture in different countries. The fact is that people in underdeveloped countries are 'crazy' for the products of these corporations and prefer their products to the products produced indigenously.

Reasons for the Growth of MNCs

Reasons for the growth of multinationals are manifold, the important ones being as follows:

1. Expansion of Market Territory. As the operations of a large sized firm expand and as its international image builds up, it seeks more and more extension of its activities beyond the physical boundaries of the country in which it is incorporated.

2. Marketing Superiorities. A multinational firm enjoys a number of marketing superiorities over the national firms; *(a)* It possesses a more reliable and uptodate market information system, *(b)* It enjoys market reputation and faces less difficulty in selling its products; *(c)* It adopts more effective advertising and sales promotion techniques, and *(d)* It has efficient warehousing facilities due to lower inventory requirements.

3. Financial Superiorities. A multinational firm enjoys the following financial superiorities over the national firm; *(a)* It has huge financial resources with which it can easily turn all circumstances in its favour; *(b)* It maintains a high level of funds utilization by generating funds in one country and using them in another; *(c)* It has easier access to external capital markets; and *(d)* Because of its international reputation it is able to raise more international resources. Even investors and banks of the host country are eager to invest in it.

4. Technological Superiorities. The main reason why MNCs have been encouraged by the underdeveloped countries to participate in their industrial development is on account of the technological superiorities which these firms possess as compared to national companies. The underdeveloped countries regard transfer of technology from MNCs useful on account of the following reasons: *(a)* Industrialization represents the most important way out of underdevelopment and the resources of these countries are insufficient to sustain the industrial progress on their own; *(b)* Local manpower, materials, local capital equipments etc. have to be optimally exploited and these countries are unable to accomplish this; *(c)* Depending totally on local companies would require heavy imports of raw materials, capital equipment, machinery and technical knowledge whereas MNCs bring these on their own; and *(d)* The underdeveloped countries have to face stiff competition for selling their products in international markets. Unless their goods meet international standards and quality specifications, they cannot sell. MNCs help them in producing such goods.

5. Product Innovations. MNCs have Research and Development Departments engaged in the task of developing new products and superior designs of existing products. Therefore their production opportunities are far greater as compared to national companies.

Domination of MNCs

MNCs have a strong hold over the Indian economy. In fact, even two decades ago these corporations controlled 53.7 per cent of the assets of the giant sector in India. According to the Industrial Licensing Policy Inquiry Committee, there were 112 companies in India in 1966 with assets worth Rs. 10 crores or more. Of these, 48 were either foreign branches or Indian subsidiaries of foreign companies. In addition, 14 Indian companies had extremely heavy loans and equity capital and, therefore, were virtually foreign controlled. These 62 companies had Rs. 1,370 crores worth of assets which constituted 54 per cent of the total companies were also under foreign domination in one way or the other. In return for technical assistance, they had promised an assured market of machines and spares to their foreign associates. Some companies were heavily dependent on international financial institutions for economic assistance.

An interesting thing about the operations of MNCs in India is that they have raised a major part of investment resources from within the Indian economy. A study on the sources of finance of MNCs was conducted by Sudip Chaudhuri for the period 1956-75. The sample selected for study included 50 largest foreign subsidiaries.

His analysis revealed that for the period 1956-75 as a whole, foreign sources (in the form of foreign share capital and foreign loans) contributed only 5.4 per cent of the financial resources of these companies, 94.6 per cent being contributed by the domestic sources. Directly comparable data are not available for the period after 1975. However, Table 5.4 of John Martinussen's study shows that the amount of capital issues consented with foreign participation declined from 61.5 per cent of all consent to public limited companies in 1976 to a mere 29.5 per cent in 1980. John Martinussen indicates that 20 TNC affiliated companies even reduced their foreign funding. Several of these companies obtained no foreign funds at all during the period from 1974 to 1983. This fact about the financing behaviour of MNCs explodes the myth that they bring in large amounts of foreign capital with them.

Foreign Collaboration and MNCs

A common form of MNC participation in Indian industry is through entering into collaboration with Indian industrialists. Foreign collaboration agreements are made between Indian companies and foreign parties, involving sale of technology, as well as use of foreign brand names for the final products. The enormity of foreign collaborations entered into by the Indian companies would be clear from the fact that in nearly all of the new industries in the large or medium size group, privately or publicly owned, set up after Independence, some collaboration agreement was present. Trends of liberalisation in the 1980s gave a substantial spurt to foreign collaborations. This would be clear from the fact that of the total 12,760 foreign collaboration agreements approved in 40 years between 1948 and 1988, as many as 6,165 (*i.e.* 48.3 per cent) were approved during the eighty years between 1981 and 1988. As a result of liberalised foreign investment policy announced in July-August 1991, there has been a further spurt in foreign collaborations. The value of approvals of direct investment proposals rose considerably from \$ 325 million (Rs. 739 crores) in 1991 to \$ 4.3 billion (Rs. 13,591 crores) in 1994. The total direct foreign investment proposals approved since 1991 till September 1995 amounts to \$ 15.0 billion (Rs. 46,580 crores), against just under $ 1.0 billion (Rs. 1,274 crores) approved during the whole of the previous decade (1981-90).

A study of the foreign collaborations reveals certain interesting results. Thus, a large number of agreements were concluded for the manufacture of products which were non-essential or which could be produced with the help of local technology. These items included vacuum flasks, lipstick, toothpaste, cosmetics, brassiers, ice-cream, gin, beer, biscuits, dry batteries and readymade garments. Not only were collaborations granted for these products, they were often in multiple numbers and were renewed on expiry.

In addition to this 'orientation' of foreign collaborations, they also suffered from a number of other drawbacks as is clear from the following considerations:

(i) The government permitted multiple collaborations, *i.e.* repetitive import of the same or similar technology. This resulted in repetitive payments without adding to the stock of technical knowledge in the country;

(ii) The terms of agreements were mostly weighted in faovur of the foreign collaborators and were against Indian interests. This arose on account of the lack of bargaining power in the Indian side and the government's eagerness to acquire foreign participation in the fact of foreign exchange shortage;

(iii) The practice of multiple collaborations led to the introduction of standards of various countries (in raw materials, spare parts, deigns, specifications, and even terms of measurement) into the Indian industry even for very similar products or within the same firm. This multiplicity led to large inventory accumulation and uneconomic locking up of working capital. It also hindered standardisation and variety reduction which are so essential for raising industrial productivity;

(iv) Since the responsibility of specification and supply of equipment was entrusted to the foreign collaborators, there was close tie-up between the designers and suppliers resulting not only in price mark-up but also in over-import of equipment. Sometimes equipments were imparted even when they were available locally, sometimes they remained idle for want of spares, and often the processes were more highly mechanised and sophisticated than was desirable or necessary. At times, obsolete technology was imported;

(v) The terms of payment were also drawn up so as to squeeze out the maximum payment under one head or other. Generally 5 per cent of the annual turnover for 10 years as royalty plus 5 per cent of the imported plant cost as technical fees in the case of royalty-cum-technical fees, or 10 per cent of the issued capital as lumpsum payment for technical fees alone, were the limits of official policy. However, these tended to become routine;

(vi) The most important part related to the presence of various restrictive clauses in the agreements. Some restrictions imposed were: *(a)* the technology cannot be passed on to any one else, in some cases even after the expiry of the agreement; *(b)* manufacturing is to be carried out according to the specifications laid down by the collaborator and no local adaptations can be made; *(c)* control over overseas purchased was exercised through the provision that it had to be made directly or indirectly through the collaborator; *(d)* production was tightly controlled at times through the posing of foreign technicians; *(e)* controls over the pricing and marketing of the products were exercised by requiring that a part of the production was to be sold to the collaborator's subsidiary in India at a fixed commission or that specified firms were to be made the sole selling agents; and *(f)* right to export was also restricted by provision that exports could be done only to specific countries or on certain preconditions; and

(vii) Foreign collaborations have helped the growth of monopolies and concentration. They joined hands with the big business houses and the latter were only too eager to enter into understanding with them since the presence of foreign links often conferred certain strategic advantages (patent, resources, foreign exchange, etc.) enabling the big business houses to diversify and expand.

Harmful Effects of the Operations of MNCs on Indian Economy

The operations of MNCs open up the possibilities of interference in the industrial (and other) activities of the recipient country and are thus resented by the 'nationalist' thinkers. Their arguments against the operations of MNCs can be summed up as follow:

1. Payment of Dividends and Royalty. A large sum of money flows out of the country in terms of payment of dividends, profits, royalties, technical fees and interest to the foreign investors. For instance, remittance made abroad by private sector companies stood at Rs. 72.26 crores in 1969-70. This rose to Rs. 398.9 crores in 1981-82 and further to 813.5 crores in 1989. A study by N.K. Chandra shows that over three fifths of private corporate, or about two fifths of factory sector dividends were paid out by the foreign firms in the mid-1980s.

2. Distortion of Economic Structure. MNCs can inflict heavy damage on the host country in various forms such as suppression of domestic enterpreneurship, extension of oligopolistic practices (such as unnecessary product differentiation, heavy advertising, or excessive profit taking), supplying the economy with unsuitable technology and unsuitable products, worsening of income distribution by distorting the production structure to meet the requirements of high-income elites, etc. Modern Marxist economists (Paul Baran, for example) argue that foreign investment (especially through multinational corporations) opens up the doors of 'neo-imperialism' and 'exploitation'.

3. Technology Transfer not Necessarily Conducive to Development. As far as transfer of technology to underdeveloped countries is concerned, the behaviour pattern of MNCs reveals that they do not engage in R & D activities within the underdeveloped countries. Their R & D efforts are concentrated in laboratories in the home county or in other industrialised countries. Though R & D activities continue to be centralized in the parent country, the host countries have to bear the bulk of their costs since the affiliates of the MNCs in these countries remit payments on this account generally in relation to their sales volume. Such payments by the affiliates are generally over and above those remitted in the form of royalties and technical fees to the parent firm. The satisfaction expressed on technology transfer is partly misconceived also on account of the fact that MNCs which generally command a semi-monopolistic position in their product lines do not transfer their first-line or most advanced technology until foreign firms compel them to do so. In many cases, the technology transferred is of a capital intensive nature which is not useful from the point of view of a labour surplus economy. In fact, continued insistence on the import of such technology can have serious consequences for the economy of the host country since unemployment will increase.

4. Political Interference. Because of their immense financial and technical power, the MNCs have gained the necessary strength to influence the decision making processes in underdeveloped countries. Though they do help in transferring technology to underdeveloped countries. It has been often found that models and patterns of industrial development and technologies transferred are not in harmony with the interests of the host countries. The governments of underdeveloped countries have also felt threatened by the direct and indirect interference of MNCs in their internal affairs. The autonomy and sovereignty of the host countries is in danger. Because of these reasons, the governments of various countries have sought to restrict the activities of MNCs in their economies through a battery of administrative controls and legal provisions.

Control over Multinational Corporations

The responsibility of controlling the activities of Multinational Corporations in India rests on different government agencies. These agencies are: *(i)* the Ministry of Company Affairs, *(ii)* the Reserve Bank of India, *(iii)* the Ministry of Industrial Development, and *(iv)* the Ministry of Finance. However, these agencies do not work in close cooperation with each other. As a result, there is no coordination in their functioning. Each case is discussed on its own merits by the authorities.

As a result of a study of Michael Kidron entitled Foreign Investment in India published in 1965 (and the follow up discussions in which many economists participated) and the appearance of the Industrial Licensing Policy Inquiry Committee Report in 1968, the belief got strengthened that imports of foreign technology were overpriced and were designed to perpetrate dependence. As a consequence, the government policy was progressively tightened in the following directions: *(1)* Some industries were not allowed to import technology at all, the underlying principles of the policy being that *(a)* no 'inessential' article should be produced with fresh imports of technology (this gave the existing domestic and foreign producers automatic protection against fresh imports of technology) and *(b)* where domestic capacity was 'adequate' no technology should be imported; *(2)* Among industries where technology imports were allowed, the maximum rate of royalty was laid down; *(3)* In some designated industries, foreign investment was allowed in principle, but sanction in individual cases was a matter of administrative decision; *(4)* The normal permissible period of agreements was reduced form ten years to five, and renewals were generally frowned upon; *(5)* Exports and other marketing restrictions were generally not allowed, and often an obligation to export a certain proportion of the output was insisted upon; *(6)* A clause was often inserted in the agreements granting permission to the importer to sub-licence the technology; *(7)* The CSIR was allowed to look at applications for approval of technology imports, and if it expressed willingness to supply the technology, approval was withheld or at least delayed.

FOREIGN COLLABORATIONS

Need for Foreign Collaboration. Lack of capital is a serious handicap in the way of economic development of underdeveloped countries. The internal resources are not sufficient, so they have to rely on foreign capital in the initial stages of their development. The pace of economic development primarily depends upon the rate of capital formation. But in the underdeveloped countries the per capita real income being very low, the rate of saving investment is very low. Therefore, these countries are obliged to depend upon external sources of capital for initiating them process of economic development. External capital cards in the form of *(i)* Direct Business Investment commonly called, private Foreign Capital and *(ii)* International Loans and Grants more commonly known as Foreign Aid or External Assitance. In the earlier years more direct business investment was the major form of foreign capital. The private industries and multinational corporations made direct investment in various fields of economic activities—agriculturc, industries, plantation, mining, etc. in the underdeveloped countries. However, the flow of direct business investment or foreign capital has declined in the recent years and therefore, now the major form of foreign capital comes by way of international loans and grants. At one time there was great opposition to the use of foreign capital in India. It was said there was the danger of domination and economic exploitation.

Contribution of Foreign Capital. The underdeveloped countries are always capital scarce countries and that is a perpetual need of capital for economic development projects. The degree of dependence on foreign capital depends on the extent to which domestic resources could be mentioned. India has required foreign capital to speed up economic growth. There was considerable opposition to the use of foreign capital in India. This was mainly due to the political role it played in the past. The colonial empires of the 19th and 20th centuries were built by European countries on the basis of trade and identity. The Government of India at one time was subjected to the pressure of foreign companies and foreign government.

Arguments in Favour of Foreign Capital. India is a developing country, and has adopted the path of economic planning for growth. Her natural resources and labour forece are in abundance but there is lack of capital. Our technological knowledge is outdated and industrial productivity is very low under these circumstances, the importance of foreign capital increases. This can be explained as under:

1. Encouragement to Domestic Savings. In a developing country like India the level of domestic savings is low because of low income of the people. Naturally it suffers from scarcity of investment and in this way is caught in the vicious circle of poverty. With the help of foreign capital, the savings and investments can be pushed up.

2. Proper Exploitation of Natural Resources. India possesses abundant natural resources but due to lack of technological know how and capital, the natural resources cannot be properly exploited. Thus it is necessary that the help of foreign capital is sought in order to accelerate the pace of economic development.

3. Availability of Foreign Technology and Managerial Techniques. Developing countries also lack new technology and modern scientific managerial techniques. With the help of foreign capital these can also be gained. This process is essential for the economic development of the country.

4. Establishment of Basic and key Industries. Basic and capital intensive industries cannot be set up for want of sufficient capital. The domestic capital is shy and does not come forward. Thus foreign capital can easily contribute to the development of such industries. Economic history of India is an evidence that foreign capital has played a vital role in the establishment of basic and key industries.

5. Solution of Unemployment Problem. Unemployment is increasing constantly in India was the help of foreign capital. New industries can be set up and chance of expanding the old ones also increase. Thus the level of employment opportunities also increase.

6. Lack of Enterprising Spirit. In an underdeveloped country like India, capital is shy. Capitalists are apperehensive of investing this capital in risky enterprises. Foreign capital is welcomed to face the initial rests.

7. Control over Inflation. India needs more money for its economic growth. So she has been adopting a policy of deficit financing. This leads to increase of money in circulation and the prices level goes up. Thus a state of inflation arises (High prices) foreign capital including capital goods, machinery and equipment can easily control and check inflation.

8. Helpful in Accelerating the pace of Economic Development. To accelerate the pace of economic development the policy of comprehensive economic planning has to be followed. It need cannot be met with domestic reasons. Thus foreign capital becomes Assesstial in boosting the level of capital formation.

9. Improvement in the Balance of Payments Position. In the early stages of economic development of India machines, equipment and raw materials had to be imported. This led to adverse balance of payments. If India imports foreign capital it can make the balance of payments favourable in the short run as well as in the long run.

Arguments against Foreign Capital

1. Obsolete Machines of Technology. Foreign capital is responsible for obsolete machines and technology being passed on to Indian partners by the foreign collaborations.

2. Dependence on Foreign Countries. Foreign collaboration has made Indian industries dependent to a considerable extent on imports and intermediate goods and parts of machinery. It has destroyed self-reliance.

3. Foreign capital offer Prize Posts and superior jobs to their own nationals. They disregard the claims of highly qualified Indians and thus follow the policy of discrimination.

4. Foreign capital derives the industrial profits out of the country. This may lead to the exhaustion of country's valuable resources and the progressive impoverishment of the country.

5. Foreign capital and enterprise brings about economic development by the foreigners. Economic domination may entail political domination in some form. Foreign capital may thus give rise to vested interests which may oppose the political and economic advancement of the country.

6. Foreign capital bound tò beat to great dependence on foreign countries. This may, it is apprehended, impede the attainment of socialist pattern of society.

7. Foreign capital can prove highly prejudicial to national defence if have and key industries are monopolized by the foreigners.

These are the disadvantages that accrue to the country from the use of foreign capital. But in spite of strong reaction in the country against the import of foreign capital we have to considered our need to foreign capital in the light of requirements of a backward country like India.

Foreign Investment in Recent Years. Till the end of 1980, foreign investment was generally allowed only in areas of hi-tech sophisticated industries and Indian industries which were in a position to export substantial part of their production. The normal ceiling for forign investment was then 40 per cent of total equity capital of companies, though a higher percentage of foreign equity capital was favoured in private sector industries, if the technology was highly sophisticated and not available in the country, or if the industrial unit was largely export-oriented.

New Liberal Policy. Government of India has adopted a more liberal policy in regard to foreign investment in India as part of the New Industrial Policy of July 1991.

The new regime of foreign investment contains the following: *(i)* As against the past policy of considering all foreign investment on a case-by-case basis and that too within the normal ceiling of 40 per cent of total equity investment, the new policy provides for automatic approval of direct foreign investment up to 51 per cent foreign equity holding in 34 specified high priority, capital-intensive hi-technology industries provided the foreign equity covers the foreign exchange involved in importing capital goods and outflow on account of dividend payments are balanced by export earnings over a period of seven years from the commencement of production; *(ii)* Foreign technology agreements are also liaberalised for 34 industries with industrial units left free to negotiate the terms of technology transfer without the need for prior Government approval for hiring of foreign technicians; *(iii)* Foreign equity holdings up to 51 per cent would be permitted for foreign trading companies with a view to exploit world markets adopting professional marketing activities; and *(iv)* Boards of Investment Promotion has been set up to look into large foreign investment projects and expedite their approval or non-approval.

Consequence. Though as a consequence of the New liberal economic and industrial policy of July 1991, much foreign equity investment was expected to flow into India, the response though increasing to some extent, has not been as expected. The main reason is that in spite of the announcement of the liberal foreign investment policy, persistence of bureaucratic cobwebs and delays and sticking to rules and regulations still persist obstructing free and abundant flow of foreign equity capital into India. Also Western countries with funds to invest abroad have different priorities such as increasing investments in East Germany, Taiwan and some other Asian countries where there is political stability and greater chances of financial success.

Dangers of Private Foreign Capital. From the Indian experience since her independence, the following dangers of private foreign capital operating in India (through their Indian collaborators) have come to be noticed:

1. Foreign companies from the West European countries and from the United States are generally reluctant to enter into collaboration with public sector companies (*i.e.* Government companies) in India, mostly on ideological grounds. If insisted to do so, they would rather not come to India than offer their participation with the Public Sector Indian companies.

2. In certain areas of industrial production, Indian technology is fairly well developed. Callaboration with foreign companies in low

priority areas like cosmetics and luxury goods has only meant duplication of technology which is unnecessary and often costly. Indian companies or entrepreneurs have the necessary technology in such low priority industries which means any collaboration in such areas is superfluous.

3. The rate of return on initial foreign investments in India is very high, making it possible to return the entire amount of foreign investment within 2 to 4 years. It is, therefore, argued that unless foreign collaboration agreements help to increase India's exports and result in descrease in dependence on foreign countries for imports, outflow of foreign exchange might far outweigh initial gain from foreign collaboration agreements.

4. Often technology that is passed on by private foreign collaborators of Indian partners is obsolete on not appropriate to Indian conditions; often import of capital equipment was far in excess of India's requirements. Thus, technology appropriate to Indian conditions or development of such technology in Indian itself through collaboration with foreign companies has not become possible to any very great extent.

5. It is noted that royalty payments and fees for technical services rendered by foreigners all result in increasing claims on India's foreign exchange earnings and reserves which are relatively small in relation to the country's requirements. One estimate is that total outgoings due to private foreign collaboration agreements were more than the inflow of foreign capital. For example, Coca Cola with a small investment of foreign currency used to send abroad many times that amount annually by way of profit until permission to continue its activities was refused to the country. The same is true of the US oil companies like of ESSO and Caltex. For example, the ESSO with an investment of Rs. 30 crore (with Indian holdings of only Rs. 57 lakh) took away from India profit (in foreign currency) of Rs. 83 crore during 1968 to 1970 only.

6. On the whole, the impact of foreign private collaboration on India's balance of payments has not been favourable. The main

reason for his has been the substantially high level of imports consequent on foreign collaboration agreements as compared to the low level of exports, such foreign collaborations hardly adding to India's export earnings.

For long under the private foreign collaboration agreements, as excessive number of technicians, often not suitable to Indian conditions were sent to India and designs and machines were not suitable to Indian conditions; but under the agreements, they were imposed on India.

7. There is also the myth of the policy of Indianisation. Under Section 29(1) of the Foreign Exchange Regulation Act, all foreign companies are required to dilute their ownership to 74 per cent and under Section 29(2) of the FERA, the Indian branches of foreign companies are to be converted into Indian companies with non-resident share in equity capital not exceeding 40 per cent.

It is observed that the dilution of equity form 100 per cent to 74 per cent (or from 100 per cent to 40 per cent) has hardly made any difference to the drain of foreign exchange from India to foreign countries in which the head offices of foreign collaborations are situated. It is observed, for example, that Ponds and Warren Tea were able to send home net worth of their company's investment every two yers. In the case of Colgate-Palmolive, the highest limit of profit was 89 per cent which meant that the entire net worth of assets invested in India was repatriated within less than 14 months. The new issues of such companies are excessively oversubscribed on the pretext of broadening the Indian of these companies are able to raise plenty of local capital and the Indian Shareholders with their personal interest only in view and in diviend, provided support to the functioning of multinational companies whenever the bogey of expropriation was raised in Indian Parliament. It was not the existing equity capital that was shared with India national, but the new equity that was issued to Indians. The Indian shareholders were scattered all over India and even if they wanted, they could not take any concerted action against the policies of the company. In fact, Indian shareholders were only interested in dividend and hardly took any interest in the functioning of the company. Thus, the domination of foreign collaborators continued unabated in India.

The myth of Indianisation can be exposed by the fact that foreign partners or the parent companies in their collaboration agreement retained the absolute power of appointing chairman and managing directors of their Indian subsidiaries even when the dilution of shareholdings was brought down to 25 per cent.

It is also observed that by adopting the practice of wide dispersal of equity holdings and ownership rights, the foreign collaborators have also significantly blunted Indian people's opposition to multinational foreign companies with subsidiaries in India while repaying very high returns on their investments. It may be said that garb or covering of Indianisation is being cleverly exploited by many foreign multinational companies to convert the business environment in India in their favour and thus continue to make and transfer home enormous profits made in India annaully.

Michael Kidron has estimated that dring 1948 to 1961, foreign companies as a whole had taken out of India total funds worth three times their investments in india. It may be said that the situation did not change much during the 1970s.

8. Instead of allowing foreign private capital and its participation on a selective basis and only in the case of essential capital equipment and other essential imputs, foreign collaboration agreements were permitted out of overenthusiasm to bring foreign capital into India into lines of production of commodities such as chewing gum, cosmetics, boot-polish, cigarettes, hotels and so on.

Though government assumed powers under the FERA, no concrete results have followed and foreign companies continue to make enormous profis in India and remit them to their mother countries as before.

Government's Policy in Regard to Foreign Capital

After India became independent in August 1947, Jawaharlal Nehru, the then Prime Minister of India, made a statement in April 1949 giving the following assurances to foreign capital.

1. There would be no discrimination between foreign companies and purely Indian companies which meant that foreign capital would get the same treatment as indigenous capital.

2. Foreign investors would be permitted to remit profits and repatriate capital, taking into consideration India's position in regard to availability of foreign exchange.

3. In case a foreign company was nationalised, far and equitable compensation will be given to foreign investors.

The above policy was based on several considerations. There was a shortage of indigenous capital and that needed supplementing by foreign capital, if rapid industrial and economic development were to be brought about. Also, there was need of capital goods and equipment and technical know-how from abroad as India then lacked these essential requisites of growth and development.

Tax Concessions

In the initial stages, with a view to attract foreign capital (that is, foreign companies) to India, Government offered various tax concessions and to avoid delays in finalising foreign collaboration agreements, streamlined its licensing policy of procedures to quickly approve foreign collaboration agreements.

In 1961 the Indian Investment Centre was opened, the objective being to bring together Indian and foreign businessmen and appraise foreign investors of the vast business opportunities in India.

In 1972 the Government of India took another major step to attract foreign capital into the country. It permitted wholly-owned subsidiaries in India of foreign companies, provided they undertook to export 100 per cent of their production.

Export Liability

If the export liability was less than 100 per cent of its output, the extent of permissible foreign capital was to be decided by negotiations between the foreign companies and the Government of India.

Thus, the Government of India had to choose between the Indianisation of foreign subsidiary companies in India or boosting up export through their help. Government preferred the second of the above two possible courses. But Government's choice of the second policy was beset with many difficulties. What if export targets laid down were not fulfilled by foreign companies? Have not, with the promise of boosting, exports, a large number of foreign companies opened their branches or entered into collaboration agreements with Indian companies, thus dominating the Indian industrial scene, making the country dependent on foreign countries and creating problems of balance of payments?

Limits on the Role of Foriegn Capital and Foriegn Collaboration Agreements

While for a developing country like India, foreign capital as also foreign technical knowledge are important for the industrial development of the country, there are clear limits on the use of foreign capial and on foreign industrial collaboration agreements as instruments of industrial development in a counry like India.

The limits on the above two or on the absorptive capacity of foreign capital and technical know-how for industrial development in a country like India are fixed by considerations such as availability of industrial raw materials in the country, level of industrial and economic development already attained, availability of skilled pesonnel in the country, availability of various infrastructural facilities, the extent to which industrial and commercial projects are prepared or can be prepared with speed, availability of local or indigenous capital, experience of Indian companies in the industrial and commercial fields and their willingness to enter into industrial collaboration agreements, capacity of the country to pay servicing and other charges in foreign currencies to foreign collaborators, political stability and political ideology governing industrial and economic policy of the government of the country, willingness of foreign investors and companies to enter into collaboration agreements with local companies (which depends upon the extent to which Indian companies inspire confidence among foreign investors and foreign companies) and above all, on Government of India's policy in regard to foreign capital and foreign collaboration agreements in the industrial field.

Instruments of Industrial Growth

World Bank Loan. Due to an unprecedented drought in the country in 1987-88, the World Bank has agreed to give India a loan of dollar 350 million to help India to pay for the imports necessitated by the drought. This is in additon to a dollar loan from Japan amounting to 200 million.

The crucial point is that, for the first time, India is borrowing from international lending institutions to pay for current consumption. In the past such borrowing were intended for creating assests that would be productive in future, and thereby enhance the country's capacity to repay the loans in future. Now, however, India has taken another step towards the dreaded debt trap.

External or Foreign Debt of India—Latest Position. Exconomic Survey of the Government of India for 1991-92 has following things to say about India's foreign or external debt:

"India's medium and long-term external debt, consiting of external assistance on Government and non-Government accounts external commercial borrowings and the IMF liabilities amounted to Rs. 1,004 hundred crores (*i.e.* US dollars 51.1 billion) at the end of 1990-91 and constituted about 19 per cent of GDP. Including NRI deposits, the country's external debt (other than shor-term debt) stood at Rs. 1,212 hundred crores (US dollars 61.7 billion) constituting about 23 per cent of GDP.

Adding the estimates of short-term debt of maturities to one year, India's aggregate external debt amounted to Rs. 1,307 hundred crores or US. dollars 66.5 billion on march 31, 1991 which was around 25 per cent of the country's GDP."

External Assistance or Foreign Aid

In recent decades, particularly after the World War II, whereas the flow of private foreign capital to the underdeveloped countries has gone down sharply, that of public development assistance (foreign aid), both from the individual national governments and multinational donor agencies (like IBRD, IDA, etc.) has gone up tremendously. Foreign aid or external assistance is that flow of capital funds to the underdeveloped countries whose objective is non-commercial from the point of view of the donor agencies. Further, such assistance is characterised by concessional terms *i.e.*,it has a low rate of interest and its repayment period is considerably large. These 'softer' terms of borrowings of foreign aid are in contrast to commercial borrowings which have high interest rate and stringent repayment schedule. During nearly five decades of her planned economic development, India has utilised substantial quantities of foreign aid. In the First Five Year Plan, the need for external assistance was not felt to greater degree because we heavily relied on the withdrawal of our accumulated foreign exchange reserves for supplementing the domestic capital. The withdrawal of our foreign resources continued right till the middle of 1958, when they became so low that they were not considered sufficient even to meet the minimum requirements of the economy. It was at this time that the need for procuring foreign capital was urgently felt and the friendly countries along with the international institutions like the I.B.R.D. were approached for help. Ever since that time, there has been a continuous flow of external assistance to India which has come in the form of *(a)* loans, *(b)* grants, and *(c)* aid under U.S. Public Law 480 commonly known as PL 480 which was discontinued around the year 1971-72.

External Assistance : Authorisation and Utilisation

The total external assistance authorised to India till the end of March 1998 amounted to Rs. 1,82,319 crores, of which Rs.1,61,326 crores or 88.5 per cent of the total authorisation were in the form of loans and Rs. 18219 crores or 10 per cent of the total were by way of grants, Rs.2,774 crores or 1.5 per cent being in the form of PL 480/665 U.S. assistance to India. The actual Utilisation of total assistance of the end of March 1998 amounted to Rs. 1,29,352 crores which was only about 71 per cent of the total authorised assistance. In the total, aid utilised loans accounted for Rs. 1,13,851 crores (88 per cent of the total, assistance utilised) and grants Rs. 11,682 crores (9 per cent of the utilised assistance). The balance Rs. 2,819 crores (3 per cent of the total utilisation) was PL 480/665 assistance which was fully utilised by the end of 1971-72.

Aid in Pipeline. Aid available in pipeline represents assistance committed over the years which has remained undisbursed and is available for disbursement in future. Total aid in pipeline, both in the form of loans and grants, amounted to Rs. 52,967 crores at the end of March 1998. The World Bank group's share in the total undisbursed loans was over 50 per cent.

Low Utilisation of Aid. Not only there is a decline in the quantum of fresh aid, but also the country has not been able to fully utilise the already committed aid. Utilisation of total authorised aid upto the end of March 1995 was only about 70 per cent. Among the reasons for lower utilisation are:inadequate provision of matching rupee resources from the Government organisational and administrative inefficiency; undue delay in completion of projects, etc.Cost-overruns consequent to inordinate delays in completion of projects in critical areas have not only slowed down timely utilisation of aid available in the pipeline, but has also started adversely affecting fresh commitments by donors.

Source-wise External Assistance. India has been receiving assistance from a number of countries/country groups and international agencies. As at the end of March 1998, the share of World Bank Group (IBRD and IDA) in the total authorisations was 42.8 per cent. Japan has emerged as the second largest contributor (16.2 per cent) followed by the Asian Development Bank (9.1 per cent). Among the other major donors are the U.K., Germany and the OPEC Group.

Problems of Foreign Aid. External assistance, which plays a crucial role in the economic development of the underdeveloped countries, has also some problems that dilute its good impact. Foreign aid is largely uncertain and fluctuating and, therefore, it becomes difficult to plan your development by placing much reliance on such aid. It has been seen that the quantum of foreign aid has not much relation with the requirements and absorption capacity of the aid receiving country as much of it is governed by the political considerations. And then the tied-aid, which is the common form of aid these days, restricts the country's choice of projects or choice of markets for import of necessary goods as the donor countries give aid only for specific projects on the condition that the equipment and machinery required for these projects will be bought only in the market of the donor country. This naturally reduces the impact of such aid as the prices of goods in the donor countries may be higher and their technologies inappropriate for underdeveloped countries. Another problem of foreign aid is the debt-servicing burden it imposes. Interest has to be paid regularly and instalments must be paid on time. All these payments have to be made in foreign currency. With the meager export earnings of the underdeveloped countries such debt servicing may consume a substantial proportion of their export-earnings. For example, debt servicing payments in India now use almost 30 per cent of our export earning. This leaves less foreign exchange for importing other essential items required for development. Thus, foreign aid is not an unmixed blessing; it has its evil consequences as well.

ROLE OF MNC'S

International flow of funds to the less developed countries takes the form of either *(i)* Direct Foreign Investment or Private Foreign Capital which is the investment made by foreign companies or Multinational Corporations in various economic sectors of the less developed countries, or *(ii)* Official Development Assistance or Foriegn Aid provided by the donor countries or multilateral institutions like IBRD, IDA, etc. to the less developed country's governments in the form of concessional loans and outright grants. The first one *i.e.*, direct foreign investment is called Foreign Capital and the second one *i.e.*, international loans and grants is known as Foreign Aid.

Multinational Corporations (MNC's). Private foreign investment or foreign capital takes the form of direct foreign investment by huge multinational corporations. These are the mighty big firms with their headquarters in North America, Western Europe or Japan who have their massive network of subsidiaries spread over many nations. These firms are so big that in many cases their annual sales turnover is greater than the entire GNP of the nations in which they operate.

Advantages of Direct Foreign Investment. Direct foreign investment coming from these MNC's having much experience, standing and efficiency can confer great benefits on the less developed countries where they operate. They by providing capital, supplement the domestic resources, provide the much needed foreign exchange resources for essential capital goods imports; provide necessary and up-to-date technology and knowledge and general employment and incomes in the countries where they operate. They can benefit the consumers by offering better quality goods at lower prices due to the high levels of efficiency in their production processes. In brief, foreign capital supplements domestic savings to achieve higher levels of investment and facilitate import of capital goods and technology, which are not domestically available and thus promote the diversification of economic structure and its efficiency. Apart from finance and technology, foreign capital brings with its marketing and management skills which are so scarce and undevelopd in the underdeveloped economies.

Drawbacks of Direct Foreign Investments. Our distrust of MNC's. However as the experience in India under the British rule has shown, foreign capital has not been of much help. No doubt, many of our industries own their growth to British Multinational firms, but the fact is that such foreign investments have only developed our export items like tea, jute, rubber, etc. where the clientele were foreign and profits were high. Not much was done to develop those industries that provided necessary goods to the teeming millions of poor Indians. The pattern of development that took place was essentially dualistic where some packets were growing while the rest of the economy remained backward.

Because by nature the MNC's are big industrial gaints, they can exercise their semi-monopoly power to oust local producers and exploit the consumers. They, through massive publicity and propoganda, promote inappropriate products and cause misallocation of country's resources. By using inappropriate technology brought from and suited to their home country resource endowments, cause unemployment to rise and dualistic structure to rigidity. By their sheer money power they can corrupt the politicians and bureaucrats and seek large concessions for themselves. They cause drain on our resources in the form of repatriation of their large profits and export of goods made form raw materials which may be scarce in the country and hence needed to be preserved for our own development.

(1) Reasons for Preferring. Since our experience with foreign capital has not been satisfactory in the past, the Government of India showed a distinct preference for the other means of international capital transfers viz., foreign aid. Over the years India has received massive foreign aid from various countries and international agencies. The good thing about foreign aid is that India can use it in accordance with its own plans and priorities. None of the evils that accompany direct foreign investment are found in foreign aid. We can invest according to our own plans, produce the goods that we think to be necessary, use the technique that is most suited to our conditions and keep the profit within the country to prevent drain of resources.

(2) Problem of Foreign Aid. But the problem with foreign loans (most of the foreign aid is in the form of loans) is that they have to be serviced, *i.e.*, interest has to be paid on them and the loan returned in instalments. Besides, most of the loans are tied loans, that is they can be used for specific projects for which they are given and equipment for those projects has to be purchased in the country that gives the loan. This reduces the freedom of the borrowing to use the loan the way it likes.

(3) Mounting Indebtedness. Indiscriminate borrowings have led to growing international indebtedness. Total external debt of India outstanding as at the end of 1991 was around \$83801 million. This increased to about $ 99008 million at the end of 1995 but came down to 93908 million by the end of March 1998.

As a ratio of GDP at current market prices, India's external debt which was 28.0 per cent in 1991, rose to over 33.1 per cent at the end of March 1994 but declined to 26.3 per cent in March 1996 and further to 23.8 per cent at the end of March 1998.

International Debt Trap. Since a country that takes loans has to return that in instalments and pay interest on that loan regularly, it means every year a part of our foreign exchange earnings will have to be used for debt servicing, *i.e.*, amortisation and interest payment. And when the country contracts large amounts of loans year after year, then a situation may arise where the country has a raise to new loan to pay the interest and instalments of the old loans. In such a case the new inflow of aid (gross aid minus debt servicing) will become small and hence development process would suffer.

Lately such a situation has emerged in India. Every year almost one half to two thirds of gross foreign aid received is used for debt servicing thereby reducing the net aid to extremely low levels.

Net foreign aid which was only about 51 per cent of the gross aid disbursed in 1980-81, came down to only 36 per cent of the gross aid in 1990-91. The position detriorated sharply and became worse during 1994-95 and 1995-96 when gross aid inflow was less than the outflow on account of debt servicing. The same was the situation in 1997-98. This means the country has come to that position where it has to raise loans just to meet the repayment obligations *i.e.*, it has come into the grip of debt trap.

Debt Service Ratio. Debt service payment take away a substantial part of our foreign exchange earnings. Debt service payments as a ratio of country's current receipts are an important indication of its international indebtedness. A situation where a country may have to pay about 40 to 45 per cent of its current receipts for debt servicing is an indication that it has virtually been caught in a dept trap. In India the Debt Service Ratio *i.e.*, the ratio of debt servicing to export of goods and services (current receipts) increased from 9.3 per cent in 1981 to about 35 per cent in 1991. Though this ratio gradually declined after that year, it was still high at 26.4 at the end of March 1998. This shows that a quarter of country's foreign exchange earnings were used to meet repayment obligations.

India's mounting external indebtedness and increasing debt servicing obligations have caused tremendous strain on our balance of payments position. There was a virtual crisis in 1990 and 1991 when India's position to meet its external commitments became precarious and the country had to rush to IMF and World Bank to bail it out. Due to such mounting pressures on balance of payments and foreign exchange rerserves, the Government of India decided to liberalise its policy towards direct foreign investment with a view to encouraging its inflow.

One great advantage of direct foreign investment to the recipient countries lies in the fact that servicing of this capital begins only when the investment reaches a profit-making stage unlike foreign loans and commercial borrowings where servicing begins shortly after disbursement. While borrowing go to augment investible resources in the short-term and medium-term, direct investment in the form of equity capital provides reasources on a much longer basis.

In view of this, the Government has announced liberal terms and incentives to foreign investors. According to the Industrial Policy announced in July 1991, there will be automatic approval for direct foreign investment upto 51 per cent equity holding in 34 specified high priority industries. Many additional concessions have been given to attract foreign direct investment in India.

India, undoubtedly, has a number of advantages to offer to the potential foreign investor. Among these are political stability in a democratic framework; and economy characterised by steady growth; a vast domestic market; a large and growing pool of trained manpower;

fairly well developed physical and social infrastructure; a vibrant financial system and a diversified industrial base.

Liberalisation in India

The recent policy of the Government is that of liberalisation. The policy has been pursued with a view to have rational and fuller utilisation of resources in the different sectors of the economy, promotion of exports, development of backward areas, development of small-scale sector, larger opportunities to the new enterprises, etc.

Steps towards Liberalisation. The Government, in the recent past, has announced a number of concessions and incentives which tend to lieberalise the different producing sectors of the economy. Some of the major concessions in this direction are given below:

(1) Except for a short list of industries in the high priority ares, all other industries have been deregulated. Industrial licensing would be compulsory only for 15 industries in the high priority sector.

(2) Automatic approval up to 51 per cent equity extended to trading companies primarily engaged in export activities, to hotels and tourism-related industries, exploration/development, refining and marketing of petroleum oil and gas.

(3) Fully-owned foreign enterprises will be allowed to set up gaint power project without the requirement to balance dividend payments with export earnings.

(4) The list of the industries exclusively reserved for the State has been pruned. Only 6 industries have been reserved for the public sector. In the Union Budget 1993-94, even the generation of power and processing of minerals has been left open to private sector.

(5) Automatic approval by the Reserve Bank for foreign direct investment up to 51 per cent for foreign equity in 34 selected areas.

(6) NRIs and overseas corporate bodies predominantly owned by them are permitted up to 100 per cent foreign equity in high priority areas.

(7) Foreign Exchange Regulation Act companies have been brought at par with Indian companies. The existing FERA companies have also been extended the facility of 51 per cent equity. Companies have also been allowed to use foreign brand names and trade marks on goods for sale within the country.

(8) Condition of dividend balancing thorugh export earning has withdrawn except for 22 industries under the consumer goods category.

(9) Automatic approval for technology agreements related to high priority industries, if such agreements do no require the expenditure of foreign exchange.

(10) Threshold limits of assets (Rs. 100 crores) in respect of MRTP companies and dominant undertakings stands withdrawn. This eliminates the requirements of prior approval of Central Government for establishment of new undertakings, expansion of undertakings, merger, amalgamation and takeover and appointment of directors.

(11) All existing registration schemes (Delicensed, Registration, Exempted Industries Registration, DGTD Registration) have been abolished.

(12) Investment in fixed capital by SSI unis raised to Rs. 60 lakhs, in case of ancillaries to Rs. 75 lakhs. and for tiny sector units to Rs. 5 lakhs.

(13) Free float of Indian ruppee in the international market.

(14) A concessional tax rate of 10 per cent on short-term capital gains for foreign institutional investors was introduced to enhance the level of foreign investment in Indian stocks.

(15) New export-import policy announced for the five-year period 1997-2002, has made a major thrust towards trade liberalisation. The new policy substantially eliminates licensing quantitative restrictions, and other regulatory and discretionary

controls. Exports and imports are allowed freely, subject only to a negative list of imports and a negative list of exports. The list of canalised items imported and exported through public sector undertakings drastically curtailed.

(16) A five-year tax holiday for new industries in industrially backward States and Union Territories and for power generation anywhere in India was produced.

All these measure suggest liberalisation of the Indian economy in a big way. In spite of certain defects associated with liberalisation, it is likely to accelerate the pace of economic development in the Indian economy.

❐

9

New Economic Policy

The New Economic Policy (NEP), in brief, is the policy of Liberalisation, Privatisation and Globaliation. The policy of economic liberalisation was, in fact, initiated by the Late Prime Minister Shri Rajiv Gandhi during mid-eighties when with a view to increasing investment and efficiency in the economy he opened up more areas to the private sector, simplified licensing system and provided more facilities to foreign capital to give a big boost to the modernisation of the economy. But the measures adopted were by and large piecemeal and half-hearted. It was only in 1991, under the Prime ministership of Shri P.V. Narsimha Rao that concrete efforts were made in this direction. By abolishing requirements of industrial licensing (except for a short list of 18 industries related to security, strategic and environmental concerns), removing restrictions on expansion of large industrial houses under MRTP, allowing unfettered entry of private sector, etc. the government have moved towards greater liberalisation of the economic activity.

The New Economic policy seeks to encourage gradual privatisation of the economy. Privatisation may mean many things such as induction of private ownership in public sector industries, induction of private management (with or without private ownership) in publicly owned industries. It is in general a process that involves the private sector in the ownership and operation of state enterprises. Denationalisation of public enterprises is another way to privatisation. The NEP however does not seek to bring about privatisation through any of the above methods. The process of privatisation under the NIP involves; *(i)* reduction in the sphere of industries reserved for the public sector and *(ii)* disinvestment of a part of the equity of public enterprises. Under the new policy only 8 industrial sectors of strategic and infrastructure nature have been kept reserved for the public sector as against the 17 sectors reserved earlier. The rest has been left free for the private sector thereby considerably expanding the area of operation of private industries. Also the government has taken recourse to disinvestment to the tune of 20 per cent in many public sector undertakings. Private enterprise has also been allowed to participate, if the government so requires, in areas reserved for the public sector even under the new policy.

The New Economy Policy aims at globalisation of the Indian economy. Globalisation means integration of the national economy with the world economy. Ever since independence we had protected our domestic industries against foreign competition through a variety of devices such as tariff and quota restrictions import licensing and canalising of trade through a number of public sector institutions such as State Trading Corporation, Mineral and Metals Trading Corporation, etc. Over the years these controls and restrictions were so much tightened that the cost and quality structure of Indian products became highly incompetitive. Our goods could not be sold in the world market without the crutches provided by export subsidies and credits. Our domestic buyers had no option except to purchase the high cost low quality goods produced by obsolete technology used by the inefficient and unimaginative producers who were well protected form the outside competition. The NEP substantially reduces import restrictions, curtails tariff walls, abolishes licences for a large number of import goods and eliminates many regulatory and discriminatory trade controls. With these, there will be a relatively free inflow of imports that would compete with the domestic goods and induce domestic entrepreneurs to improve their quality and reduce costs through technology upgradation and other innovative measures. It is also believed that the new and better quality goods produced by the competitive economy will find a place in world market and thus expand our exports.

The New Economic Policy also aims of attaining macroeconomic stabilisation through reducing the gross fiscal deficit. Gross fiscal deficit refers to the gap between the total government expenditure over its revenue receipts (tax revenue and non-tax revenue) and grants. It excludes capital receipts like market borrowings and external assistance because such receipts only add to the indebtedness of the government. Excessively high gross fiscal deficit represents fiscal indiscipline in the sense that governmental expenditure (some of which may be non-productive) is being kept much above the normal fiscal receipts (taxes, non-tax revenue and grants) by taking recourse to loans and deficit financing. A high fiscal deficit may land the government into a debt trap where it may have to borrow more just to pay off the instalments of an interest on the past loans. This naturally means unproductive use of national resources. Thus, the NEP emphasises the need to exercise economy in public expenditure by curtailing government's administrative expenditure, reducing and ultimately eliminating all subsidies on food, fertilizers, exports, etc. If fiscal deficit is allowed to reach continuously higher magnitudes, as has been happening in the past, it will lead to increased deficit financing, more money supply, higher prices, higher deficits in balance of payments, internal and international debt traps thereby weakening the structure of the whole economy.

New Economic Policy: Expected Gains

The New Economic policy seeks to initiate an era of market oriented system which would be different from the one that prevailed in the past. The private sector has been assigned a larger role while the public sector no more holds the commanding heights of the economy. The new market friendly economic policy is expected to benefit the economy and contribute to its rapid development in many ways.

The NEP will lead to improved efficiency in the use of precious economic resources of the country. With the private sector earlier being subjected to faulty controls and regulations and inefficiencies in the public enterprises, the overall productivity of capital is very low, capital output is high and many industrial units are sick. Removal of controls coupled with lure of private profits will channelise flow of capital into more efficient uses. hence, more economic use of capital would ensure greater flow of output and faster growth of the economy. Not only this, with controls, licences and permits abolished, much of the time and energy that was wasted in fulfilling cumbersome formalities and governmental requirements will now be fruitfully used for productive activities. Again privatisation of even a part of the public enterprises would lead to a more professional approach to their management thereby improving their efficiency and contribution to the nation's economy.

Relaxing of controls on foreign investment and liberalizing terms regarding foreign participation in Indian industries is bound to attract more foreign equity capital. This will supplement domestic capital, and give us the benefits of modern technology through technology transfers and also help us in learning scientific ways of modern management. Thus, with the impetus given by the NEP, we shall be able to simultaneously fill up the saving gap, the foreign exchange gap, the technology gap and the management gap, all of which would help in promoting rapid development of our economy. Private domestic capital and foreign capital together under a liberal policy regime are expected to boost production, increase employment and lead to allround progress.

Removal of import restrictions would make the domestic industry more competitive through efficiency improvements because tariff protection and other shelters from foreign competition will no more be available to producers. Specific trade policies like convertibility of the Rupee, devaluation, etc. would boost exports and create more employment and income.

Macroeconomic stability will create fiscal discipline, curb inflationary pressures and reduce balance of payment deficits. It will add to building up of confidence of foreign investors in India's economic stability and increase flow of foreign funds. This would surely help us to expand out trade and industry and thus contribute to faster economic development.

The overall effects of the liberalised economic philosophy embodied in the NEP are bound to help the economy by improving its growth rate and reduce pressure on the balance of payments. But such improvements may take time to materialise. In the short run, some problems may be faced and some shortfalls may occur in production and employment as the economy tries to adjust to the new system. But the things are bound to look up over time as the economy will move faster in future.

NEW POLICY FOR SMALL INDUSTRIES

While announcing the New Industrial policy Statement on July 24, 1991, the Government had promised that it will shortly come out with a separate policy statement for the small scale sector. keeping her promise, the Government of India, on August 6, 1991, announced a new package for the small-scale, tiny and village industries.

Objectives of the New Policy Statement

The primary objectives of the Small scale Industrial policy during the nineties will be as follows:

(i) Impetus to the growth of small-scale sector to enable it to contribute its mite fully to the economy, particularly in terms of growth of output, employment and exports.

(ii) Encouraging modernisation and technological upgradation to make them more competitive.

(iii) Deregulation and debureaucratisation of the sector with a view to remove all fetters on its growth potential.

Highlights of the New Policy Statement

Several policy measures have been announced in the New Policy to achieve the various objectives set for the small sector. The major highlights of the New Policy Statement are as follows:

(1) Infrastructural Facilities. A Scheme of Integrated Infrastructural Development (including Technological backup Services) for small scale industries will be implemented to facilitate location of industries in rural/backward areas.

A Technology Development Cell (TDC) would be set up in the Small Industries Development Organisation (SIDO) which would provide technology inputs to improve productivity and competitiveness of products of the small scale industries.

Adequacy and equitable distribution of indigenous and imported raw materials would be ensured to the small scale sector, particularly the tiny sub-sector.

(2) Marketing and Exports. National Small Industries Corporation (NSIC) would concentrate on marketing of mass consumption items under common brand name and organic links between NSIC and SSIDCs would be established.

With a view to establish complementarity between large and small-scale units production of components, spares, sub-assemblies, etc. will be encouraged for production in a techno-economically viable manner through small-scale ancillary units.

The SIDO will operate as a nodal agency to support the small-scale industries in export promotion. An Export Development Centre would be set up in SIDO for this purpose.

(3) Modernisation, Technological and Quality Upgradation. Industry associations would be encouraged and supported to establish quality counselling and common testing facilities. Technology Information Centres will provide knowledge on technology and markets.

A reorientation programme of modernisation and technological upgradation aimed at improving productivity, efficiency and cost effectiveness in the small-scale sector would be pursued. IITs and selected Engineering Colleges will serve as Technological Information, Design and Development Centres in their respective command areas.

(4) Simplification of Rules and Procedures. Procedures would be simplified, bureaucratic controls effectively reduced, unnecessary interference eliminated and paper work cut down to minimum to enable the enterpreneurship to concentrate on production and marketing functions.

(5) Promotion of Enterpreneurship. Large number of Enterpreneurial Development Programme (EDP) trainers and motivators will be trained to significantly expand EDPs, EDP would be built into the curricula of vocational and other degree-level courses. Women entrepreneurs will receive support through special training programmes. Additional employment opportunities would be generated through training of multi-disciplinary barefoot managers to suit the special requirements of the small-scale sector.

(6) Financial Support. The investment limit for small-scale, ancillary and tiny sector units has been fixed at Rs. 300 lakhs and Rs. 25 lakhs respectively. With a view to provide access to the capital market the Government has decided to allow equity participation by other industrial undertakings in the SSI, not exceeding 24 per cent of the total shareholding.

It has also been decided to widen the scope of the National Equity Fund Scheme to cover projects up to Rs. 10 lakhs for quity support (upto 15 per cent). Single Window Loan Scheme has been enlarged to cover projects up to Rs. 20 lakhs with working capital margin up to Rs. 10 lakhs. Composite loans under Single Window Scheme, now available only through SFCs and twin function State Industries Development Corporations (SSIDCs), would also be channelised through commercial banks.

(7) An ordinance was promulgated on September 23, 1992 making payment of interest obligatory on delayed payments to small scale and ancillary industrial undertakings.

(8) Development of Village Industries. Several schemes have been announced in the New Policy to promote the growth of village industries. Some of the new packages are as follows:

(i) Promotion of handloom sector to sustain employment in the rural areas.

(ii) Project Package Scheme for handloom sector for product development upgradation of technology, improvement of marketing facilities, etc.

(iii) National handloom Development Corporation (NHDC) would operate as the nodal agency for increasing the supply of hank yarn and of dyes and chemicals.

(iv) Expansion of marketing infrastructure, exhibitions, publicity, etc. through Centre and State Handicrafts Corporations.

(v) Measures to sustain an increased exports of handicrafts through new marketing channels, like trading companies, departmental stores, etc.

(vi) Development of village industries for stepping up non-farm employment opportunities.

(vii) For improving marketing of handloom products, a more intensive implementation of schemes for design and product improvement by national level publicity, exhibitions and design exercise will be undertaken.

(viii) Integrated development of the handicrafts sector so that it could contribute towards a faster pace of rural industrialisation.

(ix) Through the setting up of craft development centres, extension of services like supply of raw materials, design and technical guidance, market support, training and procuring of related materials/inputs will be provided to the handicrafts.

(x) Better flow of credit from the financial institutions to village industries for improving their productivity.

(xi) Agro-processing and food processing industries would be promoted with a viw to utilise locally available agricultural produce and promote employment.

Latest Incentives for SSI Units

1. Excise concessions for both registered and unregistered units on a graded scale depending upon turnover up to Rs. 300 lakh.

2. A scheme of Integrated Development was launched in March, 1994 to strengthen infrastructural facilities in rural and backward areas.

3. Financial support is extended to SSI units to acquire ISO-9000 certificate.

4. Seven-point Action Plan has been initiated to improve flow of credit to SSI sector.

5. Concessional/fixed rate of interest for loans up to Rs. 2 lakhs.

6. Single Window Scheme of SIDBI for project outlays up to Rs. 50 lakhs.

7. Scope of NEF scheme enlarged to cover the whole country to support expansion, modernisation and technology upgradation.

8. Forty per cent of advances to SSI sector have been reserved for tiny sector and village and cottage industries.

9. 822 products reserved for exclusive manufacture in the SSI sector.

10. NRIs, OCBs, FIIs, etc. allowed for equity participation up to 24 per cent in the SSI units. However, such participants shall have prior SIA approval and export obligations.

11. 40 per cent of advances to SSI sector reserved for tiny sector and village and cottage industries.

12. Steps to be taken to ensure that composite loans (covering both term loans and working capital) are sanctioned to SSI entrepreneurs as far as possible.

13. Export obligation of non SSI units producing reserved items has been reduced from 75 per cent to 50 per cent.

14. Infrastructural support to Entrepreneurship Development Institutes (EDIs) to augment their training capacities.

Evaluation

The new package for the small-scale sector announced by the government has been welcomed by small producers. Deregulation and debureaucratisation will accelerate the rate of growth of small units. Equity participation in small units and widening of the scope of the National Equity Fund Scheme will improve the resource position of small scale units. Technological upgradation, development of infrastructural support, improvement in marketing facilities and development of enterpreneurial skill are the steps in the right direction to improve efficiency and productivity. The Government efforts to preserve the traditional richness of crafts and hereditary skills of caraftsman would protect the interest of poor craftsmen. The new policy has outlined various schemes for the promotion of handicrafts and handloom sectors. The policy, has ignored the interests of the modern small scale sector which is the major foreign exchange earner. Modern small scale industries will now be entitled to only one time concession such as the purchase of land at concessional prices, access to technology upgradation, etc.

The Federation of Association of Small Scale Industries of India (FASII) has criticised the new policy for totally ignoring the problem of the rehabilitation of sick SSI units.

Integration between large and small scale units is essential for a balanced industrial development of the country, and also to improve industrial productivity. The new policy has recognised the need for an effective and close relation between large and small scale units and suggested suitable strategy to achieve this end.

In brief, the new policy is a landmark in the history of small units. It is a move to restore the pride position that the small scale sector used to enjoy in the past. The various measures suggested in the new policy are likely to make small scale industries more competitive, cost-efficient and productive.

INDUSTRIAL SICKNESS

A sick unit may be defined as one which fails to generate an internal surplus on a continuing basis and depends for its survival upon a frequent infusion of external funds. The following are the important symptoms of sick unit:

(i) Slow turnover in the accounts of the unit;

(ii) frequent requests for overdrafts;

(iii) Failure to honour its bills on maturity;

(iv) Inexplicable delays in the submission of stock statements;

(v) Slow off-take of stocks; and

(vi) Overvaluation of stocks, diversion of stocks, etc.

Magnitude of Industrial Sickness Both large and small-scale industrial units suffer form sickness. According to the latest data available as at the end of March 1995, the total number of sick units identified by banks as sick stood at 2.71 lakhs with outstanding bank credit of Rs. 13,739 crores. These included 1,915 large sick industrial units (*i.e.* units individually enjoying credit limits of Rs. 1 crore and above from the banking system) with aggregate outstanding bank credit of Rs. 5,786 crores as compared to 1,461 units with outstanding amount of Rs. 5,106 crores at the end of December 1991. As at the end of March, 1995, there were 2,68,815 sick small scale industrial units involving bank credit of Rs. 3,100 crores as compared to 2,21,472 units involving bank finance of Rs. 2,792 crores 4 years ago.

The president of All India Sick Small Scale Industries Association (AISSIA) said, the banks were largely responsible for the condition of over 90 per cent of the small sick units.

Causes of Industrial Sickness

Industrial sickness is caused by a number of factors, the more important among these are as follows:

(i) High cost of manufacture and the low sales revenue;

(ii) Inadequate availability of raw materials or availability at high prices;

(iii) Lack of regular supply of crude inputs, such as power, transport, etc.;

(iv) Recessionary trends in the economy as reflected by a sharp fall in demand;

(v) Inability of an industrial unit to raise sufficient financial resources to withstand operational losses;

(vi) Managerial inefficiency;

(vii) High rate of taxation affecting the profit margins; and

(viii) Wrong choice of technology, unsuitability of product mix and wrong location of industry.

In brief, the shortage of raw material and other inputs, high cost of production, poor marketing techniques, and inefficient management are mainly responsible for industrial sickness.

Rehabilitation of Sick Units

The following measures can be adopted to solve the problem of industrial sickness and to rehabilitate the sick units:

(i) Credit agencies should extend loans only when they satisfy themselves about the technical feasibility and economic viability of project.

(ii) There should be proper coordination between the different credit agencies so that there remains no scope for overfinancing on under-financing.

(iii) Lending institution should sacrifice the major dues by way of reducing the rate of interest on loans, writing off excess interest charges, sanctioning of loans at concessional rate of interest, etc.

(iv) The Government can take over a sick unit and operate it as a State enterprise.

(v) The Government can also provide consultancy services to the sick units to strengthen their organisational set-up.

(vi) Competent technical and managerial personnel should be appointed in key positions in production, finance and marketing.

(vii) No sympathy should be shown for deliberate sickness.

(viii) A sick unit should be merged with a financially sound unit in order to make both of them work.

It is of great interest to know that the Margin Money Assistance Scheme has been introduced from January 1, 1982 for providing margin money on soft terms for the revival of sick small scale units. Under the scheme, the State Government provide margin money assistance ranging from Rs.10,000 to Rs. 20,000 to sick small scale units in the form of long-term loans.

The Board for Industrial and Financial Reconstruction (BIFR), set up under the Sick Industrial Companies (Special Provision) Act, 1985, became operational on 15th May, 1987. Industrial companies whose net worth has eroded completely and those which have net worth eroded has been by 50 per cent or more are required to make a reference to the BIFR. BIFR may recommend the winding up, merger, change of management, leasing and rehabilitation of the sick units. Financial institutions such as IDBI, ICICI, IFCI, IRBI and the State Government can be requested to formulate policy packages for rehabilitation of sick industrial unit.

Reserve Bank's Guidance to Banks

The Reserve Bank has issued the following guidelines to scheduled commercial banks regarding the revival of sick units:

(1) Banks which have entered into a consortium arrangement for financing, a healthy unit should also agree to participate in the rehabilitation package when the unit become sick.

(2) Banks have been given the opinion either to help the rehabilitation package or to sell their debts to other willing banks at a discount as per the guidelines issued by the RBI.

(3) In case workers of the sick unit are interested in taking over the management by forming worker's co-operatives, banks should actively support the rehabilitation package.

(4) The present system of prior approval by the RBI for extending reliefs/concessions beyond the parameters fixed by it has been withdrawn for the grant of reliefs/concessions as part of the packages evolved for the rehabilitation of sick/weak units.

(5) It has been decided that existing/additional facilities provided to sick/weak units under rehabilitation packages could be exempt from application of the existing ceiling prescribed under the prudential norms for single group exposure limits.

In October 1989, the Government announced a scheme for excise relief for weak industrial units. The rehabilitation package includes granting of excise duty actually paid for 3 years. The total amount of excise loan shall not in any case, exceed 25 per cent of the overall cost of the rehabilitation package. The excise loan is interest free and is repayable within 7 years in installments.

The scheme was further liberalised in September 1990 for sick industrial units employing more than 1,000 worker and recommended by the BIFR for excise relief as part of an approved rehabilitation package. These units will be eligible for excise loan not exceeding 50 per cent of the excise duty actually paid for 5 years from the date of approval of the rehabilitation package subject to a ceiling of 33 per cent of the total cost of the rehabilitation.

In sum, industrial sickness is the result of external factors. The Government should make all out efforts to rehabilitate units having genuine sickness. However, the deliberate sickness should not allowed to flourish at any cost.

In order to examine the problems of the sick industrial units and corporate restructuring, the Government appointed a Committee on Industrial Sickness and Corporate Restructuring in May 1993. The Committee submitted its report in July 1993. It suggested measures for early detection of incipient sickness, and recommended that reference to BIFR may be made voluntary rather than compulsory. It also recommended a number of measures to expedite decision making in BIFR and facilitated closure of unviable units.

RECOMMENDATIONS OF COMMITTEE

The Government, in May 1993, appointed Committee under the Chairmanship of Prof. Omkar Goswami to look into the various aspects of industrial sickness and issues relating to corporate restructuring. The Committee submitted its Report in July 1993. The major recommendations of the Committee are as under:

(a) The responsibility of industrial and corporate reorganisation must shift from secured creditors and the State to the defaulter debtor firms, for bringing about corporate and industrial restructuring.

(b) The Board for Industrial and Financial Reconstruction (BIFR) should be a fast track facilitator by taking decisions instead of seeking clarifications and explanations. The Government should go in for organisational changes in BIFR by appointing eight members who are experts from areas like finance, taxation and corporate law in BIFR at the branch level.

(c) BIFR should make use of the winding up provisions of Sick Industrial Companies (Special Provisions) Act of 1985 (SICA) so as to facilitate the sale of unviable units and thereby speeding up the pace of decision-making among the affected parties.

(d) There should be five self-financing recovery tribunals exclusively for recovering corporate debts in secured creditors.

(e) The financial sector requirements should be closely monitored and expedited so as to quicken the process of industrial restructuring. The following measures can be taken to achieve the aforesaid objective:

(i) the non-written off exposure to be charged and discounted at market rate of interest.

(ii) there should be no write-off of new loans;

(iii) if a partial write-off is necessary, it should be explicit and only on part debt;

(f) The Central Board of Direct Taxes (CBDT) should remove all tax hurdles that prevent banks and financial institutions from converting debt to equity of sick companies.

(g) The definition of sick unit should be modified as follows:

(i) default of 180 days or more on repayment to term lending institutions, or

(ii) irregularities in cash credit or working capital for 180 days or more.

(h) In order to detect sickness at the incipient stage, the Committee has recommended that the Irregular Statement (IS) has to be revised and further the Revised Irregular Statement (RIS) should be examined by RBI. Also, the health coding system presently used has to be replaced with four categories (satisfactory, irregular, suspect and Managerial Input Required (MIR) instead of earlier two categories (satisfactory and irregular).

(i) All financial institutions and scheduled commercial banks should prepare a list of defaulting creditors depending upon the frequency and magnitude of defaults and the list should be updated every quarter.

(j) Instead of interest specific norms the credit rating agencies should prepare guidelines for prescribing company specific, technology specific, demand specific and product specific guidelines.

(k) The Companies Act, 1956 should be suitably amended in order to enable the secured creditors to implement de facto changes in management and/the Board of Directors in instances of repeated debt defaults.

(l) The Committee has also exhorted the government to seriously consider introducing summary procedures in winding up cases.

(m) The Provisional Liquidator (PL), to take care of the company's assets, should be appointed by the High Court as soon as BIFR's recommendations are forwarded.

All these recommendations will help early restructuring of sick units and also check further incidence of sickness in industrial units.

❐